Oracle® Designer

ISBN 0-13-015343-5

Oracle Designer

A Template for Developing an Enterprise Standards Document

Mark A. Kramm
Palindrome Solutions, Inc.

Kent Graziano
ARIS Corporation

Prentice Hall PTR
Upper Saddle River, NJ 07458
www.phptr.com

Library of Congress Cataloging-in-Publication Data

Kramm, Mark A.
Oracle developer : a template for developing an enterprise standards document / Mark A. Kramm, Kent B. Graziano, Jr.
p. cm.
ISBN 0-13-015343-5
1. Application software- -Development- -Standards. 2. Designer. I. Graziano, Kent II. Title.
QA76.76.D47 K73 1999
005.2--dc21 99-40531
CIP

Acquisitions editor: *Tim Moore*
Cover designer: *Talar Agasyan*
Cover design director: *Jerry Votta*
Manufacturing manager: *Maura Goldstaub*
Editorial assistant: *Julie Okulicz*
Marketing manager: *Bryan Gambrel*
Project coordinator: *Anne Trowbridge*
Compositor/Production services: *Pine Tree Composition, Inc.*

Prentice-Hall, Inc.
Upper Saddle River, New Jersey 07458

Prentice Hall books are widely used by corporations and government agencies for training, marketing, and resale.

The publisher offers discounts on this book when ordered in bulk quantities. For more information contact:

Corporate Sales Department
Phone: 800-382-3419
Fax: 201-236-7141
E-mail: corpsales@prenhall.com

Or write:

Prentice Hall PTR
Corp. Sales Dept.
One Lake Street
Upper Saddle River, New Jersey 07458

Printed in the United States of America
10 9 8 7 6 5 4 3 2 1

ISBN 0-13-015343-5

Prentice-Hall International (UK) Limited, *London*
Prentice-Hall of Australia Pty. Limited, *Sydney*
Prentice-Hall Canada Inc., *Toronto*
Prentice-Hall Hispanoamericana, S.A., *Mexico*
Prentice-Hall of India Private Limited, *New Delhi*
Prentice-Hall of Japan, Inc., *Tokyo*
Prentice-Hall (Singapore) Pte. Ltd., *Singapore*
Editora Prentice-Hall do Brasil, Ltda., *Rio de Janeiro*

To my loving and understanding wife Bonnie.
Thank you for inspiring me by giving me the most
beautiful and precious gift of all, our daughter Emily.

To my college professor, Mr. Louis Mercuri,
whose enthusiastic instructions and unceasing
encouragement moved me and motivated me.

And of course, to my parents. Thanks for supporting me through
the years. My father's most memorable and inspirational quote was
"It doesn't matter what you are in life, as long as you strive
to be the best." Thanks Dad. —Mark

To my wife Arlene for having the patience to let me
get involved in too many projects and to my parents
(whatever you did it appears to have worked). —Kent

CONTENTS

PREFACE

This book is for those of you in the Oracle world that use the Designer tool to get your jobs done, but dread that one task we all must do: **develop a corporate standards document.** If you *like* doing these sorts of things, chances are you already have one, so this book is not for you (unless you are in need of a good sleep aid).

The idea to write this book came from our own painful experiences trying to create these documents on every major project undertaken. We found ourselves constantly writing the same thing over and over again. Each time we had to try to remember all the things we included the last time. What was that one little standard that we used two projects back that helped so much? What was that one we forgot to include the last time that nearly ate our lunch? Sound familiar? This, along with numerous e-mails from the Oracle Development Tools User Group e-mail list asking for standards, led us to conclude that there is a need for a book that will help Oracle Designer teams get off on the right foot.

If you have had any experience with large (and medium-sized) projects, you already know how critical good, comprehensive standards are to the success of the project. **This book is for you!** If you have not had that experience, trust us; you need this book, too. This book and the template on the CD-ROM will save you hours of thankless drudgery.

As with any project, there are many people to acknowledge and thank, not the least of which is Tim Moore from Prentice-Hall for believing two geeks when we told him he could make money from this book (please don't prove us wrong).

Kent would like to thank Mark for asking him to help with this project in the first place. It is not a project Kent would have come up with on his own. He would also like to thank Len Silverston and W.H. (Bill) Inmon for introducing him to the wonderful world of technical publishing by letting him co-author a book with them a few years back (*The Data Model Resource Book*).

He would also like to thank his managers at ARIS Corporation, Mark Devlin and Mike McDonough, for all their encouragement and flexibility, as well as all his colleagues at ARIS who contributed in many ways to the completion of this work.

Lastly, Kent would like to thank his loving wife Arlene for encouraging him to take on the project (she likes being married to a published author), for helping edit the work, for creative title suggestions (our first title was really BORING), and for her endless patience as he continued to take on one task too many.

Mark (not to be outdone), would like to thank Carrie Anderson at Oracle Corporation for allowing him the opportunity to instruct Oracle Designer courses for Oracle Corporation. The many students' comments and broad industry requirements helped him recognize the need for this type of book. He would also like to thank Kent for accepting his challenge. Without Kent's past authoring skills, this book would never have been completed.

We both owe a great debt to Paul Dirksen and Ken Atkins for their extraordinary work on the technical reviews for this book. Both of these men contributed greatly to the project, often pointing out what should have been obvious gaps. Without them this book would not be nearly as complete as it is.

FOREWORD

Today, business and technology change are causing organizations to rethink who they are and how they do business. Traditional brick and mortar businesses are focusing on eBusiness initatives, while new internet start-ups are opening virtual storefronts, literally overnight. The demand for qualified technology professionals is at an all time high, and is projected to continue to spike over the next 5 years. These factors are placing unparalleled demands on Information Technology (IT) groups everywhere. Now, more than ever, organizations need to reevaluate their use of technology to gain a competitive advantage, not simply to maintain the status quo. No longer can organizations rely solely on the business knowledge that members of their IT staff possess. They must focus on knowledge management, creating repositories that contain the years of collective business knowledge that the IT staff has gathered. The organization then begins to retain the organizational knowledge, lessening the risk associated with staff turnover and enabling it to more adeptly manage technological change.

This is where Computer Aided System Engineering (CASE) tools, such as Oracle Designer can really help. They are repository-based products, capturing as default documentation, a level of information that can only be dreamed of on some development efforts. Oracle Designer is currently the front runner in this arena, and in my opinion is by far and away the most feature-rich of all the CASE tools in the marketplace today. Its integration of analysis, design and generation capabilities are truly unmatched by competing products. However, the key to Oracle Designer's power is not simply using it, but using it effectively—and that is one of the benefits you will derive from this book.

One of the keys for successfully using Oracle Designer is using common naming standards, consistently across all projects within your organization. Naming Standards are a fundamental building block that allows an IT department, and more importantly, an organization to build its intellectual capital. Organizations benefit from this practice by reducing the time lost during the transition of IT staff from project to project. Maintenance time is reduced. Training of new staff becomes easier as does accounting for staff turnover. You spend much less time debating what an object is called and more time addressing the business need at hand.

Kent and Mark have taken a very practical approach to the application of naming standards using Oracle Designer. They have compiled a solid list of recommendations based on years of IT project experience. All levels of readers will benefit from this book. I believe the working template is a must for organizations using Oracle Designer. It will serve you well to work through the entire template from beginning to end, and then apply it to your work. This should be a living document that you continue to refine and update as your organization evolves.

PAUL DIRKSEN
ARIS CORPORATION
OLYMPIA, WASHINGTON
JULY, 1999

Oracle Designer

Chapter 1

STANDARDS? WE DON'T NEED NO STINKING STANDARDS!

This book is about a subject that most analysts and project directors hate. People who don't actually hate standards definitely find the development of standards a boring, repetitive, and tedious task (at least one of the authors does). Hence the goal of this book is to eliminate (or at least reduce the duration of) all those negative emotions from your job by making the development of a standards document a snap.

Seriously, the purpose of this book is to provide a common basis for analysis and development of complete business systems at any company using Oracle Designer. The book (and CD-ROM) can be used as a template for the establishment of a corporate standards document, which could then be customized by the individual organization. The standards and conventions established by this document are intended to assist in the integration of methodologies and applications across all business areas within the company.

WHO NEEDS STANDARDS ANYWAY?

Everyone who is contemplating doing a project in Designer needs to consider developing a standards document. No matter what the size of the project, a standards document is a necessity. *Standardization is critical to the successful achievement of quality in the system engineering process.* A good standards document is a communication tool that allows the project team to work together in a cohesive manner. It ensures that team members are all indeed "on the same page." Having established standards:

- Provides consistency across all projects.
- Eliminates guesswork on the part of new team members as to how things are supposed to be done.
- Improves the maintainability of models and systems over time (i.e., less guesswork).
- Reduces long-term costs (because systems are easier to maintain).
- Promotes reusability (because objects within the Designer Repository can be easily identified).

Early establishment of appropriate standards can improve the effectiveness of Oracle Designer. The tool itself was built with the expectation that certain naming conventions would be adhered to (based on CASE*Method as established by Richard Barker and Oracle's Custom Development Methodology [CDM]). In addition, the new database transformer utility generates repository objects that are named using a specific standard. The resulting object names are affected by the names of the analysis objects they are based on. This book contains standards that have been adopted, developed, and used by the authors in numerous engagements and so are based on real-life experiences using Designer. Using the standards proposed in this book will save you from wasting time editing or redoing tasks in Oracle Designer.

THE COST OF CREATING AND IMPLEMENTING STANDARDS

From our past experiences in developing Oracle Designer naming standards, we have seen clients who have spent from $50,000 to $500,000 over a period of 6 months to 2 years. Some of the expenses may be attributed to contracting outside consultants and to wading through company politics.

The use of our standards template will drastically reduce the time, cost, and frustration of defining standards.

HOW CAN YOU USE THIS BOOK AND THE CD-ROM?

This book is designed to provide a template that can be used to jump-start the development of your own project or corporate standards document. It is broken into various parts that correspond to several of the stages of the Oracle*CASE Method and/or CDM (which is often used on Designer projects). Each part/chapter contains several excerpts from the template standards document (enclosed in a text box) along with explanations about why the section is important, screen shots of the dialogs in Designer where the information is entered, and any potential variations that could be incorporated. You can then pick and choose which sections to use in your document and which to ignore. Keep in mind that if you are doing a full life-cycle development project; you will probably need most of the sections we provide. Application designers and developers should use this handbook in conjunction with the enterprise-wide standards that are available on the CD-ROM.

The document on the CD-ROM (standards.doc) is an extremely valuable tool. It is a completed standards document for an Oracle Designer project, containing all the document text included in this book.

USING THE DOCUMENT AS IS

If you like (and agree with) what we have written here, you will only need to make a few minor changes to the document to make it your own. Copy the file from the CD-ROM to your hard disk, open MS Word, do a global replace on *Company-Name,* save the file, **and you are done!** You now have a completed standards document. Your life should be so easy.

USING MOST OF THE DOCUMENT

Likely, you will need to make changes to the existing document. Your company may already have some standards in place (whether you like them or not is another story). In that case, you can use the document as a template, replacing our standards with yours. Simply search through the document for the various standards and edit the text to reflect your standard. If you have additional standards that we did not include, you can add new sections where they are needed. Remember the template is a MS Word document and can be easily changed.

USING ONLY PART OF THE DOCUMENT

It is also possible that you may not be using Oracle Designer for a full life-cycle project. If, for example, you are using it only for logical data modeling, then you will need only the entities, attributes, and relationship sections. You can delete the rest. If your organization does not use a particular tool that we provided standards for, you can remove that section. For example, if you will not use the Process Modeler, you can delete that section.

Different groups within your company may be responsible for maintaining standards specific to their domain (e.g., the Database Administrator's [DBA's] maintain all standards related to physical object names). If this is the case, you may need to cut the document up into several independent (but not overlapping) documents. Again, this is not a problem.

If you are not sure what standards you should set, the document table of contents can be used as a guide or checklist to work through the process.

DOMAIN DEFINITIONS

Also on the CD-ROM you will find an application extract from Designer that contains predefined domains we have found useful in our consulting practices. Once they have been restored to your own Designer repository, these domains can be the basis for attribute naming and sizing standards (see Chapter 6 for details on domains). The name of the file is domains.dmp and it was extracted from Designer 2.1.2.

WHERE DID THESE STANDARDS COME FROM?

The standards presented in this book were developed as a result of more than 20 years combined experience doing Oracle systems development, primarily using Oracle's CASE tools (Designer and Oracle*CASE). There is nothing magical or sacred about what we have written. In some cases, the standards came from suggestions and examples in other sources (which we will cite), although some came about through trial and error (read: we made them up because we needed a standard, any standard). There are no right answers when it comes to these sorts of things, only good suggestions and "best practices." The information in the chapters and in the template document is only a suggestion for standards based on what we have used and found effective in projects we have delivered.

ASSUMPTIONS

This book is not about how to use Oracle Designer. For great books on that topic see *Oracle Designer/2000 Handbook,* by Dorsey and Koletzke, and *Oracle Designer Generation,* by Atkins, Dirksen, and Ince.

This book is also not about CASE*Method (or any methodology per se). Books that address this topic include *CASE*Method: Tasks and Deliverables* by Richard Barker, *Oracle: A Database Developers Guide* by Ulka Rodgers, and *Designer/2000 Handbook* by Dorsey and Koletzke.

Finally, this book is not about data modeling or function modeling. A few references here (no offense to the many we did not list) include *CASE*Method: Entity Relationship Modelling* by Richard Barker; *The Data Model Resource Book* by Silverston, Inmon, and Graziano; *Data Modeling Patterns* by David Hay; and *CASE*Method Function and Process Modelling* by Barker and Longman.

In writing this book, we assumed that you have used Oracle Designer (or Designer/2000) before and that you know your way around the tool (although the book is full of screen shots, just in case). We also assumed you are familiar with some methodology resembling CASE*Method, CDM, or CADM (Case Application Development Method). In general, we assumed that you are indeed a technical professional developing custom software using Oracle tools and databases.

OVERVIEW

Part 1 of the book outlines standards for system development and sets naming conventions for logical and physical objects as well as for data and process elements. It is expected that the standards contained herein will continue to evolve to support the changing needs of any organization that adopts them.

Part 2 documents recommended conventions for use with the primary diagramming tools found in Oracle Designer. There are conventions presented for the Business Process Modeler, the Function Hierarchy Diagrammer, the Entity Relationship Diagrammer, and the Server Model Diagrammer. We did not, however, include conventions for the Data Flow Diagrammer (DFD), the Matrix Diagrammer (MD), or the Module Data Diagrammer (MDD). Besides the fact that conventions for data flow diagrams have been available (and documented by its proponents) for a long time, we have minimal experience with the tool and could not do it justice. The same holds for the MD; we usually use other tools and approaches that we find more useful for accomplishing the same tasks. The MDD required no conventions, as the tool automatically lays out the pictures based on an internal Designer algorithm.

Combined with the template on the CD-ROM, we hope this book and its ideas will help you deliver a successful project.

Part I OBJECT NAMING STANDARDS

The primary goal of any standards document is to provide a common ground for project participants to work from. In developing a standards document for Oracle Designer projects, we need to first consider the naming of objects in the Designer repository. Everything we do in Designer revolves around these objects that we enter through the various interfaces (i.e., diagrams, RON, Design Editor). So to get off on the right foot, we need to establish standard naming conventions for these objects. This part of the book presents standards for the objects we have found to be most useful in our project experiences.

Note that since Oracle Corporation is constantly upgrading and enhancing this product, there may be new objects in the version you are using that we do not cover here.

Chapter 2

DOCUMENT OVERVIEW AND GENERAL NAMING RULES

Where do you start when building a standards document? At the beginning of course, with a title page! This chapter walks through the structure of the template document provided in Appendix D. It briefly discusses the various components of the document, the relevance of the up-front material, and then provides some general naming standards that apply across the board. If your corporation already has a standard for document layout, you may need to rearrange or reformat part of the document (which you can easily do in MS Word using the document on the CD-ROM).

TITLE PAGE

The title page of course names the document and gives a version number. This assumes that the development of standards will be an ongoing effort, so it will be important to track the changes so that all the teams are using the same version. You will notice that in several places there is the phrase "Company-Name." This feature enables you to do a global search-and-replace to put your company name into the template more easily.

The information contained in this box is key to ensuring that everyone is using the same guidelines. Of particular importance is the "last updated" value and the "control number."

Document identification information:

Company-Name

Version 1.0

Author: *Company-Name Information Resources Standards Team*

Creation Date: Sept. 18, 1999

Last Updated: Sept. 18, 1999

Control Number: 1.0

The title page also includes a reference to this book so that readers of the standards document may get more detail if desired. In addition there are boxes for various approvals. The titles of the approving authorities should be changed to match titles and processes in your organization.

On the second page of the document are standard text tables for the change record, reviewers, and a distribution list. Again you may alter or remove this information as needed.

Approvals:

Project Manager

Project Team Representative

TABLE OF CONTENTS

Next in the document is the table of contents, which details the various sections of the template document. The template starts with a general section, followed by sections for naming strategy and analysis objects, design objects, and then build objects. (This roughly follows the standard Oracle*CASE Method designations, although the standards are appropriate for any methodology you use.) The document continues with a section of diagramming guidelines (covering all the major diagramming tools in Oracle Designer), followed by three appendices.

Once you have made modifications to the template, you may need to rebuild the table of contents. This is easily done in MS Word by clicking anywhere inside the table of contents and then pressing F9.

GENERAL INFORMATION

This section of the template standards document contains an introduction, objectives, applicability, references, authorization, access, and document organization.

INTRODUCTION

This part sets the stage and context for the standards document.

> This document establishes naming conventions for *Company-Name* for logical and physical objects generated from the Oracle Designer CASE tool. It also establishes diagramming conventions to be used with the various diagramming tools provided with Oracle Designer. These standards are based on the functionality available with Oracle Designer 2.1.2 but may be applicable to both earlier and later versions.

This paragraph clearly states the scope of the document. If you wish to expand the document to cover other corporate standards, add that information to this paragraph. Given that Oracle tools are constantly changing (and being renamed), it is likely that at some point you will also need to modify this section to reflect those changes as well. For a standards document to have real value to an organization, it must be constantly reviewed and updated.

OBJECTIVES

The objectives defines the purpose and goals of the document. This will help those developing the document, as well as those using it, to understand more completely what and how the standards document fits into the overall systems development architecture.

The last paragraph of this section is optional. It presupposes that once an organization starts developing standards, it will continue the effort into other areas beyond Oracle Designer. This, we believe, is a *good* idea. If that is not the intention in your organization (or it is in the unforeseen future), then you will want to delete that paragraph from the document. Additionally you may want to delete any of the subject areas marked '(TBD)'.

The purpose of this document is to provide a common basis for analysis and development of business systems at *Company-Name*. The standards and conventions established by this document are intended to assist in the integration of methodologies and applications across all business areas within the company. Standardization is critical to the successful achievement of quality in the system engineering process.

This document establishes standards for system development and sets naming conventions for logical and physical objects as well as for data and process elements. It is expected that the standards contained herein will continue to evolve to support the changing needs of *Company-Name*.

The initial version of this document establishes the standards and conventions needed to support the processes of business reengineering and documentation of the corporate Enterprise using Oracle Designer. Subsequent efforts will focus on expanding the contents to incorporate standards for all automated systems and tools purchased and/or developed at *Company-Name*. Appropriate subject areas have been named in paragraph headings in this document to indicate future additions. These are marked '*(TBD)*' to indicate that the content is to be developed at some future time.

APPLICABILITY

This section contains one sentence to clearly state where the standards in the document can be applied.

This document applies to all custom development efforts that will be developed using Oracle Designer.

If in the future, the scope of the document were expanded to other areas of systems development, this section would need to be updated to reflect that change.

REFERENCES

Again, this is one sentence in the template to cite the effort from which these standards are derived. If standards were derived from other sources, documents, books, etc., then it would be appropriate to list them in this section. Where the phrase 'Enterprise Standardization Efforts' appears, you should substitute the actual name of your standards development project.

This document includes and adopts selected standards that were developed as a result of *Company-Name's* Enterprise Standardization Efforts.

AUTHORIZATION

This section establishes who will be responsible for maintaining and approving changes to the established standards. We recommend that you establish a Systems Architecture Committee if possible. In a small organization, this committee may be limited to only one or two people. In most organizations, the committee should be led by the Data Architect or Data Administrator. Whatever the title, these people are responsible for ensuring the consistency and appropriate use of data across all systems in the organization. If you do not have such a person, you need to name one if you want to integrate your organization's data.

In the case of standards related to module names, database objects, and security, the committee should also include other people such as the Application Architect, the lead DBA, and the Application Administrator.

The System Architecture Committee is responsible for the establishment of these Standards and Naming Conventions. This committee will consist at a minimum of the Lead Data Architect, the Lead Application Architect, and the Lead Database Administrator (when appropriate). All future additions and amendments to this document will be controlled by this committee.

Changes to these standards will go through the following process:

1. Requests for change(s) must be submitted, in writing, to this committee.
2. The committee will review the requested changes, and either accept or reject them. If the requested changes are rejected, the committee will inform the requestor and tell them the reasons for rejection.
3. If the changes are accepted, the standards document will be updated, and all of the analysts, designers, and developers will be informed that the standards have changed, and given a brief summary of the changes. This step can be done on a periodic basis if there are many changes in progress.

Deviations from the standards must be reviewed and approved by the committee prior to implementation.

This section also establishes the process for changing standards. The template states that requests must be in writing. Again, we recommend that you establish a clear and concise change management process that is in writing. Included in the template is a simple example of how the process might work. Depending on the complexity and size of your organization, it may be appropriate to include additional details in this section. For example, you may want to also include details regarding how long the committee has to review a request and what to do if requests are not reviewed in a timely manner.

ACCESS

For people to use the document, they must be able to find it. We recommend that you consider putting a current version of the document on the corporate Intranet for ease of access. It should be in a read-only format to prevent intentional or unintentional changes by unauthorized personnel.

> This document can be accessed by any system user on a read-only basis via the *Company-Name* Intranet or internal file system.

This section of the template document should be updated to include the actual URL of the document, if on an Intranet, or the full directory and file name if it is on a file system.

DOCUMENT ORGANIZATION

This section contains a high-level outline of the content of the document. It is somewhat redundant with the table of contents, but nonetheless provides a quick overview.

> This document is organized into six distinct sections:
>
> - ❑ Oracle Objects
> - ❑ Strategy/Analysis
> - ❑ Design
> - ❑ Build
> - ❑ Diagramming Conventions
> - ❑ Appendices

If subject areas are added or deleted from the template, those should be noted here. If your organization is using a methodology that is very different from CASE*Method, you may want to rename certain sections or perhaps organize them differently. For the document to be used within an organization, it must make sense to those using it and have some real correspondence to the methodology being followed.

NAMING ORACLE OBJECTS: GENERAL RULES

The information in this segment intends to establish the "ground rules" for the various naming standards that are detailed in later sections.

All rules established in this section must be followed when naming objects, unless **specifically** excepted by individual object descriptions in later sections.

The individual sections contain any additional rules specific to an object and one or more examples to illustrate usage.

LENGTH OF LABELS

It is important to establish a standard for label and name lengths. If the label is too long and it is eventually used for naming a database object, it may exceed the length allowed by Oracle and cause an error during database build. In addition standardizing lengths adds to consistency.

ORACLE database object names are restricted to no more than thirty (30) characters and include entities, attributes, tables, columns, views, sequence generators, and domains. However, some Designer utilities may add a suffix of 4 additional characters for example "_JNL". For this reason, the recommended length is 26 characters. The words' 'alias' and 'short name' are used to describe a codified label of two (2) to four (4) characters. The word 'name' will signify a descriptive label of three (3) to twenty-six (26) characters. Names should be meaningful, and should accurately describe the object to which they are assigned. Oracle Applications' data names for entity and attributes should be used if possible. The consistent use of abbreviations and standard acronyms will assist in this endeavor.

The statement referring to the use of Oracle Applications naming standards may be removed from the template if your shop does not use these products. It is included to ensure consistency of object naming in shops that do use these products.

How do you determine the appropriate length for specific objects? We have tried to outline most of them for you. Some of them are limits imposed by Designer; others were developed for the reasons stated previously.

> Specific formats and lengths (where appropriate) are detailed by object in **Appendix B Object Format & Flow Down Charts** in the book *Oracle Designer: A Template for Developing an Enterprise Standards Document.* These specifications are the basis of all object names and must be followed. These limits are established to promote consistency and to ensure that all objects used in module generation are of appropriate length.

The standard says these guidelines *must* be followed. That really is up to each organization to determine. Can you force people to follow standards? Not really, but a strongly worded document may make them take it more seriously.

In our experience, it almost always takes mandatory model and design reviews to enforce standards. However, it can be difficult to make this process mandatory, so it is a good idea to also stipulate a time limit for these reviews. Standards that stipulate mandatory reviews with a hard time limit for the reviewers seem to work best. For example, you could state that the System Architecture Committee has two weeks to review an application design and return recommended changes. If there is no response in that time, the project team can assume that the design is OK and can continue with the process.

ACRONYMS/ABBREVIATIONS

Every standards document must deal with acronyms and abbreviations, and every organization should maintain a list of acceptable ones. Most organizations will have their own acronyms that everybody uses. These will need to be added to the list provided in this document. Abbreviations tend to be subjective as well, but they are necessary to keep some object names from becoming too long and cumbersome to type (and stay within the length requirements).

> Full words should always be used, unless an approved acronym can be substituted or an abbreviation is required for length considerations. In other words, always substitute an acronym if an appropriate one exists, and only abbreviate when necessary because of name length considerations. (An acronym is a word formed from the initial letter or letters of each of the successive or major parts of a compound term.)

When and how do you determine abbreviations? The template offers these guidelines:

> If name length considerations mandate abbreviation of words, begin the abbreviation process from the right. If the word has an approved abbreviation, substitute the abbreviation. If, after all appropriate acronyms and abbreviations have been substituted, it is still necessary to reduce the length of a label, begin to abbreviate the last word in the label and continue to reduce one word at a time until the total length of the label is acceptable. Apply the following techniques, in the order given, to create a unique abbreviation of appropriate length.
>
> ❑ Remove internal vowels and final 'e'.
>
> Example: country is abbreviated 'cntry', object is abbreviated 'objct'.
>
> ❑ Sequentially remove consonants beginning at the end of the word.
>
> Example: address is abbreviated 'addr', abbreviation is abbreviated 'abbr'.
>
> An abbreviation should be no less than three and no more than five characters. In some instances, an abbreviation of two (2) characters is allowable if the meaning of the abbreviation is clear and/or it is in common usage such as 'oz', 'ft', or 'lb'. If the qualifying word is four or fewer characters long, it should not be abbreviated.
>
> Tables of standard abbreviations and acronyms are provided in Appendix A—Approved Abbreviations, Codes and Acronyms.
>
> If further assistance is required, contact the Data Administrator to determine the acronym(s) or abbreviation(s) required. If you have created a new abbreviation using the rules above, contact your Data Architect to update the approved abbreviation, codes and acronyms list.

Once again the Data Administrator comes into play. Whenever anything new is developed relating to these standards, you must involve the Data Administrator for approval. Otherwise, some projects may develop their own set of abbreviations while others use the standard set. This could lead to problems later if the two projects are ever merged.

USE OF SIGNIFICANT WORDS

The goal here is to limit words used in naming objects to those that are really meaningful. Since there is a limit set on the length of a name or label, use of insignificant words simply makes it harder to stay within that limit. Names should not be sentences.

Use root words wherever possible. Dropping the suffix (-age, -ence, -ance, -ing, -ant, -ity, -any, -ive, -ary, -ony, -aty, -ory, -ation, -ment, -ed, -tion) will generally leave the root word. Do this only if the remaining root word is meaningful as is.

Words such as who, what, when, or where are *not* allowed.

The use of articles and prepositions (such as **the** or **of**), adjoining words or conjunctions (such as **and** or **or**), qualifying words such as **new** or **old**, and numbers should be on an exception basis.

This rule may seem like nit picking, but it is important. It is also important when naming objects in Designer to avoid the tendency to be verbose. All objects in Designer can have long text descriptions and notes associated with them. Use this feature to explain meanings in detail. It is not necessary to define an object completely with its name.

USE OF SPECIAL CHARACTERS

Special characters rarely add meaning or value to a label and thus should be avoided. We must keep in mind length limitations and the overall goal of making names meaningful. Special characters do not help achieve these goals.

Special characters, including brackets, quotation marks, question marks, and slashes are *not* permitted. Dashes are allowed only in legitimately hyphenated words.

Underscores will not be used except where needed to separate words in physical implementation objects (like tables, columns, and modules). The Designer tool will insert underscores, when required, during transformation from logical to physical repository objects.

The general standards and guidelines presented in this chapter should be kept in mind when considering all the specific standards in the following chapters. Only rarely will you need to modify these rules. In most cases, the specific standards presented assume that these general rules are being followed.

Chapter 3

Enterprise Strategic Objects

Strategic Objects are defined by management and help define the business direction or mission (business objectives), the events that allow the mission to be achieved (critical success factors), and measurements to track the progress of events (key performance indicators).

Some of the key deliverables of the Strategy stage (in CDM and CASE*Method) other than high level data and process models are upper management's long- and short-term goals and the organization direction or mission. These Strategic Objects are defined by management and are documented during an enterprise modeling effort. The definition of these objects compel the organization to explicitly agree upon what it wants to achieve and its priorities. Three components of these Strategic Objects are captured in the form of business objectives, critical success factors, and key performance indicators. Later during the Analysis stage, one of the key deliverables of a process model is the cross-referencing of business functions to the objectives established by management for your organization. If a business function does not help to achieve the defined objectives, management may question whether, in fact, it is even necessary.

This chapter presents definitions and naming standards for the following Enterprise Strategic Objects:

- Business Objectives
- Critical Success Factors (CSF)
- Key Performance Indicators (KPI)
- Business Events

- ❑ Business Terminology
- ❑ Business Units

The chapter also discusses how to cross reference key performance indicators and critical success factors to business objectives.

BUSINESS OBJECTIVES

An Objective is a mission, goal, or target that a business is trying to achieve. To focus on the most important aspects of the business, it must be quantifiable and measurable. If it is quantifiable and measurable, then it must be possible to ascertain whether the objective has been achieved. In other words, it must be SMART: Specific, Measurable, Achievable, Relevant, and Tractable. Such objectivity also allows a business to measure its progress toward an objective at a point in time or for a given period of time. For example, a business might want to "expand to be recognized nationally." You can define a single target and unit of measure for an objective, or you can define multiple target values and units of measure by creating Key Performance Indicators.

The only standard we are proposing here is that you collect and record business objectives as part of an enterprise modeling effort.

> Business Objectives will be extracted from the Corporate Strategic Plan and maintained in the Corporate Level Enterprise Model. Business Objective names can be up to forty (40) characters in length.
>
> **Example:** EXPAND TO BE RECOGNIZED NATIONALLY.

Business objects can be created only in the Repository Object Navigator (RON) (Figure 3.1). The standard of 40 characters is due to limitations imposed by Designer.

> If your organization does not have a strategic plan, use this opportunity to begin one. Record the business objectives in Designer as a start. Later you can use repository (or custom) reports to pull the information out as a jump-start for the plan.

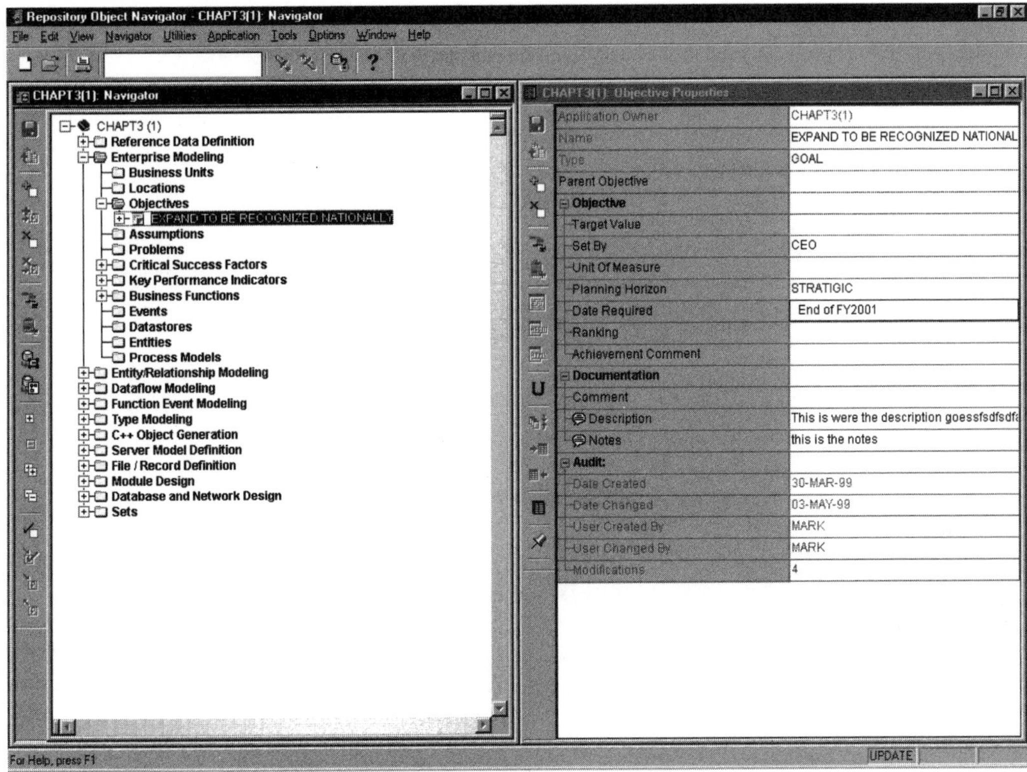

FIGURE 3.1 Defining a business objective.

All Objectives require, at a minimum, a name and a type. The type property is used to classify the objective. Some organizations use the terms, aims, targets, goals, etc. There are no list of values that you can choose from. This allows your organization the flexibility to define your own. The other properties are optional and are explained in detail using the on-line help facility.

CRITICAL SUCCESS FACTORS

A CSF is any event, deliverable or other influence, that is integral to the ultimate success of achieving an objective. For example, the ability to handle new government regulations quickly and aggressive marketing strategies are recognized critical success factors and could be associated with the example objective defined previously.

> The resources, events and conditions required to meet each Business Objective will be identified and cataloged as Critical Success Factors (CSF). CSF names are nouns or nominative phrases of up to forty (40) characters.
>
> **Examples:** AGGRESSIVE MARKETING STRATEGIES,
> HANDLE NEW GOVERNMENT REGS QUICKLY.

CSF's can be created only in the RON (Figure 3.2). The standard of 40 characters is due to limitations imposed by Designer.

All CSF's require a name and an indication whether or not the Critical Success Factor is critical. The property that is used to define the success factor as being critical or not is called Critical. The other properties are optional and are explained in detail using the on-line help facility. Keep in mind, the more information you enter, the better you will be able to report information later. This is your corporate meta-data!

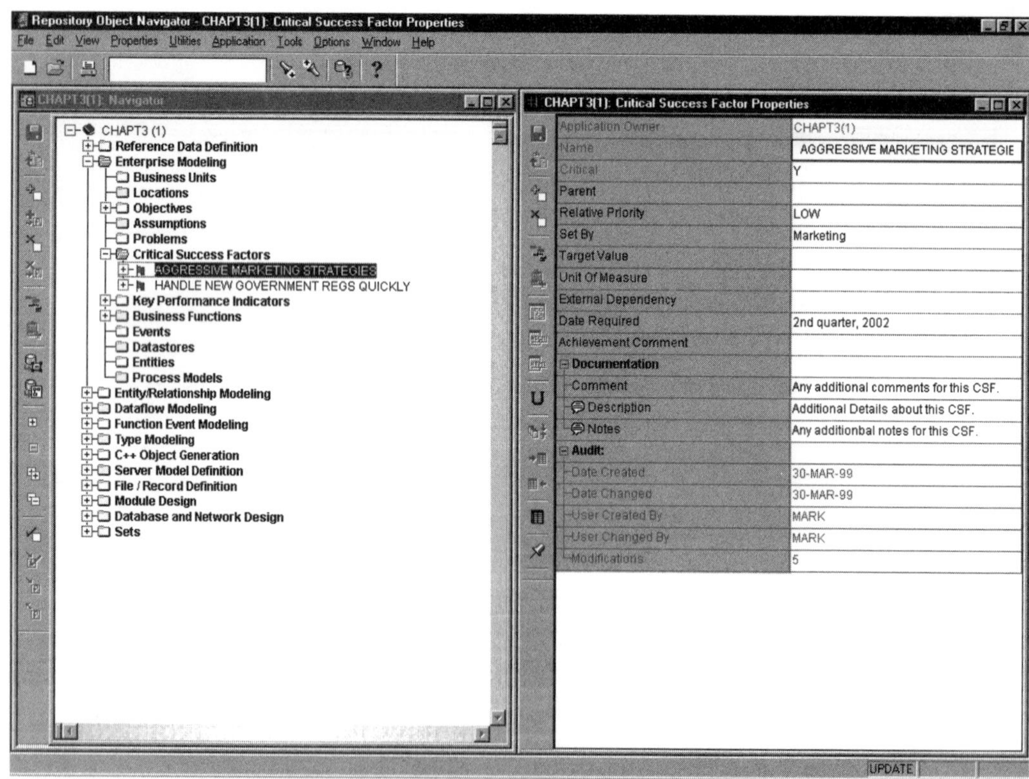

FIGURE 3.2 Defining critical success factors.

KEY PERFORMANCE INDICATORS

A KPI is a measure used to help monitor how well a business is achieving its quantifiable objectives. For example, "Open 5 new offices in new states" is a recognized key performance indicator and could be associated with the example objective defined previously.

> Deliverables, schedules, milestones and other tracking mechanisms will be assigned to each Business Objective and will be used to determine progress. Key Performance Indicator (KPI) names are nouns or nominative phrases of up to forty (40) characters.
>
> **Example:** OPEN 5 NEW OFFICES IN NEW STATES.

KPIs can be created only in the RON (Figure 3.3). The standard of 40 characters is due to limitations imposed by Designer.

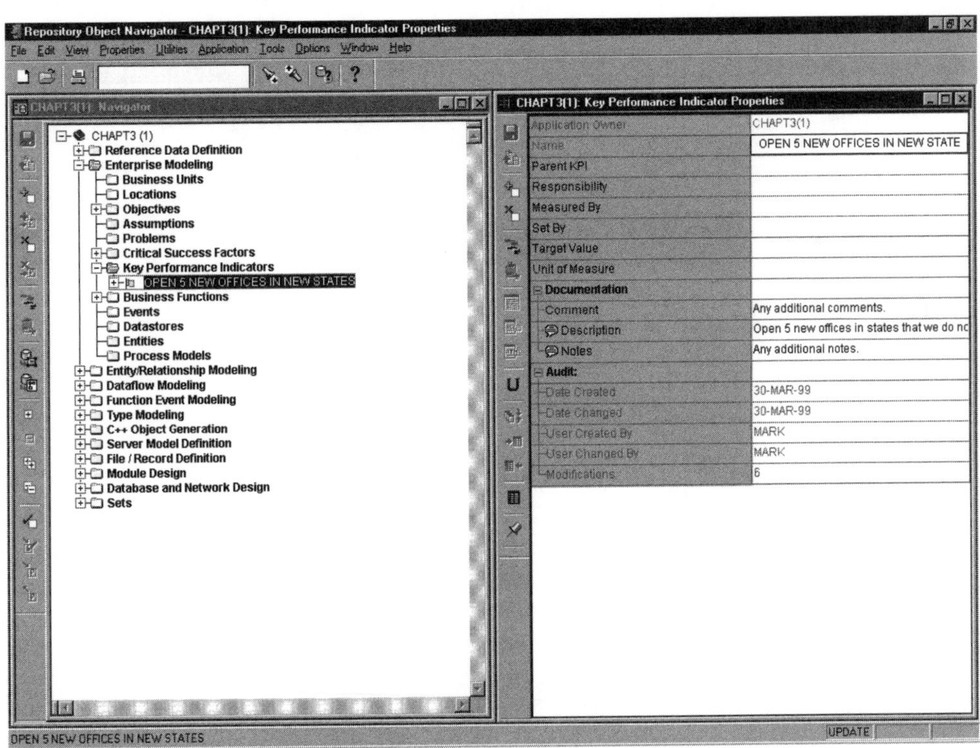

FIGURE 3.3 Defining Key Performance Indicators.

The template indicates that the standard is to actually record this type of information. Without this information, you will have no real way of measuring your success in achieving the goals and objectives.

All KPIs require, at a minimum, a name. The other properties are optional and are explained in detail using the on-line help facility.

CROSS-REFERENCING KEY PERFORMANCE INDICATORS AND CRITICAL SUCCESS FACTORS TO OBJECTIVES

Once you have defined your organization's business objectives (Objectives), you can then associate the mechanism for measuring progress (KPI) and the resources, events or conditions (CSF) required to meet a specific objective.

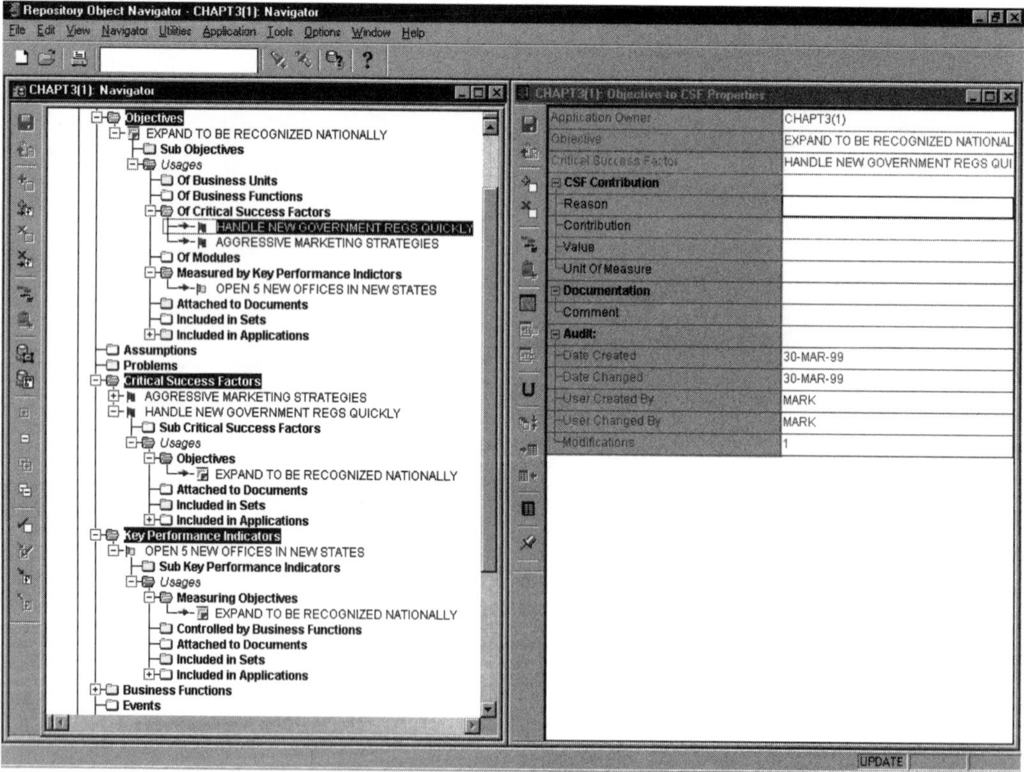

FIGURE 3.4 Cross-referencing a KPI and CSF to an Objective.

Figure 3.4 shows how the definition of the cross-referencing of KPIs and CSFs to Objectives will look in the Repository Navigator. Unfortunately there is as yet no diagramming technique or wizard for completing this task. It can be defined only using the Repository Object Navigator.

Later in the Analysis phase, one of the key deliverables of a process model is the cross-referencing of business functions to the objectives established by management for your organization. If a business function does not help to achieve the defined objectives, management would question whether it is necessary at all.

BUSINESS EVENTS

An Event is a named action that initiates the execution of a business process; for example, the arrival of a significant point in time, a change in status of something, or the occurrence of something external. In the Process Modeler, it is an element that either precedes or follows a process. A preceding event is called a trigger, and a following event is known as an outcome. (In RON, they are defined under Enterprise Modeling and Function Event Modeling as Events). Business events are also referred to as "triggers" but should not be confused with Oracle Forms triggers.

Event names must consist of a verb and an object and are restricted to thirty (30) characters.

Examples:

RECEIVE INVOICE is an example of a trigger that is an initiating event for an Accounts Payable process.

VENDOR PAYED is an example of an outcome event for an Accounts Payable process.

Business events can be created either in RON or via the Process Modeler (Figure 3.5). The standard of 30 characters is due to limitations imposed by Designer. The naming standard of using a verb and an object is simply to make the event name recognizable and understandable by business users.

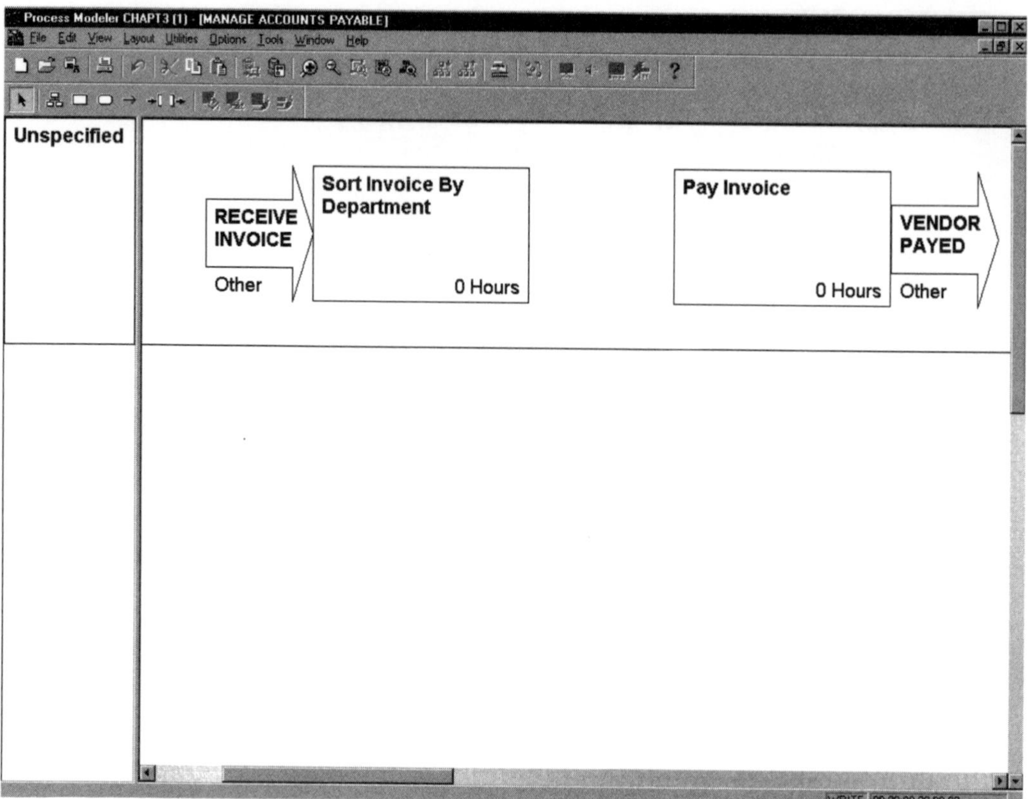

FIGURE 3.5 Create business events in the Process Modeler.

BUSINESS TERMINOLOGY

In Designer, it is also possible to record definitions of the business terminology or terms that are used throughout the organization. With the terminology defined and along with entity names and their synonyms a comprehensive glossary of terms can be produced using repository reports. The business terminology can also be generated as a glossary into the MS Help-based on-line help system used in generated Oracle Developer Forms applications.

Business Terminology is the name given to the node in the RON where the glossary of business terms will be stored (under Reference Data Definition). Entries must not be the same as entities because both entities and business terms are stored and reported together and must be unique within the group. The contents

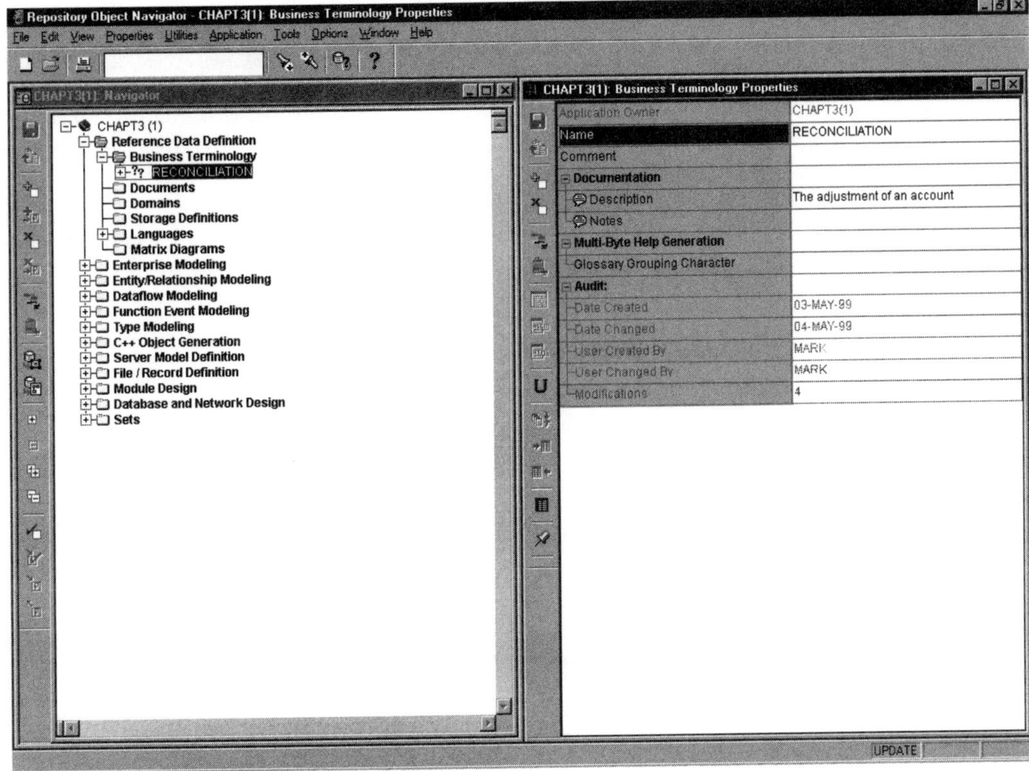

FIGURE 3.6 Defining Business Terminology.

of the glossary may be printed for ease of use but should always be viewed on-line if possible to ensure that all current information is available. Terminology names can be up to (40) characters (Figure 3.6).

The standard for recording business terminology is as follows:

> **Business Terminology** should be additional terms and associated definitions useful for understanding the enterprise being modeled.
>
> Terms entered must not duplicate entity names.
>
> Terminology names can be up to (40) characters in length.

BUSINESS UNITS

In common usage, business units are called organizations or organizational units. A Business Unit is a uniquely named resource (or group of resources) that performs one or more business functions.

A Business Unit differs from a Business Area, which is a named collection of related business functions. A Business Area, such as Procurement, may or may not be specific to a single Business Unit.

For example, Database Services is a Business Unit composed of a manager (which is a role), staff (which is a role), equipment, and material resources. This Business Unit performs the functions of the Business Area called Database Management. These functions include system installations and upgrades, data and system backup and restore, user maintenance, etc.

A Business Unit definition will contain a long descriptive name and a short name.

Business Unit short names will have a minimum of two (2) characters and a maximum of four (4) characters, two characters are preferred.

Business Unit short names are codes which you will derive from the longer, descriptive name of the Business Unit.

Example:

Long name = Database Services

Short name = DBSV

You can create business units using the RON, or you can use the Business Process diagrammer (i.e., Process Modeler) to create them. In the Business Process diagrammer, they are called Organization Units. Figure 3.7 shows how to create a business unit using the Business Process diagrammer.

In the Business Process diagrammer, select the "create organization unit" button. Then right mouse click on the unspecified organization unit. Fill in the name and the short name in the dialog box and click OK to save (Figures 3.7 and 3.8).

Hint: To resize a swim lane, shift right click on its organization unit, and then use the up and down arrows on your key board.

Hint: To reorder organizations units in a diagram, select the organization unit, and then use the up and down arrow keys on your key board.

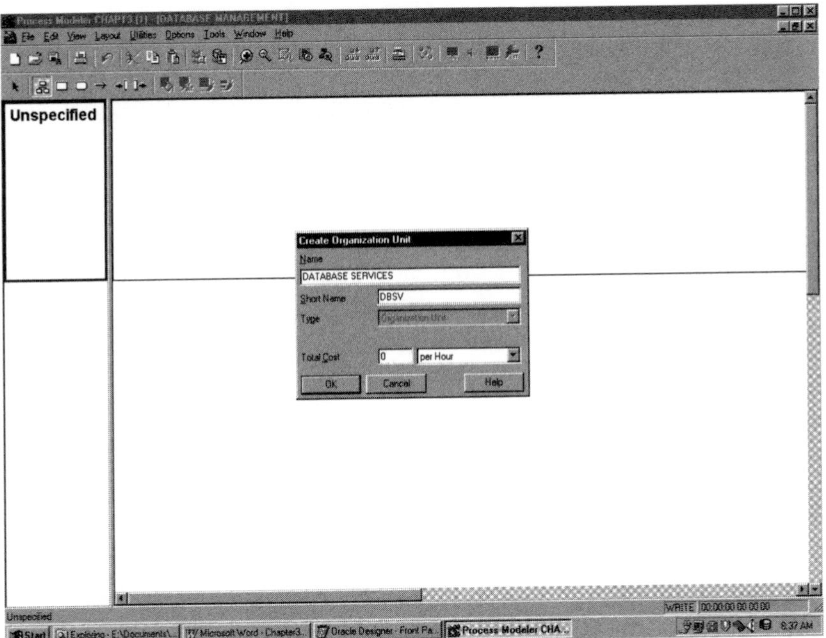

FIGURE 3.7 Creating an Organization Unit.

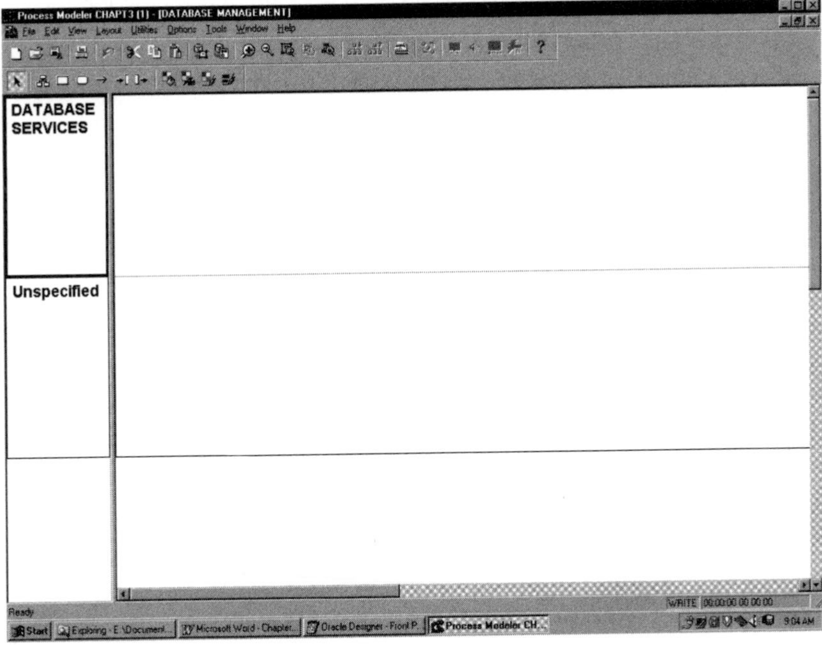

FIGURE 3.8 Organization Unit displayed in the Business Process Diagrammer.

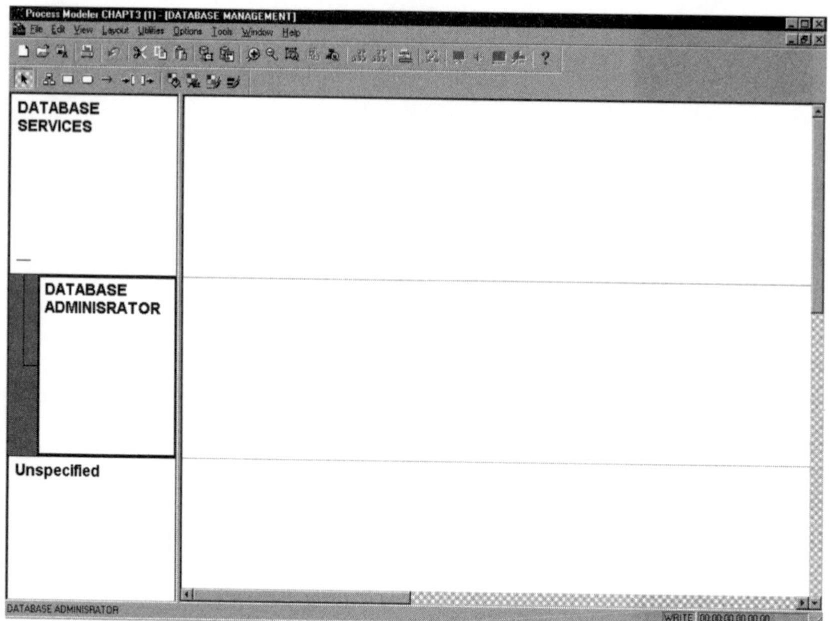

FIGURE 3.9 First step in creating a Role (suborganization unit).

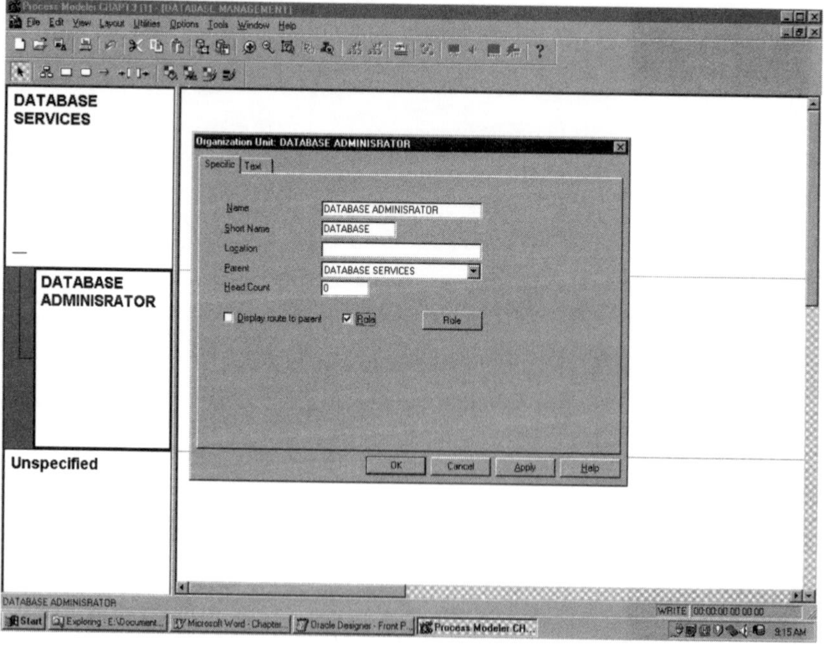

FIGURE 3.10 Create Role dialog box.

To create a Role, you must first create an Organization Unit. This is done the same way as shown in Figure 3.7 except, instead of clicking on the Unspecified Organization Unit, left click on the Organization Unit that you want to create a role for. Fill in the name and short name in the dialog box and click OK to save (see Figure 3.7 for the "create organization unit" dialog box). Now simply double click on the object you just created (Figure 3.9) and in the specific tab, check the box labeled "Role" and click the OK button to save. Figure 3.10 illustrates the creation of a Role.

Chapter 4

BUSINESS POLICIES AND RULES

Both internal and external agencies impose legal and/or functional constraints on the conduct of business. To work within those constraints, the organization must establish Business Policies and Business Rules. These policies and rules must be documented and associated with appropriate processes and functions. This information should be maintained as part of the Corporate Enterprise Model in the Designer repository.

This chapter presents guidelines for storing these kind of data and standards for recording the following:

- Business policy labels
- Business policy short definitions
- Business rule labels
- Business rule short definitions

HOW TO STORE POLICIES AND RULES IN DESIGNER

Current releases of Oracle Designer do not have the functionality to explicitly capture Business Policies or Rules and to document their (many-to-many) relationships to Business Functions. One option is to extend the repository using the User Extensibility feature of the tool to capture policies and rules. This option can make the tool upgrade process more difficult. Therefore, we generally adopt a convention of storing Business Policies and Rules as functions under a separate Rules Root Function.

This method expedites the creation and documentation of design level objects in the design phase. In Analysis, once you create the business rule, you will associate the use of the data to the Business Rule (just as you would with a normal function). Then, in the design phase, you will use the Application Design Transformer to convert the rules functions captured in the analysis phase into client and/or server side objects such as stored packages and procedures. These will later be implemented in development to enforce the application systems Business Rules.

Note: Separate analysis tasks are needed to assign data usages to the Business Rules and link the Business Rules to the appropriate Business Functions. Refer to *Linking Business Rules to Business Functions* in this chapter, and Chapter 5 *Elementary Functions: Defining function data usages* for details of these procedures.

LAYING THE FOUNDATION

A convention of storing Business Policies and Rules as functions under a separate RULES ROOT FUNCTION will be used at *Company-Name.*

All the highest-level Business Area Policies and Rules (BAPR) have been identified and entered into the Enterprise model. These BAPRs detail the highest levels of the major process areas in the Enterprise and have been modeled to establish a common environment for recording business policies and rules for the corporation. In most cases, standard industry descriptions have been used to identify BAPRs. In a changing business environment, the use of standard names and descriptions provides the flexibility needed to support a dynamic environment.

It is recommended that a high-level, enterprise-wide Business Area Policies and Rules (BAPR) model be established in the repository to facilitate the subsequent identification of policies and rules associated with the major business areas of you company. This "seeding" of the repository can be only one level deep and usually no more than twenty levels wide. This accomplishes three things:

1. It establishes a common area for recording business policies and rules in the repository and, at the same time, facilitates the grouping of related business policies and rules under a predefined BAPR.
2. Because the Business Policies and Rules are easily accessible (using RON or standard function reports), the business community policies and rules re-

view process is easier, and the duplication of policies and rules may be reduced.

3. Because we are not using the user extensibility features of the tool and creating custom reports, standard function reports that already exist in Oracle Designer can be used to view the business policies and rules.

The following two steps outline the process for developing the business rule foundation for your company.

1. Within the Enterprise Model Application, create a new root function with a short definition of "Business Policies and Rules" and a Label of "Z_BPR."
2. Create the second level, which will represent the major Business Area Policies and Rules. Generally use standard industry descriptions. The short definition last words should be "Business Polices and Rules" (Figure 4.1).

Prefixing the labels with a "Z" accomplishes two things;

1. It segregates standard business processes and functions from business functions that are created as business policies and rules. This facilitates the running of standard Repository reports, Solutron, Inc.'s product Publisher/2000 to generate reports or the creation of custom reports using the Designer API.
2. When viewing functions within the RON, the business rules are at the bottom of the list.

The Label is composed of six (6) alpha characters: the first two characters are "Z_"; the next four (4) are an acronym of the short definition.

> As business policies are identified, they will be appended to the appropriate higher level BAPR in the Enterprise Model. These extensions of the BAPR Enterprise Model may be only one level deep before business rule decompositions begins.
>
> If additional levels are required for a very complex model, the extension must be approved by the System Architecture Committee

This technique tends to create a very flat rules hierarchy diagram. Therefore, as mentioned previously, a custom API report should be created (or use Solutron's product Publisher/2000) to print the Policies and Rules for business review and verification.

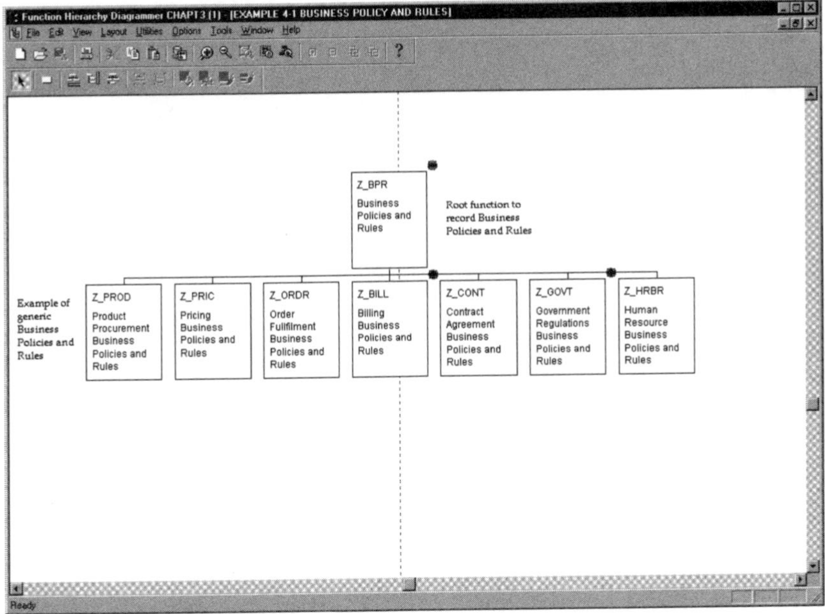

FIGURE 4.1 Seeding the repository with corporate Business Area Policies and Rules.

BUSINESS POLICY LABELS

The following is our recommendation for assigning business policy labels:

At the third level of the model, the business policy label will be composed of seven (7) alpha characters where the *first* of the six characters is the name of the level two parent and the seventh is a single number character. This digit is positional and begins with one (1).

Use of alpha characters in the positional parameter will be permitted only on an exception basis with approval of the System Architecture Committee.

Note: Level two labels are composed of six (6) alpha characters where the *first two* characters are "Z_" and the next four (4) is an acronym of the short definition. These have already been established.

Example:

Z_BILL1 is the label for the Billing Business Policy which is a child of the level two BOPR 'Z_BILL Billing Business Rules'

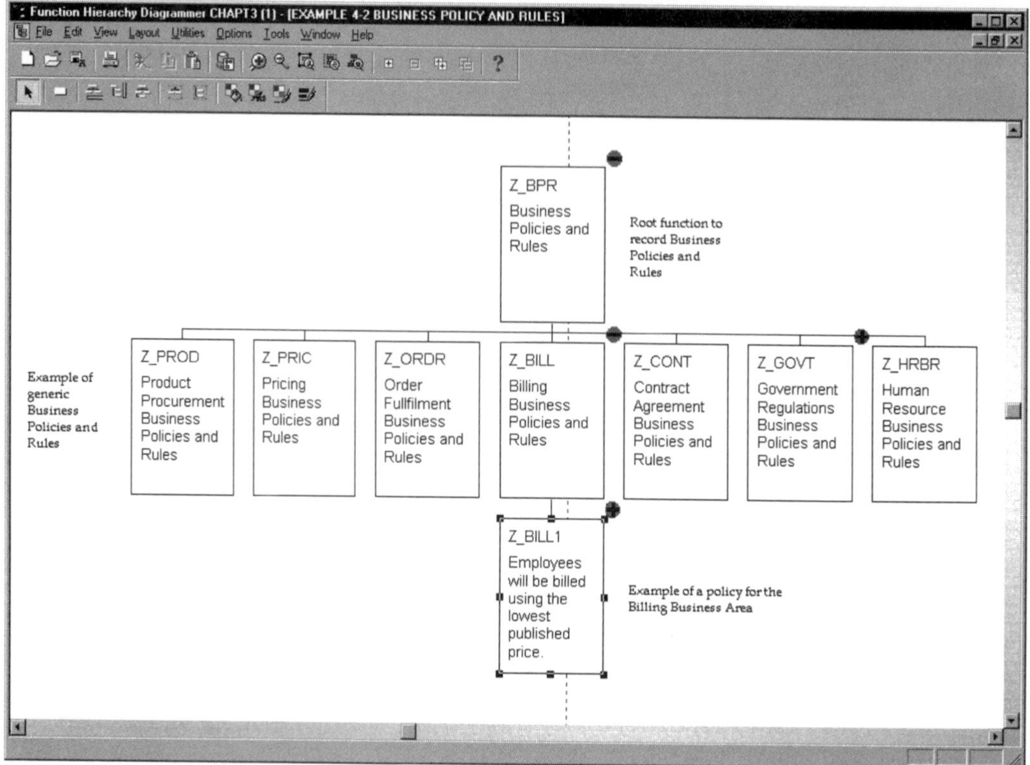

FIGURE 4.2 Illustration of a business policy in the Functional Hierarchy Diagrammer.

This standard starts with level three because the seeding of the repository (described previously) must be done before giving any one access to the company standards. You could add the procedure outlined in "Laying the Foundation" to your standards document to help clarify this point.

Figure 4.2 shows how the definition of a business policy will look in the Functional Hierarchy Diagrammer (FHD).

BUSINESS POLICY SHORT DEFINITIONS

Business Policies must not be atomic and cannot be marked as elementary; that is, Business Policies must be able to be decomposed further into Business Rules. If a policy cannot be further decomposed, it is considered a business rule by default.

Note: If you are creating custom reports to print all business policies, you would select functions where the label starts with 'Z_' and atomic = NO and elementary = NO.

Business Policies are high level statements of desired constraints and may imply one or more business rules.

The short definition of a business policy is usually a statement or phrase and can be up to (70) characters.

Business Policies *must not* be "Atomic" and *must not* be "Elementary" when defined in the Designer Repository

Example: Employees will be billed using the lowest published price.

BUSINESS RULE LABELS

Below is our recommendation for the entry and definition of business rule labels:

All business rule labels are limited to ten (10) characters.

Labels are a concatenation of the label from the parent business policy, and from one (1) to three (3) numeric characters. The digits that identify the level of decomposition within the business policy are positional and begin with the number one (1).

The examples in this section show how business rule labels are built.

Z_BILL1: Employees will be billed using the lowest published price (policy)

Where:

Z_BILL = Billing Business Rules (Business Area Policies and Rules (BAPR))

1 = Employees will be billed using the lowest published price (which is a Policy, of the Business Area Policies and Rules; Z_BILL Billing Business Policies and Rules)

Z_BILL11: If time of service was prior to employment with company, bill for the service(s).

Where:

Z_BILL = Billing Business Policies and Rules (Business Area Policies and Rules (BAPR))

1 = Employees will be billed using the lowest published price (which is a Policy, of the Business Area Policies and Rules; Z_BILL Billing Business Policies and Rules)

1 = If time of service was prior to employment with company, bill for the service(s) (left most, Business Rule, of the Policy; Z_BILL1 Employees will be billed using the lowest published price).

Z_BILL12: If service is within 2 weeks of employee termination, do not bill for service(s).

Where:

Z_BILL = Billing Business Policies and Rules (Business Area Policies and Rules (BAPR))

1 = Employees will be billed using the lowest published price (which is a Policy, of the Business Area Policies and Rules; Z_BILL Billing Business Policies and Rules).

2 = If service is within 2 weeks of employee termination, do not bill for service(s).

When we say that the digits indicate the level of decomposition and that they are "positional," we mean that the digits in the label actually identify a hierarchy that indicates the level of decomposition within the business policy. The first digit identifies the first level of decomposition; the second digit identifies the second

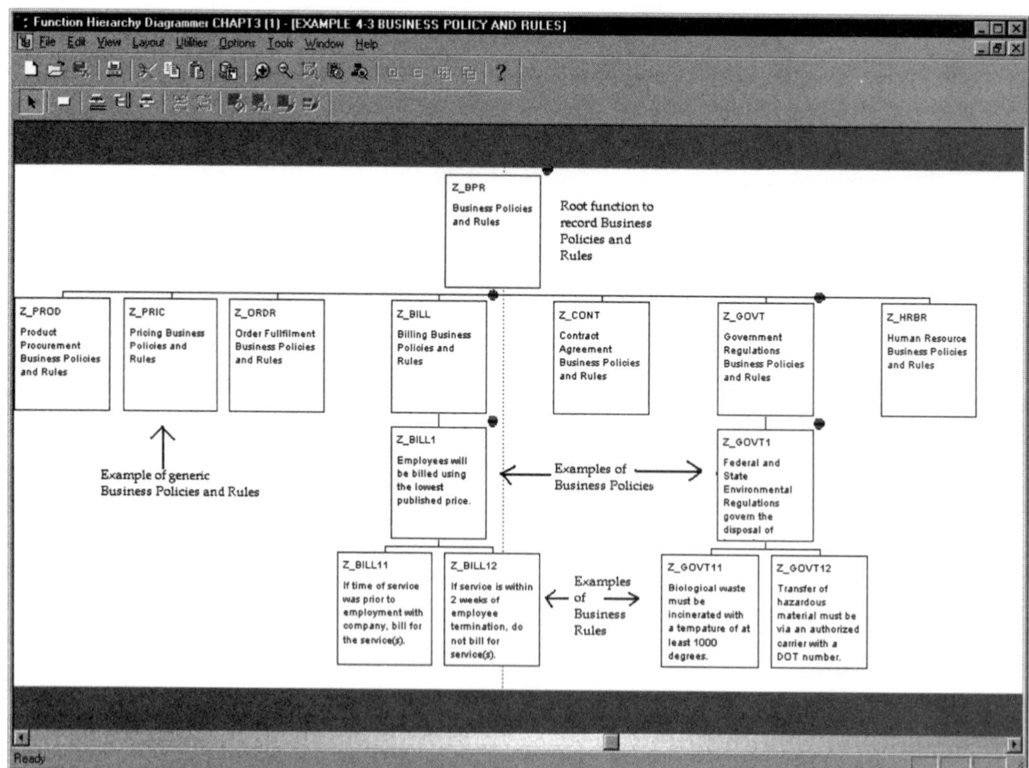

FIGURE 4.3 Illustration of Definitions of business policy and rules in the FHD.

level of decomposition, etc. Since only three digits are allowed, the decomposition within a business policy can be only three levels deep. Figure 4.3 shows how these definitions of business policies and rules look when recorded in the FHD.

BUSINESS RULE SHORT DEFINITIONS

Business Rules must be atomic and must be marked as elementary, that is, business rules must be decomposed into the lowest level. In other words, a rule must take the business from one consistent state to another or else return it back to its original state. See the template listing below for several examples of policies and rules.

(**Note:** If you are creating custom reports to print all business rules, you would select functions were the label starts with 'Z_' and atomic = YES and elementary = YES.)

A Business Rule is an elementary (single action) statement of a constraint on data that is enforced by processes.

The short definition of a business rule is usually a single statement containing actions and verbs and can be up to (70) characters.

Business Rules *must* be "Atomic"; and, they must be defined as "Elementary" in the Oracle Designer Repository

Example 1:

Business Policy:

Employees will be billed using the lowest published price.

Business Rules:

1. If time of service was prior to employment with company, bill for the service(s).
2. If service is within 2 weeks of employee termination, do not bill for service(s).

Example 2:

Business Policy:

Federal and State Environmental Regulations govern the disposal of hazardous materials.

Business Rules:

1. Biological waste must be incinerated with a temperature of at least 1000 degrees.
2. Transfer of hazardous material must be via an authorized carrier with a DOT Number.

LINKING BUSINESS RULES TO BUSINESS FUNCTIONS

The previous section detailed the tasks for documenting business policies and rules in the Oracle Designer repository. This section outlines the technique of linking Business Rules to Business Functions. Why do you need to link the rules to functions? Consider this: if the rules have no association to a real Business Function, why was the rule recorded?

> All Business Rules must be linked to at least one Business Function.

After you have documented your Business Rules, you will need to associate them to Business Functions. You do this by defining the Business Function as triggering the Business Rule via functions-triggering functions associations. To

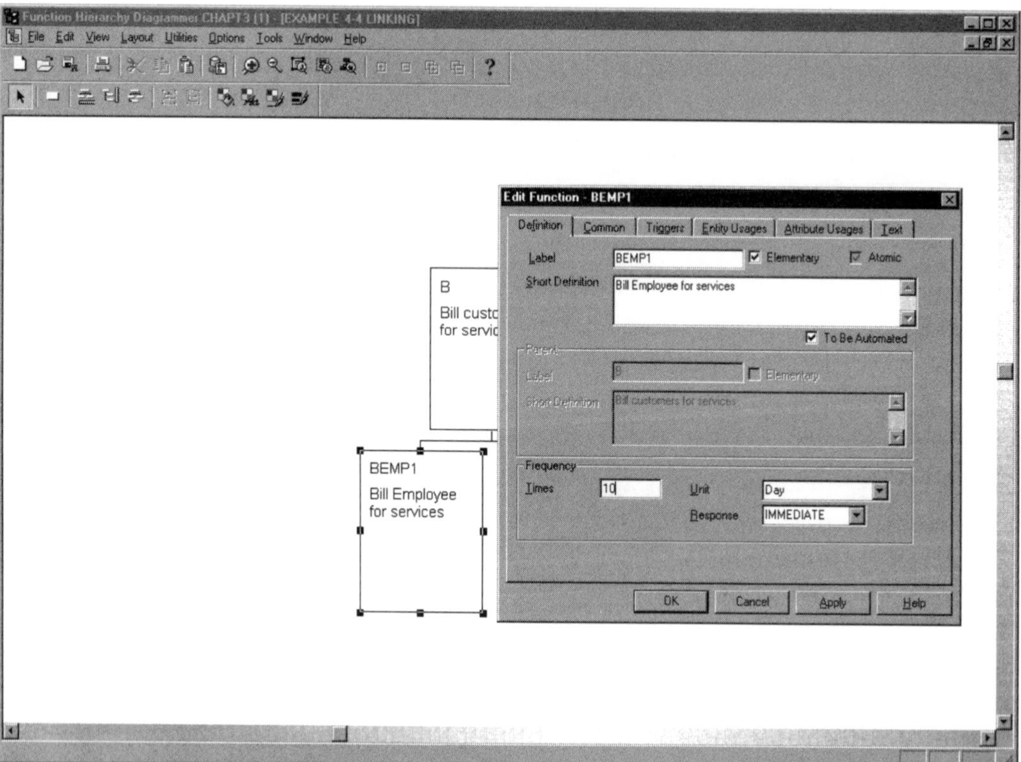

FIGURE 4.4 Edit Function dialog.

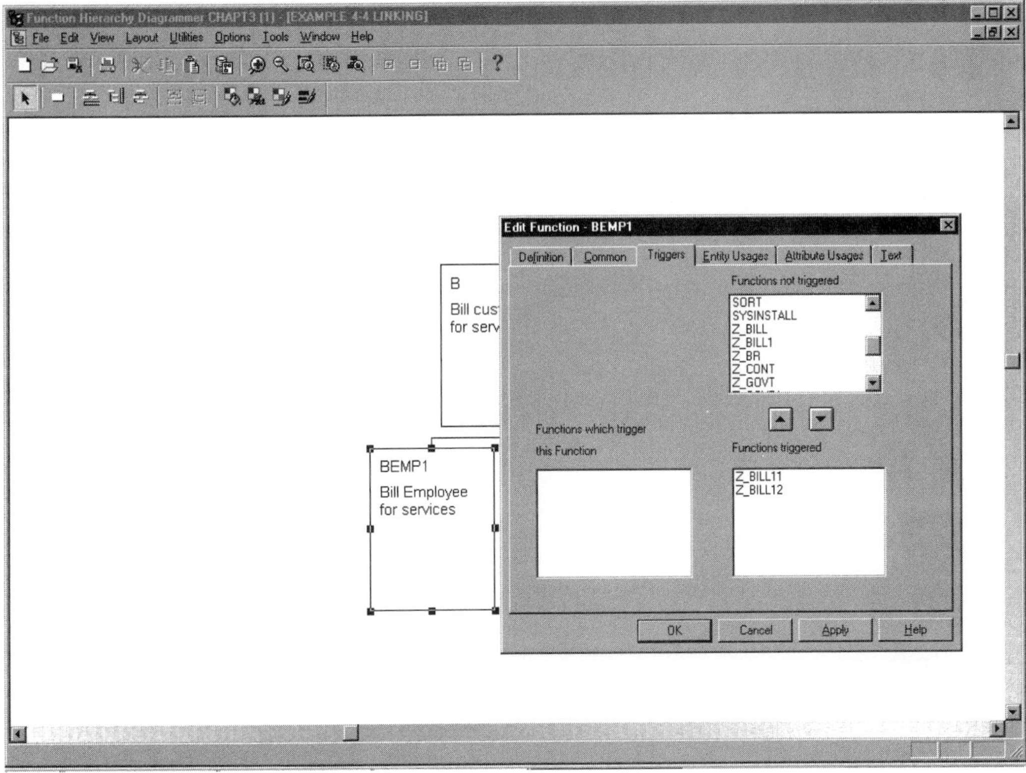

FIGURE 4.5 Selecting a "rule" to link to a function.

do this you must have already defined your Business Functions in the Designer repository (see Chapter 5).

In the FHD, activate the Edit Function dialog window by double clicking on a function (Figure 4.4). Next select the Triggers tab.

In the functions not triggered window, select the business rule(s) that you would like to associate to this business function and then click on the down arrow. Then click on OK to save. Be sure to select only "rules" where the function label contains a 'Z' and a number. For example: Z_BILL11 (Figure 4.5).

It is again recommended that a custom API report be created to print business functions and their associated business rules. An alternative is to use Solutron, Inc.'s product Publisher/2000 reporting software.

Chapter 5

Business Processes and Functions

Process and function modeling are sets of methods and techniques for capturing what your organization does. Both methods involve identifying what a business does (*processes and functions*), what triggers those activities (*events*), and which information (*entities*), or properties of that information (*attributes*) are acted on by the function. Process modeling involves developing a diagram to capture the activities of your organization and the sequence in which they take place. For more complex organizations, your model may consist of a number of diagrams, each showing the details of the higher (top) level processes.

This chapter presents standards for naming and recording information about:

- ❑ Business processes
- ❑ Process labels
- ❑ Process short definitions
- ❑ Business functions
- ❑ Function labels
- ❑ Function short definitions
- ❑ Common functions
- ❑ Elementary functions
- ❑ Data stores
- ❑ Data flows

In addition we discuss the best way to enter all this information into Oracle Designer.

GETTING STARTED

You should start by defining the top-level processes in your organization. These can be directly derived from the objectives that were defined by management. Each of these major processes are made up of a number of lower-level processes. Typically, there will be between five and ten major processes.

It is important to start with a complete picture of what your organization does, even if the picture is not very detailed in the beginning. With nothing more than the names of the major processes, you can start breaking down those processes into lower-level processes and functions.

Typically you use function hierarchies for a purely decompositional approach and process modeling for a more business process approach. However, we recommend a combined approach in which business process modeling is performed only to identify and define major high-level processes that are performed by your organization. Then, function decomposition is performed on each major process until you have decomposed the process to its elementary level. This will ensure that business users understand and contribute to the process models (business process models) and that there is sufficient implementation detail (function hierarchies and detailed elementary function definitions).

As mentioned previously, business process modeling and function hierarchy decomposition are two different methods used for performing business process modeling. Business process modeling allows the analyst to document the flow between business processes and the interaction of the business units that perform, or are responsible for, these processes. Function hierarchy decomposition entails the capturing of business processes and their lower level supporting functions without the identification of the business units that perform them. Both methods can coexist during the same business engineering/re-engineering effort. However, you need to be aware of and understand the interaction between the two methods and approaches and how they interact with the Repository Object Navigator (RON). As this topic is somewhat beyond the scope of this book, we have provided Appendix C, which contains an article that explains the relationship between the Oracle Designer Business Process Modeler (BPM) and the Function Hierarchy Diagrammer (FHD).

BUSINESS PROCESSES

> Business processes will be captured using the Process Modeler and the Function Hierarchy Diagrammer.

A business process is a set of actions performed by one or more business units. Frequently, business areas encompass the same set of actions and have the same names as related business processes. A business process may contain other business processes in addition to business functions. When creating a functional hierarchy diagram, both business processes and business functions are legitimate functional entries.

We recommend that a high-level enterprise-wide Business Process model be established in the repository. This will facilitate the subsequent decomposition of the business processes by providing pre-established high-level views of the business. This "seeding" of the repository can be from one to two levels deep and usually no more than seven to nine processes wide.

> All the highest level Business Processes have been identified and entered into the process model. Standard industry descriptions have been, and will continue to be used to identify business processes.

All the highest level Business Processes should be identified and entered into the enterprise-level process model. These processes detail the highest levels of organization in the enterprise and are modeled to establish a common environment for the corporation. In most cases, standard industry descriptions should be used to identify business processes so that the models can be easily understood by executives and managers who will need to review these models. In a changing business environment, the use of standard names and descriptions also provides the flexibility needed to support a dynamic environment.

If your organization elects not to "seed" the repository with a high-level process model, you should rewrite this section of the standards document. The following example of this standards section could be used to replace the section defined previously.

> All the highest level Business Processes must be identified and entered into the process model. Standard industry descriptions should be used to identify business processes.

Once the highest level processes have been identified and entered into Designer, you will need to continue to add additional lower level processes that extend the overall model. We recommend limiting the number of lower levels developed before switching from Business Process Modeling to functional decomposition.

> As additional process models are developed, they will be appended to the appropriate higher level process in the Enterprise Model. These extensions of the Enterprise Model may not exceed two additional levels of business processes before functional decomposition begins.
>
> If additional levels are required for a very complex model, the extension must be approved by the System Architecture Committee.

Limiting the analysis to only two levels of process definitions will simplify the model and, at the same time, expedite the decomposition of processes into functions without sacrificing business process detail.

BUSINESS PROCESS LABELS

We recommend that you establish a logical system of labels. The following is our recommendation. Refer to the section on "Entering Process Model Information" in this chapter for details on where and how to enter this information.

> At the highest two levels of the enterprise, the business process labels have a single alpha character and have already been established. All subsequent levels of business processes labels will be composed of three (3) alpha characters where the *first* of the three characters is the name of the level two parent.
>
> **Example:**
>
> CAM is the label for the Customer Account Maintenance process, which is a child of the level two process 'C' Customer Services.
>
> Labels are automatically displayed in FHDs to help identify processes and functions hierarchic relationships.

By using this labeling standard, it will be easy for business experts to identify and review processes related to their areas.

BUSINESS PROCESS SHORT DEFINITIONS

Business processes define what an organization does currently or what it needs to do in the future. These processes are expressed as nouns, whereas the actions that an organization performs currently or needs to perform in the future are captured as functions in the form of verbs. Refer to the section on Entering Process Model Information in this chapter for details on where and how to enter this information.

The short definition of a business process is always a noun or nominative phrase.

Example 1:

Accounting and Fixed Assets are standard high level processes;

Accounts Payable, Accounts Receivable and General Ledger are processes which are functions of the higher level process, Accounting;

Asset Acquisition, Asset Capitalization, Asset Depreciation and Asset Retirement are processes, which are functions of the higher level process, Fixed Assets.

Example 2:

Planning, Customer Service and Marketing are standard high level processes;

Customer Account Maintenance and Collections are processes, which are functions of the higher level process, Customer Service.

This standard helps to distinguish processes from functions, as function short definitions always start with a verb.

ENTERING PROCESS MODEL INFORMATION

Oracle Designer provides you with an extensive set of tools for capturing process information. You can enter process model information into the repository using the RON, BPM, matrix diagrammer, data flow diagrammer (DFD), or FHD. Choosing the best tool can be subjective. Based on our years of experience, we have found that using the BPM to define major high-level processes and subsequently using the FHD to decompose processes into more detail is the most efficient way to capture business requirements.

The following example shows how to enter the process model information using the BPM. Later we will show you how to decompose these processes into functions using the FHD.

When you create a new process diagram, you can base it on an existing process or you can create a new root process.

Follow these steps to create a new diagram:

1. Click on File-> New
2. In the New Diagram Dialog box either
   - ❑ Select one of the processes displayed and click on OK

   or

   - ❑ Select Create New Root Process, type a short definition and label, then click on OK to save

Note: A root process is a process that has no parent.

Figure 5.1 shows an example of creating a new root process/function.

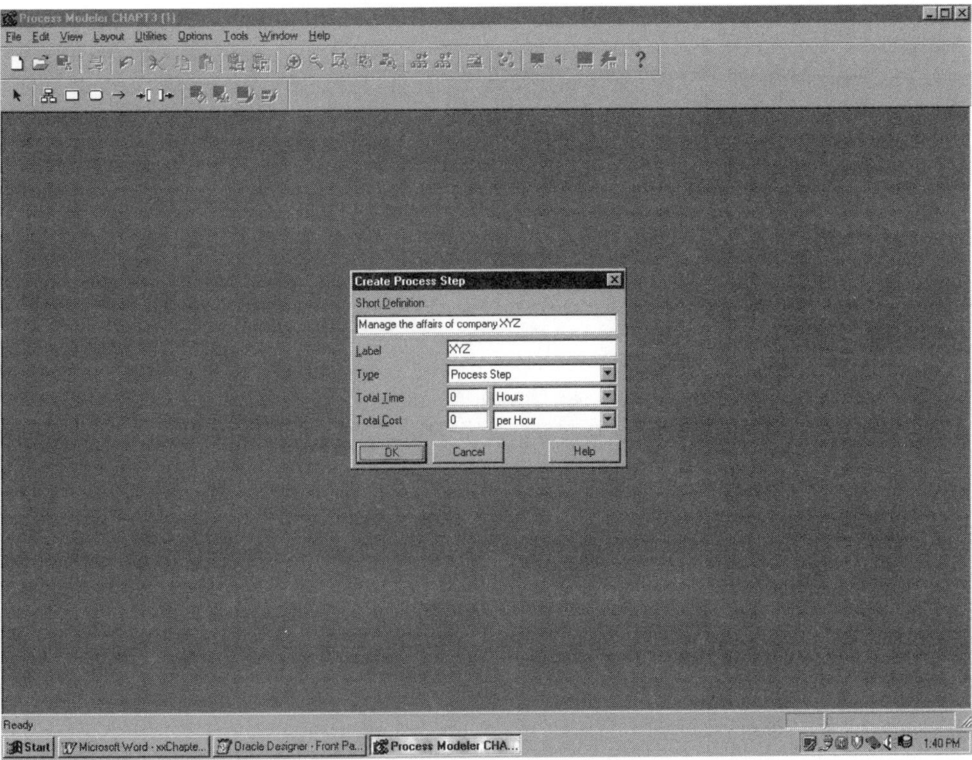

Figure 5.1 Creating a new process step.

Figure 5.2 Base process of a new diagram.

Figure 5.2 shows that the process you just created became the base process for the new diagram (i.e., it does not show up as a process in a swim lane). At the top of the diagram, you will see the short name of the process that was just created.

As you create new processes in this diagram they will become subprocesses (children) of the base processes. Follow these steps to create new processes in a diagram.

1. Include or create organization units to be shown on this diagram. The steps in performing this task are detailed in Chapter 3: Enterprise Strategic Objects, in Business Units.
2. From the tools pallet, click on the "create process step" button and click in the organization units swim lane that you want this function to be associated with.
3. Enter the short definition and the label.
4. Click OK to save

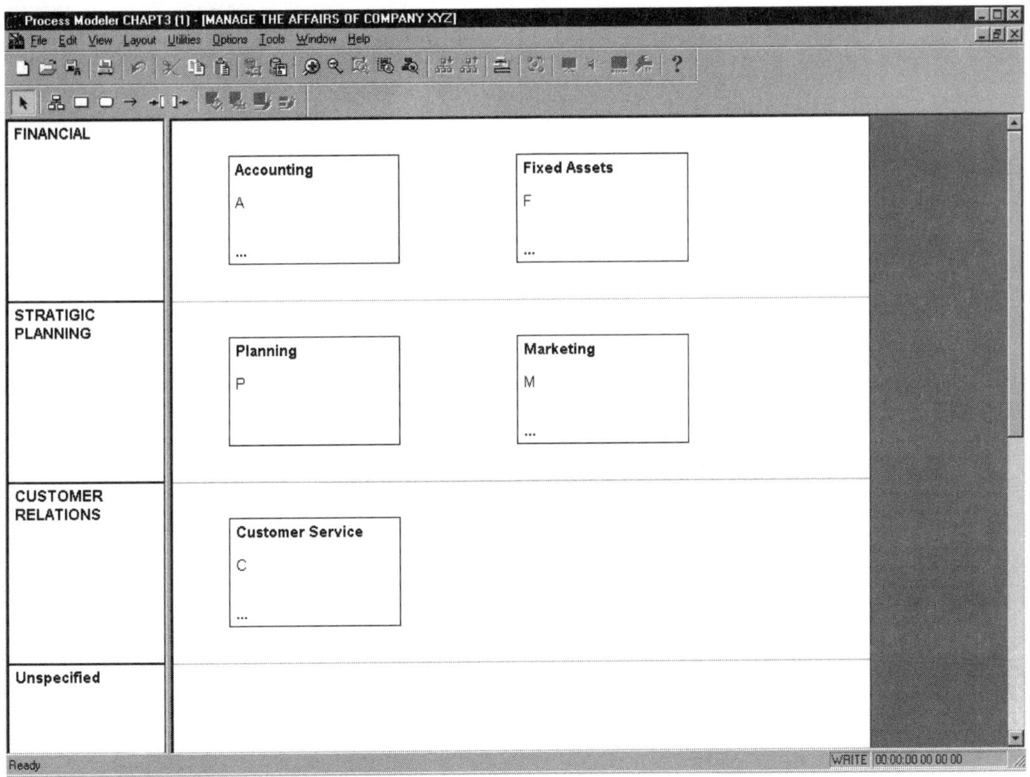

Figure 5.3 Illustration of processes in a Business Process Model diagram.

Figure 5.3 shows how the process would look in the BPM.

Each of these major processes can be broken down into lower-level processes.

The following steps outline the process.

1. Click on the process that you want to decompose.
2. Select File-> Open Down from the file menu. This action will cause a new diagram to be created with the selected process as the base process for the new diagram.

Figure 5.4 shows the major process Accounting broken down into lower-level processes.

Once you have entered the major processes and subprocesses of your organization, you can view them and start to decompose them into functions. You can create a function hierarchy diagram by following these steps:

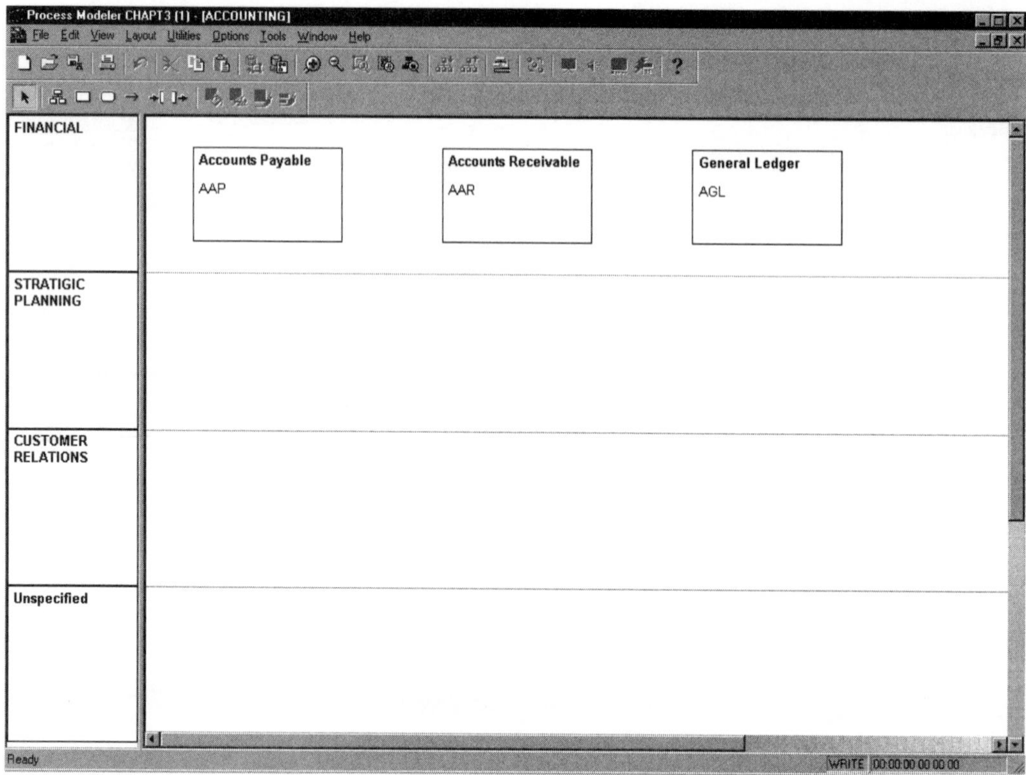

Figure 5.4 Lower-level process.

1. Open the FHD.
2. In the FHD, select File->New.
3. From the New Diagram dialog box select the root function (Figure 5.5). In our example, we are using "Manage the affairs of company XYZ."

All of the subprocesses of the selected process will automatically be included in the diagram (Figure 5.6).

The following characteristics will help differentiate a process from a function when viewed in a function hierarchy diagram:

- ❑ Process labels do not contain numbers.
- ❑ Process short definitions do not start with a verb.
- ❑ Processes usually will have subprocesses defined under them (depending on whether they have been fully decomposed).

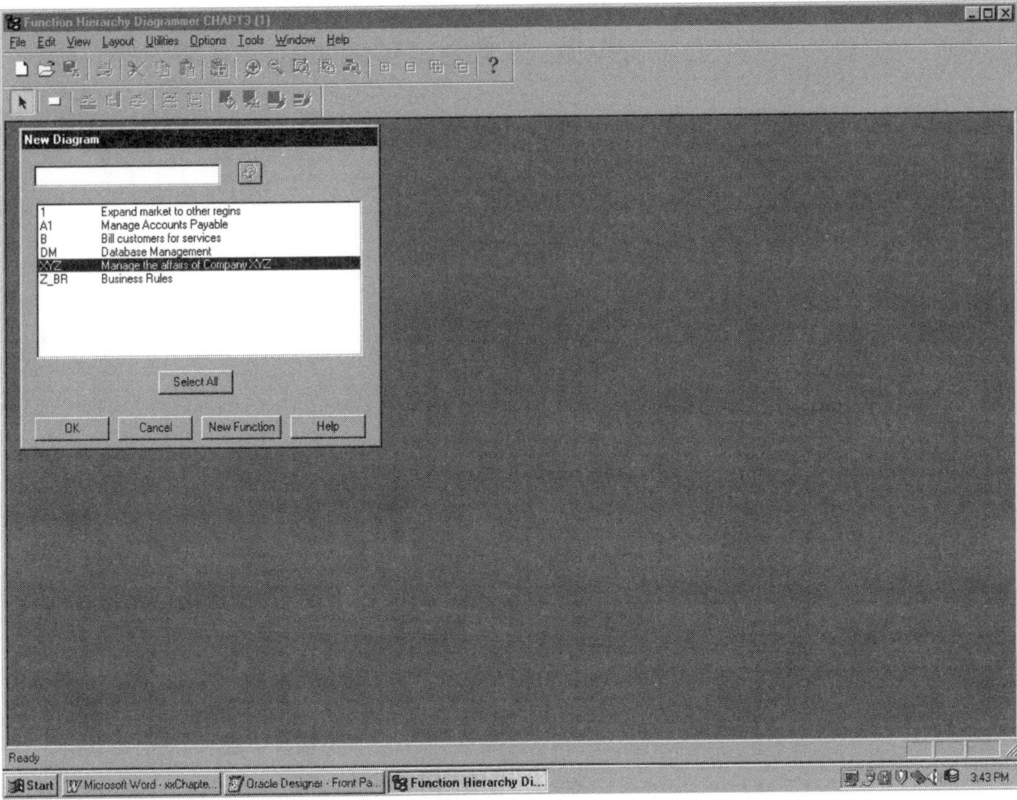

Figure 5.5 Create a new FHD from existing processes in the repository.

This convention is important because Business Processes and Business Functions are all stored as Business Function definitions in the Designer repository. If a naming standard is not applied, it can be next to impossible to discern if a function was created for use in a BPM or a FHD. This is a commonly overlooked and not widely understood problem.

BUSINESS FUNCTIONS

A business function is a named action performed by one or more business units as part of a business process. An elementary function is a function that has been decomposed to its lowest level. Elementary functions are discussed later in this chapter.

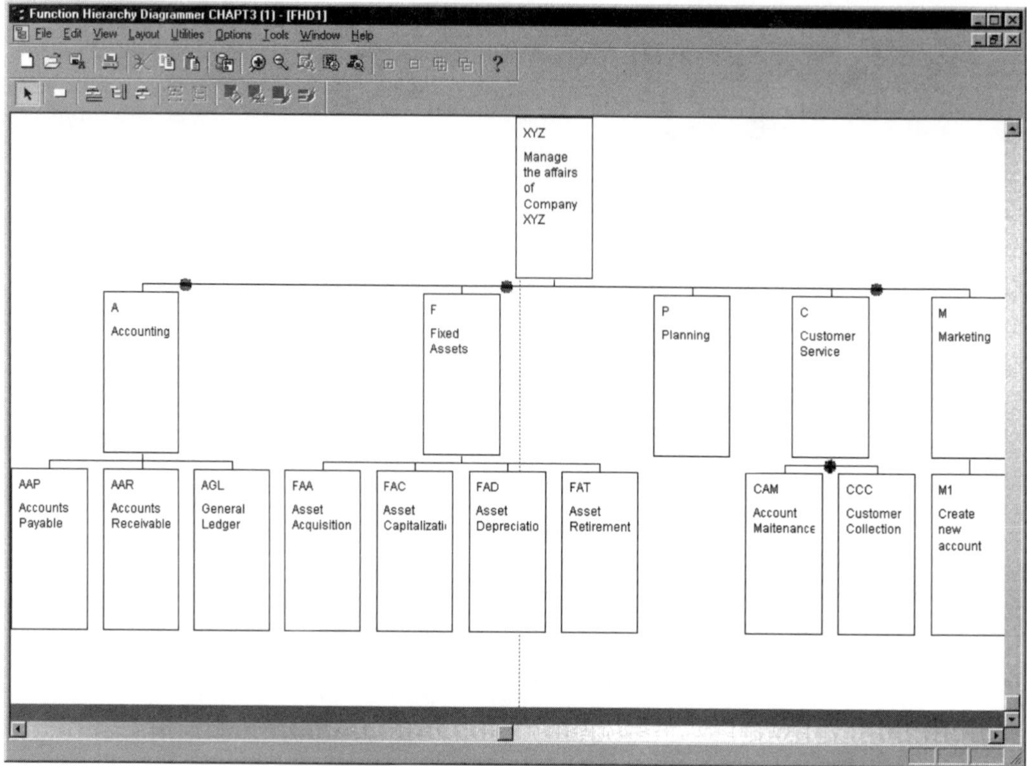

Figure 5.6 Illustration of how the major processes will look in the FHD.

BUSINESS FUNCTION LABELS

As mentioned previously, we recommend that you establish a logical system of labels. The following is our recommendation. Refer to the section Entering Function Model Information in this chapter for details on where and how to enter this information.

All business function labels are limited to ten (10) characters.

Labels are a concatenation of the label from the parent business process, and from one (1) to seven (7) numeric characters. The digits, which identify the level of functional decomposition within the business process, are positional and begin with one (1). This scheme supports a maximum of seven (7) levels of functional decomposition of a business process.

Use of alpha characters in the positional parameters will be permitted only on an exception basis with approval of the System Architecture Committee.

Examples:

CAM1: Establish New Account

Where:

C = Customer Service

CAM = Account Maintenance (Business Process which is also a function of the *primary* business process Customer Service)

1 = Establish New Account (First, First Level Function of the process CAM Account Maintenance)

CAM11: Conduct interview

Where:

C = Customer Service

CAM = Account Maintenance (Business Process which is also a function of the *primary* business process Customer Service)

1 = Establish New Account (First, First Level Function in the process CAM Account Maintenance)

1 = Conduct interview (First, Second Level Function in the process CAM1 Establish New Account)

CAM12: Record applicant data

Where:

C = Customer Service

CAM = Customer Account Maintenance (Business Process which is also a function of the *primary* business process Customer Service)

1 = Establish New Account (First, First Level Function in the process CAM Account Maintenance)

2 = Record applicant data (Second, Second Level Function in the process CAM1 Establish New Account)

BUSINESS FUNCTION SHORT DEFINITIONS

Business functions define actions that are currently performed or what needs to be performed in the future. These functions are expressed as verbs, whereas business processes define what an organization does currently or what it needs to do in the future. Refer to the section on "Entering Function Model Information" in this chapter for details on where and how to enter this information.

> Business Functions will have a short definition consisting of a verb and an object. Always describe the function starting with a verb. If you don't, it will be confused with a process. The short definition can consist of as few as two words, or it can be as long as a sentence. It should clearly describe the complete activity carried out within the scope of that function.
>
> **Examples:** Establish New Account, Revise Existing Contract

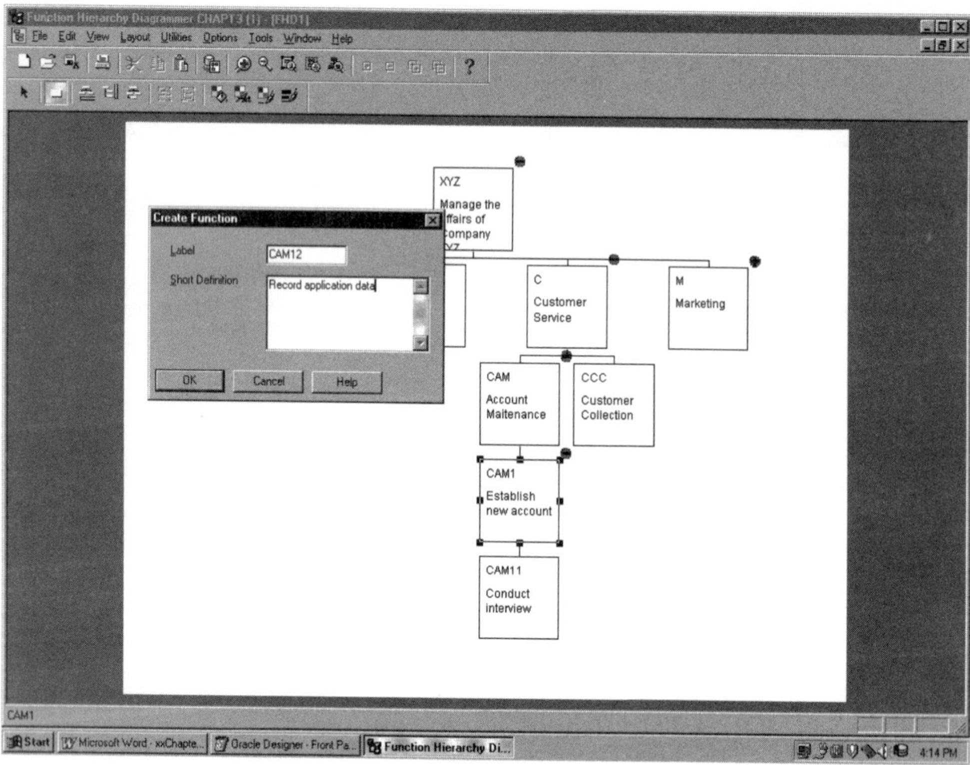

Figure 5.7 Create function dialog box.

ENTERING FUNCTION MODEL INFORMATION

As with processes, you can enter functions into the repository using the RON, BPM, DFD, or the FHD. We recommend entering functions using the FHD.

Perform the following steps to create a process or function in the FHD:

1. Select the function button on the tool palette and drop it onto the function that you want it to be a child function of.
2. Fill in the label and short definition and click OK to save.

Figure 5.7 shows the Create Function dialog box for creating the function CAM12 Record application data.

Figure 5.8 shows how the previous examples would look in the FHD. (Layout conventions for FHDs are discussed in Part 2 Diagramming Conventions, Chapter 12: Function Hierarchy Diagrams.)

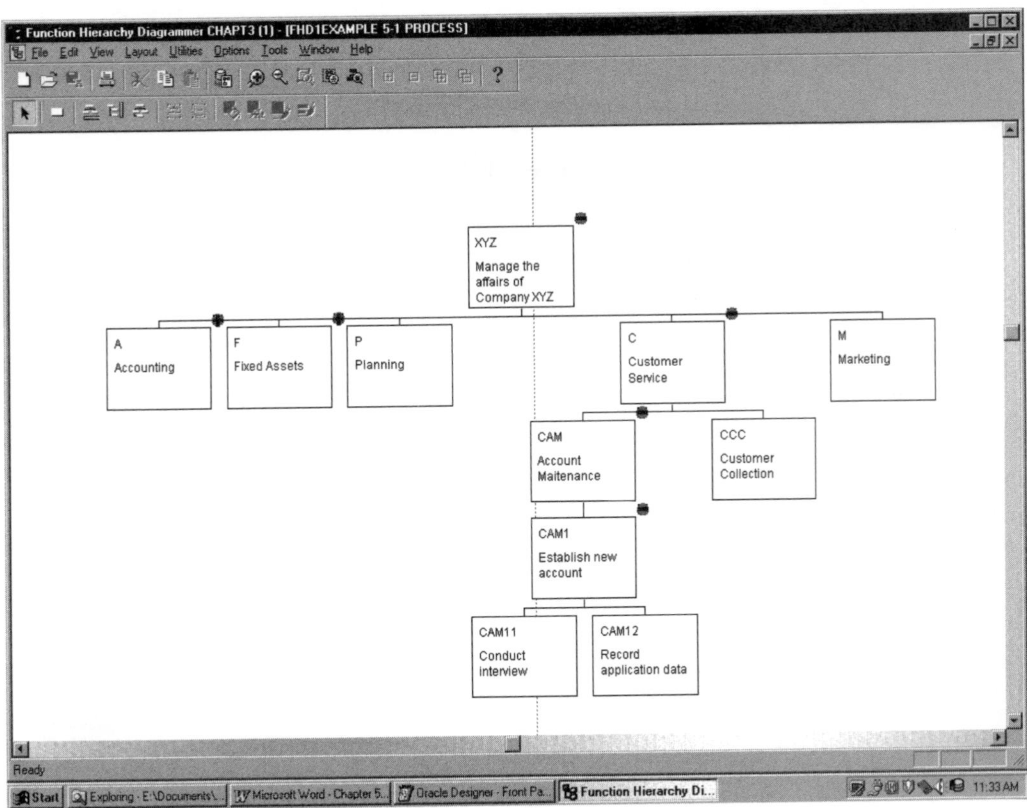

Figure 5.8 Example of a process decomposed to its elementary functions.

The following characteristics help differentiate a function from a process when viewed in a FHD:

- Function labels *must* contain numbers.
- Function short definitions *must* start with a verb.
- Functions usually will not have subprocesses defined under them (elementary function).

COMMON FUNCTIONS

Common functions are functions that are identical in what they do in terms of how they act on the same data requirements. When you perform business process re-engineering, you try to identify commonality between functions that are per-

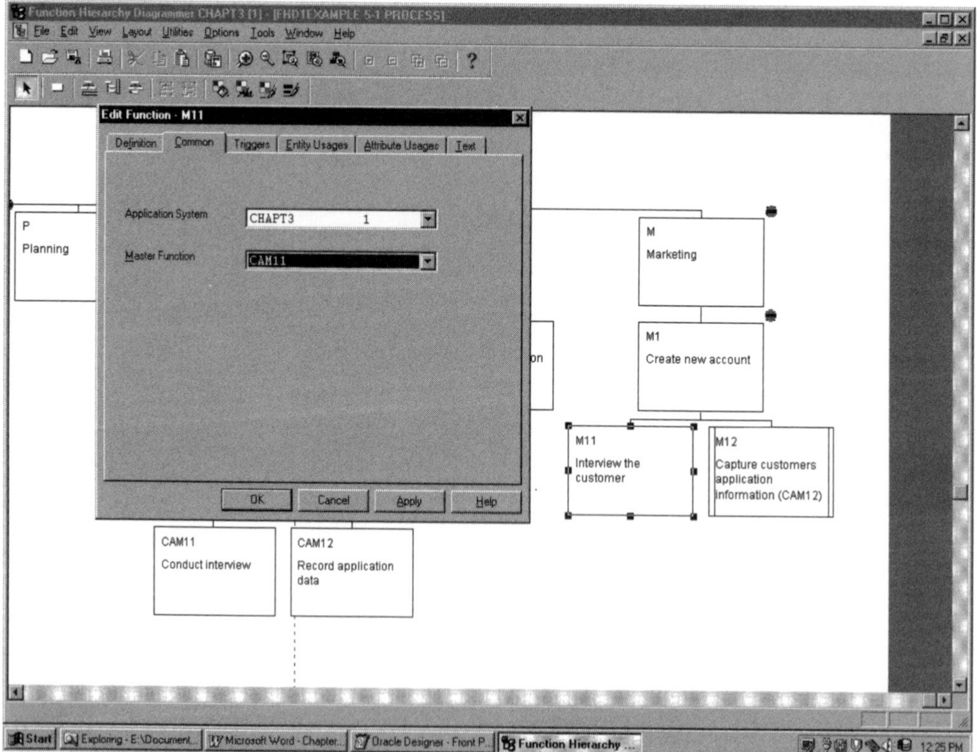

Figure 5.9 Creating common functions.

formed by different areas, or maybe even in the same area. These are areas that will be looked at for re-engineering efforts.

When a new system is developed, each process/function that can be used to satisfy more than one requirement saves development, implementation, mainte-

> All Common Functions must include the master function label as part of the short definition.
>
> **Example:**
>
> **Label:** M11
>
> **Definition:** Interview the customer (CAM11)
>
> Where CAM11 is the master function "Conduct Interview".

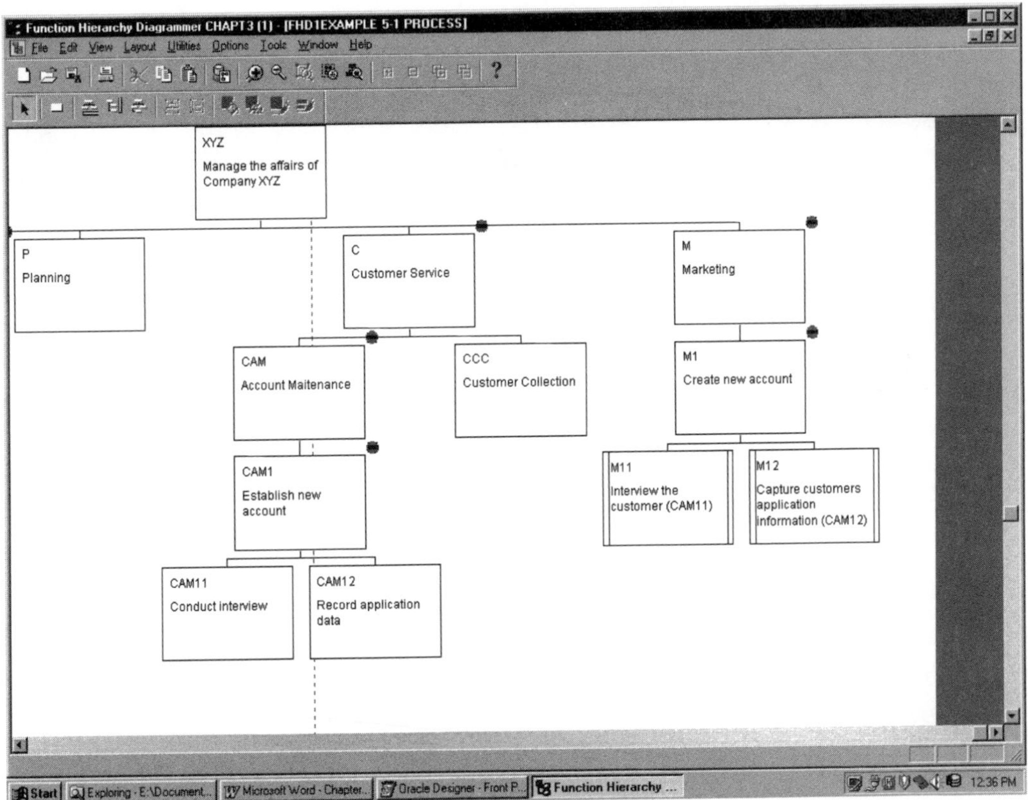

Figure 5.10 Common functions in a FHD.

nance, and enhancement time. Thus striving for common functions is a worthwhile exercise.

When common functions are shown on an FHD, you can not see the name of the master function that the common function is based on. Because of this fact, when creating a common function, you should include the master functions label as part of the function short definition. For example, an *interview* function that is performed as part of the marketing process could be defined as "Interview the customer (CAM11)," where CAM11 identifies the master function that it is based on (Figure 5.9).

CREATING COMMON FUNCTIONS

To create a common function using the FHD, you must first create the function. Next double click on the function and select the common tab. Select the current application and then select the label of the function that you want this common function to be based on (i.e., select the Master Function). The function will be displayed with two vertical lines on both sides of it (Figure 5.10).

Figure 5.10 shows that function M11 is common with function CAM11, and function M12 is common with function CAM12.

ELEMENTARY FUNCTIONS

Richard Barker in the book, *Oracle CASE*Method: Function and Process Modelling*, defines an elementary function as "A business function which, if started, must be completed. It cannot exist in an intermediate stage." Elementary business functions are at the lowest level of a function hierarchy. They must be defined as atomic and elementary; that is, they cannot be further decomposed.

This section:

- ❑ Explains how you will know when you are done with function decomposition.
- ❑ Explains and illustrates how to define a function as elementary.
- ❑ Explains and illustrates how to define function data usages.

A good elementary function test is defined as a function that leaves the business in a state of consistency; that is, if it fails for some reason, any effect it has on the information must be returned to its original state. An example of this type would be a function within an *"ATM withdrawal"* process. The function *"Give money to customer"* would include debiting the account and counting the money and giving it to the customer. It would not be a complete transaction if you only debited the account and failed to give the money to the customer. If the giving of the money to the customer failed, you would want to return the customer's account balance to its original state before the start of the ATM withdrawal process.

HOW DO YOU KNOW WHEN YOU ARE DONE WITH FUNCTION DECOMPOSITION?

Do not go too far. Each situation is different, and deciding when sufficient detail has been reached is highly subjective. We recommend decomposing functions only to a point where:

- The function can be tracked as a unit of work.
- The function passes the "elementary function test."

DEFINING A FUNCTION AS ELEMENTARY

You can capture the details of a function using the RON, DFD, FHD, or the matrix diagrammer. We recommend using the FHD, as you can visually see the leaf level functions.

Perform the following steps to define a function as elementary:

1. In the FHD, open a diagram and double click on a leaf function.
2. In the Definitions tab, click in the Elementary check box.
3. In the Response property, select the type of response required. Later in the design phase, the application transformer will use this attribute to determine the type of module to create (i.e., a response type of Immediate will cause the transformer to produce a module of type Developer Forms were as Overnight will produce a module of type Developer Reports).
4. Click OK to save.

Repeat these steps for all of the leaf level functions that you have decomposed (Figure 5.11).

DEFINING FUNCTION DATA USAGES

Once you have defined a function as elementary, you need to record the entities, attributes, and actions that the function will perform on those entities and attributes. This can be performed using the RON, FHD, DFD, and the matrix diagrammer. We again recommend that you use the FHD, as you did when defining a function as elementary. Ideally, you would perform this task at the same time you are performing the task of defining a function as elementary.

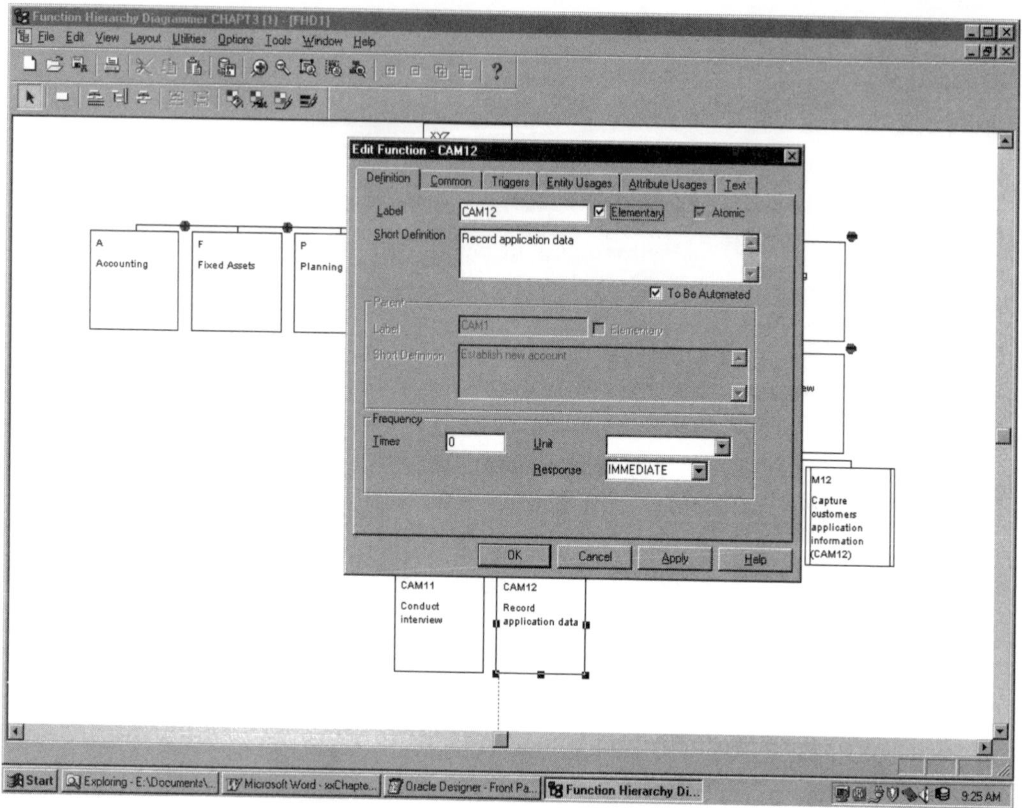

Figure 5.11 Defining a function as elementary.

Perform the following steps to define data usages for an elementary function:

1. In the FHD, open a diagram and double click on an elementary (leaf) function.
2. In the Entity Usage tab, select the entities that this function will use from the drop down list.
3. Check off the actions that the function will perform on each entity (Figure 5.12).
4. Select the Attribute Usages tab.
5. For each entity that was previously defined on the Entity Usages tab, select the attributes that this function will act on. Use the Attribute drop down list to select individual attributes, or press the "select all" button to automatically bring in all of the entity's attributes.

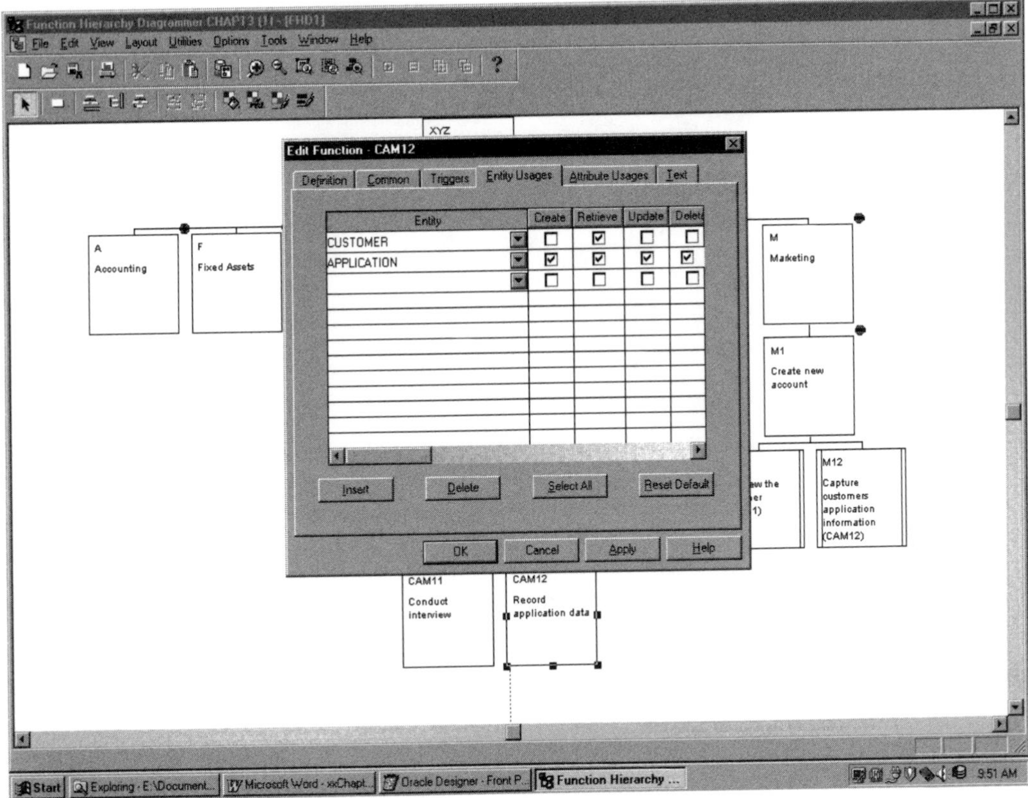

Figure 5.12 Create function entity usages.

6. You will notice that the actions that will be performed on each of the attributes were automatically filled in based on the actions that you previously defined at the entity level. You will need to review these actions to ensure that they are correct (Figure 5.13).

DATASTORES

Generally, a datastore is a collection of manual and/or system files or tables.

Datastores can be created using the RON, BPM, or the DFD.

Note: The RON and DFD will provide the functionality to define entity and attribute usage's for a datastore, however, you cannot define data usage's in the BPM.

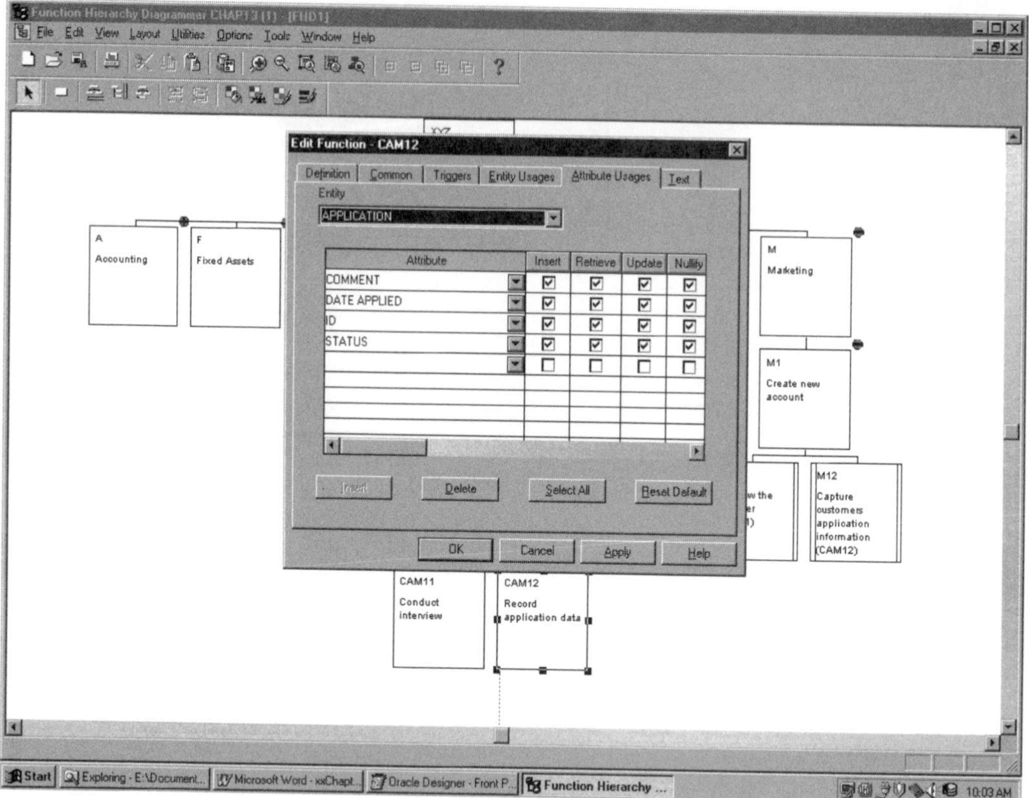

Figure 5.13 Create attribute usages.

A datastore must have a name and an ID.

Datastore names must describe the contents of the datastore and are restricted to thirty (30) characters. Datastore IDs are limited to ten (10) characters.

Example:

CUSTOMER SERVICE INFORMATION is the name of a datastore that contains files, tables, paper forms, etc. related to Customer Service.

CSI is the ID for the datastore.

Data is the type for the datastore.

Since more and more people are using business process modeling techniques over data flow diagramming, the following example will use the BPM tool to illustrate how to create datastores.

1. In the BPM, select the "create store" button on the tool pallete and click the swim lane corresponding to the organization unit to which the store belongs. If a store is used by multiple organization units, you should create it in the Unspecified swim lane.
2. Enter the datastore name and ID.
3. Select the type of "Data Store." Where physical items are held, this is called a *Material store*. Where information is held, this is known as a *Data store*.
4. Click OK to save.

Figure 5.14 shows the "Create Store" dialog box. Figure 5.15 shows how the store will look in the BPM.

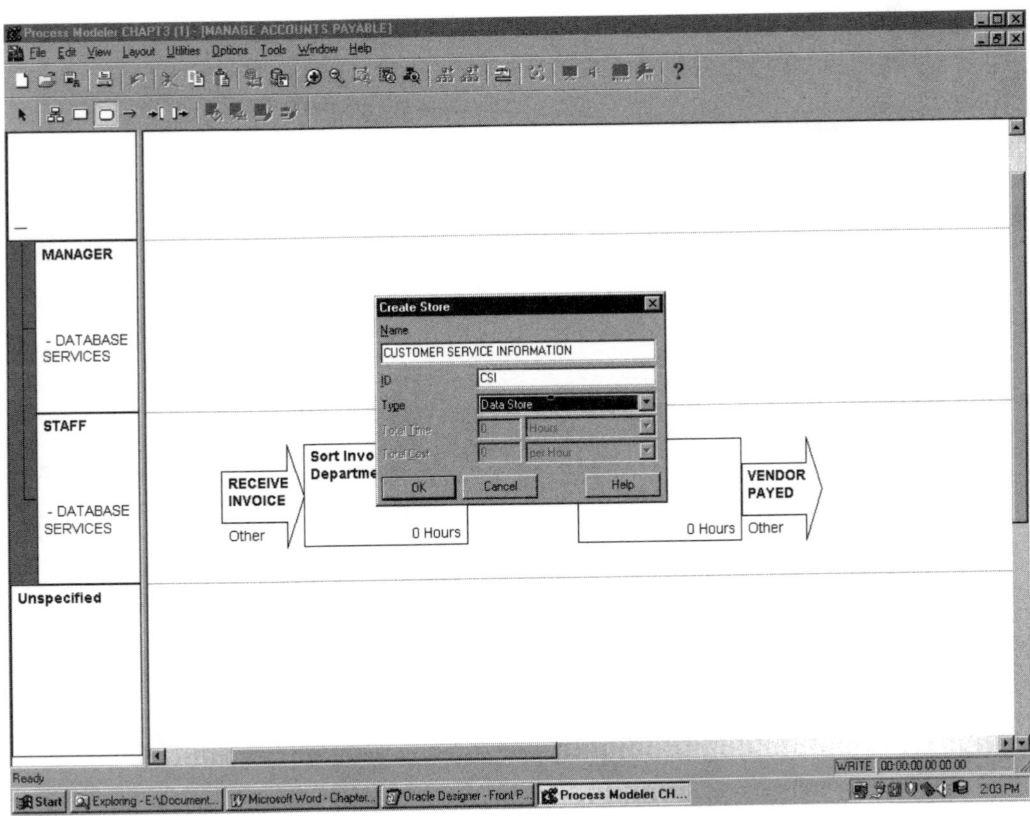

Figure 5.14 Create store dialog box.

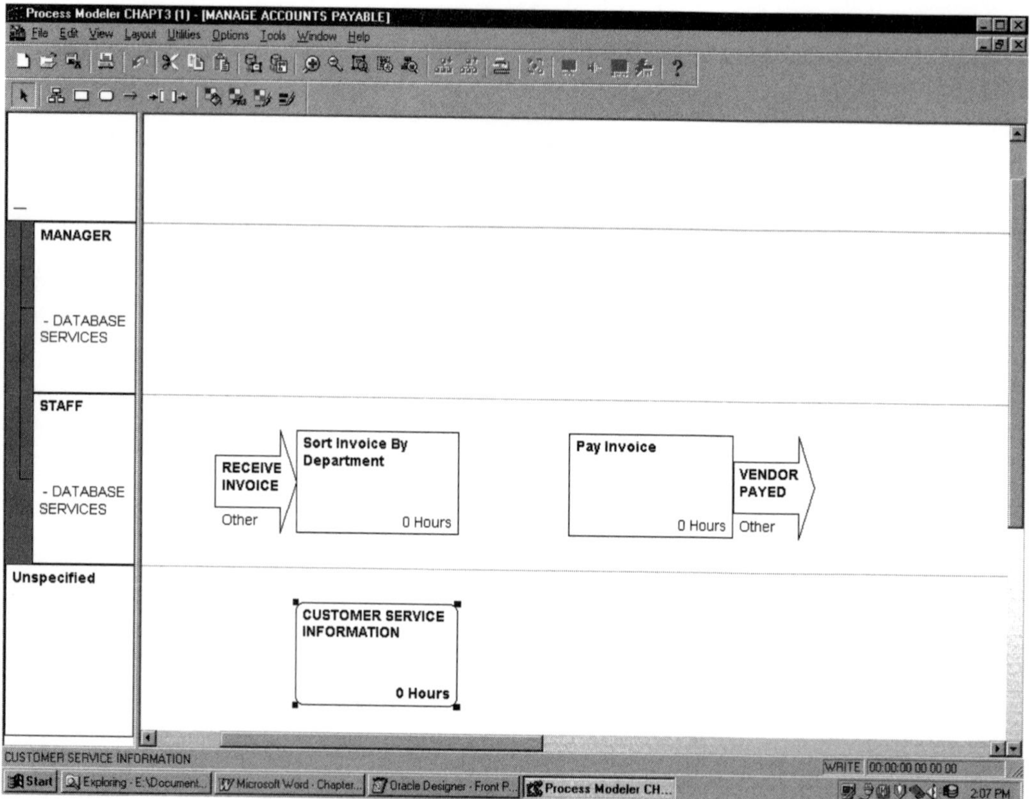

Figure 5.15 Datastore in a BPM.

You can now create flows to and from your stores. You should define any flows in and out of material stores as flows of type "material" and flows into and out of data stores as flows of type "data".

Once you have created the datastore, you can optionally define the data that the store represents in the form of entities and attributes. Unfortunately, this function is not available through the BPM; you will have to use the RON to accomplish it. The following steps must be completed to create datastore data usages. **Note:** The entities and attributes must already be defined in the repository to associate them with datastores.

1. In the RON, select the datastore that you want to define usages for under the Enterprise Modeling node.
2. Then click once on the + symbol to expand the datastore node.

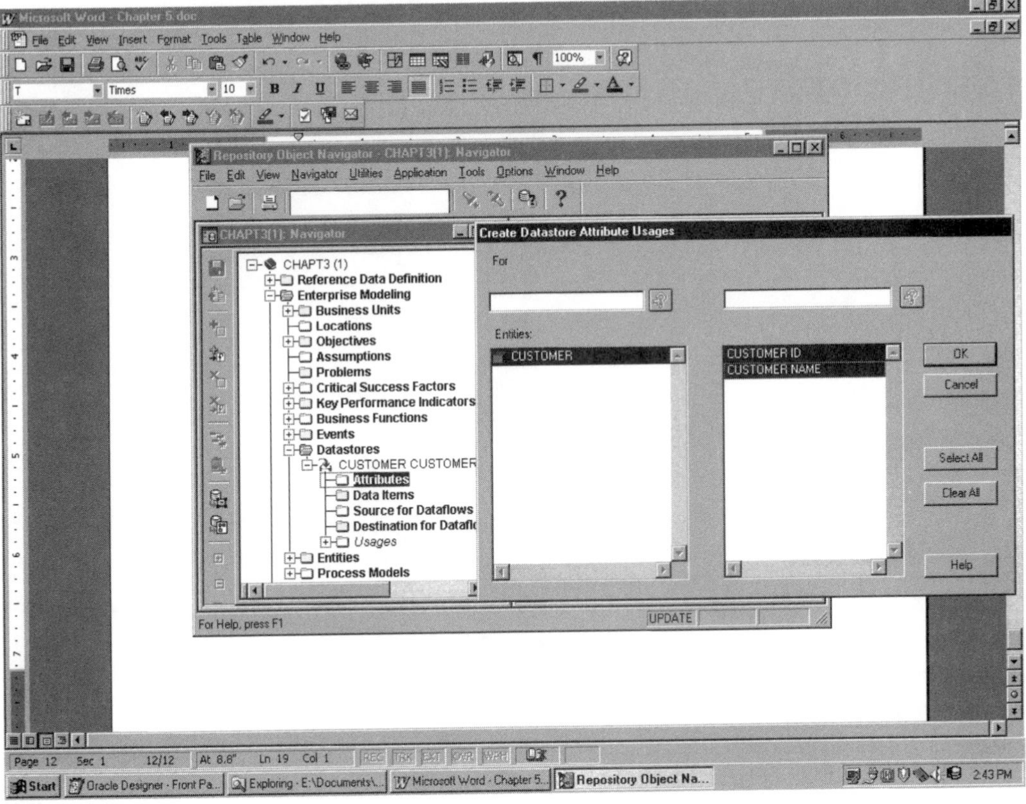

Figure 5.16 Create Datastore Attribute Usages.

3. Click on the attribute node and then click on the green plus sign to create the data usages.
4. In the Create Datastore Attribute Usages dialog box, select the entities on the left side and the attributes on the right side and click OK to save.

Figures 5.16 and 5.17 show the Create Datastore Attribute Usages dialog box and the final definition in the RON.

No specific standard states that datastores must be associated with data usages, as the information is very loosely defined (e.g., Customer Service Information datastore is a high level definition of the customer information that is captured by this store). The data usage information does not flow down into subsequent phases of the development life cycle. We recommend defining datastore usages only it if it helps communicate to the business community informa-

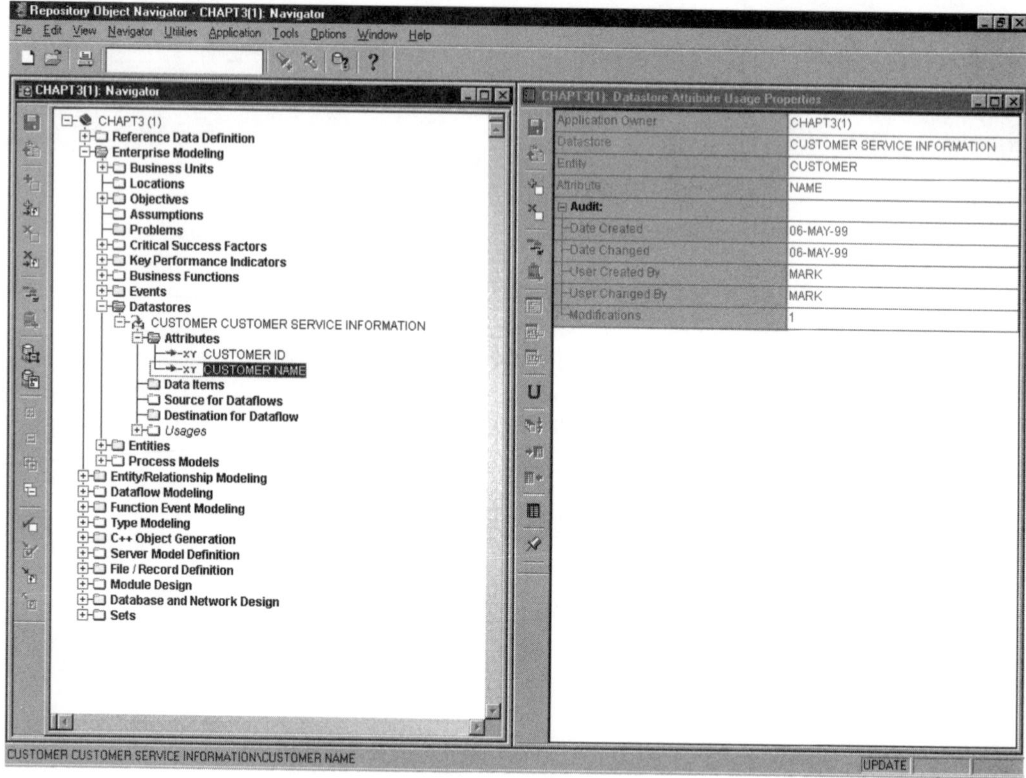

Figure 5.17 Datastore Attribute Usage in RON.

tion requirements for a specific process. However, we always recommend defining data usages at the elementary function level (see Elementary Business Functions).

DATAFLOWS

Flows record and display information about the flow between business objects. The flow between a process and a datastore is called a "data" flow. Other types of flows that can be recorded in the repository are material and temporal.

Dataflows can be created using the RON, BPM, or DFD.

Note: The RON and DFD will provide the functionality to define entity and attribute usages for a dataflow; however, you cannot define data usages in the BPM.

Data flows do not have to be named.

Flow names describe the contents of the flow and are restricted to thirty (30) characters.

Data is the type for the data flow.

Example:

CUSTOMER ACCOUNT INFO is the name of a data flow that contains information related to the Customer Service Information datastore**.** The data flow: **Customer Account Information may be the entire or just be a subset of the information defined by the data store Customer Service Information.**

Since more and more people are using business process modeling techniques over data flow diagramming, the following example will use the BPM tool to illustrate how to create dataflows.

1. In the BPM, select the "create flow" button on the tool pallete and click the source object (process or datastore) and then the destination object (process or datastore).
2. Enter the data flow name
3. Select the type of dataflow. There are three types of flows that you can use.
   - ❑ *Material flow* shows the passage of physical items, for example money.
   - ❑ *Temporal flow* shows a control sequence in which processes are performed in a particular order.
   - ❑ *Data flow* shows the flow of information between processes or stores.
4. Click OK to save.

Figure 5.18 and 5.19 shows the Create Flow dialog box and how it will look in the BPM once the flow has been added.

Once you have created the data flow, you can optionally define the data that the flow represents in the form of entities and attributes. As with the assignment to data stores, this functionality is not available through the BPM; you will have to use the RON to accomplish it. The following are the steps for creating data flow data usages. **Note:** The entities and attributes must already be defined in the repository to associate them with data flows.

1. In the RON, select the dataflow that you want to define usages for under the Dataflow Modeling node.

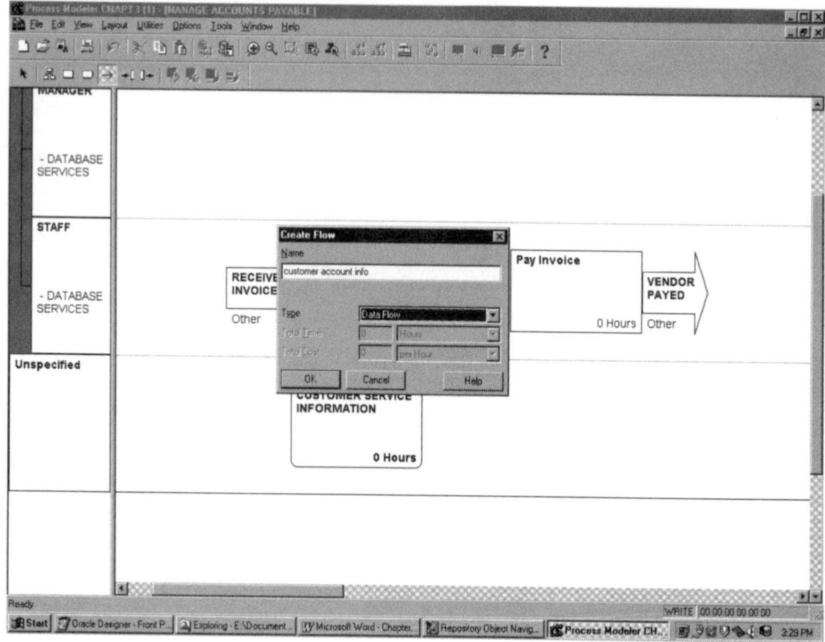

Figure 5.18 Create flow dialog box.

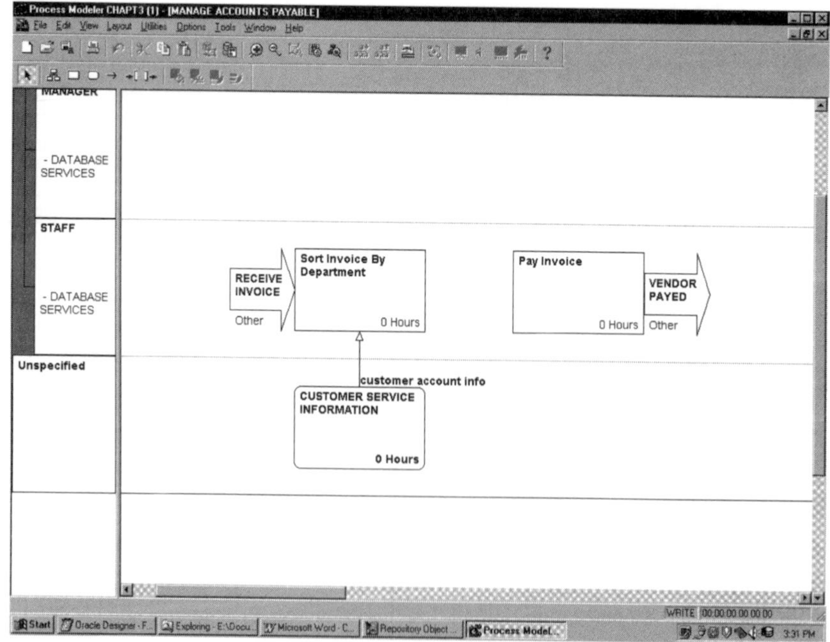

Figure 5.19 Illustration of a data flow in a BPM.

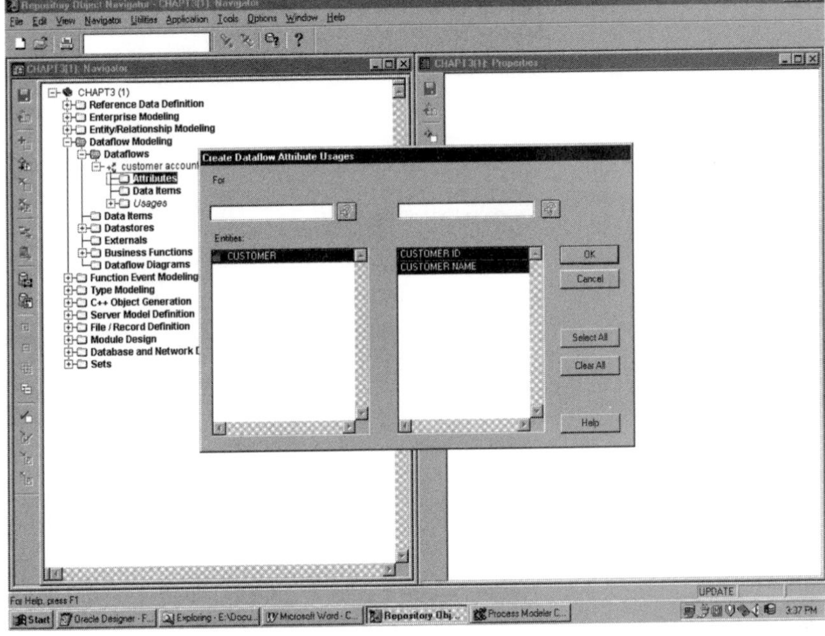

Figure 5.20 Create Dataflow Attribute Usages.

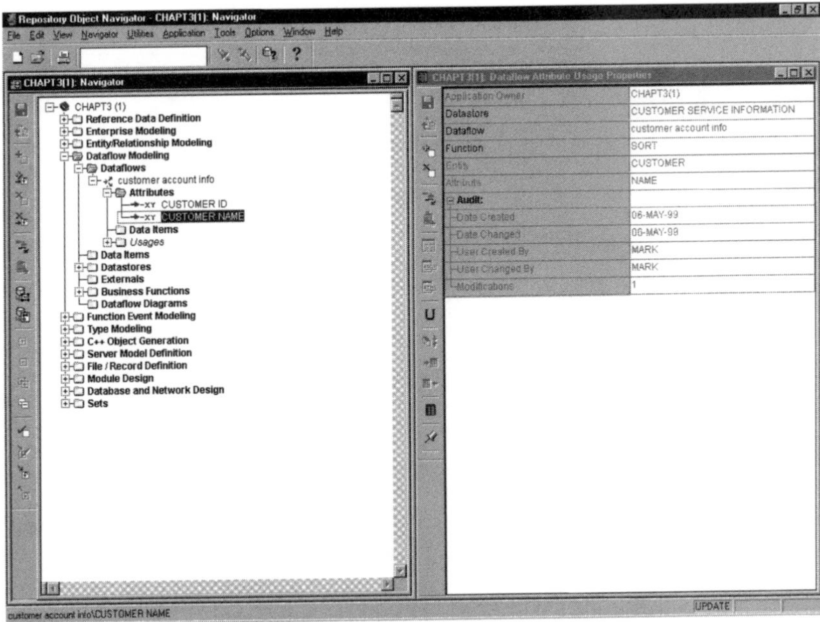

Figure 5.21 Dataflow Attribute Usage in RON.

2. Then click once on the + symbol to expand the dataflows node.
3. Click on the attribute node and then click on the green plus sign to create the data usages.
4. In the Create Dataflow Attribute Usages dialog box, select the entities on the left side and the attributes on the right side (Figure 5.20) and click OK to save.

Once you have completed these steps, you will be able to see the mappings in RON (Figure 5.21), and you will be able to produce reports from Designer for people to review your analysis.

Chapter 6

DOMAINS

A domain is a set of business validation rules, format constraints, and other properties that apply to a group of attributes. Domains are used to provide *standardized* characteristics for attributes defined in Oracle Designer. The characteristics associated with a domain will be used by the Database Design Transformer (DDT) and later by the various Designer generators. Their use decreases the amount of data entry and coding required and increases standardization across developed systems. In addition, the use of domains ensures consistency across attribute definitions (i.e., all *name* attributes are the same length, all dollar amounts are formatted the same).

Every organization should establish a predefined set of domains to be used in the development of their enterprise systems. The standards document included with this book contains an appendix with a list of domains that are applicable in a variety of situations. The CD-ROM also includes an archived Designer application with these domains already defined. Modifications to a standard domain list should be under the control of the Data Administrator.

The following sections discuss standard uses for domains and how to select which domain to use. The first section discusses naming domains as outlined in the standards document. Each additional section describes various usages and why they are important to consider. Choose the one that best fits the attribute you are defining. Generally this will be the most complex domain that fits your needs. If none of the established domains are suitable, ask the DA to establish a new domain and share them with all application systems that require it.

NAMING DOMAINS

Naming standards for domains are straightforward. The following text box contains the section from the standards document that addresses this issue.

Domain Names

Domain names may be up to (30) characters and should indicate the scope or contents of the domain. Do not place underscores between words in a domain name. If the name becomes too long, refer to the list of approved abbreviations and acronyms in the appendices of this document.

Examples:

Address

Amount

Id

Long Text (1000)

Very Long Text (2000)

Name

Domains will also be used, as required, to provide lists of values (LOVs) when generating forms from Designer. For such a domain, known as a reference domain, the domain name will be the plural of the attribute referenced.

Example: **STATES** is the reference domain for the attribute **STATE.**

SPECIFY FORMAT AND SIZE

All attributes require, at a minimum, a name, a format type, a length, and a comment. With the exception of a name, these characteristics can be supplied by the domain, hence the standard in the box on page 73.

Which domain to use is specified as a property of the attribute (Figure 6.1). In the Designer Edit Entity dialog, the domain can be selected using a standard pop-list. Once selected, the characteristics of the domain are automatically assigned to the attribute.

> The following properties are mandatory for all domains created for the enterprise:
>
> ❑ Name
>
> ❑ Attribute Format
>
> ❑ Column Datatype
>
> ❑ Maximum Length (both attribute and column)
>
> ❑ Comment (describes domain purpose, suggested uses, etc.).

Attributes, which are used for descriptive labels, generally fall into a discrete set of formats. For example, many entities will have an attribute called *description*. These attributes will fall into a category of short, medium, long, and text. Domains can be created for DESC xx where *xx* is the maximum length. When

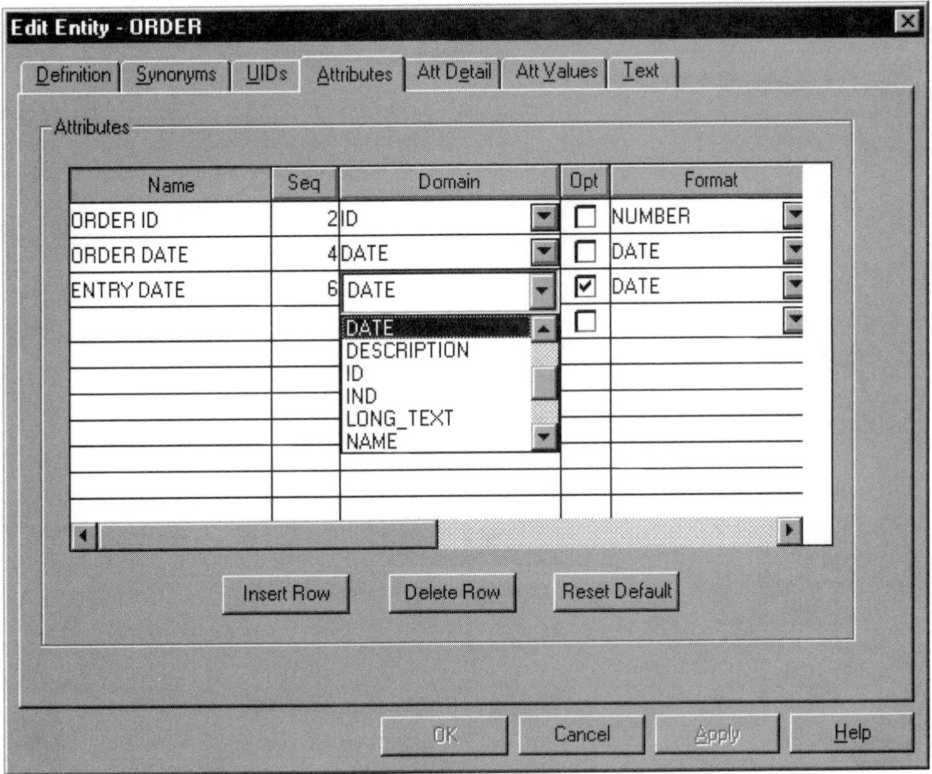

FIGURE 6.1 Assigning a domain in the Edit Entity dialog.

creating a descriptive attribute, choose the domain that best fits the length of your description. Specify that domain as a property of the attribute *instead of* specifying properties of length, and format type. Again, this will ensure standardization of size and format across the various *description* attributes in the enterprise.

Names of people (i.e., first, middle, and last), standardized number formats such as Social Security numbers, and geographical features are some of the other types of data for which domains can supply specialized formats.

SPECIFY DEFAULT VALUES

Default values are used to initialize data with suggested or anticipated values. Modules generated by Designer will incorporate any initial values supplied by domains. Domains can be effectively used to provide default values for attributes that repeatedly occur throughout an application system. By associating an attribute with a default value via a domain, the analyst is actually providing the initial specifications for the database and application design. If the analyst has done a thorough job of gathering requirements, this will actually help produce a higher quality system that users will accept.

For example, in a domain for a standard "yes/no" indicator flag, a default value of Y for yes or N for No might be specified. When entering data for a new employee, the active status is usually Y. Using this domain would default a Y for each new record. If a different status is required at creation, it can be easily substituted. However, for the vast majority of entries, this field will not need to be modified, there by saving time.

As shown in Figure 6.2, domain default values are entered using the *Detail* tab.

SPECIFY A RANGE OF VALUES

In addition to default values, domains can be useful for specifying other business rules such as a valid range of values. When an attribute using a domain has a range of values, the resulting column definition will be generated with a column level check constraint that enforces that range. Alternatively, the range could be enforced on the server using either the Table Application Programatic Interface (API) database triggers or check constraints created by the Server generator, or with client-side logic built by the Forms generator. For example, a domain of AMOUNT could be specified with maximum length of 10, money format, a column datatype of numeric with a range of values set to 0 to 999,999,999.99 (Figure 6.3). The attribute PURCHASE ORDER AMOUNT could then be assigned to that domain and inherit those characteristics. The subsequent table built with Designer would then provide check constraints in the form of in-line column check constraints, API code, and/or client side code to enforce this range.

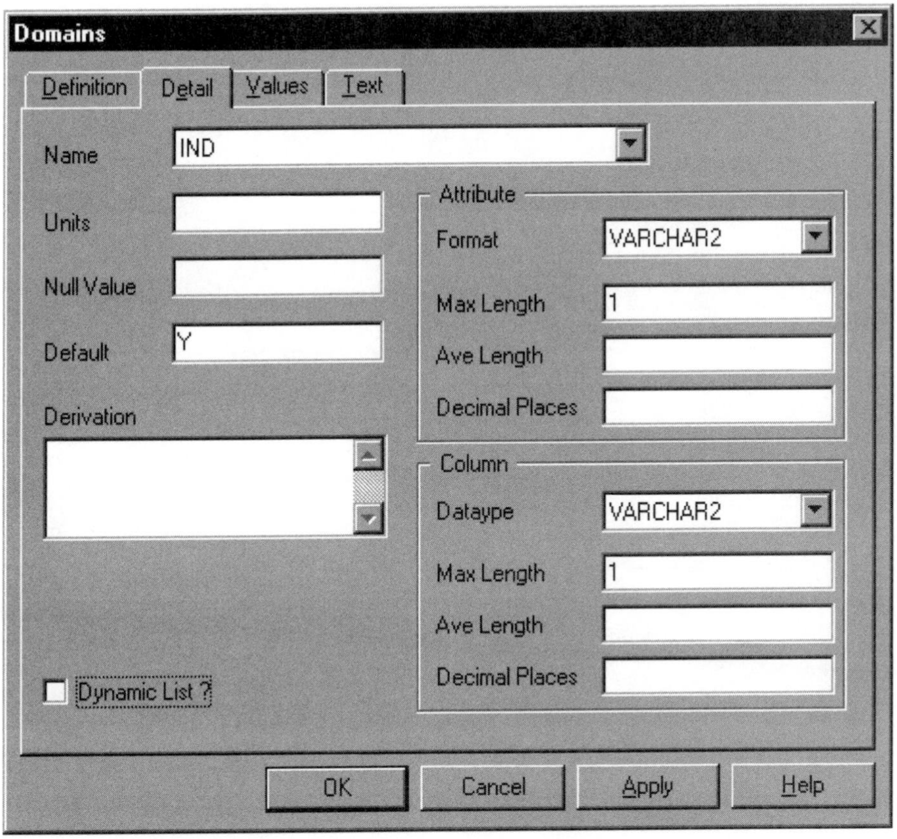

FIGURE 6.2 Entering a default value for a domain.

SPECIFY A LIST OF VALUES

A limited number of domains should be established to provide list of values (LOV) pop-up lists to help in data entry and validation. These domains can be configured to provide direct incorporation (hard-coding) into modules during the generation processes. They also can be configured to provide data via external access to a collapsed table containing the values. For a more detailed discussion regarding the implementation of domains using Designer, see the book *Oracle Designer Generation*.

The configuration method you choose depends on processing and maintenance considerations. Generally, access to an external table requires input-output that might deteriorate performance if the LOV is quite large. Direct incorporation of a domain's values into a module negates performance issues. However, if any

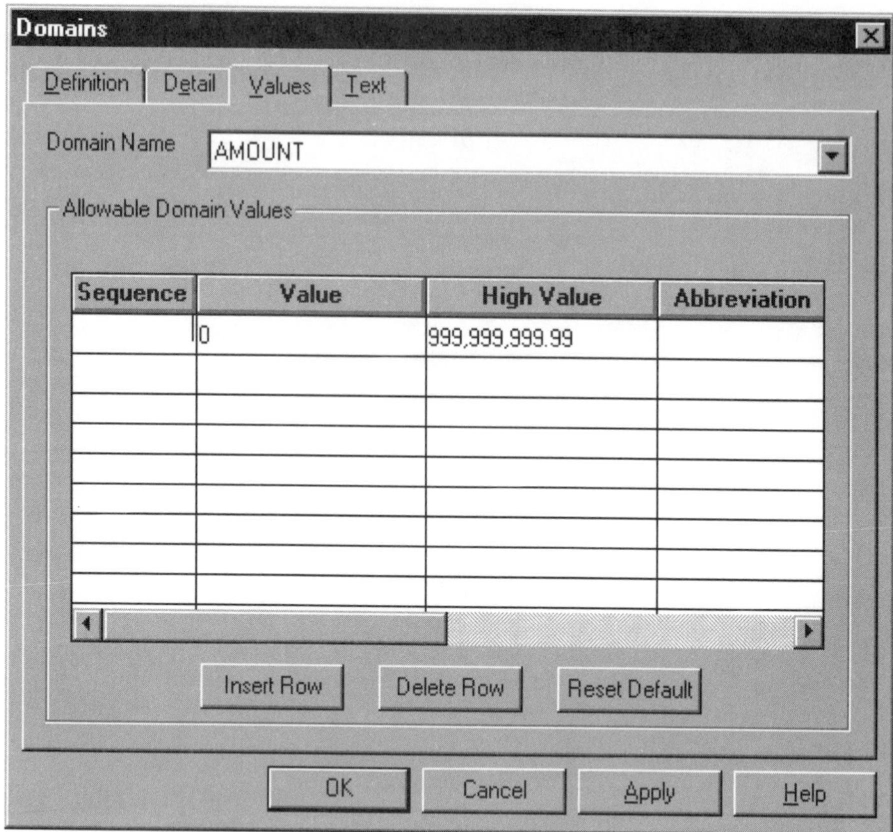

FIGURE 6.3 Setting a range of values for a domain.

entries in an incorporated LOV change, all affected generated modules must be regenerated to incorporate the changes. This information is entered into Designer in the same place as the range of values mentioned previously.

Again from the standards document:

> In general, domains will be used only if the values are relatively static and encompass fifty (50) or fewer discrete values.
>
> Examples: **STATES** is an approved LOV domain because the values are static and limited.
>
> **AREA CODES** is **not** an approved domain. The values are not sufficiently limited.

WHEN TO USE DOMAINS

Domains should be used as a rule, rather than the exception. The development time for a logical data model can be greatly reduced through the appropriate use of domains simply because of the reduction of keystrokes required to complete an attribute definition. In addition, this approach ensures consistency across attribute definitions and provides a means of validating values. The standards document states the following with regard to the use of domains:

Standard Uses for Domains

There are several things that domains should be commonly used to provide. They are:

- ❑ A list of values
- ❑ A range of values
- ❑ A specified data type and size
- ❑ Any combination of these.

You also need to consider the types of applications that will interface with your final database design when deciding when and where to use domains for valid values. That means that during the Analysis phase you must look ahead to deployment. During the Design phase, you will have the option of creating a single reference table that will house all the domains and their values or to enforce the values as column check constraints. A third option is to enforce the values using the Table API generator. As a rule, adhoc query tools will not be able to use the reference table generated by Designer. For this purpose, separate reference tables with foreign key constraints are preferred, in which case you do **not** want to use a domain with a LOV. For a more detailed discussion of the mechanics of implementing domains using these options please refer to the book *Oracle Designer Generation.*

Chapter 7

Entities, Attributes, and Relationships

According to Richard Barker (in the book *Oracle CASE* Method: Entity Relationship Modelling*) an entity is "a thing of significance, whether real or imagined, about which information needs to be known or held." An attribute "is any detail that serves to qualify, identify, classify, quantify or express the state of an entity." And a relationship is "a named, significant association between two entities." These then are the standard definitions for these objects that are generally accepted in the Oracle world. We stand by them and developed our standards from this perspective.

Entities, attributes, and relationships are the elements needed to capture the data requirements and are core to the Strategy and Analysis stages of any Designer project. Defining these completely and accurately is a critical factor for the success of the project, so it is only natural that we be concerned with setting appropriate standards for use with Oracle Designer. This chapter describes standards for:

- ❑ Entity names
- ❑ Entity plurals
- ❑ Entity short names
- ❑ Intersection entities
- ❑ Association entities
- ❑ Validation entities
- ❑ General attributes
- ❑ Primary unique identifier (UID) attributes

- ❑ Audit attributes
- ❑ Relationships
- ❑ Unique identifiers

In addition we will also point out other data that should be entered into Designer *as a standard practice* to help ensure you can get the most use from the tool.

ENTITIES

Following are the standards that apply to the creation of entities within Oracle Designer.

ENTITY NAMES

Naming standards for entities seem to vary by analysis method and even by tool. In the world of Oracle Designer (previously Oracle*CASE), most people make their entity names singular. The rational for this is that an entity represents a single occurrence of an object (while a table is a collection of data about multiple occurrences). The standard we recommend is as follows:

> Entity Names should be singular nouns or nominative phrases. They must be business-oriented, and will contain one blank space between each word. Use single or multiple full-word descriptive names, but allow exceptions for approved acronyms and/or abbreviations (e.g., CUST or ADDR) when the name exceeds 24 characters.
>
> Entity names may not contain the name of *physical* constructs such as “file” or “table” as a qualifier.
>
> Example: Use **Customer** *not Customer File* or *Customer Table.*
>
> Entities must not exceed 24 characters including spaces. See the section on use of abbreviations if your entity name exceeds this limit.

As in Chapter 2, we again reinforce the length standard to prevent the generation of Oracle object names that are too long for the database to handle. Figure 7.1 shows the main dialog you will use to create entity names.

This dialog pops up when you create a new entity in the Entity Relationship Diagrammer. Once you enter a name and press OK, the entity is created. Designer will not force you to keep the name singular, hence the need for the standard.

A particular situation might cause some problems. Oracle Designer allows the same entity name to occur in separate applications. This could happen when

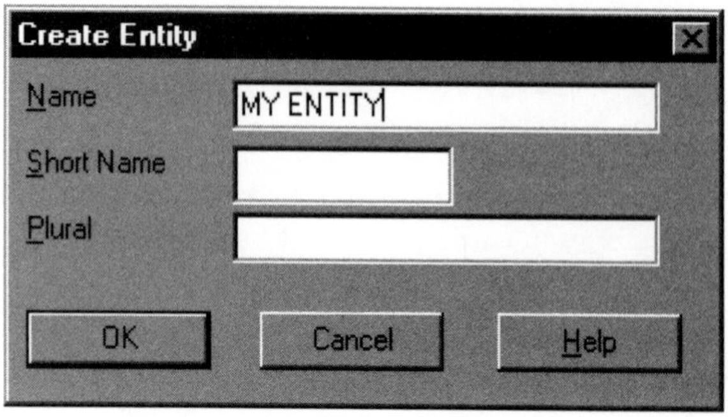

FIGURE 7.1 Create Entity Dialog from the Entity Relationship Diagrammer.

multiple projects define entities with the same name (they may or may not really be the same entity). The problem could also occur if you reverse engineer a third party application package into your repository. Even though Designer will allow you to do this, it is not a good practice. If there are two CUSTOMER entities in Designer, how will anyone know which one you are talking about?Also, duplicate entity names may also prevent you from sharing entities across multiple designer applications. Whenever you try to share an entity with the same name you will get "duplicate entity name" errors and will not able to complete the share.

Our first recommendation is to resolve the conflict. First be sure that the names chosen are the best names for the entities: Does this entity really represent customer information? If it does, then look to see if the entities could be consolidated into one. Are they really describing the same thing? If so, delete one of the entities and share the other into the second application. If you cannot eliminate one of the duplicates, then we propose the following standard:

> If you may be sharing entities from other vendor applications (e.g., Oracle Applications) with the same name as your entities, for example, CUSTOMER, you may want to prefix your entities with a two or three character application identifier. For example, if your application name is ANY COMPANY, then prefix your entities with "AC" (e.g., AC_CUSTOMER).

ENTITY PLURAL

Oracle Designer uses the entity plural to generate the associated table name when the Database Transformer utility is used. The standard proposed here is to always define a plural for each entity. In fact, Designer requires the entity plural to be entered and will create it for you if you leave the field blank (as in Figure 7.1). This of course presupposes that table names will be plural. This standard is discussed previously in this chapter and in Chapter 9.

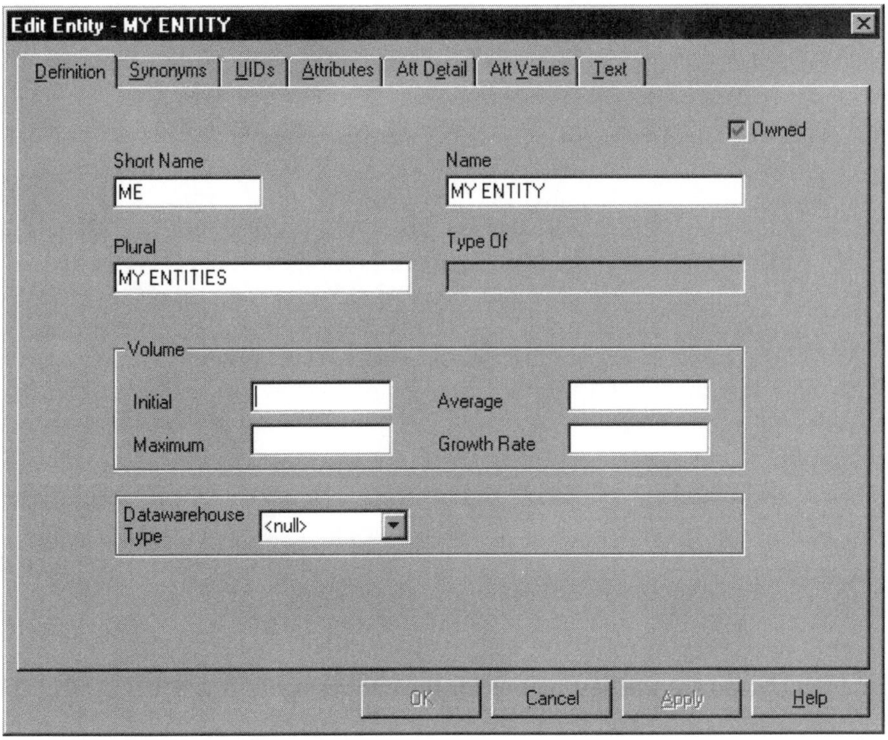

FIGURE 7.2 Edit Entity dialog showing the generated plural (and short name).

The Edit Entity dialog shows the generated entity plural (Figure 7.2). It can be overridden by user input.

The standard is:

> At *Company-Name,* it has been decided that all tables will be the plural form of the entity name.
>
> Thus the plural for each entity must also be defined at the time an entity is named (since the DDT will use this to create the table name). Some utilities impose a restriction on the length of the entity plural name. For example if you decide to create journal tables using Designer, the tool will generate a three-character suffix "_JN".
>
> Entity Plural must not exceed 26 characters including spaces.

Again, the name length is a consideration in the proposed standard.

ENTITY SHORT NAME

Also known as the "alias," the entity short name is a required entry into Designer. It is used as a table alias in generated applications. If the field is left blank during entity creation, then Designer will create a name for you using the following rules:

- If the entity is one word, the short name is the first three letters.
- If the entity is multiple words, the short name is the first letter of each word.

In the case of a duplicate, Designer will add a number to the end of the short name (e.g., CUST2). As you can see in Figure 7.2, the short name for My Entity is ME. Because of what Designer does automatically, we propose the following standard:

An entity short name is composed of a distinct word or words (10 characters or less) or a concatenation of Entity word fragments. Oracle Designer uses the short name in the generation of names for constraints, foreign keys, and sequences. A user should be able to look at an entity short name and know to which entity it refers. Since the entity short name may be used to create any migrated foreign-key column names, it is important that the short name indicate the entity from which it came. Use a standard abbreviation if one exists. Short names should be a minimum of 3 characters and a maximum of 10.

If an entity name consists of one word, the short name should be the first 3 to 6 characters, or it can be an approved acronym or abbreviation. If the entity name consists of two or more words, the short name should be the first letter of each of the words in the name not to exceed 6 characters, or each word can be an approved acronym or abbreviation with no space between them. If more characters are needed for readability, contact the Data Administrator for approval. Resolve vulgar or objectionable words with your Data Administrator as well.

Example:

CUST is the short name for the entity CUSTOMER;

ADDR is the short name for the entity ADDRESS;

PHNUM is a possible short name for the entity PHONE NUMBER. PN will be the short name automatically created.

ORDHDR is the short name for the entity ORDER HEADER. OH will be the short name automatically created.

In the case of short names that consist of only a two-letter abbreviation, we recommend that you consider expanding the name by using appropriate abbreviations so that the reference is more readily understood. If this is the case, you would need to fill in the short name field shown in Figure 7.1 (otherwise you will need to manually edit the generated short name later).

INTERSECTION ENTITIES

Because intersection entities constitute a specific classification of entities, we have established a slightly more specific standard for them.

An intersection entity associates two different entities and resolves a many-to-many relationship. It is named according to its business functionality.

Example:

If entity one is named ORDER and entity two is named PRODUCT, an intersection entity may be created called ORDER ITEM.

If there are no business terms that will work, the name is simply formed from the names of the entities which are associated.

Example:

CUSTOMER ADDRESS describes the connection of the CUSTOMER and ADDRESS entities.

ASSOCIATION AND VALIDATION ENTITIES

As with intersection entities, association entities and validation entities deserve a special standard.

Association Entities

An association entitiy is used to resolve a many-to-many **recursive** relationship between an entity and itself. It is named for its parent entity with the word ASSOCIATION appended.

Example: CUSTOMER ASSOCIATION

Validation Entities

A validation entity is one that contains "lookup" or code information. Validation entities should be suffixed with a blank space and the word "TYPE" to distinguish them from other types of entities.

Example:

COUNTRY OF ORIGIN TYPE

ORDER TYPE

CUSTOMER TYPE

VEHICLE TYPE

OTHER ENTITY INFORMATION

We also recommend entering volume information (Figure 7.2) and a detailed entity description (via the text tab). The volume information is used by the Database Transformer to populate fields associated with the table definition that can then be used to generate a database sizing report.

The detailed description serves two purposes. First, it ensures that the analysts completely understand the definition and importance of the entity and can print it out, using standard Designer reports, for the users to review. Second it can be used by the Database Transformer to populate the User Help Text property, which is then used to generate user-friendly applications. Be sure that the description entered is in business terms and is void of any techno-jargon (i.e., use real English). (Refer to Appendix B, Oracle Designer Flow Down Chart, to view how other objects flow from one phase to another.)

ATTRIBUTE STANDARDS

Following are the standards that apply to the creation of attributes within Oracle Designer.

USE OF DOMAINS

Whenever possible, use a domain to define the characteristics of an attribute (see Chapter 6).

A domain will ensure that all the required information is entered. Figure 7.3 shows the main dialog box for entering attribute information. It is actually one of

Required Domains

Whenever possible, each attribute should have a **domain type.** In some situations it is possible that an attribute may have unique characteristics that are not repeated elsewhere; in this case, use of a domain would be of little value.

If the domain associated with an attribute contains allowed values, the attribute name will be the same as the domain name, only singular.

the tabs on the Edit Entity dialog. If a domain is *not* used, be sure to enter the format, maximum length, decimal (if numeric), and a comment. Also *un-check* the 'opt' column (for optional) if it is a mandatory attribute. You should also consider entering a detailed description (via the Text tab), as this will be used by the Database Transformer to populate the User Help Text property.

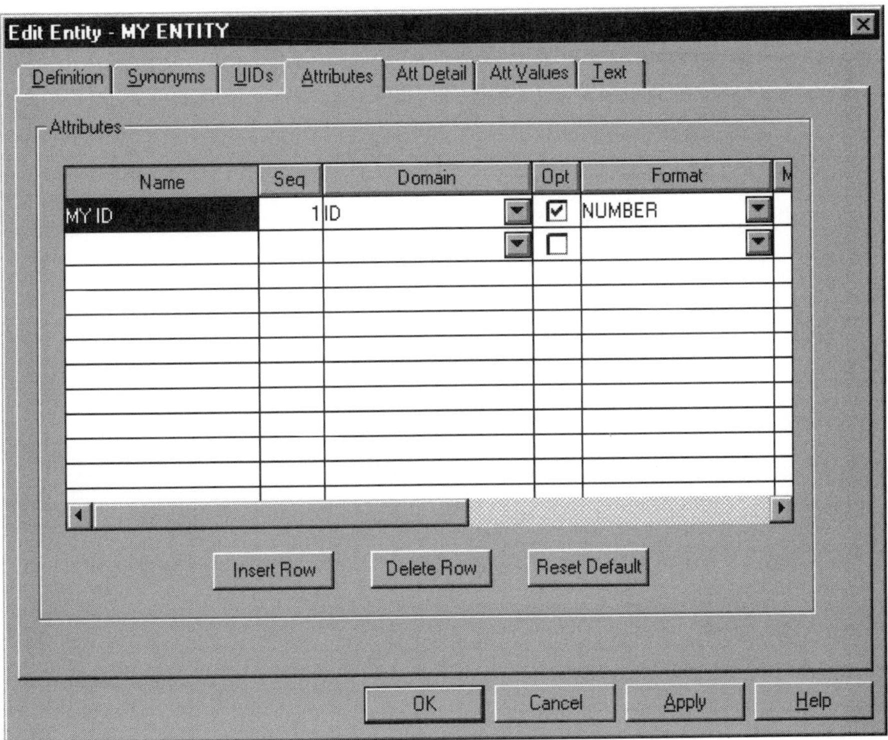

FIGURE 7.3 Attribute entry tab in Edit Entity dialog.

The basic standard for naming attributes is as follows:

Attribute names may be up to 30 characters long. Since attributes are always shown in the context of an owning entity, do not repeat the name of the entity as part of the attribute name, unless it participates in the unique identifier (UID). Attributes can have multi-part names and should not have underscores between the words. Attribute names should be as descriptive as possible without being overly convoluted. They should be named using terms an end-user will recognize as much as possible. If necessary, abbreviations and acronyms may be used to meet the length requirements.

Examples:

Start Date

End Date

Description

At one time, it was common practice to name all attributes with a prefix of either the entity name or the entity short name. It was thought that this practice helped clarify which entity (or later table) the attribute belonged to. It was really a consideration for making SQL understandable. Since attributes are part of the logical model and have nothing to do with SQL, adding the entity name to the attribute is superfluous. When the model is converted to tables and columns, there is an option to add prefixes at that time (see Chapter 9).

PRIMARY UID ATTRIBUTES

As with naming entities, special classes of attributes require more specific naming standards. Attributes that are part of a primary UID will eventually be part of the primary key of a table. The standards proposed will ultimately result in consistency in the naming of columns and therefore understandability across applications.

Primary UID Attributes

When naming an attribute that participates in the UID, use the entity name (if it is relatively short) or the entity short name plus one of the following words as a suffix:

ID is used for a UID that contains a system-generated number and is used internally during processing to access or link data. The values are meaningful only as pointers or keys, and usually do not show on end user reports or screens. *The domain for IDs is 'UID'.*

NUMBER is used for a UID that contains a number by which the end user recognizes the entity. NUMBERs **are** displayed on reports or screens to provide information to an end user. The number may be system generated but is usually determined by the user or has been provided from a legacy system. *The domain for NUMBERs in a UID is 'UID'.*

CODE is used for a UID that contains an alphanumeric value by which the end user recognizes the entity. CODEs are displayed on reports or screens to provide information to an end user. The value of the code is usually representative of the entity it identifies. *The domain for CODEs is 'CODE'.*

TYPE is used for an attribute that contains an alphanumeric value to represent a categorization of an entity (i.e., a sub-type). *The domain for TYPEs is 'TYPE'.*

Examples:

CUSTOMER ID: If the entity CUSTOMER has a system generated internal use UID, the attribute will be designated **CUSTOMER ID.**

CUSTOMER NUMBER: If the entity CUSTOMER has a system generated or user generated UID which is significant to the end user, the attribute will be designated **CUSTOMER NUMBER**.

CUSTOMER CODE: If the entity CUSTOMER were identified by an alphanumeric UID (e.g., GRAZ1), it would be called **CUSTOMER CODE.**

CUSTOMER TYPE: Account management recognizes several categories for Customers, such as commercial or residential. Each grouping is identified by an alphanumeric value called **CUSTOMER TYPE**.

Because we are prefixing the UID attributes, it is important to remember to un-check the Foreign key column prefix box on the "Other Settings" tab in the Settings dialog in the Database Design Transformer (Figure 7.4). If you leave this box *checked* (the default), all the foreign key columns built based on the UID attributes will include the entity short name as a prefix to the attribute. This would result in the FK column based on Customer Id being named Cust_Customer_Id instead of just Customer_Id.

What would be the result if you chose not to use our standard? If the UID attribute did *not* include a prefix (e.g., Id, Code) and you left the Foreign key col-

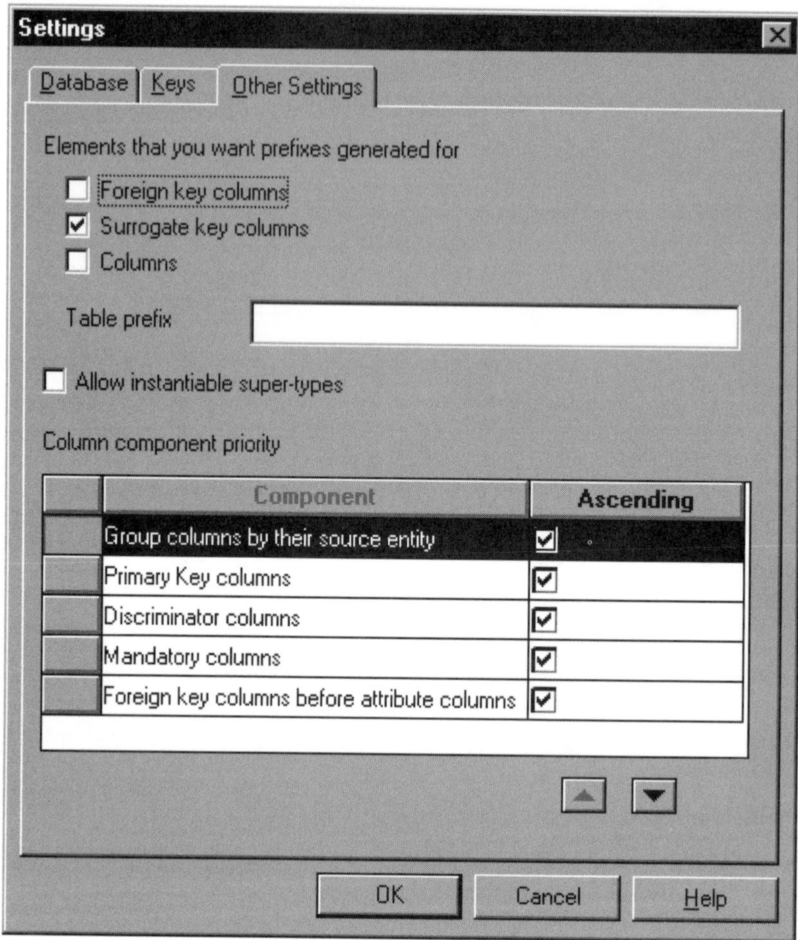

FIGURE 7.4 The Other Settings tab in the Database Design Transformer.

umn box *checked*, the foreign key column would be named Cust_Id and the source column would be named just "Id". The problem with this approach is that modern adhoc query tools build joins based on common names, so you would not be able to rely on that feature. By prefixing the UID attribute, you can achieve common column names without making any additional input or changes. If you did *not prefix* the UID attribute and you did *not check* the prefix box in the DDT, then the column names would be "Id" in both the source table and the reference table. This would also cause the query tools problems since you would likely have multiple tables in the application with a primary key column named "Id".

AUDIT ATTRIBUTES

Audit Attributes

Audit capabilities are required in all systems developed for the enterprise. Every entity **must** contain the following four audit attributes:

CREATED BY

CREATION DATE

LAST UPDATED BY

LAST UPDATE DATE

These audit attributes are to be detailed in the logical models for any entity. When tables and columns are later generated from entities and attributes, the Database Design Transformer will create the appropriate columns.

Again we consider it a "best practice" to include audit columns in a finished application. We believe they belong in the logical model because they quantify and "express the state" of the entity. You may choose not to put them on the actual diagram to avoid redundant clutter.

Others may argue that they are simply an artifact of the physical implementation of a certain style of security. You will need to address this question as part of the standards development process. You may decide that these attributes should be shown on the logical model for clarity. Whatever you decide, you may alter or delete this section of the document as fits your needs.

RELATIONSHIPS

The point of relationships in the Oracle approach to entity and relationship modeling is to make the diagram more understandable to anyone reading it, such as end-users. If done correctly, the Entity Relationship Diagram (ERD) can be used for end-user review sessions. If the naming of relationships is not taken seriously then the diagrams will be of little or no use in reviews. In fact, poor relationship names could lead the end-users to believe that the analysts do not truly understand their business. That would not be a good way to start off a project!

Since Oracle Designer was developed expecting a particular naming and "reading" convention, those are incorporated into the following standards.

Relationships should be named so that the diagram can be easily read. To read any relationship simply and definitively, the following syntax is used:

Each (and every) ENTITY-A {must be, may be} relationship-name {ONE AND ONLY ONE ENTITY-B (singular), ONE OR MORE ENTITY-B plural}

Where *ENTITY-A* is the source entity of the relationship, *ENTITY-B* is the destination end of the relationship, and *relationship-name* is the name applied to the relationship in the direction the relationship is being read. Note the following rules:

The choice between *must be* and *may be* is determined by the modality (optionality) of the relationship emanating from the source entity. A solid line represents *must be* (mandatory) and a dashed line represents *may be* (optional).

The choice between *ONE AND ONLY ONE ENTITY-B (singular)* and *ONE OR MORE ENTITY-B plural* is determined, respectively, by the absence or presence of the "crows feet" at the ENTITY-B end. This is also known as the cardinality of the relationship.

Since relationships are always bi-directional, naming a relationship requires two relationship names be supplied. Hence, the relationship must be readable using the above syntactic structure in both directions.

Examples:

Each (and every) PERSON *may be* **located at** ONE OR MORE ADDRESSES.

Each (and every) ADDRESS *must be* **the location for** ONE AND ONLY ONE PERSON.

Each (and every) DEPARTMENT *may be* **responsible for** ONE OR MORE EMPLOYEES.

Each (and every) EMPLOYEE *must be* **assigned to** ONE AND ONLY ONE DEPARTMENT.

Whenever multiple relationships are created into a single entity, from the same parent entity, the relationship labels **must be** unique to prevent duplicate index names from being created by the Database Transformer. Otherwise, the indexes will not be generated during "DDL Generation"

Do not use weak relationship names, such as "associated with", or "related to". Remember that relationships are documenting business rules and will be used to explain the model to end-users. Whenever possible, use business terminology. For example, the correct way to document a person and their address would be:

A PERSON *may be* **located at** one or more ADDRESSes, **not** a PERSON *may be* **associated with** one or more ADDRESSes.

Many of the analysis level reports from Designer include the relationships written in sentence format. It is a good idea to run these reports frequently to check the relationship names for conformity to this standard. If the standards have not been adhered to, you may find some unusual sentences!

UNIQUE IDENTIFIERS

These are logical constructs made up of attributes, relationships, or both. The sum of these must uniquely identify an occurrence of an entity. Do not confuse a UID with an attribute used in a UID.

Designer will automatically name the primary UID. This standard is presented to give you guidance when naming secondary UIDs (which later become secondary unique keys and indexes on a table). The standard is as follows:

Every entity must have at least one unique identifier that will eventually serve as the primary key. This will ensure the uniqueness of the data to be entered. It is also possible for an entity to have additional unique identifiers.

If the Primary UID of a "fundamental" entity is based on a surrogate key then the entity must also have a secondary UID, which represents the natural key for the entity.

Designer will automatically name the primary unique identifier with the Entity Short name. Any additional UIDs created against the entity should be named:

<Entity Short Name>#

Where '#' is a number indicating the sequence of the UID.

Example:

The entity PERSON has the short name PER. The primary UID will be named PER.

A secondary UID on the attribute NAME should then be named PER2.

A secondary UID is often defined to delineate the "natural" key for an entity. For example:

- The primary key consists of a system-generated UID attribute called Customer ID.
- The natural key is really the Customer Name.

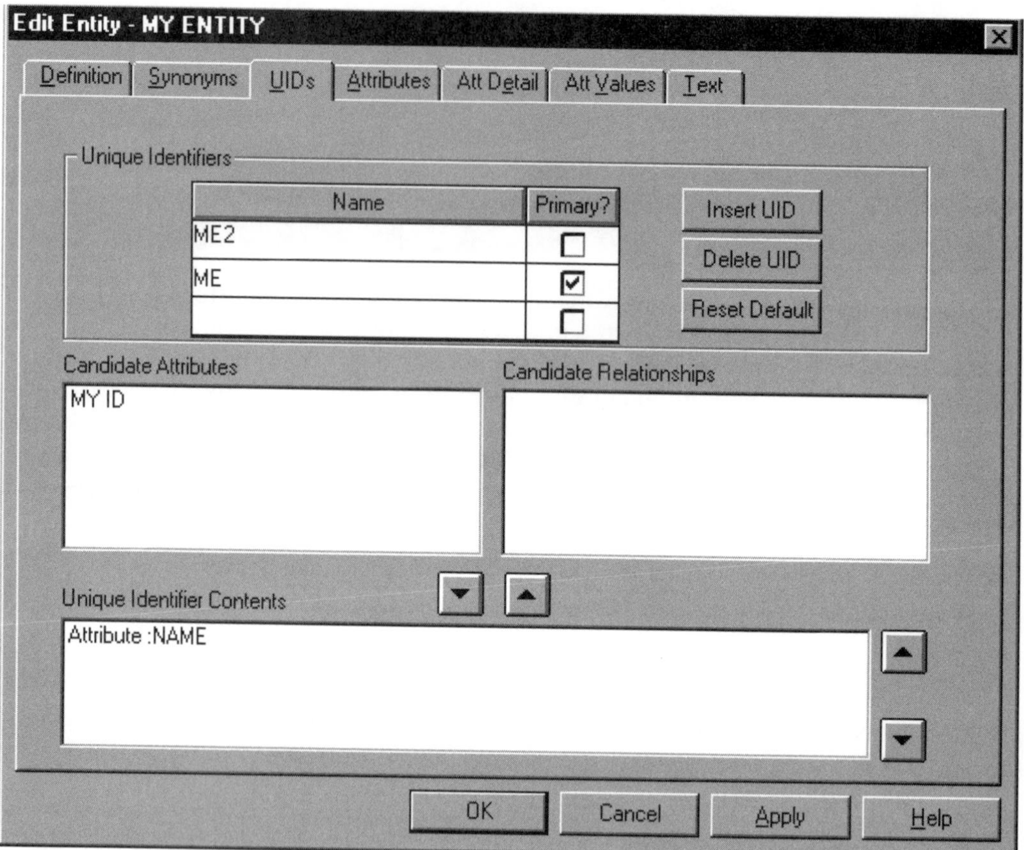

FIGURE 7.5 Tab to enter or create primary and secondary unique identifiers.

To enter a secondary UID, use the UID tab in the Edit Entity dialog (Figure 7.5).

Notice that the check box for *primary* is not checked for the UID named *ME2*. This is the only way Designer can distinguish between the primary and other secondary UIDs. The two arrows in the middle of the tab are used to select or deselect attributes and relationships that may be contained in the UID.

Chapter 8

Modules and Module Components

One of the great productivity benefits of Oracle Designer is its ability to convert analysis level information into a working application with the push of a few buttons. Once the Analysis Phase is completed, you can use the Application Design Transformer (ADT) to convert business functions and data usages into module definitions. These definitions may take the form of screens (Oracle Forms), reports (Oracle Reports), utilities, or manual processes. Once the modules are defined, you can even change the definition so that it generates as an Oracle Web Server module or as a Visual Basic program. In addition the ADT can be used to generate menu modules that can then be generated into an integrated Oracle Forms menu with role level security.

With all the different module types that can be built and the potential number of modules in an application, it is important to have a consistent way of naming them. This chapter presents a naming standard for:

- Screens
- Reports
- Web Server modules
- Menus
- Oracle Developer Libraries
- Visual Basic programs

In addition, we will address the naming of Reusable Module Components (a new repository object as of Designer 2.x), Module Components, preference sets, and other module elements.

SCOPE

The idea of naming standards for modules is not quite as straightforward as you would hope. Not all modules or applications used at an organization are going to be developed using Designer. In fact, many applications may actually be purchased from a third-party vendor. Some old applications may have been around the company since before Oracle even existed as a database. Thus it would be impossible to insist on a naming standard across all applications within the organization. So, the standards document must state this and delineate the exceptions.

> *The names of all modules developed with and generated from Oracle Designer will conform to these conventions. This includes all menus, reports, screens, libraries, webserver modules, and Visual Basic programs. In addition, all SQL*Plus reports (where documented) developed at COMPANY-NAME will also conform to these conventions.*
>
> *The following distinctions between modules developed for or associated with Legacy systems and Vendor-supplied software and those to be developed for new or replacement systems are recognized:*
>
> *All new or replacement systems developed for Company-Name will be developed using the Designer tool set. All modules, whether custom designed or generated from Designer, will adhere to standards without exception.*
>
> *Legacy modules' names will not be changed. After Legacy software is recovered into the Designer repository, any future modules created to augment the legacy system must conform to these standards.*
>
> *Vendor's modules' names will not be changed. If objects from a purchased package are recovered into the Designer repository, and any modules are generated in-house to use those vendor objects, the new modules will be developed according to this standard.*

Why is this important? First, it clearly states that all new development will use these standards and that the intention of the company is to use Designer for doing this development work. Even if a utility is not built using Oracle technology, the definition and data usages for the module can be recorded in Designer. If this is done, the impact analysis reports of Designer can still be used to assess the effect (from a programming perspective) of pending database changes.

Second, we mention legacy systems and vendor applications because even these types of systems should be at least minimally documented in Designer. If this is done across the board within an organization, then Designer can be used as the sole source of application meta-data. With all this information in one Oracle-based repository there are many options for the organization to access and use this information, including such things as ad-hoc query tools like Oracle Discoverer that could be used to publish application information to the company's intranet.

Finally, it is important to include these systems in Designer because if they are Oracle-based, you can build custom extensions and reports by defining new modules against the schema model. This could greatly increase the value your organization gets from these existing systems. See Appendix E for information to reverse engineer the database design of an existing system into Designer.

NAMING MODULES

So how should you name modules in Designer? In previous chapters we have presented standards that were based in part on how Designer named the objects. Unfortunately we cannot do that in this case. Because of the way in which the ADT creates module names, modules will need to be renamed immediately after creation. When the ADT creates module definitions from business functions, it uses the application name (or part of it) and appends a four-digit number incremented by 10 (Figure 8.1). *We do not believe that this is an adequate standard,* as it does not provide enough information to be meaningful. In addition, if the defaults are not reset, then successive runs of the utility will attempt to produce duplicate module names, and thus an error.

First, we need to be clear that when we say module name, we are referring to the Module Short Name property (Figure 8.2) as it is called in the Design Editor. The short name is often used as the implementation name as well (i.e., the file name for the executable program). In the template we decided to limit the length of the module name to eight characters (just in case anyone is still on a 16-bit platform), but we also have a recommendation on how to modify that standard if you do not have that restriction.

Module names should consist of:

- ❑ *a two character prefix representing the application*
- ❑ *two characters representing the Functional Area within the application*
- ❑ *one character identifying the type of module*
- ❑ *a sequence number*

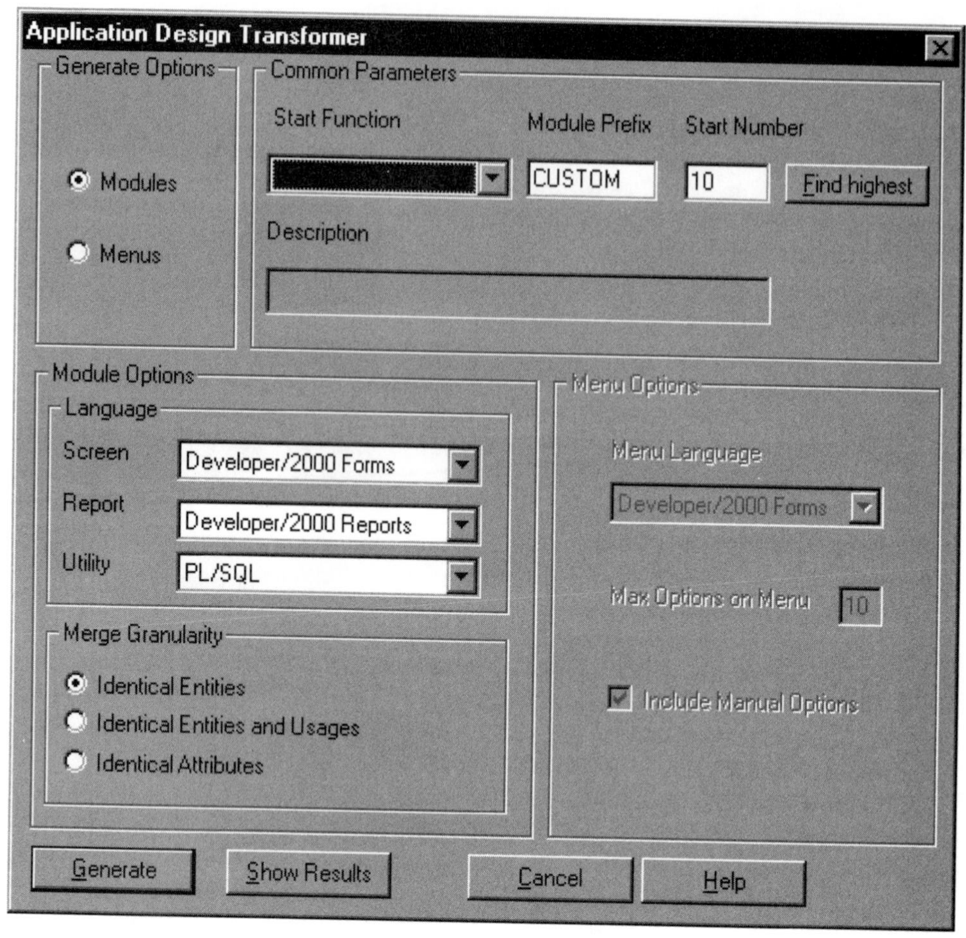

FIGURE 8.1 Default setting for the Application Design transformer utility.

To make the name meaningful, it was necessary to design a coded naming standard.

To create module names using this scheme, the standards document must also provide a list of accepted (and prescribed) abbreviations for the various segment of the name. The list of application abbreviations provided is the same as those listed in Chapter 3. You will need to modify this list to match the application names and agreed upon abbreviations at your company.

Our standard also assumes that you have broken your application down by subsystem as well. This will provide additional clarity and precision to the module names. Again, the list provided in the template document is for illustration purposes only. You will need to modify the list to meet the needs of you company.

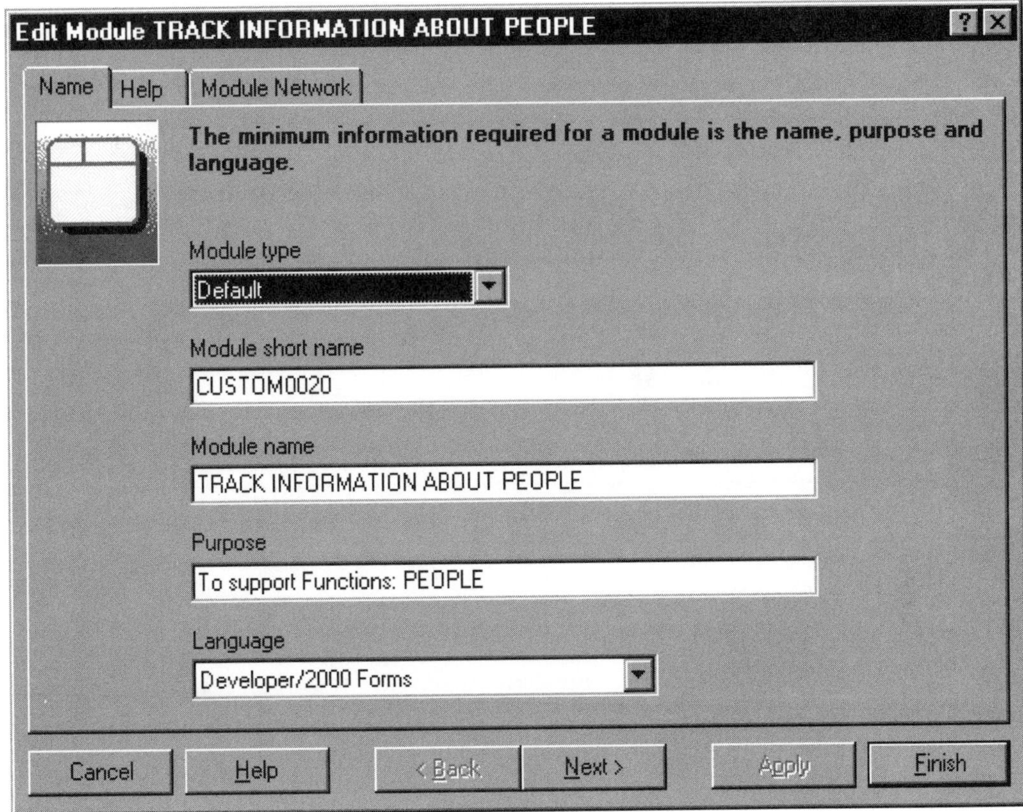

FIGURE 8.2 The Edit Module dialog showing the Module short name property (as well as others).

The following table lists the valid module identifiers for applications under development at Company-Name:

APPLICATION SYSTEM	VALUE
Logistics	LO
Acquisitions	AC
Financials	FN
Product Marketing	PM
Production	PR
Employee Relations	ER
Multiple Application Systems (common module)	CM

The third and fourth characters of the name indicate the Functional Area (within an Application System) for which the module is developed.

FUNCTIONAL AREA	VALUE
Accounts Payable	AP
Accounts Receivable	AR
Collections	CL
Cost Accounting	CA
Employee Benefits	BE
General Ledger	GL
Planning	PL
Order Entry	OE
Shared Module(common modules)	SH

The next piece of the puzzle is to indicate the type of module. The list provided here is based on our experience and will generally be recognized by most Oracle developers. If you do not like our choice of values, feel free to change them. The point is that whatever you choose as a standard, be sure to apply it consistently across the organization.

The fifth character of the name indicates the Type of the Module.

TYPE OF MODULE	VALUE
Oracle Forms	F
Oracle Forms – Query Only	Q
Oracle Reports	R
Oracle WebServer	W
Menu	M
Developer Library (pll)	L
Object Library	O
Template Form	T
Reference Form	R
Visual Basic	B
SQL*Plus Report (doc only)	P

The last piece of the name puzzle is the numeric suffix. It is basically meaningless. The sequence could be used to indicate relative importance of the module or even the order of appearance within the application. The problem with attaching this kind of meaning to the sequence is that you would find yourself constantly renumbering the modules as the design or design priorities changed. Standards are very important to the success of a project, but some things are just not worth the hassle!

The last component of the module name, the sequence number, is simply three digits, which are incremented by 10. The increment may be modified to five (5) if the number of modules per subsystem becomes extremely large.

If you are not restricted to an eight-character module name, you should consider changing this last component. Instead of using three digits as a suffix, use an underscore followed by some meaningful abbreviations that help describe the function of the module. If you choose this option, be sure to modify your final document to include it.

What do the module names look like when you put this all together? To be sure the standard is understood, the template also includes some examples. You should change them according to the various abbreviations you ultimately decide to use.

Screens

Examples:

Name: FNAPF010
Translation: Financials applications, Accounts Payable subsystem, Oracle Form

Name: ERBEF010
Translation: Employee Relations application, Employee Benefits subsystem, Oracle Form

Reports

Examples:

Name: FNAPR010

Translation: Financials applications, Accounts Payable subsystem, Oracle Report

Name: ERBER0010
Translation: Employee Relations application, Employee Benefits subsystem, Oracle Report

Menus

Examples:

Name: FNAPM010
Translation: Menu for the Financials applications, Accounts Payable subsystem

Name: ERBEM010
Translation: Menu for Employee Relations application, Employee Benefits subsystem

Libraries

Examples:

Name: FNAPL010
Translation: Oracle Developer library for Financials applications, Accounts Payable subsystem

Name: ERSHL010
Translation: Oracle Developer library containing shared program units for the Employee Relations application

When naming libraries, you may need to consider an additional factor. For many template and application architectures (like DesignAssist™) there is often a module specific library associated with many of the modules. In these cases, the library name should be the *exact* same name as the form, except for the "L" instead of the "F". For example, if you had a form named FIBEF010, the module specific library would be FIBEL010.

If you decide not to use the numeric suffix standard, your module names will be very different than those shown in the examples. Allowing for longer names would allow names such as ERBEF_ADD_BENEFICIARY (i.e., Employee Benefits, Add Beneficiary Form) or FNAPM_MAIN (for Accounts Payable, Main Menu). Again, if you prefer this option, you will need to update your standards document with appropriate examples.

If these standards are applied and used when developing new applications, you should find your development teams are able to communicate more effectively, and new team members will not be left wondering how to name their modules.

WHO SHOULD MODIFY THESE LISTS?

Since this standard relies so heavily on lists of abbreviations, this question is important. You don't want just anybody adding or changing abbreviations. This would lead to a standard that nobody could translate. For this standard to work, your organization must appoint someone (like an Application Architect or Technical Lead) to be responsible for updating these lists in the standards document. The update must be done in the shared document because it is the one point of reference for everybody. Updating must be done in a timely manner or your developers may find that they need to create a module for an application that is not listed. Then they will have to make up abbreviations that somebody will eventually have to track down and clean up.

REUSABLE MODULE COMPONENTS

These components are new objects with Designer 2.x. Essentially they represent data blocks in a module definition. The difference between these and Module Components is that they are designed to be reused in many modules. They give the development team a mechanism by which they can define a standard look, feel, and content for a set of data that is needed in multiple situations. Usually, these components contain a base data block (i.e., table) assignment and fields along with any desired validation and/or list-of-values. In addition you can also define the style of layout (Figure 8.3), number of rows displayed, etc. If you can define it for a module data block, you can define it for these objects as well. Once a module component is defined as reusable, then any changes made to the definition of the component will automatically be inherited by any modules current using it (OO anybody?). After that, the module must be regenerated so that the new changes are passed on to the executable program.

When the ADT creates a new module, it also creates module components. The name given to the component is the table name of the base table usage. This seems like a good place to start. If you build only one reusable module component (RMC) per table, this will do fine as a standard. If you build more than one, it won't be sufficient.

Why would you build more than one component? You may want to have various layouts such as spread table or overflow below. You may want different numbers of rows displayed in some situations. In some cases you may want to display some of the table's columns but not all. Another option would be to have a RMC that allows insert, update, and delete, while another is select only. For developers to have some idea of the intent of a particular component (without hav-

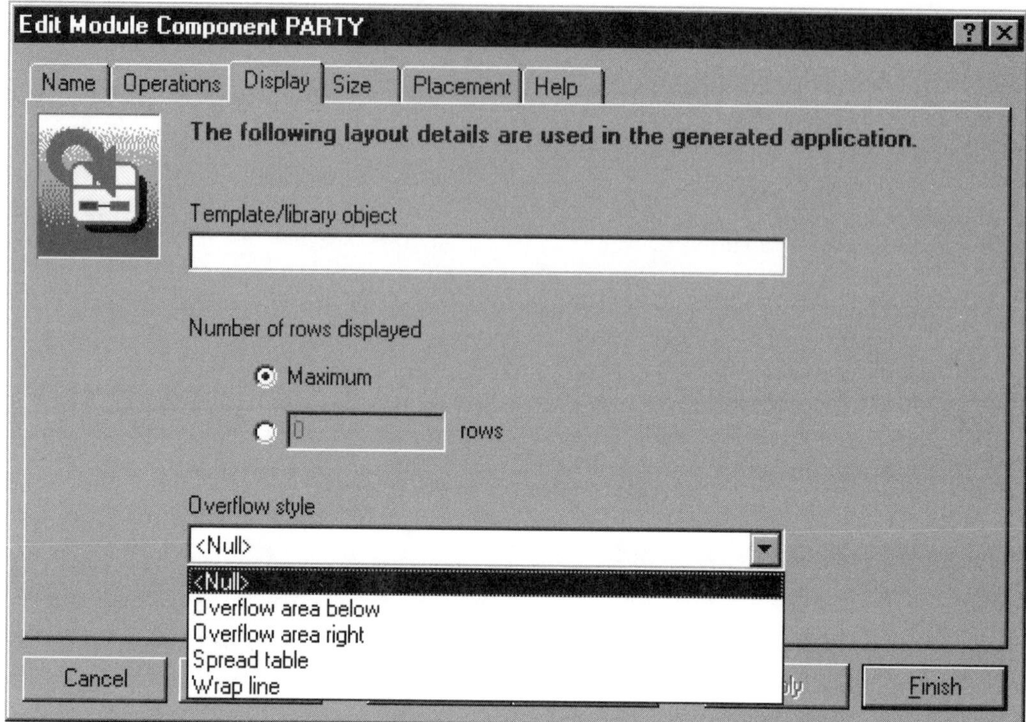

FIGURE 8.3 A view of the Edit Module Component dialog showing the available list of styles.

ing to examine it in detail), the naming standard must somehow express these possible options. What we have included in the template will accomplish this for you.

All Reusable Module Components (RMC) must adhere to the following naming convention:

- *The name must include the base table name and a prefix of R_*

***Example:** R_Invoice*

- *If there will be multiple reusable components with different layout styles, then the name will include an underscore followed by one of these abbreviations:*

  ST = Spread table

  OB = Overflow area below

OR = Overflow area right

WL = Wrap line

Example: *R_Invoice_ST*

- ❑ *If the display characteristics specify a number of rows, the name will include an underscore followed by that number, otherwise the word "MAX" will be included*

Example: *R_Invoice_ST_MAX or R_Invoice_ST_6*

- ❑ *If a RMC is "query only" then the name will include an underscore followed by the letter "Q" (_Q), if it allows insert then use "I", if update use U, if delete then D. If all of these are used then add nothing.*

Examples: *R_Invoice_ST_MAX_Q, R_Invoice_ST_MAX_QIU*

- ❑ *If there are multiple RMCs with the same base table and some contain all the possible enterable columns, these RMC's will include an underscore and the word ALL. If there is only one RMC for a base table, no notation is required.*

Example: *R_Invoice_ST_MAX_ALL*

- ❑ *If the RMC name becomes too long (over 20 characters), then use the table alias instead*

Example: *R_Invoice_line_items_ST_MAX_ALL becomes R_ILI_ST_MAX_ALL*

In some cases you may design a RMC that does not have a base table usage. This would be a control block that may contain display only context fields, action items to fire complex procedures, or nondisplayed fields that hold reference information required for the form to function correctly. Whatever the reason, there needs to be a different standard for these type of RMCs.

- ❑ *If the RMC is not based on a table (i.e., a control block) it will be named with the prefix CTL followed by a string that represents its basic functionality or usage.*

Example: *CTL_calc_totals*

A new feature with Designer 2.x is the ability to base a module component or RMC on a PL/SQL package. This too requires an additional naming standard.

- *If the RMC is based on a PL/SQL package then it will be named with PLSQL followed by the name of the package.*

Example: *PLSQL_MyPackage*

In the case of a RMC based on a PL/SQL package, all the other standards should also be applied as if the component was based on a table.

We believe that consistent use of this standard will make life much easier for your development staff and lead to better quality systems.

MODULE COMPONENTS

What about naming standards for module components? As an option, all the standards proposed for RMCs could also be applied to stand-alone module components. If most of your modules were generated using the ADT, applying these standards would require a lot of extra work. If you build your modules from scratch using the Design Editor, naming the components is work you must do anyway and could provide additional clarity to developers who may be generating or modifying your modules at a later time. The only issue here is that you may not know what style or layout the module component will use when it is finished, so you could end up renaming it later.

The standard we recommend is based on the one used by the ADT. The ADT names module components using the table alias of the base table for the component. If that table is the basis for multiple components within a module, then a numeric suffix is added to the alias. Our standard states that in this case that you should include a suffix indicating the purpose of the second usage (rather than the generated number).

All Module Components (MC) must adhere to the following naming convention:

- *The name must include the alias of the base table name upon which the module is based.*

Example: *INV is the MC name for a component based on the Invoices table*

- *If there will be multiple components within a module using the same base table, then the name will include an underscore followed by an abbreviation of the purpose.*

Example: *INV_QRY is the MC name for a second component based on the Invoices table that will be query only*

If you choose to use the RMC naming standard instead for stand-alone module components, be sure to modify this section of the template document to reflect this choice.

MODULE COMPONENT ELEMENTS

There are several elements found in module components and reusable module components that can also be named. They are:

- Item groups
- Unbound items
- SQL Query sets
- Navigation action items
- Custom action items
- Application Logic Event code segments
- Application Logic Named Routines
- API Logic code segments

Because these elements have their own nodes in the Design Editor, it is quite easy to distinguish them from other objects. Since naming standards are often designed to impart some descriptive information about the object (i.e., this is an unbound item), it seems to us that a strict standard may not be needed here. However, if a developer needs to modify a module outside of Designer, for example, using Oracle Developer, some naming standards could prove useful. Because of this possibility, we present these standards as an option. You will need to determine their usefulness and then either include them in or eliminate them from the final standards document as appropriate.

Module Component Elements

Item Groups

- *Item groups may be named to represent a functional grouping of data. The name may be multiple words with no underscores between them.*

Example: *The item group encompasses columns that make up the information for a mailing address so the item group is named MAILING ADDRESS*

- *If the layout item group is a horizontal item group, the name will prefixed with an "H". If it is a vertical item group, it will be prefixed with a 'V'. (Additional prefixes may be developed to represent the additional functions for which item groups are used in reports generation.)*

Example: *H MAILING ADDRESS is a horizontal item group containing columns for a mailing address*

- *If the purpose of the item group is to enable the generation of a specific layout then the name will be LAYOUT #, where # represents an integer.*

Example: *V LAYOUT 1 is a vertical item group used specifically for layout generation*

- *If nested item groups are used to achieve a complex layout then the name of the nested item groups will be NESTED LAYOUT #-#, where the first # represents the number associated with the parent layout group and the second # is a sequential integer within that group*

Example: *H NESTED LAYOUT 1-2 represents the 2nd nested item group within the item group named LAYOUT 1. It is a horizontal item group.*

Example: *V NESTED LAYOUT 1-2-1 represents the 1st nested item group within the 2nd nested item group within the item group named LAYOUT 1. It is a vertical item group.*

Unbound Items

- *All unbound items will be prefixed with UB and an underscore followed by text that describes its function. Approved abbreviations and acronyms may be used as necessary.*

Example: *UB_TOTAL_PRICE is an unbound item that will contain the results of a calculation for total price*

SQL Query Sets

- *All SQL Query sets will be named with the word UNION and the table alias of the base table usage in the module component.*

Example: *UNOIN EMP is the name of the query set containing a reference to the EMPLOYEES base table usage*

Navigation Action Items (Buttons)

- *Navigation action items will be named using a prefix of NA followed by the module component name followed by the target module component or module name with an underscore in between.*

Example: *NA_CUST_FNAPF010 indicates a button to navigate from the CUST component in the current module to the module FNAPF010*

Custom Action Items (Buttons)

- *Custom action items will be named using the prefix CA followed by text that describes the function of the action item. Approved abbreviations and acronyms may be used as necessary.*

Example: *CA_CALC_TOTAL indicates a button that when pressed will cause a total to be calculated*

Application Logic Event Code Segments

- *All code segments entered to implement custom application logic will be named using a text string that defines the purpose of the code. Approved abbreviations and acronyms may be used as necessary.*

Example: *Use parameter value when present*

Application Logic Named Routines

- *Named routines will conform to the same standard set forth for PL/SQL procedures.*

API Logic Code Segments

- *API Logic code segments will conform to the same standard set forth for Application Logic code segments.*

NAMED PREFERENCE SETS

Using preference sets is a good way to manage the multitude of preferences that you must deal with to get your desired layout and functionality. Whenever you find yourself using the same set of preference settings many times, you should define and save a named preference set and use that instead. Named preference sets can save time during module development and can be used to help enforce layout and functionality standards. In addition, it will help novice developers learn how to leverage the advanced features of the generators.

When you use preference sets to help with your development, you create many different preference sets and will use them in many different places in the module. A naming standard for the preference sets can help you locate the preference set you need in a particular situation.

All preference sets will be named with one of the following prefixes that indicate at what level the preference set is intended to be used:

AP = Application

MD = Module

MC = Module Component

IG = Item Group

IT = Item

The rest of the preference set name should use abbreviations to describe the purpose of the set or the major preference settings for the preference set.

For example, if you have an item group (IG) preference set that sets the preferences to create a horizontal item group, allowing 2 items in each row, with a rectangle decoration and left justified title, you could name it "IG_H_2_REC_LEFT".

If you have a preference set that is intended to be used for modules (MD) that consist of only tab canvases, you could name it "MD_TAB_ONLY".

As you gain experience with the generators and preferences, you may want to add more specific guidelines to these standards. If you do, be sure to add them to your document.

Chapter 9

SERVER MODEL OBJECTS

Often we find Information Technology (IT) shops that are *not* managing their server objects in Designer. These same shops also have a difficult time keeping developers up to speed on the current database design. If a company is using Oracle Designer for their data modeling efforts, there is no reason not to continue to use it for database design and maintenance. The Database Design Transformer (DDT) converts the logical data model (entities, attributes, and relationships) into a physical database design (tables, columns, indexes, and constraints) with the press of a button. To do this, the DDT must have a set of rules to use when generating these database object definitions. The standards we use are based on those rules. One goal of this book is to help save you time and money by providing a template that can be readily used to develop your corporate standards. If the standards we proposed were in conflict with what the Designer utilities generated, we would be creating additional work for you and not saving you anything.

In addition to the objects generated by the DDT, you can also build several other server-based objects using Designer. This chapter presents a naming standard for the following:

- Tables
- Columns
- Constraints
- Indexes

- Sequence Generators
- Views
- PL/SQL Definitions
- PL/SQL Arguments and Program Data

TABLES

Following are the standards that apply to the creation of tables within Oracle Designer.

TABLE NAMES

As with many objects, different people have different ideas about how a table should be named. In the world of Oracle Designer, many people make their table names plural. The reasoning behind this decision is that a table represents a collection of data about multiple occurrences of an object type. When the DDT is used to generate table definitions, the entity plural is used to create the table name. If the entity plural contains multiple words, then an underscore is substituted for the space. We recommend the following standard:

> Table names must be the plural of the Entity names, with the spaces translated to underscores. If the resulting name has more than 26 characters, see **Appendix A** and **Appendix B** for a list you can use to acceptably shorten the table name.
>
> Table names will not be prefixed with an application abbreviation unless that prefix is inherited as part of the original entity name.

Some organizations find that 26 characters are too long for table names, resulting in excessive errors when a lot of SQL code is written manually. In this case, you may consider shortening the maximum length to 12 or 15 characters, as you deem appropriate. To achieve a shorter length, you will need to use more abbreviations in your naming efforts. Be sure to update the document to match your standard.

Notice too that where prefixes are concerned, we rely on the standard that was set for entities. Using standards in this manner helps promote a top-down approach to systems development. We believe that it is important to base the database design on a logical model that was developed during analysis. Consequently our standards work best in an environment that takes the same approach.

TABLE ALIAS

The table alias is inherited directly from the entity short name when the DDT is used. If the table was reverse engineered or built from scratch, the alias must be entered and should conform to the same standard used for the entity short name.

> All tables must have an alias. The alias must conform to the same standard set forth for entity short names. If the table is based on an entity, then the alias must be the same as the entity short name.

TABLE COMMENTS

Oracle Designer is a repository of information gathered and used during systems development. Much of it falls into the category of meta-data, or data about data. Designer allows you to enter a lot of this type of information via free form text entry. If the standards for entities were followed, there should be a description and help text already in place for a table. The table comment, however, does *not* get populated automatically by the DDT because no logical equivalent is entered at the entity level. Hence this explicit standard:

> To ensure that appropriate meta-data is included in the Oracle data dictionary, all tables must have a comment entered into Designer. This comment should describe the basic information stored in the table.

The comment is a description of the table that can be entered only through the table definition property sheet in the Design Editor (Figure 9.1). The text can be up to 2000 characters long. It often represents a summary of the detailed description inherited from the entity definition.

This particular property is used by the Server Generator to build a "CREATE TABLE COMMENT" command. Once executed this command stores the comment in the Oracle data dictionary where it is then accessible via SQL or many ad-hoc query tools. For example, if a Business Area is built from the data dictionary using Oracle Discoverer, this comment will be imported and used as a description for a folder based on the table.

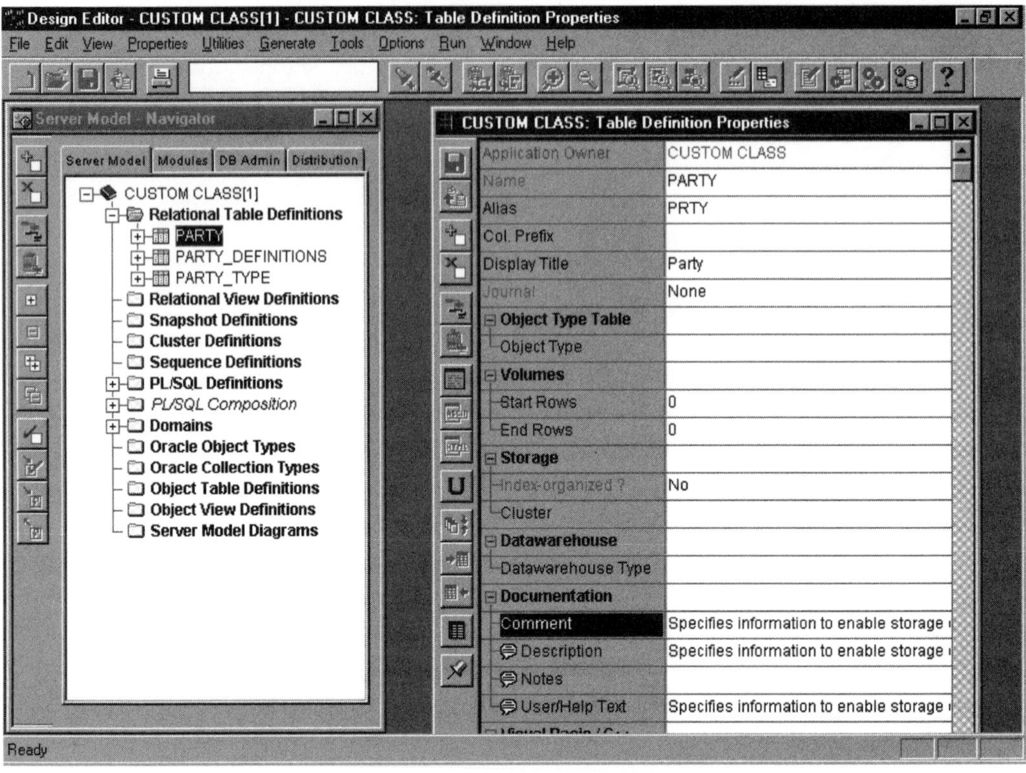

FIGURE 9.1 A table comment is entered using this property sheet.

COLUMNS

If you have tables, you must have columns, so you also need a standard for naming them.

A column name must be the same as the name of the attribute from which the column was mapped, with the spaces translated to underscores. The column name must not be a plural. If the resulting name has more than 30 characters, use the approved acronyms and abbreviations in the appendices to shorten it.

If the column is not based on an attribute, then it should be named using the naming standard set forth for attributes with the exception that an underscore is used instead of a space between segments.

In some cases when using the preceding standard combined with the table-naming standard, you will end up with a very long string. If this happens, typing SQL statements could become cumbersome. The solution is to make more use of abbreviations and acronyms to shorten the table name, the column name, or both.

Another naming standard is to avoid the use of column prefixes. Since our entire approach is geared toward getting the most use out of Oracle Designer, we have also included some guidance on how to use the tool to achieve the standard presented.

> Column names will **not** be prefixed with the table short name. This can be controlled via a checkbox in the 'Settings' dialog on the Database Design Transformer.
>
> The Database Design Transformer will also prefix foreign key column names with the parent entity's short name by default ***unless the check box for this option is unchecked*** in the 'Settings' dialog. Since the standard for naming primary UID attributes already includes using the entity name or entity short name, this option must be de-selected or the resulting foreign key column will be redundantly prefixed.

Again note that the standard for naming foreign key columns relies specifically on the standard set for primary UID attributes. So if the one standard is ignored, it will have consequences in trying to apply another standard later (i.e., the foreign key columns must match the UID attribute names). The dialog box and setting required are shown in Figure 9.2.

CONSTRAINTS

Given that our approach assumes the use of Designer and that there are many possible ways to name the various constraints, the template states explicitly that our standard is based on what the DDT will generate (the only exception is check constraints). The best reason to accept these standards is that if you don't, you will have to manually rename every constraint generated by the tool. If you have a large system, that could mean a lot of time (and therefore money) that could be better spent on other tasks. This standard has been developed for very *practical* reasons.

> Constraint names will conform to the default Designer constraint naming conventions that are automatically created when using the Database Design Transformer. Any manually created constraints must conform to this standard.

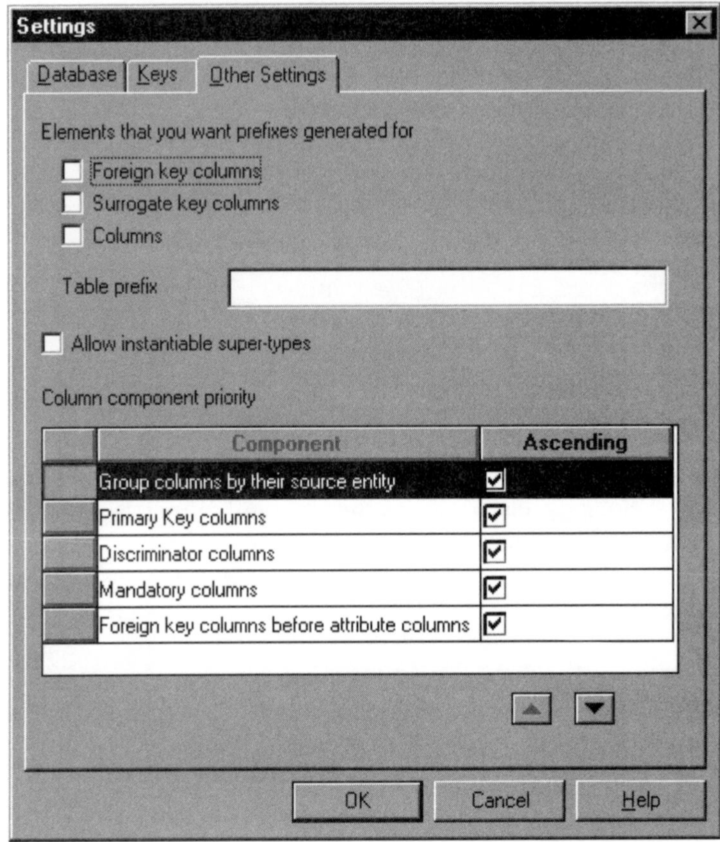

FIGURE 9.2 The settings dialog (Other Settings tab) from the Database Design Transformer.

As most of these are truly generated standards, they are presented here with a minimum of additional text. Where the standard cannot be generated, explanatory notes are included.

PRIMARY KEY CONSTRAINTS

The naming convention used by Designer is:

Primary key = <table alias>_PK

Example: For the table CUSTOMER with the alias CUST the primary key will be:

CUST_PK

UNIQUE KEY CONSTRAINTS

As for unique key constraints, the naming convention used by Designer is:

Unique key = <table alias>_<UID Name>_UK

where the UID Name is the name specified for a secondary unique identifier on the entity.

Example: The table called ORDERS (ORD) has two unique identifiers named ORD2 and ORD3. The unique key constraints will be named:

ORD_ORD2_UK

ORD_ORD3_UK

FOREIGN KEY CONSTRAINTS

Designer will generate one of two possible names depending on the number of relationships between two entities. Foreign key names are usually generated with the following algorithm:

Foreign key = <table alias of the target table>_<table alias of the originating key>_FK

Example:

ORDER _LINES (ORDLIN) >------------------- ORDERS (ORD)

The foreign key constraint on ORDER_LINES will have the foreign key constraint name generated as ORDLIN_ORD_FK.

Since it is possible to have several foreign keys between the same two tables, there is an exception to the preceding standard based partially on what the DDT will do with some additions we believe will make the resulting design more understandable.

However, if a table has multiple foreign keys to one other single table, then the algorithm for the first foreign key constraint will be the same as above. However, the second constraint with be generated as follows:

Foreign key = <table alias of the target table>_<table alias of the originating key>_relationship name_FK

Where 'relationship name' is the text associated with the relationship as depicted on the logical model.

Example:

shipped from

ORDERS >------------------------ LOCATIONS (LOC)

(ORD) >------------------------ LOCATIONS

returned to

The foreign key constraints on ORDERS will have the foreign key constraint names generated as:

ORD_LOC_FK

ORD_LOC_RETURNED_TO_FK

For the sake of clarity, in this case the first FK constraint should be renamed to:

ORD_LOC_SHIPPED_FROM_FK

Once again we have developed a standard that assumes you are following a top-down design approach that produced a logical model. If you did not, then you may find it difficult to resolve the multiple foreign key scenario without resorting to a naming standard such as ORD_ORD_FK2. Since one of the goals of establishing standards is to increase the ease of understanding systems, this approach really won't help much.

If you have occasion to build foreign keys from scratch in the Design Editor, you will note that the foreign key wizard generates a constraint name using the same standards as the DDT in most cases (Figure 9.3).

If you were to build a second foreign key between two tables using this wizard, it unfortunately simply appends a '2' to the end of the constraint name. This is understandable since the key being created has no reference to a relationship in the logical model. In this case, you will have to override the default name to conform to the standards presented.

CHECK CONSTRAINTS

The DDT does not generate these constraints. They must be manually created in the Design Editor. They are used to enforce data-dependent business rules. There

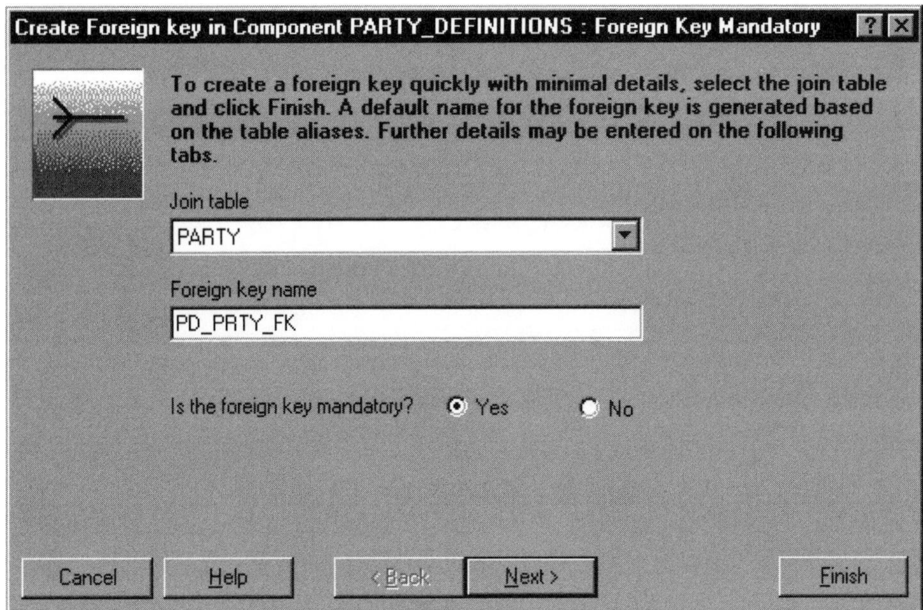

FIGURE 9.3 The foreign key creation wizard.

is no place on the logical model to depict these types of business functions. These functions should not be confused with in-line column level check constraints that the Server Generator will build as a way of enforcing valid values (see Chapter 6).

> This standard applies to table level check constraints as defined in the Design Editor.. The naming convention is:
>
> Check constraint = <table alias> _ *what is being checked_CHK*
>
> Where 'what is being checked' is either a column name or some abbreviated text to describe the condition being validated.
>
> **Example:** The table called Location_History (LOCHIST) has a check constraint to enforce an arc relationship. The check constraint will be named:
>
> LOCHIST_ ARC_ CHK
>
> **Example:** The table called CP_X_Competitors (COMPET) has a check constraint on the column END_DATE to insure it is greater than the start date. The check constraint will be named:
>
> COMPET_ END_DATE_CHK

INDEXES

This section describes standards that apply to the creation of index definitions for the various types of indexes within Oracle Designer.

PRIMARY AND UNIQUE KEY INDEXES

Because of the features of the Oracle RDBMS, this is a simple negative standard. That is, the standard indicates something you will *not* do instead of something you will do.

> Designer does not create primary or unique key indexes. Oracle7 and newer versions implicitly create the index when creating primary and unique key constraints in the database. Do not create primary key indexes in the repository as this will result in problems when running the DDL scripts generated from Designer.

If you do build and generate these indexes, when you try to load them into Oracle you will be told that those columns already have a constraint on them.

FOREIGN KEY INDEXES

If the DDT is used, and relationships are defined between entities, then along with foreign key constraints, you will also get index definitions.

> The Oracle Designer naming convention for foreign key indexes is the foreign key constraint name with "_I" appended at the end. Designer will automatically create foreign key indexes through the Database Design Transformer if it is specified in the run options.
>
> Foreign key index = <foreign key constraint name>_I
>
> **Example:** For the foreign key ORDLIN_ORD_FK, the resulting foreign key index name would be ORDLIN_ORD_FK_I

The creation of indexes by the DDT is controlled by a check box on the 'Run Options' tab (Figure 9.4). If you do not want indexes created on your foreign key columns, you must uncheck the 'create indexes' box. If you later change your mind, you can rerun the DDT later with the create box checked.

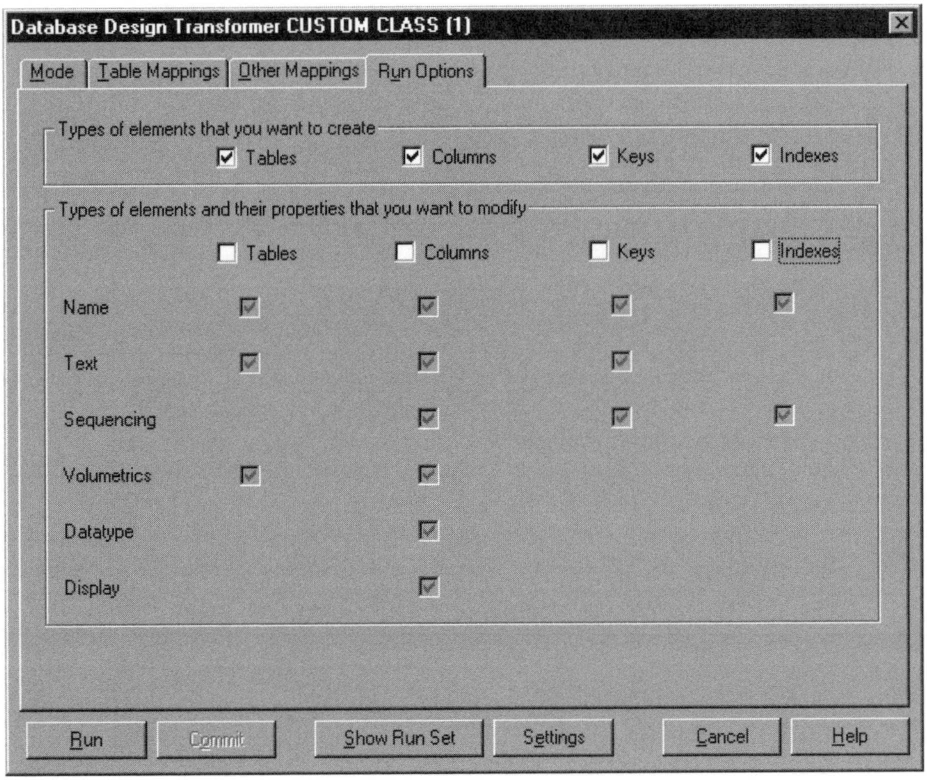

FIGURE 9.4 The Database Design Transformer—Run Option tab with create indexes on.

As with the foreign key constraints, there is a similar exception to naming the associated indexes.

In the case where multiple foreign key constraints were generated, and one was subsequently changed, it will be necessary to manually modify the associated index name so that it matches the renamed constraint.

Example:

Designer created:
ORD_LOC_FK with index ORD_LOC_FK_I

You modified the constraint to:
ORD_LOC_SHIPPED_FROM_FK

So you will need to modify the index to be:
ORD_LOC_SHIPPED_FROM_FK_I

One index is automatically generated for every foreign key constraint. You need to determine if you really need all those indexes. If they are built on small tables or columns that will not be frequently queried, then you may want to delete then from Designer so they do not waste space in your database later on. You will definitely want to eliminate the set of indexes generated on the initial columns of the primary key in a child table that has inherited part of its key from a parent table. Since the primary key constraint of the child table will also have an index, the additional foreign key index on the inherited columns is redundant and will not be used (if this does not make sense, talk to your friendly neighborhood database administrator [DBA]).

NON-KEY INDEXES

If the system you are building is going to perform adequately, you will likely need to create additional indexes to improve performance. These must be created manually using the Design Editor. You can create unique, nonunique, and bit mapped indexes.

Note: You should never create a unique index. If you need one, create a unique key constraint.

The standard we propose is as follows:

For indexes created manually that are not related to any keys, the naming convention will be:

Non-key index = <table alias>_<column name>_NU_I

Where 'NU' stands for non-unique.

If the index to be created is a bit-mapped index then the standard is:

Non-key index = <table alias>_<column name>_BM_I

Where 'BM' stands for bit-mapped.

If the index is on multiple columns, then <column name> will be the first column in the series.

Example: To improve query performance, an index on the column Employee Name in table Employee (EMP) is created. The index name will be:

EMP_Employee_Name_NU_I

SEQUENCE GENERATORS

Sequence generators (or sequences) are database objects that produce a sequence of numbers used as a nonmeaningful unique key for a table. Following are the standards that apply to the creation of sequences within Oracle Designer.

In most cases sequence names will be created as follows:

Sequence = <table name>_SEQ

Where <table name> is the table for which the sequence will provide values to the primary key.

Example: CUSTOMERS_SEQ

Additionally, sequences may need to reflect functionality because a single sequence may be used with multiple tables. In this case, the standard is:

Sequence = <common functionality>_SEQ

Example:

Three tables are generated from sub-types of the entity MODEL. They each represent a different type of model but to avoid potential key conflicts, the decision is to use one sequence for all the primary keys because they will all be mapped to a common cross-reference table. So the sequence name is MODEL_ID_SEQ since the sequence will generically represent a model identifier.

One sequence is now being used for multiple tables more often than before. In the past it would be used when logical subtypes were split into separate tables because of either sizing considerations or differences in column requirements. Today, some designers are resorting to using one sequence to emulate an object oriented environment by creating a primary key called Object_id on all tables in a system. Using our standard the sequence for this situation would be called OBJECT_ID_SEQ.

VIEWS

Since views are like tables, they have some similar standards. They must be plural, and the names must be less than 26 characters long. Additional requirements for naming views are included in the template. These additions will help ensure that end users accessing view names via a query tool will be able to at least guess at the data contained in the view.

All views must be named as follows:

View name = V_<table name>_<criteria>

Where the table name is the name of the root (or 'master') table the view is based on. The *criteria* qualifier is optional.

The maximum length for a view name will be 26. If the name of the view exceeds 26, then use the table alias, abbreviations and acronyms as needed. View names must be plural just like tables.

Example:

V_EMPLOYEES is a view on the EMPLOYEES table

The qualifier, if used, should give the end users a clear idea of the purpose and contents of the view. Use the *criteria* qualifier if

1. Using the table name alone is not unique
2. The view is based on a join of 2 or more tables
3. The view contains a where clause
4. The view is unusually complex.
5. The view is a summary.

Examples:

V_ACTIVE_CUSTOMERS provides information on only active CUSTOMERS.

V_EMPLOYEES_DEPARTMENTS is a view joining the EMPLOYEES tables and the DEPARTMENTS table.

V_CUSTOMER_COMPLAINTS provides information about CUSTOMERS and their NOTES of type 'complaint'.

V_TOTAL_CUSTOMER_SALES provides summary information on customer sales activity

Since Designer can generate applications and code against a view definition just like a table, you should also adhere to the other standards set for tables. This means including a view alias, a comment, a description, and user help text. All of these properties can be accessed in the Design Editor either through the dialogs or the property palette.

PL/SQL DEFINITIONS

A variety of PL/SQL definitions can be defined in Oracle Designer. Below we provide naming standards for them. As a general *procedural* standard, we recommend entering these into the repository using the declarative method rather than the free format method. As a friend of ours once said: "Free Format Baaaaaaad...Declarative Method Gooooood!!"

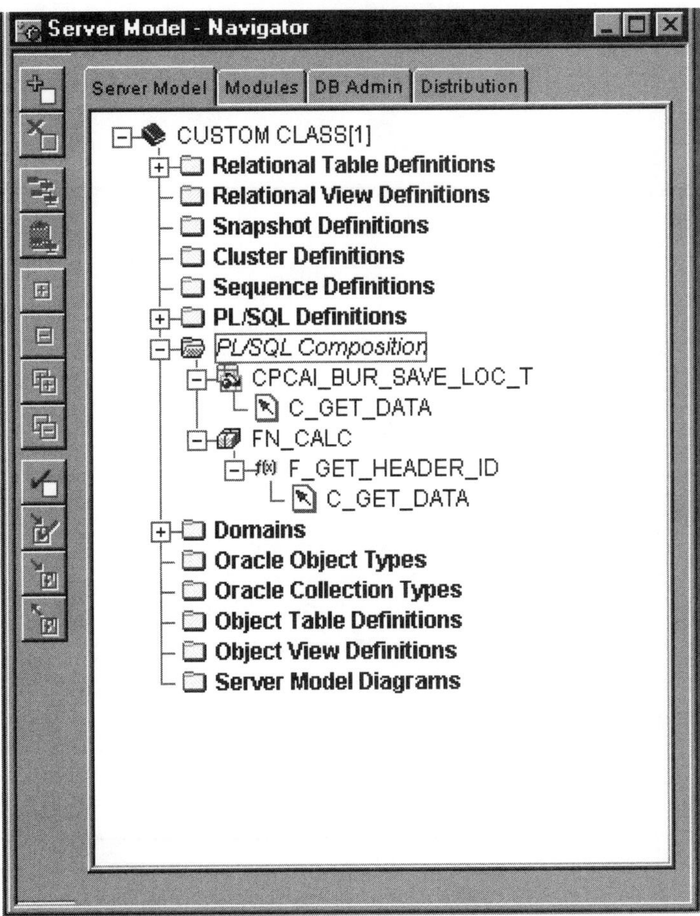

FIGURE 9.5 The PL/SQL Composition node in the Design Editor.

Why is this true? The free format method effectively hides all the interface aspects of your package and its component cursors, procedures, and functions (Figure 9.5). That means the code you write is less reusable and less traceable. Anyone wanting to use any of those components must go digging around in the package code to discover functions and procedures that would have been obvious in the Design Editor if you had declaratively specified those separate definitions and linked them as subprograms.

In addition if the declarative method is used, you can easily view arguments and variables that have been specified (Figure 9.6). Also, with free format,

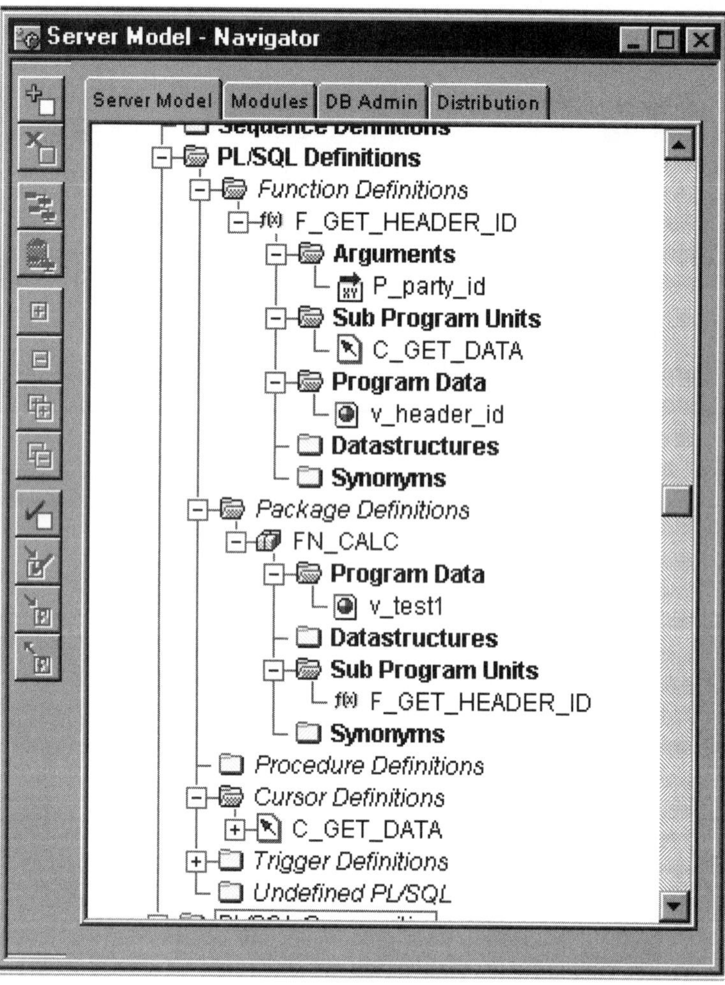

FIGURE 9.6 Expanding the PL/SQL Definitions node in the Design Editor reveals arguments and variable definitions as well as subprogram usage.

you don't get any of the nice "automatic" documentation from Designer's reports and diagrams (see *Oracle Designer Generation* for more information on using the various methods of defining PL/SQL definitions).

Designer limits the length of the short names of PL/SQL definitions to 21 characters, *so all short names must be unique within 21 characters.* It is acceptable to abbreviate the proposed standards for the short name, but you *must* use the full standard for the long name.

PL/SQL PACKAGES

Packages should be the base program unit for most of your PL/SQL code. We believe that you will increase not only the reusability of your code but your productivity if you incorporate most of your PL/SQL into packages with clearly defined uses. The naming standards proposed here (and in following sections) will help you achieve that goal.

> Packages will be named according to this standard:
>
> Package name = <app>_<description>
>
> Where <app> is the Designer application abbreviation and <description> is a one or two word explanation of the purpose. Select a description that will help simplify the naming of procedures stored within the package.
>
> Additional restrictions are:
>
> 1. **Stored Package** (i.e. Packages stored in the database) names must be 24 characters or less.
> 2. **Library Packages**, (i.e. Packages stored within a Oracle Developer library file) the package name must be unique within 27 characters.
>
> **Example**: FN_CALC is a package containing various calculation routines for the Financial application system

PL/SQL PROCEDURES

For packaged procedures (i.e., procedures to be included in a package body), the standards are seen in the box on the following page.

Remember that you will invoke these procedures from a package, so including the package name or application abbreviation would be redundant. For example, to calculate the gross profit in the Financial application the call would be to FN_CALC.GROSS_PROFIT.

> Packaged procedures will be named using the following standard:
>
> Procedure name = verb or noun or both
>
> Where the verb or noun is a brief explanation of the purpose of the procedure. Do not reuse the application abbreviation or any part of the package name in the procedure name.
>
> **Example:** GROSS_PROFIT is a procedure to calculate the companies gross profit.

A similar standard is provided for stand-alone PL/SQL procedures:

> Stand-alone procedures will be named using the following standard:
>
> Procedure name = <app>_<verb or noun or both>
>
> Where the verb or noun is a brief explanation of the purpose of the procedure. The <app> is the application abbreviation of the owning Designer application.
>
> **Example:** ER_TERMINATE_EMPLOYEE is a stand-alone procedure for the Employee Relations applications that processes an employee termination.

This standard is included for completeness. Do not use stand-alone procedures if possible. If a procedure does not appear to belong to a package, create a new package. Eventually you will find other procedures that belong with it. If you choose to adopt our approach, this section could be deleted from the template.

PL/SQL FUNCTIONS

In keeping with our previous statement, part of the standard here includes the fact that functions should be subprograms within a package. If that standard is followed, there is no need to reference an application in the function name. Additionally, we have recommended the use of a prefix to prevent potential naming conflicts (you will see this in subsequent standards as well).

All PL/SQL functions must be sub-programs within a PL/SQL package.

All PL/SQL function names will conform to the following standard:

Function = f_<noun or verb phrase>

Where the verb or noun phrase is a brief explanation of the purpose of the function. Do not reuse the application abbreviation or any part of the package name in the procedure name.

Precede the <noun or verb phrase> with "f" so that there are no conflicts with other PL/SQL program units (like procedures).

Example: f_get_header_id is a function that returns the header id column

Example: f_check_total_units is a function that returns TRUE if the total unit count is greater than zero.

CURSORS

Individual cursors can be defined in the Design Editor and reused by multiple PL/SQL program units. A function, a procedure, and a trigger could actually use the same cursor definition. This certainly promotes code reuse, but the cursor must be named intelligently to make its purpose easily recognizable.

All cursors defined for PL/SQL programs will conform to the following standard:

Cursor = c_<cursor name>

Where <cursor name> is a logical, meaningful, and concise name representing the function the cursor serves.

Precede the <cursor name> with "c" so that there are no conflicts with other PL/SQL program units (like functions).

Example: c_get_header_id is a cursor that selects the header id column into a variable

Example: c_check_total_units is a cursor that checks to ensure the total count is greater than zero.

Since cursors can be used only as subprograms in other PL/SQL definitions (and those will ultimately be referenced by a package), there is no need to reference an application.

DATABASE TRIGGERS

Another PL/SQL definition that can be entered into Designer is that of the database, or table level, trigger. There are two definitions that we will apply a standard to: that of the trigger itself and that of the trigger logic definition. When you create

All database trigger names and trigger logic definitions will conform to the following standard:

Trigger = <table alias>_ <when><type><level>_<further description>_T

Where <table alias> is the alias of the table on which the trigger is based and <type> is the action performed by the trigger. Valid types are: Insert, Update, and Delete. <Level> indicates if the trigger is fired for every row in the table or once for every DML executed. <When> refers to whether the trigger is executed before or after an insert, update, or delete. The rest of the name, which must end with an underscore and a "T", is to describe the purpose of the trigger.

Types should be abbreviated:

- ❑ Insert = I
- ❑ Update = U
- ❑ Delete = D

When should be abbreviated:

- ❑ Before = B
- ❑ After = A

Level should be abbreviated:

- ❑ Row = R
- ❑ Statement = S

Examples:

CPCAI_BUR_SAVE_LOC_T = A before update trigger to save previous location information for every row updated

CPCAI_AIUDS_CHG_STATUS_T = An after insert, update or delete trigger to change the status code in an audit table after each DML statement

a trigger on a table, in the Design Editor, a trigger logic definition is automatically created with the same name; thus the proposed standard is the same for both.

It is possible to define trigger logic independent of a trigger. This would allow you to reuse the logic in multiple triggers if you had an application the required it.

PL/SQL ARGUMENTS AND PROGRAM DATA

In addition to being able to define all these PL/SQL program types, Designer also allows you, using the declarative method, to define inputs, outputs, variables, and constants for them. Although these cannot be reused, specifying definitions at this level clarifies the design for developers who have to do maintenance work later in the project. With the exception of the prefixes proposed, the standards for these objects are the same.

ARGUMENTS

Arguments, also known as parameters, are used to pass data into or out of PL/SQL programs.

All arguments for PL/SQL packages and procedures will conform to the following standard:

Argument = P_<argument name>

Where <argument name> is a logical, meaningful, and concise name representing the value that will be passed to the program unit. Where the argument will be used to hold the value of a column in a SQL statement, then <argument name> must be the same as the column name.

Precede the <argument name> with "P" so that there are no conflicts with database object names or confusion as to which are PL/SQL arguments and which are database objects. All arguments must be in lower case, excluding the prefix.

Example: P_header_id

VARIABLES

PL/SQL variables are one type of program data that can be recorded against a PL/SQL definition. They are created within the context of the program unit, rather than passed in as arguments, as placeholders for data created, or used during the program execution.

All PL/SQL program variables will conform to the following standard:

Variable = v_<variable name>

Where <variable name> should be a logical, meaningful, and concise name representing the value the variable will hold. Where the variable will be used to hold the value of a column in a SQL statement, then <variable name> must be the same as the column name.

Precede the <variable name> with "v" so that there are no conflicts with database object names or confusion as to which are PL/SQL variables and which are database objects. All variables must be in lower case, including the prefix.

Example: v_header_id

CONSTANTS

PL/SQL constants are a second type of program data that can be recorded against a PL/SQL definition. They are also created within the context of the program unit and assigned a constant value that is used during the program execution.

All PL/SQL program constants will conform to the following standard:

Constant = c_<constant name>

Where <constant name> should be a logical, meaningful, and concise name representing the use of the value the constant will hold. Where the constant will be used to hold a value to be assigned to a column in a SQL statement, then <constant name> must be the same as the column name.

Precede the <constant name> with "c" so that there are no conflicts with database object names or confusion as to which are PL/SQL constants and which are database objects or variables. All constants must be in lower case, including the prefix.

Example: c_header_id

GLOBAL VARIABLES

Global variables are specific to Oracle Forms application program units. They are used for passing values between forms, similar to arguments or parameters. Although they are not stored in Designer as PL/SQL program data, they are included here for completeness since many people program PL/SQL in Oracle Forms.

All Oracle Forms global variables will conform to the following standard:

Variable = global.<variable name>

Where <variable name> should be a logical, meaningful, and concise name representing the value the variable will hold. Where the variable will be used to hold the value of a field in the data block, then <variable name> must be the same as the field name.

Global variables must always be referenced with ':GLOBAL.' preceding the variable name. Therefore, no additional prefix is required to distinguish global variables from local or standard variables. In order to avoid confusion, do not use the same name for both a global and a local variable.

Example: header_id (i.e., :global.header_id)

Chapter 10

Other Database Administrator Objects

In addition to all the server objects mentioned in the previous chapter, Designer allows you to store definitions on a variety of other objects that have traditionally fallen under the auspices of the database administrator (DBA). These objects are generally encountered in the Build phase of a project. Using the features of Designer, including the Server Generator, it is actually possible for the DBA to define and maintain these objects in the repository. This allows less experienced DBAs to build syntactically correct Data Definition Language Scripts (DDL) without having to refer to a DBA handbook. In addition, if the DBA uses Designer to at least store the basic definitions of these objects, then the corporation will have a central location to examine in order to determine the architecture if that DBA decides to leave. To the best of our knowledge, few DBAs use Oracle Designer in this way, but we hope that this will be a trend in the future.

This chapter presents a naming standard for the following DBA objects:

- ❏ Database Names
- ❏ Tablespace Definitions
- ❏ Tablespace Datafile Names
- ❏ Rollback Segments
- ❏ Clusters
- ❏ Snapshots
- ❏ Users
- ❏ Roles

- Profiles
- Synonyms
- Control Files
- Database Links

Since these objects are the responsibility of the DBA, the standards that are finally accepted should be developed in cooperation with the lead DBA. Deviations from and changes to these standards must be approved by the lead DBA. The standards presented here, like all the standards, are based on our experiences at various sites. Note that they do not necessarily follow the Oracle Flexible Architecture (OFA) guidelines and will need to be modified if your DBAs prefer that standard.

DATABASE NAMES

With the release of Oracle Designer 2, you now have the ability to record implementations of server model objects against multiple schemas in multiple databases. Because of this feature, it is important to name the database definitions in a way that is clear to those who will be building the objects so that they build them in the right database.

> The database name should reflect the very broad domain of the database. Examples would be PROD, DEV, and TEST.
>
> - Database names should not indicate a version (of application/domain/software).
> - Database names should refer to the domain of the data rather than the application or project. Databases are generally shared by multiple projects and, if they are not, application/project names are likely to change over time.

Since you can generate a CREATE DATABASE command from Designer, and since you likely already have a database in place, the names recorded should reflect the actual name of the database. This will allow you to rebuild the database if needed, but more importantly ensures that the developers know in which database the designers wanted the objects to appear. There is a wizard that allows you to define default characteristics and a property sheet for filling in details.

TABLESPACE DEFINITIONS

When Oracle is installed using the default database, certain tablespaces are created and named for you. The standards here are for all those other tablespaces you have to build as you install addition tools (such as Designer or Discoverer) and as your applications grow and multiply.

A tablespace name should reflect the contents of the tablespace. Some standard tablespace names are USER_DATA, TEMP, SYSTEM, RBS, and TOOLS. These are usually named during a standard Oracle installation and should not be changed.

Tablespace names that are reserved for application specific table data and indexes should reflect the following information:

- ❑ Ownership
- ❑ The growth pattern of the database objects
- ❑ The type of database objects it contains (i.e. data or index)

Tablespaces can be in one of many ranges of growth patterns. For tables/indexes which have a limited range of growth patterns, the range can be (s)mall, (m)edium, and (l)arge. For tables/indexes needing a wider range of growth patterns, the range can be 1-9, with "1" being the smallest growth. A decision must be made on which range of growth patterns is needed for the database. This decision should be based on detailed analysis of the growth patterns of the tables and indexes. Once the growth pattern range has been decided, then the growth pattern range and size should be indicated in the tablespace name. The tablespace name should also indicate whether it contains table data or index data. The tablespace name should be constructed as follows:

<3-char abbr. of THE OWNER ACCOUNT NAME>_<growth pattern range/size>_<object type>

Where <object type> is DATA or IDX

Example 1:

Tables are owned by PERSONNEL

Growth pattern range is limited and contains S, M, L

Object type is Table Data

<u>TABLESPACE NAME</u>

PER_S_DATA

PER_M_DATA

PER_L_DATA

Tables are owned by PERSONNEL

Growth pattern range is limited and contains S, M, L

Object type is Index data

<u>TABLESPACE NAME</u>

PER_S_IDX

PER_M_IDX

PER_L_IDX

Example 2:

Tables are owned by PERSONNEL

Growth pattern range is wide and contains 1,2,3,4,5,6,7,8,9

Object type is Table Data

<u>TABLESPACE NAME</u>

PER_1_DATA

PER_2_DATA

PER_5_DATA

PER_9_DATA

Tables are owned by PERSONNEL

Growth pattern range is wide and contains 1,2,3,4,5,6,7,8,9

Object type is Index Data

<u>TABLESPACE NAME</u>

PER_2_IDX

PER_3_IDX

PER_9_IDX

The growth pattern is included in the name of the tablespace to allow DBAs to put objects of similar size and growth into a tablespace with default storage parameters appropriate to that table. This eliminates the need for table level storage parameters and reduces tablespace fragmentation because all the objects have the same extent size. This strategy is often recommended in database tuning classes, as it can improve system performance (for more information refer to *Oracle8 Data Warehousing* by Dodge and Gorman). If your DBA disagrees, you will want to modify this standard and perhaps exclude the growth pattern indicator.

SINGLE TABLE TABLESPACE

Another performance tuning strategy involves creating a separate tablespace for a large table. This allows the DBA to perform backup and recovery operations at a more granular level and potentially increase availability. It also gives the DBA more control over how the data are stripped across disks and I/O devices. Another special case occurs when table partitioning features are used. This could lead to a requirement for one tablespace per partition. The decision to use this approach is made by the DBA (again refer to *Oracle8 Data Warehousing* for more on this topic). Since this is a special case, we have a special naming standard to handle it.

In a very large databases (VLDB), such as a data warehouse, it may be necessary to assign certain tables to their own tablespace. **This is a decision that should be made by the DBA.**

In this case the naming standard will be:

<Table alias>_DATA

Example: Table name: ORDER_SUMMARIES

Alias: OS

Tablespace name: OS_DATA

In the case where table partitioning is being used and the system requirements indicate that each partition should have its own table space, then the standard is modified to include a suffix on the table short name to indicate the partitioned data that is included.

Example: Table name: ORDER_SUMMARIES

Alias: OS

Partitioned by: Month and year

Tablespace name: OS_JAN98_DATA

SINGLE INDEX TABLESPACE

As there are tuning considerations with data tablespaces, similar consideration arise with indexes on very large tables. Again, we propose a special standard for that situation.

In the same manner, it may be necessary to create a tablespace for a very large index. Again this is a call for the DBA to make. In this case the naming standard will be:

<Index name>_IDX

Where <index name> is the actual name of the index being stored.

Example: Index name: ORD_LOC_FK_I

Tablespace name: ORD_LOC_FK_IDX

TABLESPACE DATAFILE NAMES

To have a tablespace in the first place requires that data files on the system be created. Those should also be named according to a standard for consistency.

Tablespaces can contain anywhere from 1 to many data files. The names for the data files should reflect the tablespace name, an incremented number, the instance name, and the database file extension (.dbf or .ora). The tablespace data file name should be constructed as follows:

<Tablespace name>_<n><SID>.dbf

Where <n> is an integer, starting from 1 and <SID> is the database instance name.

Example 1:

Tablespace name = PER_S_DATA

Number of data files = 3

Instance name = ORCL

Data file names:

per_s_data01orcl.dbf

per_s_data02orcl.dbf

per_s_data03orcl.dbf

Example 2:

Tablespace name = PER_3_IDX

Number of data files = 2

Data file names:

per_3_idx01orcl.dbf

per_3_idx02orcl.dbf

Figure 10.1 shows how the definitions of tablespaces and data files will look in the DB Admin tab of the Design Editor when completed. As with most objects in Designer, datafile definitions are easily entered using the wizards.

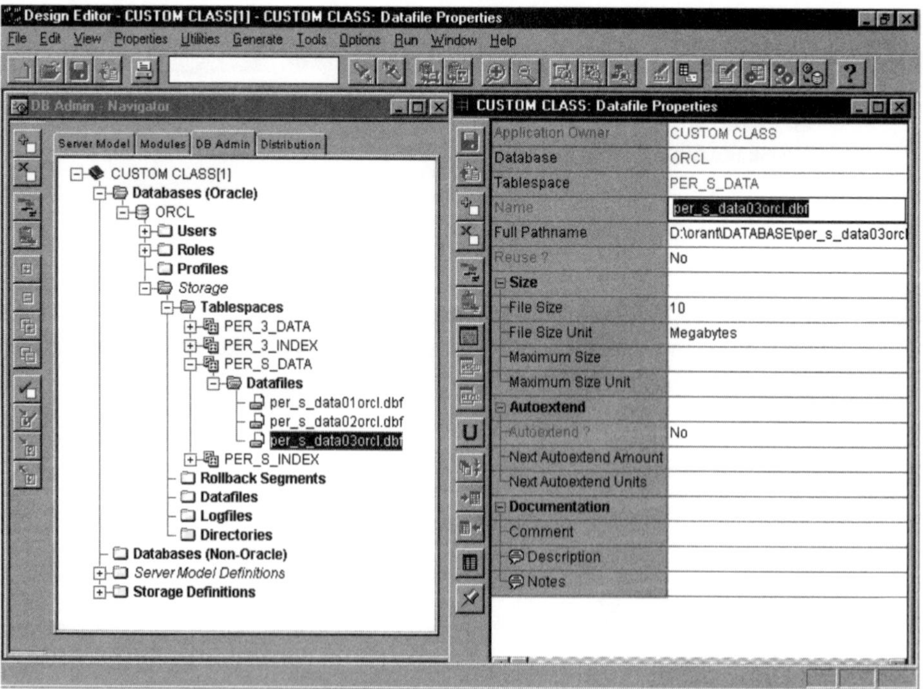

FIGURE 10.1 The DB Admin tab showing tablespace and datafile properties.

ROLLBACK SEGMENTS

Oracle Designer allows you to provide specifications for the construction of rollback segments within the Design Editor. Following is the standard for naming these objects. As always, these standards should be subject to approval by your lead DBA.

The naming convention for rollback segments is:

Rollback = <size>_RBS<number>

Where:

- <number> is a sequentially increasing integer, starting at 01. The sequence is specific to the "size" type of the rollback segment
- <size> is one of: SM(all), MED(ium), LA(rge), and VL(very large)

Examples:

SM_RBS01

SM_RBS02

MED_RBS01

VL_RBS02

Once the rollback segment is defined inside the repository, it is possible to generate the SQL code to build the rollback segment. Below is a sample of the code generated.

```
PROMPT Creating Rollback Segment 'SM_RBS01'
CREATE PUBLIC ROLLBACK SEGMENT SM_RBS01
 TABLESPACE RBS_DATA
 STORAGE(
 INITIAL 100K
 NEXT 100K
 PCTINCREASE 0
 MINEXTENTS 2
 MAXEXTENTS 505  OPTIMAL 100M
 )
/
```

As you can see the correct code can be generated even if you do not know the syntax. Be sure to tell your DBA!

CLUSTERS

Clusters are objects built for specific performance improvements. Their design and construction are best left to the DBAs of the world. In Designer, you can specify two types of clusters, index clusters and hash clusters. Both provide a way of grouping common columns in several tables so that the columns are actually stored in the same physical data block on the hardware. If done correctly, this can improve performance when tables are frequently joined on these common columns. For example, if you always process employees by department number, and join them to the Department table, it may help performance to build a cluster on the Employee and Department tables using the Department Number(DEPTNO) column.

Clusters are specified in the Server Model tab of the Design Editor. We recommend using the Dialog mode if you are unfamiliar with their construction, as it will walk you though the various pieces.

Clusters should follow this naming convention:

Cluster = <Table1 alias>_<Table2 alias>_<Common Column>_C

Where 'C' is for cluster and <common column> is the name of the column the cluster is built on.

Example:

Table 1 name = EMPLOYEES

Alias = EMP

Table 2 name = DEPARTMENT

Alias = DEPT

Common Column = DEPTNO

Cluster name = EMP_DEPT_DEPTNO_C

SNAPSHOTS

Another useful database object that DBAs can specify and design in the Design Editor is snapshots. Basically, a snapshot is a point in time copy of another table, view, or snapshots data. A snapshot contains a recent copy of the data from the object on which it is based and can be refreshed at specific intervals, if desired. It can also combine data from several tables at once (like a view). Snapshots can be a useful facility for improving performance in a reporting or decision support environment because the snapshot can be physically located in a separate instance or at a remote site (and thus does not compete for resources with the On-line Transaction Processing [OLTP] system). In addition the snapshot can provide a backup mechanism if it resides on a different machine that is potentially at a different site.

> There are two kinds of snapshots that can be defined in Designer: simple and complex. Simple snapshots (ones accessing only one table or view) will be named in this way:
>
> Snapshot name = SS_<table name>
>
> Where 'SS' represents 'snapshot' and the table name is the name of the table or view the snapshot is based on.
>
> The maximum length for a snapshot name will be 26. If the name exceeds 26, then use the table alias, abbreviations and acronyms as needed. Snapshot names must be plural just like tables.
>
> **Example:**
>
> SS_EMPLOYEES is a snapshot of the EMPLOYEES table
>
> Complex snapshots will be named in this way:
>
> Snapshot name = SS_<table name>_<criteria>
>
> The qualifier, if used, should give the end users a clear idea of the purpose and contents of the snapshot. Use the *criteria* qualifier if
>
> 1. Using the table name alone is not unique
> 2. The snapshot is based on a join of 2 or more tables
> 3. The snapshot contains a where clause
> 4. The snapshot is unusually complex.
> 5. The snapshot is a summary
>
> **Examples:**
>
> SS_ACTIVE_CUSTOMERS provides information on only active CUSTOMERS.
>
> SS_EMPLOYEES_DEPARTMENTS is a snapshot joining the EMPLOYEES tables and the DEPARTMENTS table.
>
> SS_CUSTOMER_COMPLAINTS provides information about CUSTOMERS and their NOTES of type 'complaint'.
>
> SS_TOTAL_CUSTOMER_SALES provides summary information on customer sales activity.

USERS, ROLES, AND PROFILES

This next section provides some brief guidelines for naming these objects. All of these can be defined and generated from the DB Admin tab in the Design Editor.

DATABASE USERS

The naming standard for users is quite simple. If your organization already has a different standard, simply change the text in the template to match.

> ORACLE usernames will consist of the user's first initial and last name, with no space between.
>
> **Examples:** LPHILLIP, RJAHR, BJOHNSON

When you define a user in Designer, we also recommend that you record the default tablespace assignment, the temporary tablespace assignment, any tablespace quotas, roles assignments, and at least the primary system privileges. If you want to go all the way with server generation, it is possible to record security privileges against any of the database objects defined in the application. If you record the information, you can generate reports against the repository to compare it to what has been deployed in a production system. You can also generate fully functional DDL scripts to implement the security.

ROLES

Roles are a convenient way of grouping system and object privileges to make security administration easier. If you have more than a few users on your system, you should already be using roles. If not, ask your DBA about them.

The naming standard for roles requires input from whoever is responsible for application security. This could be an Application Administrator or Application Technical Lead. This person determines who gets what kind of access to the system.

> Application specific roles should be named in this manner:
>
> Role = <Application abbreviation>_<Access level>
>
> The access levels must be determined by the Application Administrator.

Examples of access levels might be ADMIN, USER, and REPORT. So examples of role names might be:

PM_ADMIN

PM_USER

ER_REPORT

AC_USER

PROFILES

A database profile is used to provide a set of limits on various database resources and password control parameters. In Designer it is done in the DB Admin tab of the Design Editor. You currently can use only the property palette to maintain profiles; there is no wizard. Some examples of settings include number of logins per user, CPU per session, idle time allowed, number of failed logins before lock-out, and so on (Figure 10.2). These profiles can then be applied to one or more database users.

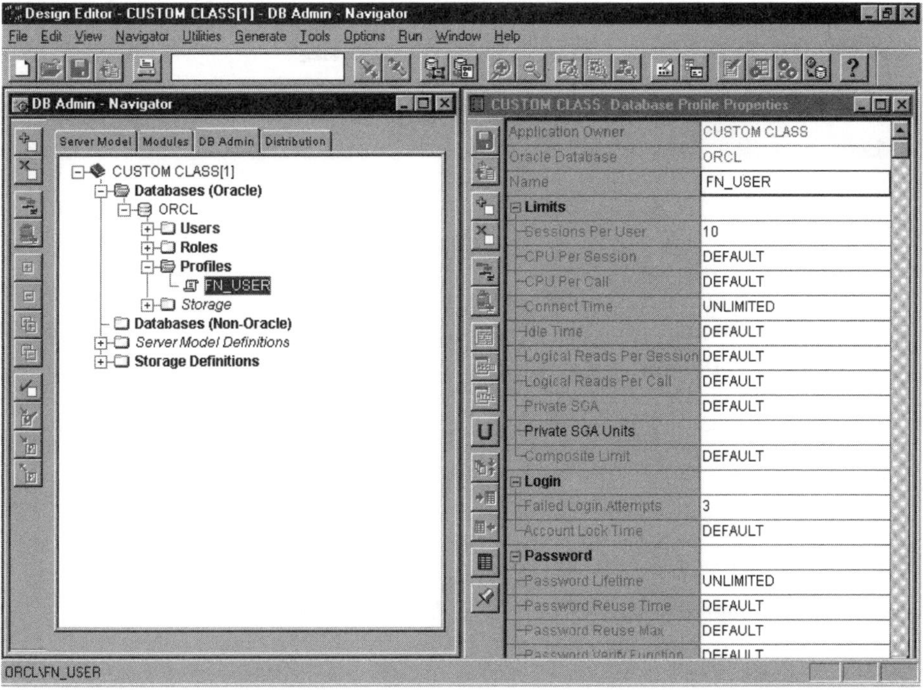

FIGURE 10.2 Using the Design Editor to create a profile in the DB Admin tab.

Defining profiles requires input from the Database Administrator and the Application Administrator (for profiles specific to an application).

Profile names should describe the interaction of the ORACLE user with the database. The DBA and the Application Administrator should determine profile definitions together.

Some recommended profile names are:

- USER—Profile for end users. May be broken into multiple profiles if application warrants different resource limits for different types of users.
- SUPPORT—Profile for developers supporting the application.
- DBA—Profile for DBAs.

If the profile is application specific, then it should be prefixed with the application abbreviation.

Example: FN_USER

As you can see, these standards are loose and will need to be refined for use in your site.

SYNONYMS

Synonym names should match the name of the underlying table or view. Using two different names (the synonym name being different from the underlying object name) is confusing. If you have a need to change an object's name (i.e., because it does not comply with current standards), you should modify your code rather than create synonyms. Oracle's mechanisms for configuring and installing distributed applications are not designed to resolve synonym chains of indeterminate length. This will not be a problem if code owners maintain codes properly. The Impact Analysis report in Designer is useful for identifying areas affected by object name changes.

The naming convention for synonyms is:

Synonym name = *table or view* name

Synonyms, whether public or private, should always match the underlying object name that the synonym is referencing.

Note that synonyms can be defined in the Design Editor using the palette mode, or they can be defined directly on a server model diagram.

CONTROL FILES

Although there is no place to specify control files in Designer (that we found), the template document contains the following standard for completeness. Even though control file data are not stored in the repository, you still need a naming standard.

The convention for a control file name is:

Control file = CTL<n><SID>.ora

Where <n> is an integer, starting from 1 and <SID> is the database instance name.

Examples:

CTL1ORCL.ORA

CTL2ORCL.ORA

DATABASE LINKS

In release 2.1 of Oracle Designer, the Database Link Name allows you to specify only the remote database name that you are linking to. You can document the name of the remote database you have a link to in the Design Editor and generate the DDL to build the link. Go to the Distribution Tab, then the Databases (Oracle) node, then the -> Public Database Links node. (Or in Repository Object Navigator go to Databases (Oracle), open the node for a database then open the Distributed Options node, then the Public Database Links node.)

A database link should be the same as the name of the remote database to which it points. The naming convention for a database link is:

Link = <remote database>

Where:

- <remote database> is the name of the remote database

Example: ORCL_DEN

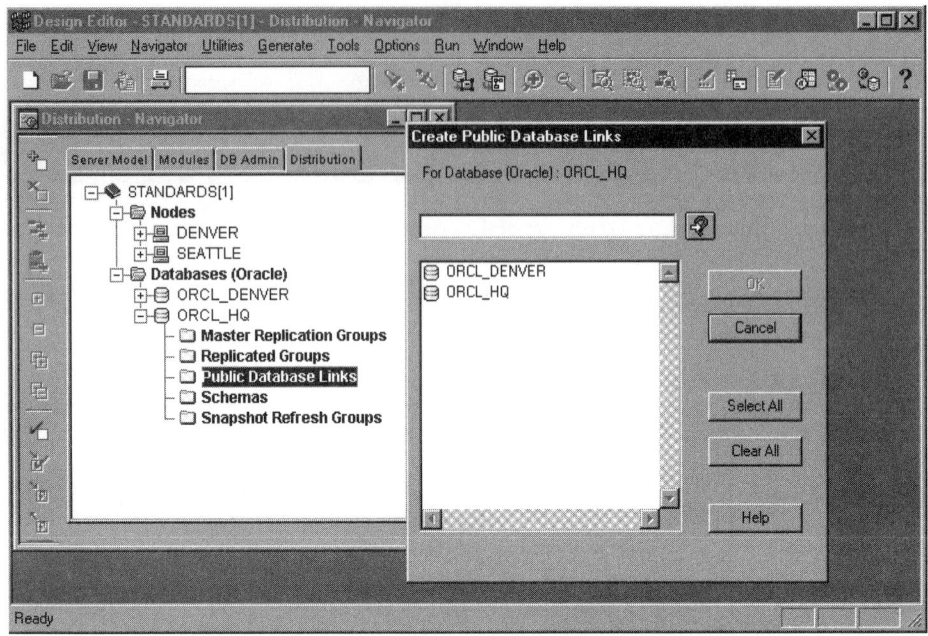

FIGURE 10.3 Creating a public database link.

To create the Database Link definition, be sure the remote database definition exists in Designer and has the TNS Alias specified. This service string should be found in the TNSNAMES.ORA file for the SQL*NET network (or the Oracle name server configuration). Now you can create the Public Database Link by selecting the Public Database Links node for the local database and then pressing the create button. You will then get a dialog where you can select the remote database (or databases) to create the link(s) for (Figure 10.3).

Once this is done you can then generate the DDL to build the link. This can be done only by selecting *Generate -> Generate Database Administration Objects* from the Design Editor menu. The generated DDL file for the database link looks like this:

```
-- d:\designer\link.dbl
--
-- Generated for Oracle 8 on Wed Apr 28 09:22:20 1999 by
Server Generator 2.1.24.4.0

PROMPT Creating Database Link to 'ORCL_DENVER'
CREATE PUBLIC DATABASE LINK ORCL_DENVER USING 'orcl_den'
/
```

Unfortunately, the release we were using does not include the connect string (even though it was specified in Designer) in the link definition, so this code would have to be modified to actually work. Even though you can generate DDL, the link definition can really be used only for documentation.

Part 2 DIAGRAMMING CONVENTIONS

Since so much work in Oracle Designer revolves around the various diagrammers (e.g., Process Model, ERD, FHD, and Server Model Diagram), it seemed appropriate to include a section on diagramming conventions. There is no magic formula here. These standards are again the result of our experience with the tools combined with advice from various other sources that we have encountered over the years. We are simply documenting them for you so that you have a place to start.

The importance of diagramming conventions may be less obvious than naming standards. The goal here is to create a consistent look for the diagrams you show to your customers or end users. If each entity relationship diagram has a different look and flow, customers will never be comfortable trying to read them in a review session. In addition by imposing standards on the diagrams, analysts are forced to carefully examine their contents. In doing so, they may uncover errors or omissions that may otherwise have been missed until later in the project. This process in and of itself will not only save hours of rework, but will then also save money.

Chapter 11

Business Process Model Diagrams

This chapter presents some conventions to be used when creating Business Process Modeler Diagrams in Oracle Designer. As was discussed in Chapter 5, in the strategy planning stage, you analyze and model the high-level processes of the enterprise. This activity helps in understanding and documentation of the major processes that your organization performs. Later in analysis, you break down these major processes into functions using the Function Hierarchy Diagrammer (FHD). Our goal here is to not obscure the high-level process model (enterprise picture) with details.

The following guidelines should be applied when performing business process modeling using the Oracle Designer Process Modeler (BPM).

MULTIPLE MODULAR DIAGRAMS

One of the goals of creating Business Process Modeler (BPM) diagrams is to make it easier for end users and business people to understand the processes in their organization and help you verify that you do, too. You don't want them to be overwhelmed by your diagrams. The first rule is keep it simple. The details of the business processes should be identified and modeled using a drill down approach as discussed in Chapter 5, and Appendix C.

As discussed elsewhere, one large process model diagram would create a very large flat function hierarchy diagram, which should be avoided. In addition to keeping the diagrams simple to read, the use of subdiagrams will ultimately make the Function Hierarchy Diagram (FHD) more readable (and useful) as well.

> Rather then creating one large business process diagram, create many subdiagrams. This will eliminate the need to maintain one large diagram that will over time become unreadable and unmanageable. Also, each process step of a business process diagram will appear as a function on a function hierarchy diagram.

AVOID OVERCROWDING

How many processes are too many? Despite the complexity of your business, each diagram should contain only six to nine business processes. The diagram will become more crowded and complex as you add stores, flows and events. As stated previously, a modular approach to process modeling will inherently build a usable function hierarchy diagram.

> Do not crowd many processes onto a single business process diagram. In general, one diagram should contain no more than six to nine process steps.
>
> If a single diagram contains more than nine process steps, consider drilling down on one of the more complex process steps into a new diagram.

Again, you will need to use your own judgment when implementing or enforcing this standard. One major factor to consider is that the processes, along with the number of process steps included on a process diagram, will affect the inherited functions and layout structure of your organization's FHD.

DISPLAY A LEGEND ON THE DIAGRAM

Since you are likely to have more than one diagram (if you follow our suggested convention), it will help to label them. Labeling allows you to go back to the tool, find the diagram (after being shown the error of your ways in a review session), and then change it. If you have a large system with many diagrams, it could be hard to identify one in a list without some reference. Designer offers a nice feature for identifying diagrams (Figure 11.1). We recommend the following:

Under *File-> Summary Information*, check the following to be displayed:

- ❑ Diagram
- ❑ Title
- ❑ Created
- ❑ Last Modified
- ❑ Author

The legend must appear under and to the right of the Unspecified business unit.

While the diagram name may be somewhat cryptic, the diagram title should be indicative of the business area being modeled and be understandable by business users.

Example:

Diagram Name = INTERVIEW APPLICANTS

Title = Interview Applicants Process

Why display both the diagram name and title? The diagram name cannot be entered in mixed case, but the title can. You need the name to find it in the tool, but the title can be more descriptive to the users. If you don't care about the case of the title, just use the diagram name (which should be equal to the base process short definition for clarity).

After you have selected the items to display, the summary information will appear in the upper left-hand corner of your diagram. The summary box can be moved to anywhere in the diagram, but we recommend you drag it so that it appears under and to the right of the Unspecified business unit for consistency (Figure 11.2).

BPM DIAGRAM LAYOUT CONVENTIONS

This section describes some helpful layout conventions for creating diagrams. These conventions aid in making your diagrams consistent and easier for the business community to understand.

Summary Information

Summary Details | Text

Show

- [x] Diagram — INTERVIEW.APPLICANTS
- [x] Title — Interview Applicants Process
- [x] Created — 30 September 1998 — 10:57:42
- [x] Last Modified — 20 May 1999 — 15:54:51
- [x] Author — Mark A. Kramm
- [ ] Application System — DEMO — 1
- [ ] Username — mark
- [ ] Connect String
- [ ] Process — Interview Applicants

OK | Cancel | Apply | Help

FIGURE 11.1 Summary information dialog in the Business Process Modeler.

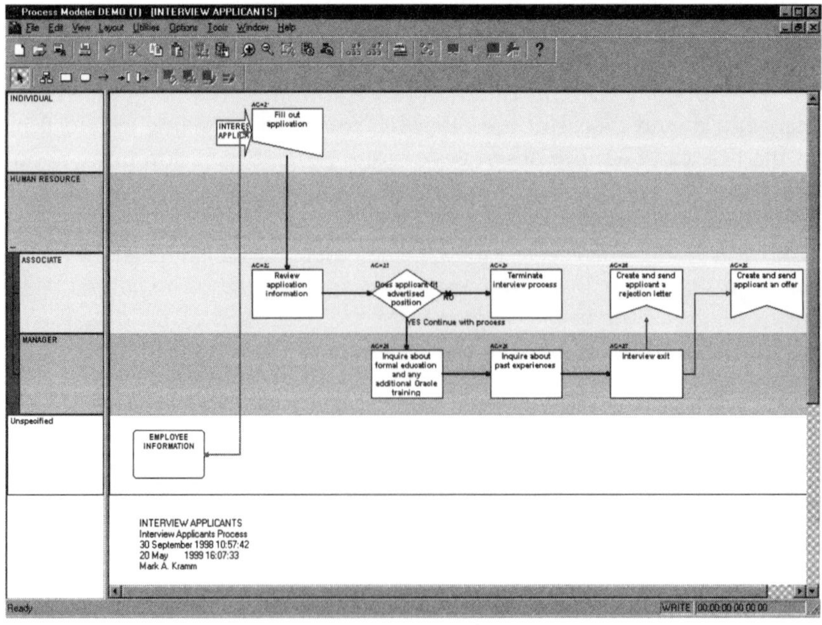

FIGURE 11.2 Sample business process model with summary information displayed.

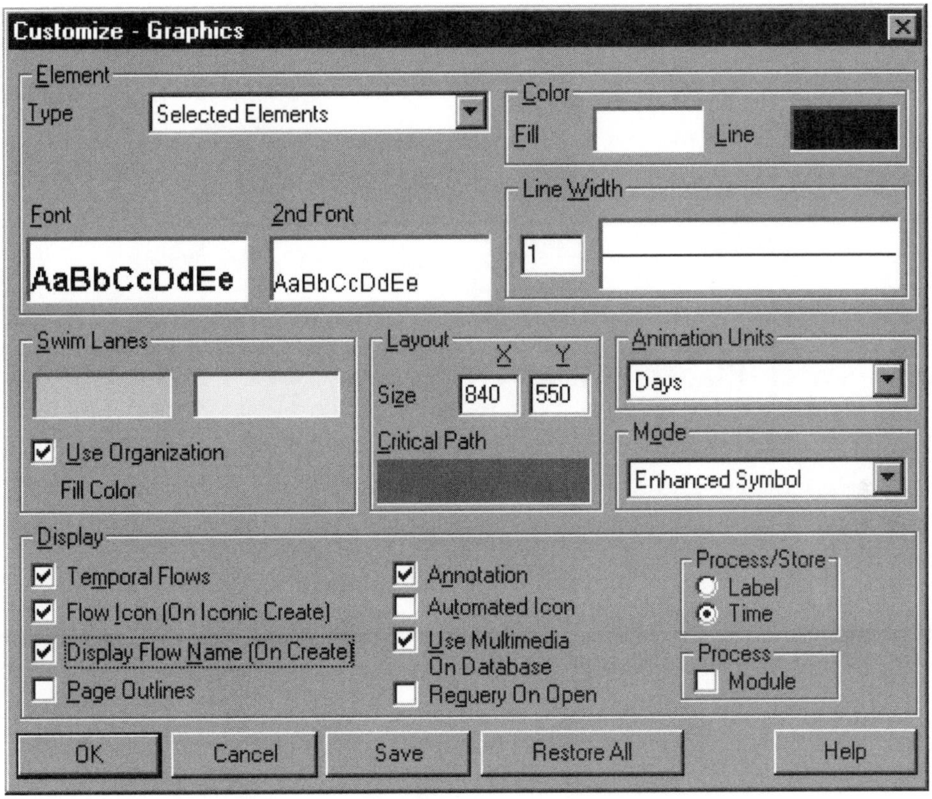

FIGURE 11.3 The Customize - Graphics diagram dialog.

DISPLAY OPTIONS

Oracle Designer gives you many options for display on a BPM diagram (Figure 11.3). These options are set by selecting *Options-> Customize->Graphics* from the BPM Diagrammer menu and then checking or unchecking the various display options.

As a rule, when creating a diagram we use the default settings, which include the settings for the following display options: Temporal Flow, Flow Icon, Display Flow Name (On Create), Annotation, and Use Multimedia On Database.

Diagrams should include:

- ❑ Major process steps (i.e., no functions)
- ❑ Flows (i.e., data, material or temporal)

- ❑ Flow names
- ❑ Process labels
- ❑ Triggers and outcomes
- ❑ Stores (data and material)

Process Step Placement

- ❑ Place process steps in the business unit's swim lane that performs it.
- ❑ When possible, place process steps to the right of a dependent process step rather than under it. This will reduce the swim lane height.
- ❑ Place process steps that are associated with a trigger one extra grid-snap to the right of the business unit. This will make the printout more readable.
- ❑ Before creating a new process step, always use the *Edit->Include* facility first to prevent duplicate processes.

OBJECT PLACEMENT

The following conventions state where to place the various objects that need to be displayed in the BPM diagram. When these conventions are followed, all of you diagrams should look consistent and will conform to a printable size.

As a general practice, you should always use the Include facility before building a new process step. When you invoke *Edit->Include->Global Process Step,* a list of existing processes not already associated with this root process appears. If you pick something from this list, the tool automatically creates a shared/common process step and includes it in your diagram. If you use *Edit->Include->Process Step,* the step will simply be added to the current diagram.

By adhering to this practice, you will reduce potential conflicts. In some cases, the same process exists in another application that you are unaware of. That's where peer reviews come in handy. If during a review you find that you have duplicated a process step, delete your process and have the previously existing one shared into your application (with the permission of the Application Lead or System Architect).

If the first process step in a process model is modeled as being triggered by an event and is placed up against the business unit area, it is hard to read the trigger name. To resolve this problem, do not place the trigger and process step up against the business unit area; place it over to the right a little.

We have also found that it is a good practice to lay out all process steps in the diagram first, before including their flows.

When drawing flows, apply the following rules:

Drawing Flows

- ❑ Face arrowheads to the right if at all possible.
- ❑ Avoid line crossings if at all possible.
- ❑ Before creating a new flow, always use the *Edit->Include* facility first to prevent creation of duplicate flows.

The reason for these rules should be obvious: They keep the diagram easy to read. Crossing and bent lines make it harder to trace a flow when the diagram is being reviewed.

The last layout issue to consider is that of the placement of flow names.

Flow name placement

When flow names are used, place flow names in the middle of the flow.

Place flow names in the middle of the flow so that they may be read easily. In places where the flow name cannot be displayed in the middle, display the name at the source side of the flow. As always the goal is to make the diagram more easily readable. See Figure 11.6 later in this chapter for an example of this convention.

Label placement

Place the label of the process above and to the left of the process step using this method:

1. Copy label to the annotation text field, set annotation type to 'TEXT' in multimedia tab.
2. Check Display Annotation in *Options->Custimize->Graghics* menu item.

Hint: Oracle Designer 2.1.1, has an option that allows you to show the labels of processes in your diagram. Because the Designer tool places the label inside of the process step box, the process step short definition may overwrite it. The convention mentioned above eliminates this problem.

The following are the steps to display labels on a BPM diagram based on the convention mentioned previously.

1. Select *Options->Customize->Graphics* from the menu tool bar of the BPM diagrammer.
2. Check the Annotation field in the Display group.
3. Check Time in the Process/Store group within the Display group (Figure 11.4).
4. Double click on a process step.
5. In the Specific tab, highlight the value in the Label field. Press Ctrl-C to copy the value.

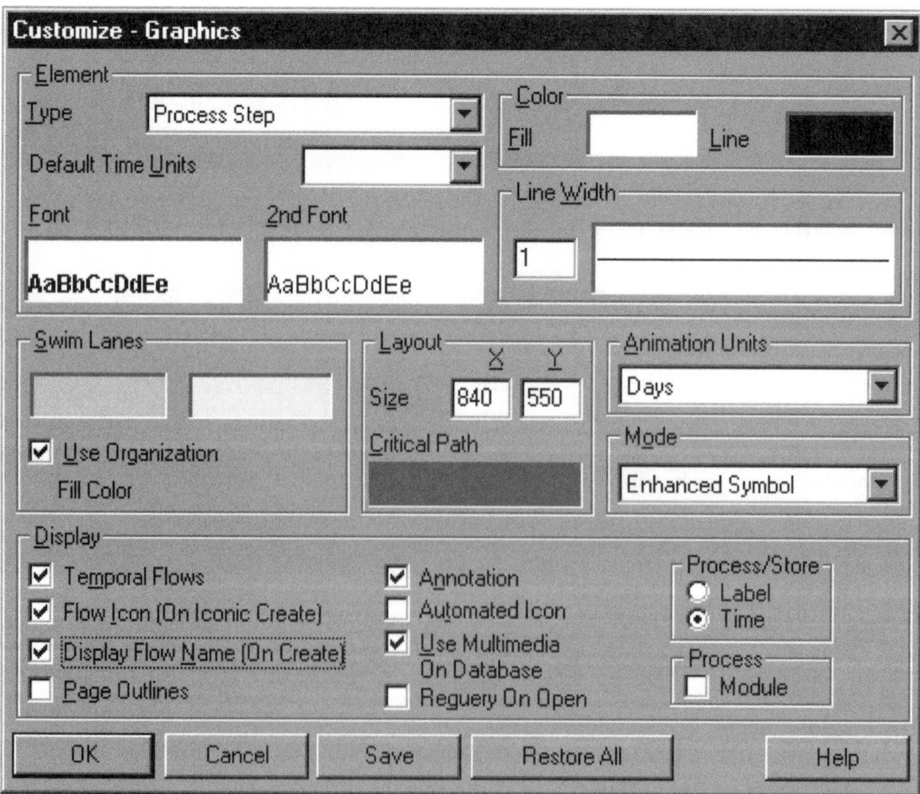

FIGURE 11.4 Using the Customizing Graphics option to show the process labels.

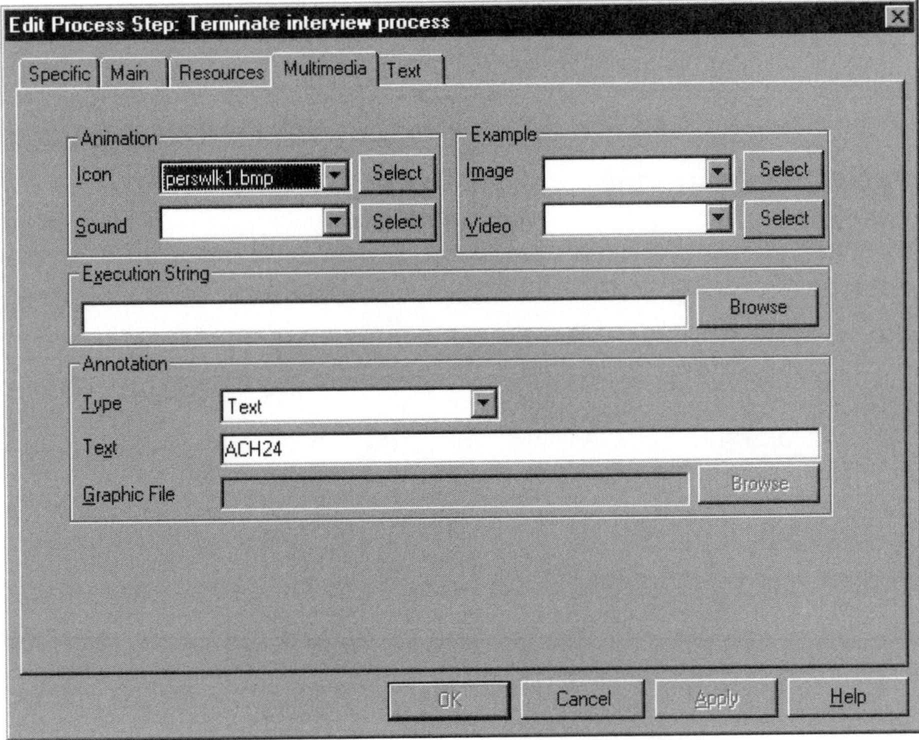

FIGURE 11.5 Including label as Annotation Text.

6. Select the Multimedia tab.
7. In the Annotation group, use the drop down list to set the Type field to: Text.
8. Place your cursor in the Text field of the Annotation group and press Ctrl-V on your keyboard to paste in the label. (Figure 11.5)

Material Store placement

Before creating a new material store, always use the *Edit->Include* facility first to prevent creation of duplicate material stores.

Place material stores in the Business Units swim lane to show that they are responsible for the material.

If you cannot explicitly identify a Business Unit that will take ownership of the material store, place it in the Unspecified swim lane.

Data Store placement

Before creating a new data store, always use the *Edit->Include* facility first to prevent creation of duplicate data stores.

Place data stores in the Unspecified swim lane.

A datastore (in other words, information) is generally used by many business units via the process steps that they perform. Therefore, to reduce the politics involved in data ownership, we recommend showing datastores in the Un-

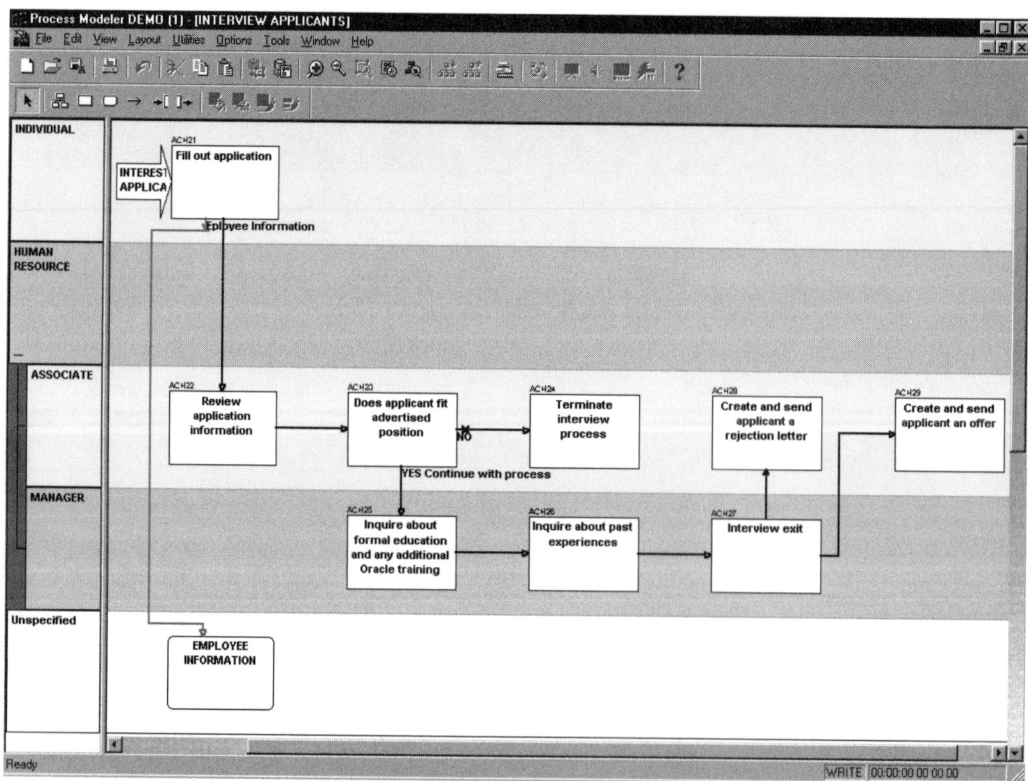

FIGURE 11.6 Example BPM diagram using layout conventions.

specified business unit swim lane. However, if clear ownership of the store can be established, then it should be put in the appropriate swim lane.

This standard also makes viewing data stores and reading the diagram easier. Figure 11.6 shows a completed model using the conventions mentioned so far.

OTHER CONSIDERATIONS

Once you have built all these diagrams, you need to maintain them. This can be quite a large task, so to help you, we have included a few other tips in the template that you should include as standard practices.

Consolidating Diagrams

Consolidate Diagrams frequently using *Edit->Requery*

In general, it is a good practice to consolidate a diagram each time you open it to ensure that you are working with current information. At a minimum, diagrams should be consolidated when there is a change to the Designer Repository relative to business functions, flows, stores, events (triggers) and business units. **If you wish to keep historical views of diagrams, save them under another name and do not consolidate them.**

Unlike the Entity Relationship Diagrammer, if a change is made in the Repository Object Navigator (RON) while a diagram is open, any objects affected by the change will *not* appear with a red dot to signify that it has been updated in another tool. Therefore, it is a good practice to select *Edit->Requery* from the menu in the diagrammer to get the diagram objects back in sync with the repository (Figure 11.7).

There is a property that you can set in the Business Process Modeler (*Options->Customize->Advanced*) to automatically requery the diagram when it is opened. *If you are going to keep a history of diagram changes, do not set this property.*

As you can see in the figure, there are several options for requery. You generally want to select the ALL option to ensure that your diagram is totally up to date.

If changes were made while the diagram was closed, you will not be notified of them until you double click on an object that has been changed. Because of this feature, we recommend that you consolidate diagrams every time you open one.

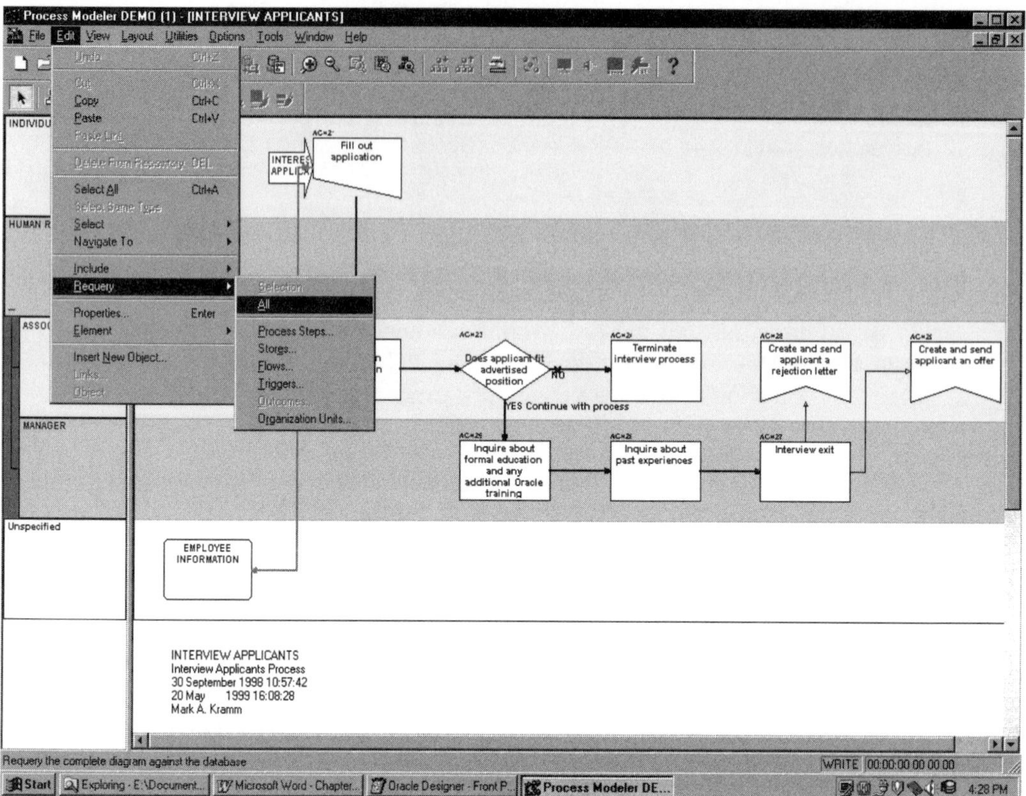

FIGURE 11.7 The BPM Diagram requery options.

Delete Unneeded Diagrams

If a diagram is no longer needed, delete it from the Repository.

This practice may seem obvious, but you would be surprised how many people create multiple versions of the same diagram and then forget which one is the most current. Once the diagrams have been opened, the dates in the legend will of course make this clear, but you may have to open several diagrams before you find the right one. Be sure to clean up after yourself (just make sure someone else did not need the other diagrams first).

COLOR CODING

As more people gain access to color printers and plotters, a new convention is emerging: people are color coding their diagrams. Colors (or even shading) of objects can be a nice way to visually distinguish among different types of processes, stores, flows, triggers, business units, and swim lanes. If this sounds like a useful convention to you, get your lead process analyst involved to determine specific colors or shading patterns to use (or avoid) and the detailed rules by which they should be applied.

To get you started, the template document includes the following guidelines:

> Use color coding or shading to distinguish the following:
>
> ❑ Process steps that are drilled down (open down) into subdiagrams.
>
> ❑ Different type of flows (Data flows from material flows)
>
> ❑ Alternating business units and/or swim lanes
>
> Do not use colors on the Unspecified business unit or its swim lane.

Selecting an object, then clicking on the CHANGE FILL COLOR button on the diagrammer toolbar easily sets colors for the selected object.

Hint: To change the color of all occurrences of the same type of object in a diagram, perform the following steps:

1. Select one of the objects in the diagram
2. Select *Edit -> Select Same Type* from the menu tool bar.
3. Click on the CHANGE FILL COLOR button on the diagrammer toolbar.

The standard for not coloring the Unspecified business unit and its swim lane makes distinguishing it from real business units easier. You can return a selected object's graphical settings to the default settings for that object type by selecting *Utilities -> Restore Graphical Preferences* from the menu.

ANNOTATIONS

> Use annotation in the form of notes or graphics to facilitate communication.

You can add a note or a graphic to a diagram object as an annotation. To reduce the complexity of the diagram, this should be done only if it facilitates communicating business requirements with the business community. Enter the text or the filename of a bitmap on the Multimedia page for a selected object. Refer to the section "BPM Diagram Layout Conventions - Label placement" for the steps on adding annotations on a diagram. **Note:** *Graphical annotations are not as useful when in Iconic mode.*

SETTING SPECIFIC OBJECT TYPES

Each object that you create in the BPM can be further defined as a specific type. For example, a process could be a type of process step, decision point, data entry, report, external, or internal. Specific types can also be set for flows, stores, triggers, and outcomes. You can set the type in the Specific tab in the property dialog. In the case of process steps and stores, the specific type determines how the object appears in Enhanced Symbol mode, so as a convention, we recommend that you set the specific type (if it is known).

Specific Types

Set the specific type for all objects in the BPM whenever the type is known.

DISPLAY MODES

You can display a diagram in one of three different modes (Figures 11.8 through 11.10). You can choose the mode from the View menu on the menu tool bar. The modes and their applicability are as follows:

- **Symbol Mode:** Use Symbol mode for simple diagramming. This mode shows the time required to complete a process step along with the short definition. **Note:** *This mode does not distinguish visually among specific types of objects.* For example, process steps of type report or decision point are displayed in the same way as a regular process step (Figure 11.8).
- **Enhanced Symbol Mode:** Use Enhanced Symbol Mode for flowcharting. Objects are displayed with distinctive symbols for different types of objects using standard flow chart symbols (Figure 11.9).
- **Iconic Mode:** Use iconic mode to display associated icons for process steps, stores, and flows. Because it is more colorful than the other modes, this mode tends to be good for upper management and end user presentations (Figure 11.10).

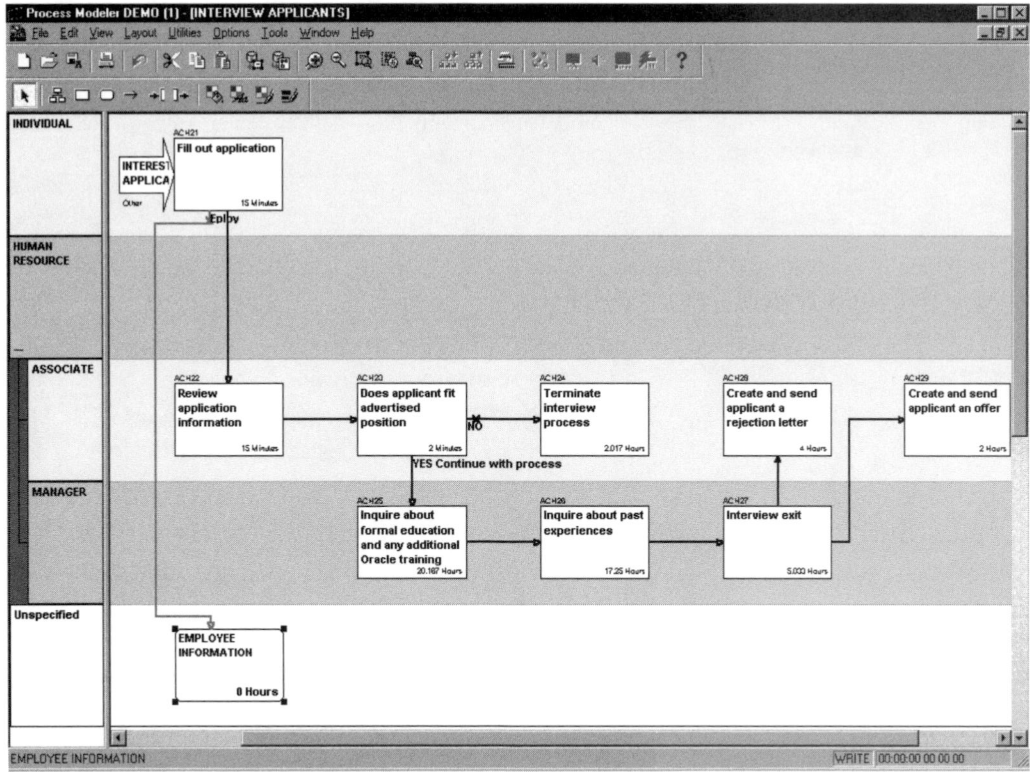

FIGURE 11.8 BPM Diagram in Symbol mode.

Display Modes

Display Diagrams in the following modes:

- **Symbol Mode:** Use Symbol mode for simple diagramming. This mode is appropriate for presentations to the non-technical business community.
- **Enhanced Symbol Mode:** Use Enhanced Symbol mode for flowcharting. This mode is appropriate for presentations to a more technical audience.
- **Iconic Mode:** Use Iconic mode to display associated icons for process steps, stores, and flows. This mode is appropriate for upper management and end-user presentations.

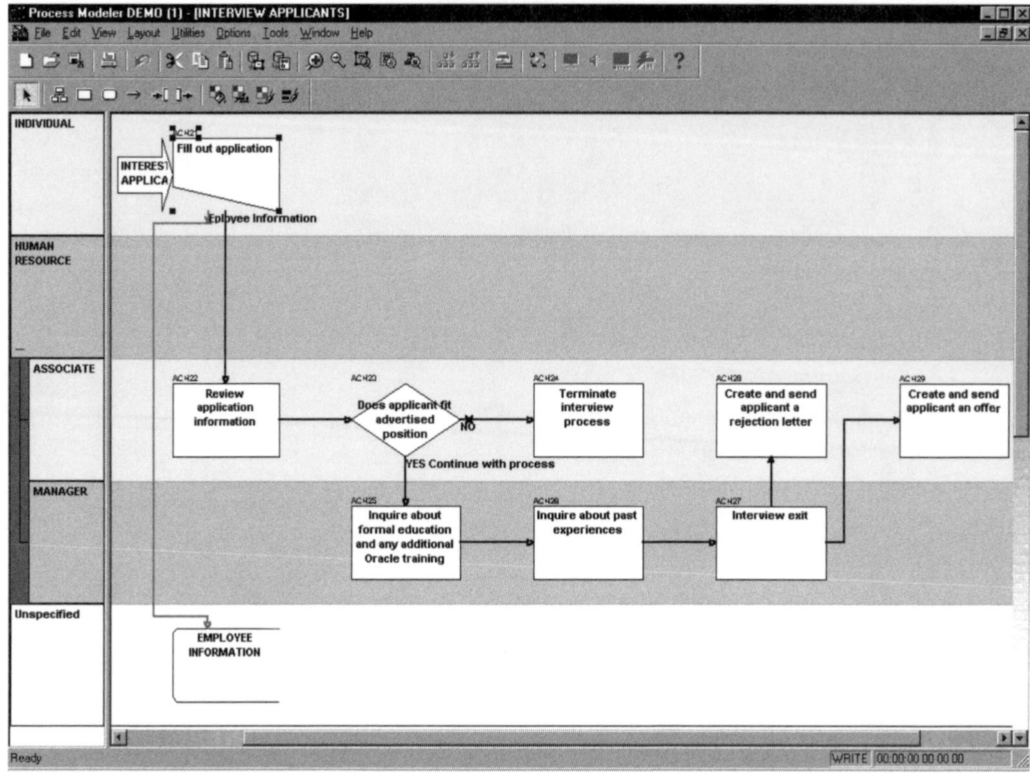

FIGURE 11.9 BPM Diagram in Enhanced Symbol mode.

VISUALIZING A PROCESS

The BPM Diagrammer in Designer has a number of other options that can be used to enhance the presentation of a diagram. Below are some additional recommendations for using these features.

IMAGES

You can display images associated with an object in your diagram. Enter the graphics filename on the Image field in the Multimedia page. This is a particularly good technique for showing photographs of actual people, buildings, documents, or vehicles associated with a process or flow. To show the image for an object, click on the SHOW IMAGE toolbar button.

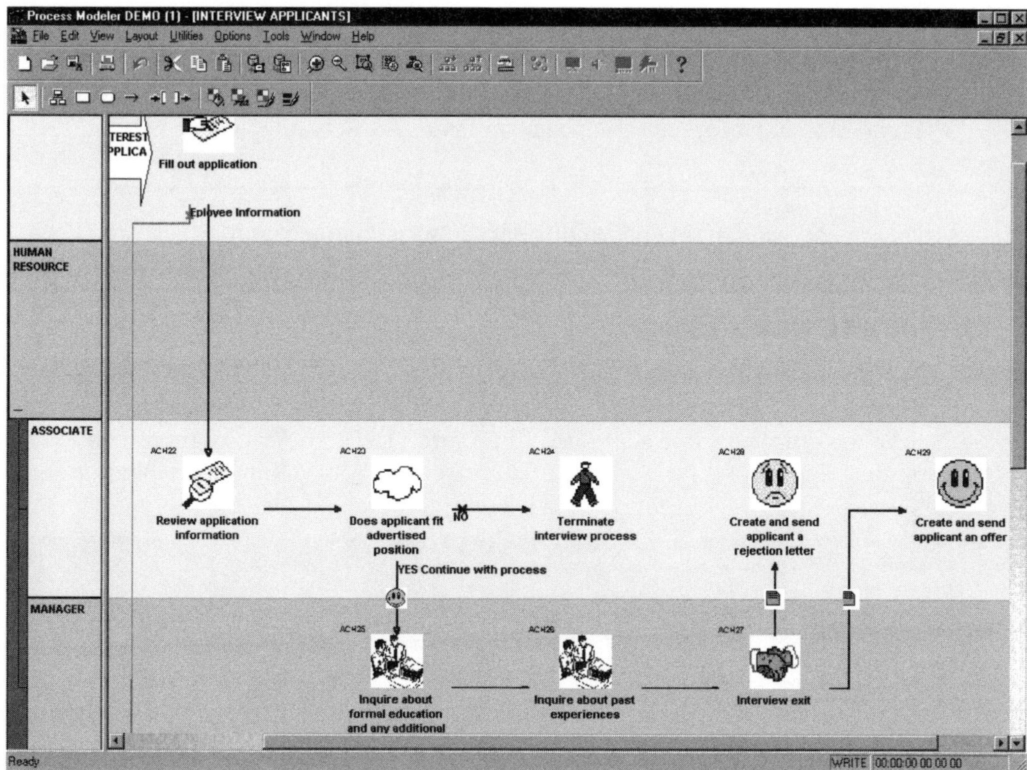

FIGURE 11.10 BPM Diagram in Iconic mode.

> Use images only if it facilitates communication.

VIDEO

You can play back digital video from within a process model using Video for Windows. Files must be in an .avi format. Enter the filename in the Video field on the Multimedia page. **Note:** *Video clips are big; even a 10-second clip takes up about 1 MB of disk space.* To play the clip for an object, click on the PLAY VIDEO toolbar button.

> Use video clips only when it facilitates communication.

SOUND

Digital sound is a particularly effective way to emphasize a diagram. Enter a .wav filename in the Sound field on the Multimedia page for the selected object. To play the sound for an object, click on the PLAY SOUND toolbar button.

> Use sound (digital recordings) only when it facilitates communication.

ANIMATION

If you want to add some pizzazz to your diagram for presentation, you can animate it. For animation to work, you have to fill in the time information in the Main tab of the processes, flows, and stores (Figure 11.11). You can begin animation by selecting the starting process step and click on the ANIMATION toolbar button.

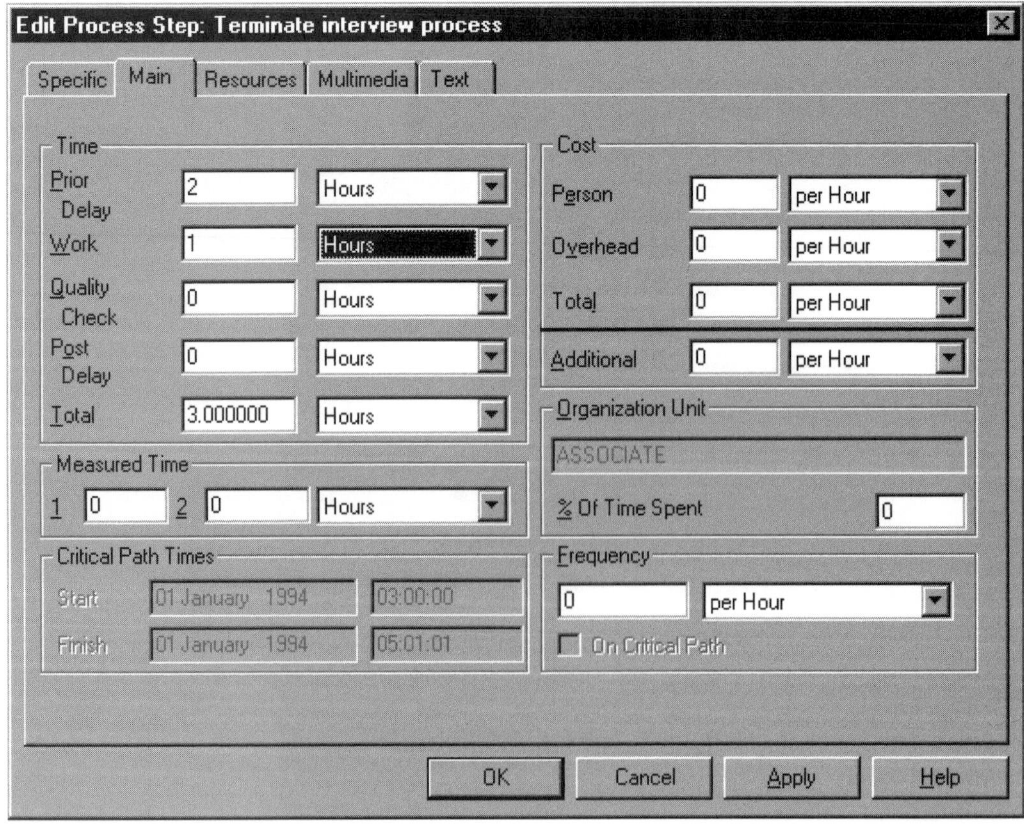

FIGURE 11.11 Entering time information (for use in animation) in the Main tab of a process step.

> Use animation only when it facilitates in communication.

It requires a lot of resources, time, and money to create the objects (i.e., video clips, images, and sound waves) to be used in animation. A saying to remember is "just because you can does not mean you should." The type of visual effects that you incorporate into your diagram should be on the same level as the complexity of the process.

Understand your audience needs before showing them animation or other visual effects. A real spiffy presentation could have managers wondering if the cost of creating the presentation is worth the effort.

Many good books are available that describe the detailed steps for visualizing and animating your process models. Two worth noting are *Oracle Designer Handbook* Second Edition, Koletzke and Dorsey, *Oracle Press,* and *Inside Oracle Designer/2000,* Lulushi, Prentice Hall.

Chapter 12

FUNCTION HIERARCHY DIAGRAMS

This chapter will describe some conventions to use when creating Function Hierarchy Diagrams (FHD) in Oracle Designer. As discussed in Chapter 5, in the strategy planning stage, you analyze and model the high-level processes of the enterprise. This activity helps in understanding and documentating the major processes that your organization performs. These high-level major processes should be documented via the process model before function decomposition is started, as described in the "Getting Started" section of Chapter 5. The next step is to break down these major processes into subfunctions using the function hierarchy-diagramming tool. Our goal here is to further decompose the processes that were captured during business process modeling into elementary functions. These elementary functions will record user interface requirements and business rules.

HOW IS THE FUNCTION HIERARCHY DIAGRAMMER DIFFERENT FROM THE BUSINESS PROCESS MODELER?

The FHD displays the higher-level processes and lower-level functions in your organization in a multilevel view. The higher-level processes represent the same higher-level processes that were defined as process steps in the BPM. The lines between functions do not represent flows but rather parent-child relationships. The function at the top of the diagram represents the highest level function that you are displaying in this diagram. The next row of functions represents the decomposition of that function. In turn, each of those functions could be decomposed into subfunctions, which would appear in the next lower row of the hierarchy. A red circle with a + sign appears next to a function if there are levels under it that are not shown. When you double click the + sign, the diagrammer displays the lower-level functions and the red circle changes to a – sign. Double clicking the – sign hides the lower-level functions.

MULTIPLE MODULAR DIAGRAMS

One of the goals of creating FHDs is to make it easier for end users and business people to understand the functions in their organization and help you verify that you do, too. You don't want them to be overwhelmed by your diagrams. The details (i.e., elementary functions) of the higher-level processes should be identified and modeled using a drill down (subfunctional) approach as discussed in Chapter 5, and Appendix C. Each process should be decomposed into at least two, but no more than nine functions.

Diagrams in this tool are hierarchical. Each diagram is associated with one function that serves as the context function of the diagram. Subfunctions of the context function are listed under the context function in the form of a tree.

> Rather then creating just one function hierarchy diagram, create many subdiagrams.
>
> - ❑ Create one diagram that will function as a view of the entire enterprise.
> - ❑ Create a diagram for each of the major processes that are subfunctions of the root function.

To create a new FHD, select *File->New* from the FHD menu tool bar. The dialog box New Diagram is then displayed (Figure 12.1). This box allows you to select a function to become the root of your diagram and this will only display root functions (functions that do not have any parent function associated with it). As mentioned in Chapter 5, if you followed the recommendations of creating high-level process models before creating function hierarchy diagrams, the top-level function of your organization is displayed.

By selecting the existing function, a diagram and all of its subfunctions are created (Figure 12.2).

At this point, you can save this diagram by giving it a name of "Enterprise" (*File->Save Diagram*). This will be the diagram that will display all of the high-level functions of your organization.

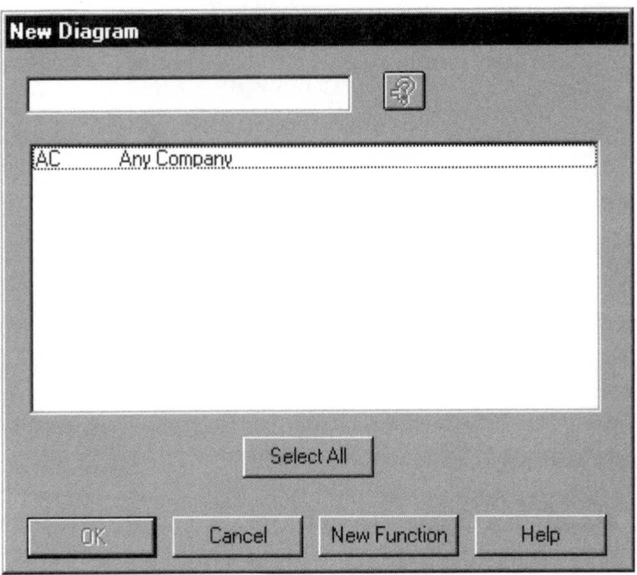

FIGURE 12.1 New Diagram dialog box.

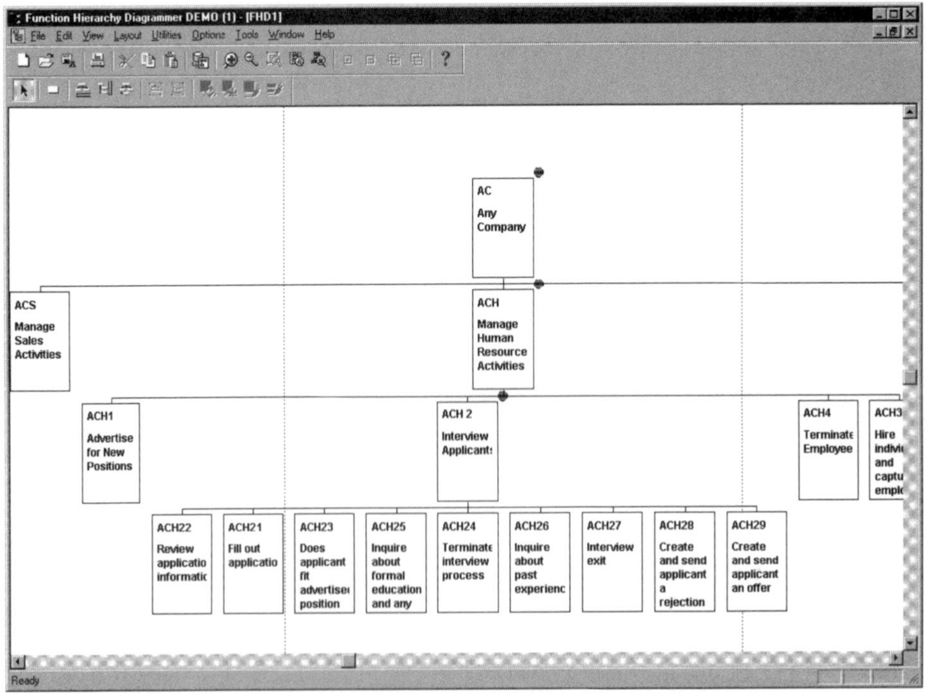

FIGURE 12.2 New Function Hierarchy diagram.

Now you can create subdiagrams for each of the next level functions. Using the previous example, one diagram that you could create would be for the function: Manage Human Resource Activities.

Follow these steps to create the diagram:

1. Select the function that you would like to become the context (top level) function of the new diagram. (For this example, we are using Manage Human Resource Activities.)
2. Select *File->Focus on Selection* from the menu tool bar (Figure 12.3). This will create a new diagram based on the context function.
3. Select *File->Save Diagram As* from the menu tool bar and name the new diagram with the same name of the context function. (For this example it will be Manage Human Resource Activities) (Figure 12.4).

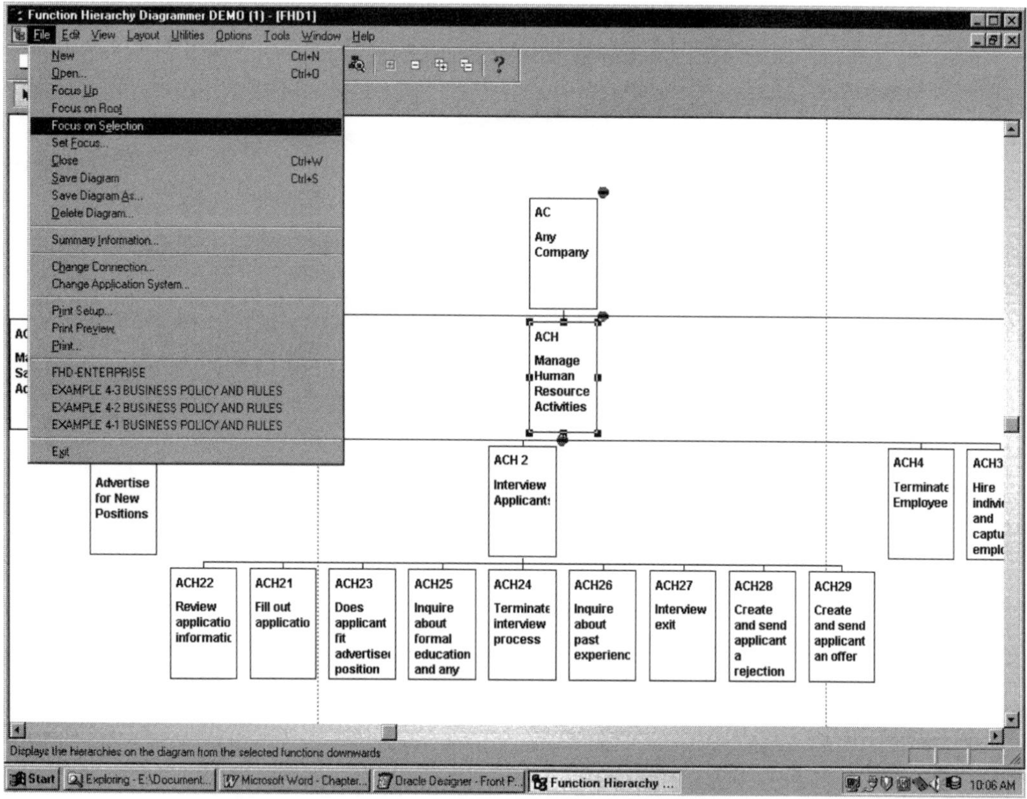

FIGURE 12.3 Creating a subfunction diagram.

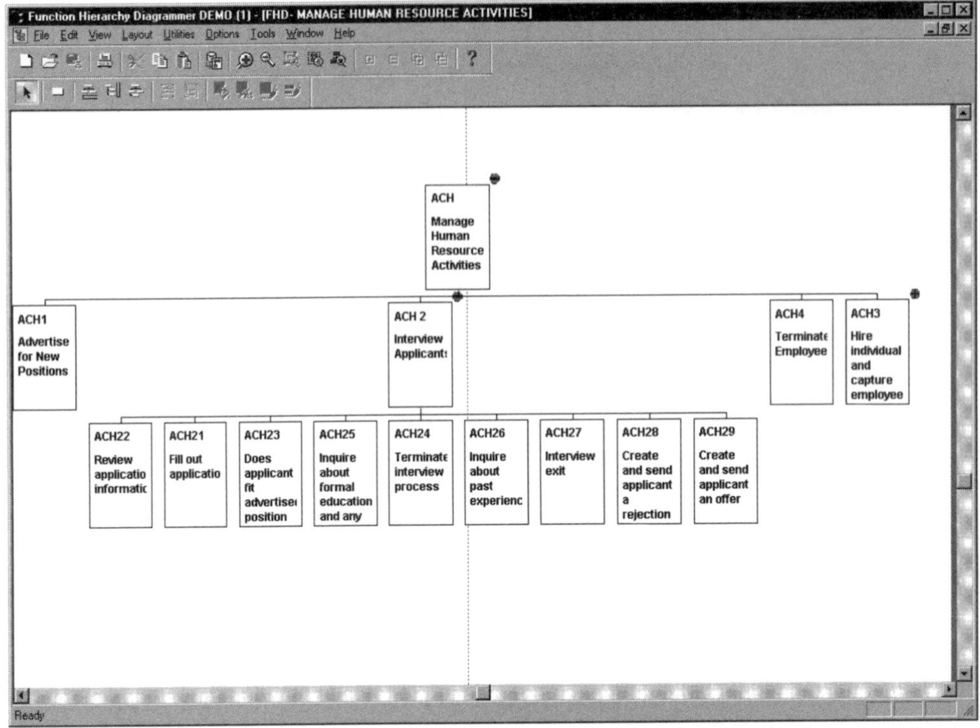

FIGURE 12.4 New lower-level Diagram showing new context function.

It is important to save the diagram using the *Save Diagram As* option rather than the *Save Diagram* options, as this option would overwrite the original diagram.

AVOID OVERCROWDING

The more functions that you display on a diagram, the harder it is to read when you print the diagram. As stated previously, a modular approach to function modeling inherently builds a more readable FHD.

> Do not crowd many functions onto a single function hierarchy diagram. In general, one diagram should contain no more than twenty functions.
>
> If a single diagram contains more than twenty functions, consider drilling down on one of the more complex functions into a new diagram.

You need to use your own judgment when implementing or enforcing this standard. You may want to consider displaying your functions in different display formats to facilitate printing. Refer to the section *FHD Layout Conventions* in this chapter for details on layout options.

DISPLAY A LEGEND ON THE DIAGRAM

Since you are likely to have more than one diagram, it will help to label them. Labeling allows you to go back to the tool, find the diagram (after having it "destroyed" in a review session), and then change it. If you have a large system with many diagrams, it could be hard to identify one in a list without some reference. Designer offers a nice feature for identifying diagrams (Figure 12.5). We recommend the following:

Under *File-> Summary Information,* check the following to be displayed:

- ❑ Diagram
- ❑ Title
- ❑ Created
- ❑ Last Modified
- ❑ Author
- ❑ Application System

Display the legend in the upper left-hand corner of the diagram.

While the diagram name should be the same as the context function label, the diagram title should be indicative of the functional area being modeled and be understandable by business users.

Example:

Diagram Name = ANY COMPANY

Title = "Any Company" Enterprise Function Model

Why display both the diagram name and title? The diagram name cannot be entered in mixed case but the title can. You need the name to find it in the tool, but the title can be more explanative to the users.

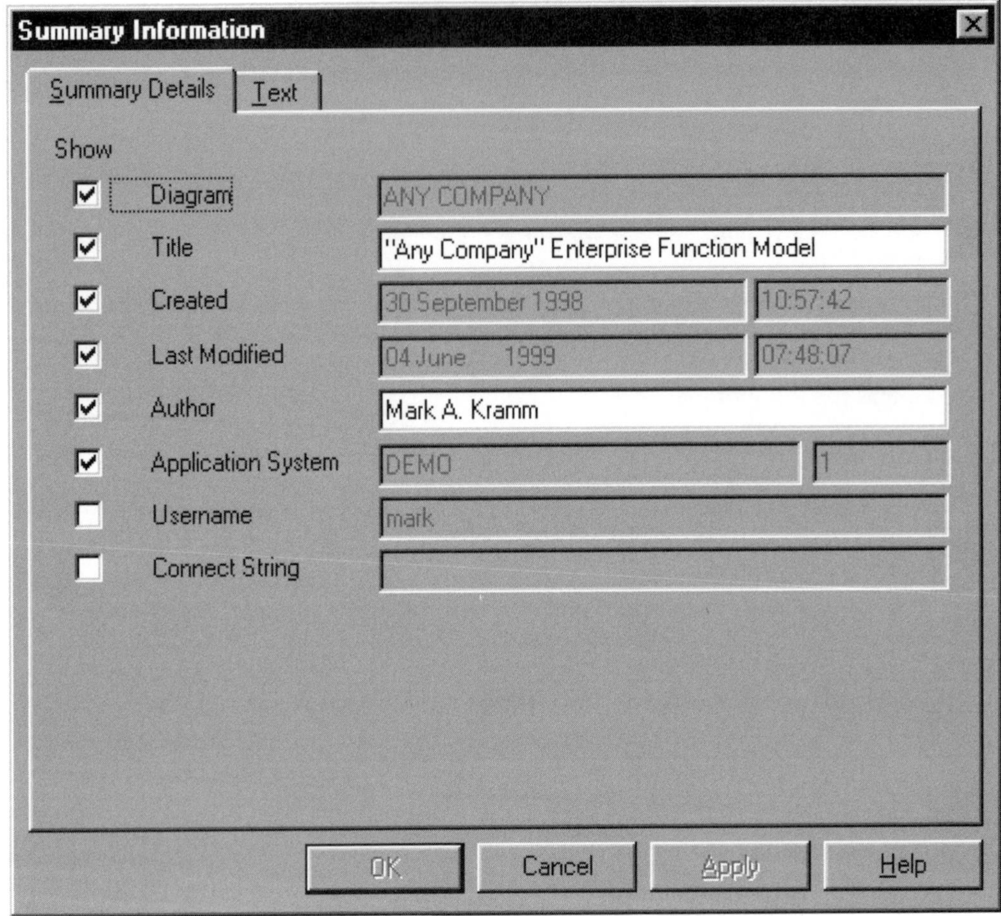

FIGURE 12.5 Summary information dialog in the Function Hierarchy Diagrammer.

After you have selected the items to display, the summary information will appear in the upper left-hand corner of your diagram (Figure 12.6).

FHD LAYOUT CONVENTIONS

This section describes some helpful layout conventions for creating diagrams. These conventions aid in making the diagrams easier for you to print and the business community to understand. The three layout styles are shown in Figures 12.7 through 12.9.

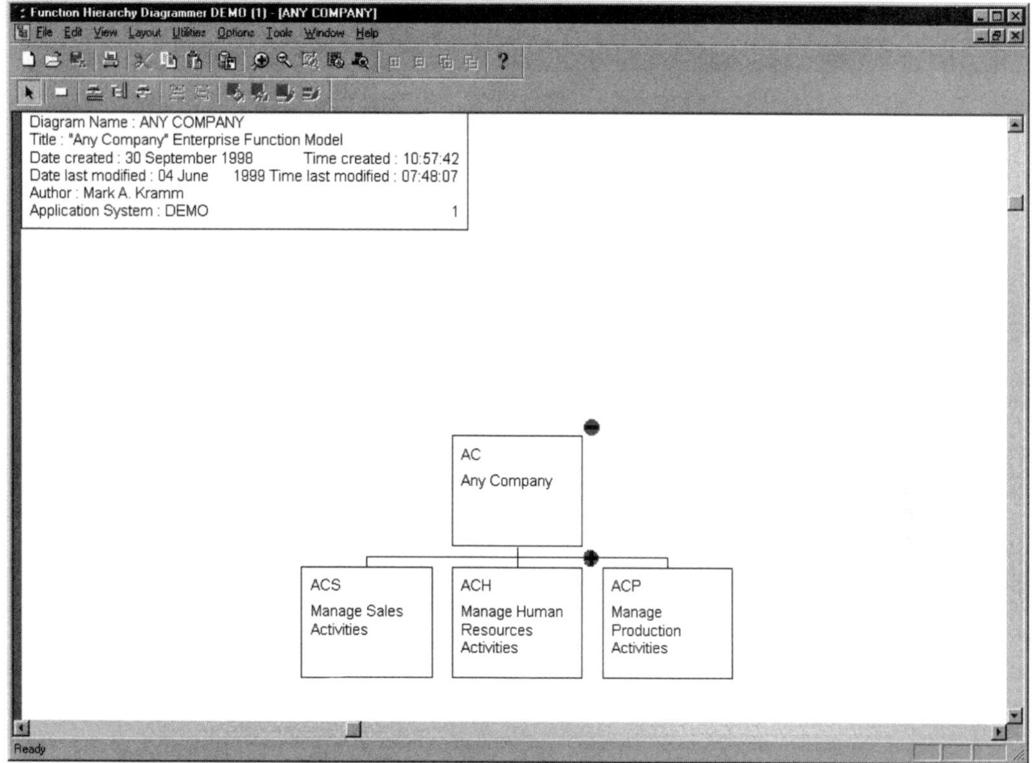

FIGURE 12.6 Sample function hierarchy diagram with summary information displayed.

Horizontal Layout is the default layout. This style shows each level of the hierarchy in a horizontal row.

Vertical Layout displays each level of the hierarchy in a vertical line, with each level indented slightly to the right of the one above it.

Hybrid Layout is a combination of vertical and horizontal layouts that shows parent functions in a horizontal layout and elementary (childless) functions in a vertical layout. This style is the best of the three options for reading and printing multilevel hierarchies.

In most cases, we recommend using the hybrid option, as it is the most efficient option. The choice really depends on the depth of your function model. If it is shallow and wide, the horizontal layout will often look good. In general the vertical style should be avoided unless the model (or model segment) is very small.

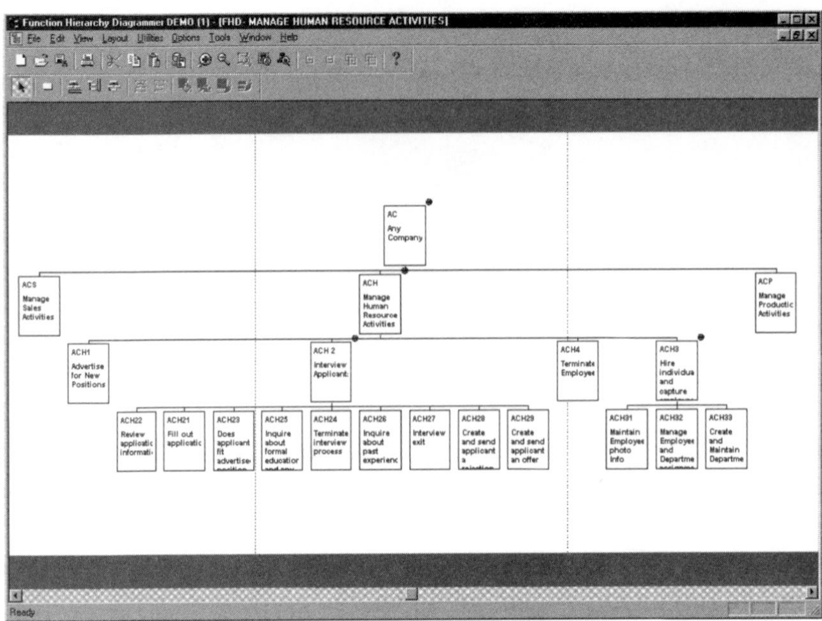

FIGURE 12.7 Example FHD displayed in horizontal layout style.

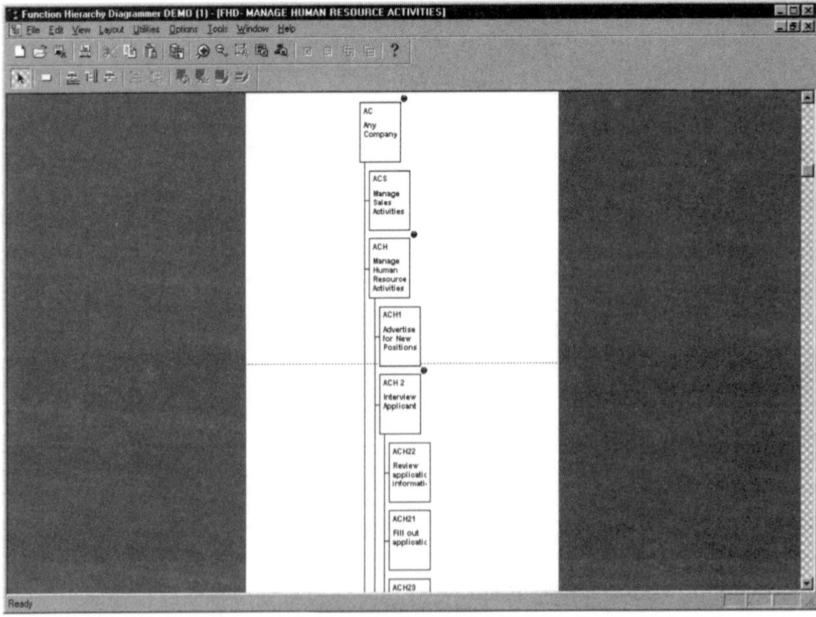

FIGURE 12.8 Example FHD displayed in vertical layout style.

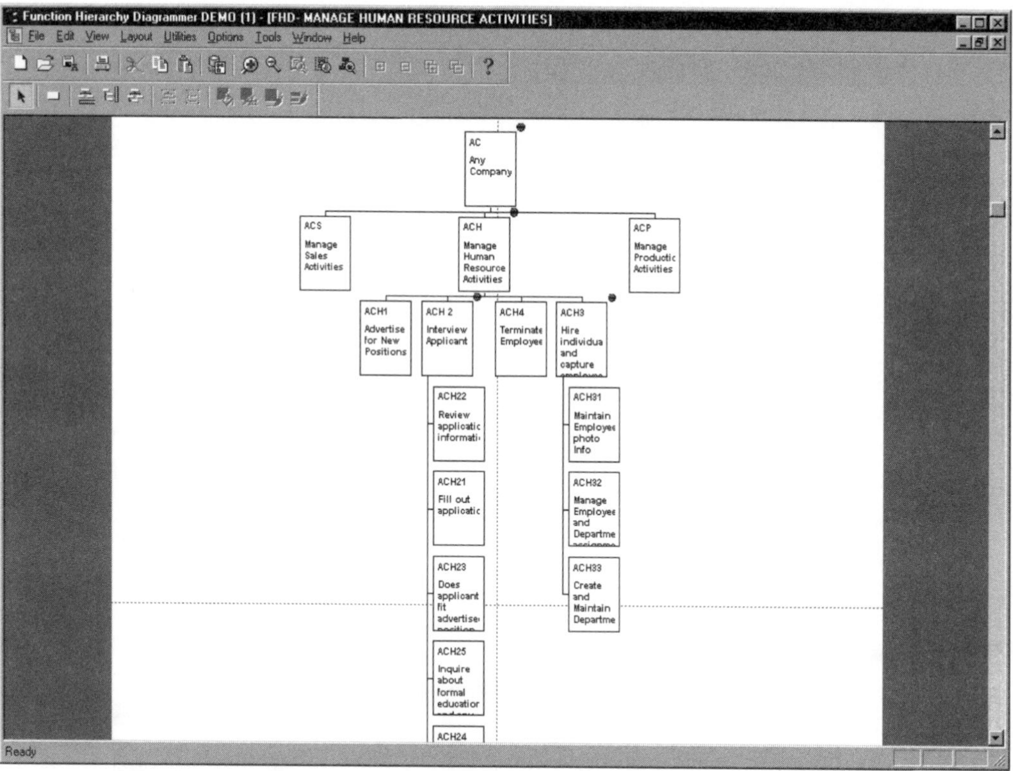

FIGURE 12.9 Example FHD displayed in hybrid layout style.

In addition to setting the layout for the entire diagram, you can select one or more functions and cause the functions under them to be displayed either in a horizontal or vertical layout. This is done by selecting a function or group of functions and then selecting the *Horizontal Layout Selection* or *Vertical Layout Selection*, respectively, from the *Layout* tool bar menu (Figure 12.10). Creative use of this feature can often enable you to get a lot of information on one page.

OTHER CONSIDERATIONS

Once you have built all these diagrams, you need to maintain them. This can be quite a large task, so to help you, we have included a few other tips in the template that you should include as standard practices.

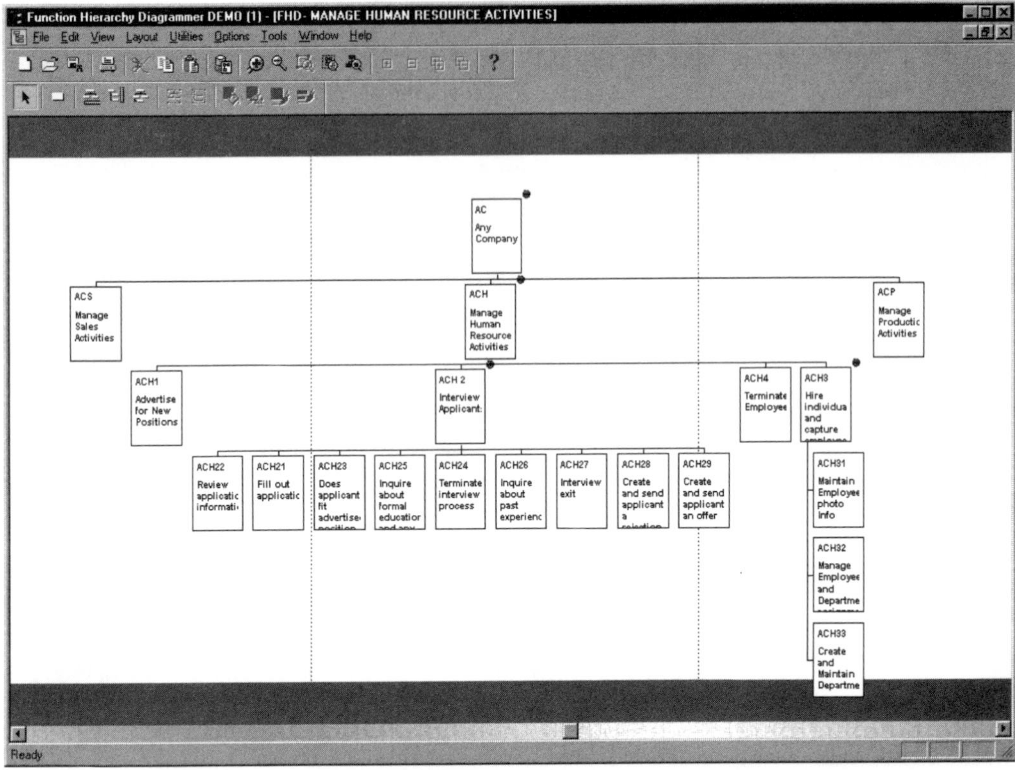

FIGURE 12.10 Example FHD displayed with combined layout styles.

Consolidating Diagrams

Consolidate Diagrams frequently using *Edit->Requery*

In general, it is a good practice to consolidate a diagram each time you open it to ensure that you only work with current information. At a minimum, diagrams should be consolidated when there is a change to the Designer Repository relative to business functions. **If you wish to keep historical views of diagrams, save them under another name and do not consolidate them.**

If a change is made in the Repository Object Navigator (RON) while a diagram is open, any objects affected by the change will have a red dot appear to signify that it has been updated in another tool (a new feature in release 2). At that

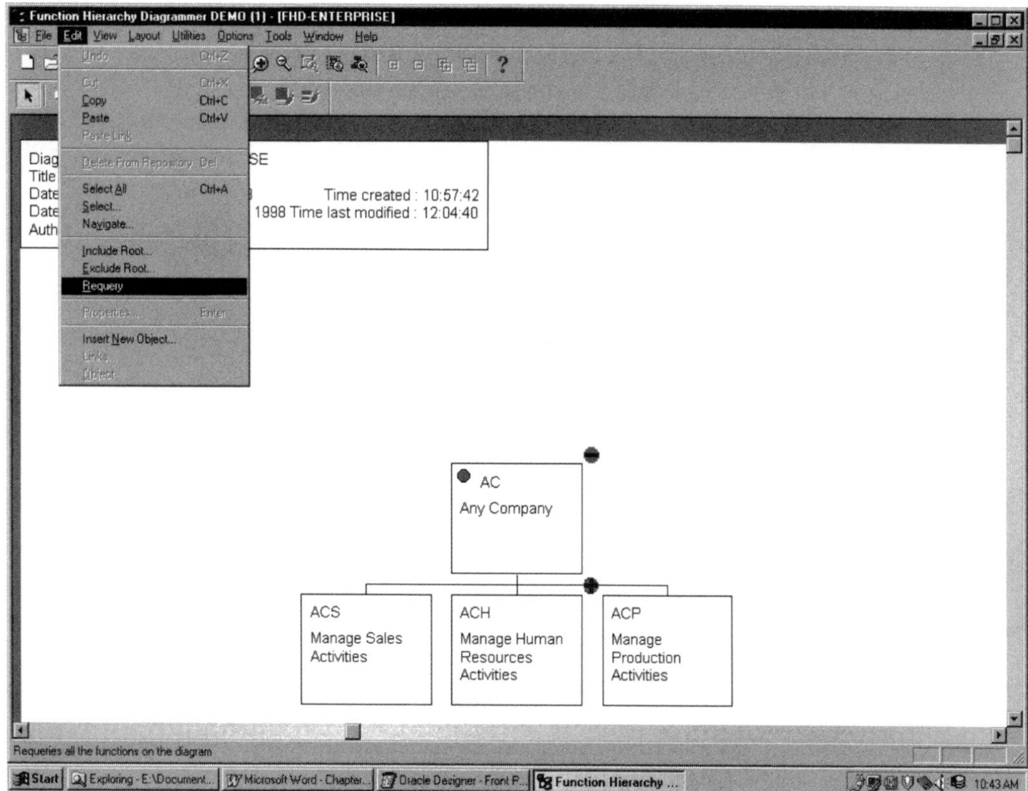

FIGURE 12.11 The FH Diagram requery options.

point you will need to select *Edit->Requery* from the menu in the diagrammer to get the function definitions back in sync with the repository (Figure 12.11).

There is a property that you can set in the function hierarchy diagrammer (*Options->Customize*) to automatically requery the diagram when it is opened. *If you are going to keep a history of diagram, changes do not set this property.*

If changes were made while the diagram was closed, you will not be notified of them until you double click on an object that has been changed. Because of this feature, we recommend that you consolidate diagrams every time you open one.

Delete Unneeded Diagrams

If a diagram is no longer needed, delete it from the Repository.

This practice may seem obvious, but you would be surprised how many people create multiple versions of the same diagram and then forget which one is the most current. Once the diagrams have been opened, the dates in the legend will of course make this clear, but you may have to open several diagrams before you find the right one. Be sure to clean up after yourself (just make sure someone else did not need the other diagrams first).

COLOR CODING

As more people gain access to color printers and plotters, a new convention is emerging: people are color coding their diagrams. Colors (or even shading) of objects can be a nice way to visually distinguish among different types of functions. If this sounds like a useful convention to you, get your lead process/functional analyst involved to determine specific colors or shading patterns to use (or avoid) and the detailed rules by which they should be applied.

To get you started, the template document includes the following guidelines:

> Use color coding or shading to distinguish the following:
>
> - ❑ Elementary functions, functions that have been decomposed to their lowest level
> - ❑ External functions, functions that are performed by external organizations but may have an effect on our organizations processes
> - ❑ Functions that are the basis of other diagrams (i.e., indicate the ability to open down)

Selecting a function, then clicking on the CHANGE FILL COLOR button on the diagrammer toolbar easily sets colors for the selected object.

Chapter 13

Entity Relationship Diagrams

This chapter presents some conventions to be used when creating Entity Relationship (ER) Diagrams in Oracle Designer. As with naming standards, these conventions can be subjective (i.e., beauty is in the eye of the beholder). In fact, we will present two slightly different conventions in this chapter. Both are used in the Oracle world (when any are actually used); one is a minor variation of the other. There are pros and cons to both approaches. You will ultimately have to decide which one you like the best, and then include that one in your standards document. The template on the CD contains both, so you will have to delete some sections once you decide. First let's discuss some basic guidelines that should be applied regardless of the convention you choose.

MULTIPLE MODULAR DIAGRAMS

One of the goals of creating ER diagrams is to make it easier for end users and business people to understand the data in their organization. By walking through the diagram with the end users you verify that your understanding of their business is correct. Your diagrams must be well organized and easy to understand to accomplish this goal. You don't want your end users to be overwhelmed by your diagrams. The first rule is keep it simple. Don't try to put all the information in one picture. Break it up into smaller, more easily understood segments of the overall model. On top of that, it is easier to maintain and manage smaller diagrams.

Rather than creating one large diagram, create many smaller diagrams. This will eliminate the need to maintain one large diagram that will over time become unreadable, unmanageable, and overwhelming to non-technical users. If you need to answer questions such as, what entities are related to other entities, use the Repository Object Navigator or the Entity Definition report. Do not rely on one large diagram.

DIAGRAM CORRESPONDENCE TO BUSINESS MODEL

If you are going to break up the model into smaller diagrams, it helps to have some guidelines on how you will determine what goes on each diagram.

Each diagram should correspond to a logical section of the overall business model. They could represent a specific business area or logical data view (In data warehousing terms these would be subject areas). For example; If you have a high level function called "Capture Customer Information", create a diagram that will depict the data needed to support that business function.

Do not include entities that are not needed to support that high level function. The entity CONTRACT should appear on a diagram called "Customer Contract" along with all the other entities to support the creation and administration of a Contract, but it may not be needed on a diagram showing customer invoicing.

These are just guidelines, not standards per se; they are open to interpretation. A good Data Administrator can be invaluable in providing additional guidance for the development of specific diagrams.

AVOID OVERCROWDING

How many entities are too many? That really depends on the complexity of the relationships between the entities and how many attributes each entity has. A diagram with simple master detail type relationships and short attribute lists can have more entities than a diagram with multiple recursive relationships, arcs, and long attribute lists. Building good, usable ER Diagrams can be more of an art than a science (even with standards).

Do not crowd many entities onto a single diagram. In general, one diagram should contain no more than 15 to 20 entities.

If a single diagram contains more than 15 entities, consider a logical refinement (e.g., the CUSTOMER INFO diagram would be subdivided into two diagrams: CUSTOMER INFO1 and CUSTOMER INFO2).

Again, you will need to use your own judgment when implementing or enforcing this standard. One factor to consider is the size of paper you will print the diagram on. If you have a plotter capable of printing larger diagrams, you can have many more than twenty entities and it will still be very readable (of course, it may then be too large to manipulate on your monitor). If you only have a standard laser printer with 8.5 × 11 paper, and want the diagrams to print on one page, you are limited. That points to a second factor: the size of your monitor. If you have a small monitor, you will not be able to easily or clearly view a diagram with too many entities.

DISPLAY A LEGEND ON THE DIAGRAM

Since you are likely to have more than one diagram, it will help to label them. Labeling allows you to go back to the tool, find the diagram (after having it "destroyed" in a review session), and then change it. If you have a large system with many diagrams, it could be hard to identify one in a list without some reference. Designer offers a nice feature for identifying diagrams (Figure 13.1). We recommend the following:

Under *File-> Summary Information,* check the following to be displayed: Diagram, Title, Created, Last Modified, and Author.

While the diagram name may be somewhat cryptic, the diagram title should be indicative of the business area being modeled and be understandable by business users.

Example:

Diagram Name = ERD-CUST. INFO

Title = Customer Definition Information.

Why display both the diagram name and title? The diagram name cannot be entered in mixed case, but the title can. You need the name to find it in the tool,

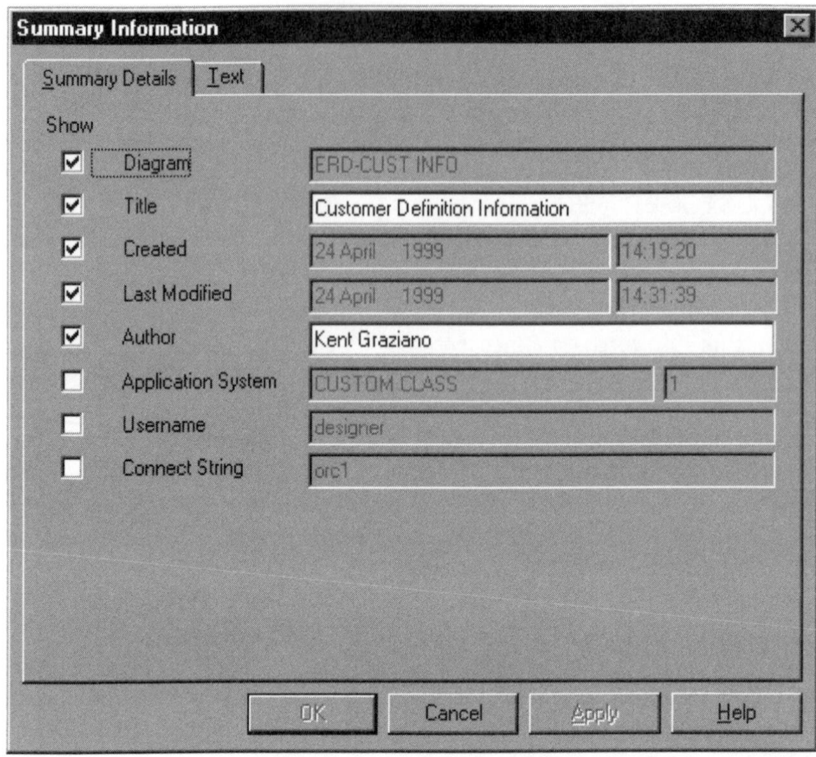

FIGURE 13.1 Summary information dialog in the Entity Relationship Diagrammer.

but the title can be more explanative to the users. If you don't care about the case of the title, just use the diagram name (assigned when you save the diagram). If you do this, be sure to give it an appropriate "name" since it will also double as the diagram title.

After you have selected the items to display, the summary information will appear in the upper left-hand corner of your diagram (Figure 13.2). The summary box can be moved to anywhere in the diagram, but we recommend you use the default location for simplicity.

ER DIAGRAM LAYOUT CONVENTIONS

As mentioned at the beginning of the chapter, two conventions are commonly used. They are discussed here, with some rationales for using each. Both are also included in the template document, so you will need to decided which you prefer to use and delete the other one.

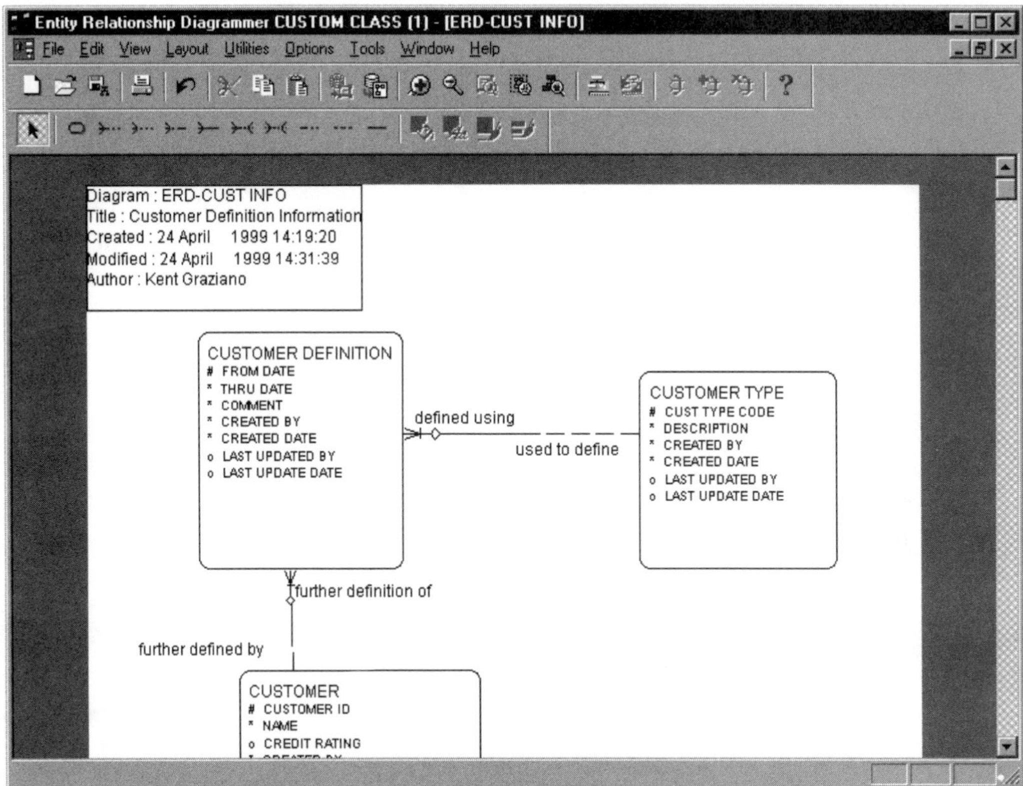

FIGURE 13.2 Sample ER Diagram with summary information displayed.

LAYOUT CONVENTION #1

Entity Placement

- ❑ Place fundamental entities to the right of the diagram.
- ❑ Size entities to reduce clutter and provide clear paths for relationships.
- ❑ Before creating a new entity, always use the *Edit->Include* facility first to prevent creating duplicate entities and relationships.

When this convention is followed, if all of the fundamental entities are placed on the right side of the diagram, the crow's feet will naturally open to the left. Any entity to the left of the fundamental entities will tend to be transactional. As you move to the left, the entities become more transactional. To enforce this layout convention, you will likely have to experiment with the size (length and width) of the entities to make it work.

As a general practice, you should always use the Include facility before building a new entity. When you invoke *Edit->Include*, a list of existing entities and relationships appears. By adhering to this practice, you will reduce potential conflicts. In some cases, the same entity exists in another application, but you are unaware of it. That's where peer reviews come in handy. If during a review you find that you have duplicated an entity, delete your entity and have the previously existing one shared into your application (with the permission of the Database Administrator).

We have also found that it is a good practice to lay out all entities in the diagram first, before including their relationships. Once the relationship lines are on the diagram, it can become quite confusing to sort out all the crossed lines as you try to rearrange the entities. If you do encounter this situation, simply cut the relationship lines from the diagram, then include them again.

When drawing relationships, apply the following rules:

Drawing Relationships

- ❑ Face crow's feet to the left (West).
- ❑ Avoid line crossings if at all possible.
- ❑ Keep relationship lines horizontal; do not angle them.
- ❑ Minimize the use of bent lines (straight lines are preferred).

The reason for these rules should be obvious: they keep the diagram easy to read. Crossing and bent lines only make it harder to trace a relationship when the diagram is being reviewed. If there are no bent lines and all crows' feet are to the left, all lines will be horizontal.

The last layout issue to consider is that of the placement of the relationship names.

Relationship name placement

Place relationship names in a clockwise pattern.

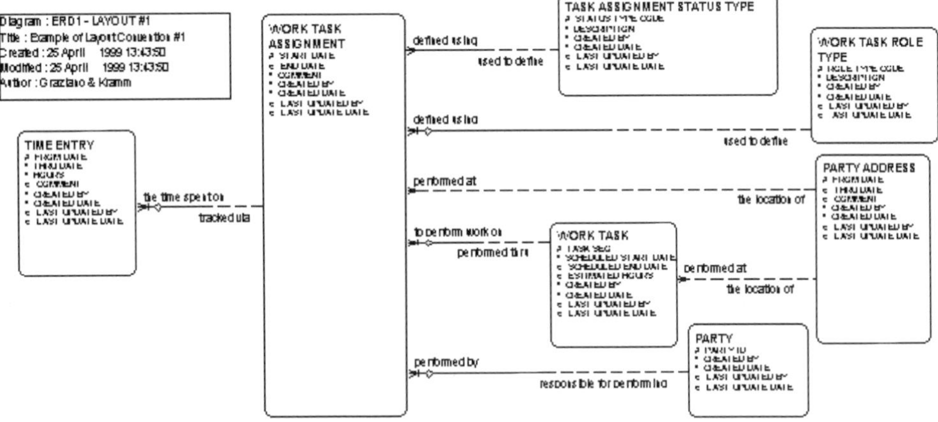

FIGURE 13.3 Example ER diagram using layout convention #1.

Place relationship names so that they may be read in a clockwise manner. That is, for a horizontal relationship line, the relationship name at the terminating crows foot end is above the line and the relationship name at the originating end is below the line. For a vertical relationship line (if you can't avoid it), the relationship name at the terminating crows foot end is to the right of the line, and the relationship name at the originating end is to the left of the line.

Hint: In Oracle Designer release 2.1.2, if you select a relationship and click on the Autolayout button, it will place the relationship name in the pattern mentioned previously.

Where possible, size the text blocks for a relationship name so that the entire relationship name appears as a single line. In places where the relationship name must be displayed with more than one line, use the minimal number of lines possible. As always the goal is to make the diagram more easily readable (Figure 13.3).

LAYOUT CONVENTION #2

Entity Placement

Place fundamental entities to the right or the bottom of the diagram.

Size entities to reduce clutter and provide clear paths for relationships.

Before creating a new entity, always use the *Edit->Include* facility first to prevent duplicate entities and relationships.

When this convention is followed, if all of the fundamental entities are placed on the right side or bottom of the diagram, then the crow's feet will naturally open up and/or to the left. Any entity to the left or above of the fundamental entities will tend to be transactional. As you move to the upper left of the diagram, the entities will become more transactional. The result is that most transaction entities are in the upper left-hand corner of the diagram. To enforce this layout convention, you also have to experiment with the size (length and width) of the entities to make it work.

The use of the Include facility and other principles mentioned in the previous section also applies to this layout convention.

When drawing relationships, apply the following rules:

Drawing Relationships

Face crow's feet to the left (West) or up (North).

Avoid line crossings if at all possible.

Keep relationship lines horizontal or vertical; do not angle them.

Minimize the use of bent lines (straight lines are more preferred).

The reason for these rules is the same as mentioned before: they keep the diagram easy to read. Crossing and bent lines only make it harder to trace a relationship when the diagram is being reviewed, especially if there are both horizontal and vertical lines.

The last layout issue to consider is placement of relationship names.

Relationship name placement

Place relationship names in a clockwise pattern.

This rule is the same regardless of the convention used. Place relationship names so that they may be read in a clockwise manner. That is, for a horizontal relationship line, the relationship name at the terminating crows foot end is above the line, and the relationship name at the originating end is below the line.

For a vertical relationship line, the relationship name at the terminating crows foot end is to the right of the line, and the relationship name at the originating end is to the left of the line (Figure 13.4).

We have noticed that people sometimes interpret the standard as allowing them to have crows feet go up and to the left, as mentioned, or all go up or all go left. If you choose convention #2, you may want to refine it to specify which of those is allowed (or not allowed).

WHAT'S THE DIFFERENCE?

The main difference between these conventions is that in convention #1, all lines are horizontal, with the crow's feet facing left. In convention #2, lines may be vertical or horizontal, with crow's feet facing either up or left. The real question is which do you like better?

Convention #2 is the standard recommendation that was originally made by Richard Barker in *CASE*Method Entity Relationship Modelling;* it is used by many people in the industry. Convention #1 is a refinement of convention #2 and is preferred by some of our end users because it is a simple standard to enforce, i.e., the lines go only in one direction. Drawing diagrams with either convention can present challenges, but with time and practice it can become nearly second nature. The benefit is creating diagrams that are easier to read and understand.

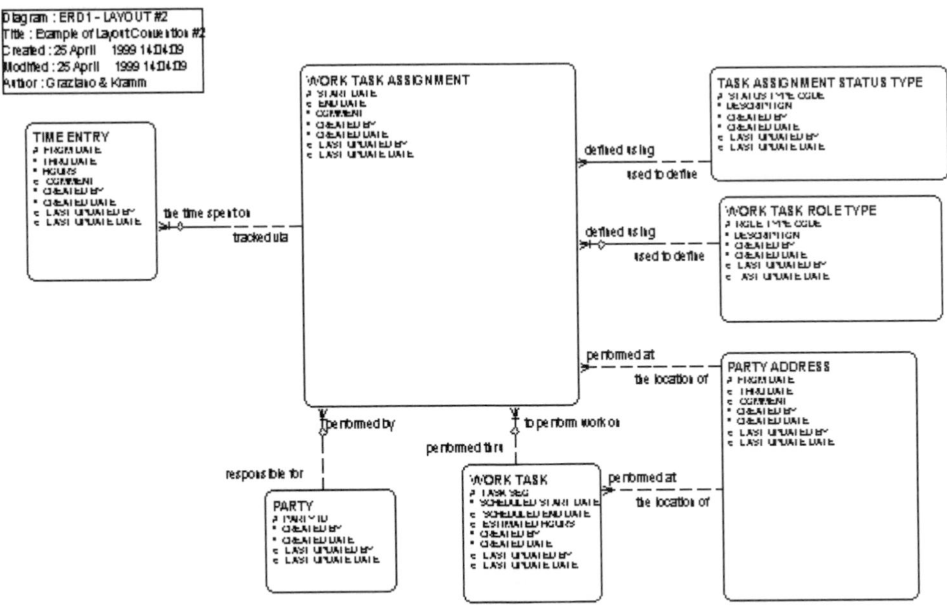

FIGURE 13.4 Example ER diagram using layout convention #2.

OTHER CONSIDERATIONS

Once you have built all these diagrams, you need to maintain them. This can be quite a large task, so to help you, we have included a few other tips in the template that you should include as standard practices.

Consolidating Diagrams

Consolidate Diagrams frequently using *Edit->Requery*

In general, it is a good practice to consolidate a diagram each time you open it to ensure that you work only with current information. At a minimum, diagrams should be consolidated when there is a change to the Designer Repository relative to entities or relationships. **If you wish to keep historical views of diagrams, save them under another name and do not consolidate them.**

It is possible for someone to change the definition of an entity, attribute, or relationship in the Repository Object Navigator (RON) as well as in a diagram. If a change is made in RON while a diagram is open, any objects affected by the change will have a red dot appear in the corner of the entity box (a new feature in release 2). At that point, you need to select *Edit->Requery* from the menu in the diagrammer to get the diagram objects back in sync with the repository (Figure 13.5).

As you can see in the figure, there are several options for requery. You generally want to select the ALL option to ensure your diagram is totally up to date.

If changes were made while the diagram was closed, you will *not* be notified until you double click on an entity that has been changed. Because of this feature, we recommend that you consolidate diagrams every time you open one.

An additional point to consider around consolidation is the tracking of historical diagrams. As mentioned, if you want to keep previous versions of a diagram you will need to save them under another name before doing the consolidation (or "version" the entire application!). If you choose to do this, an additional naming standard should be implemented so that all Data Analysts can easily discern the diagram hierarchy, for instance:

ERD-CUST INFO V1
ERD-CUST INFO V2

If you decide to implement such a standard, be sure to add it to your standards document.

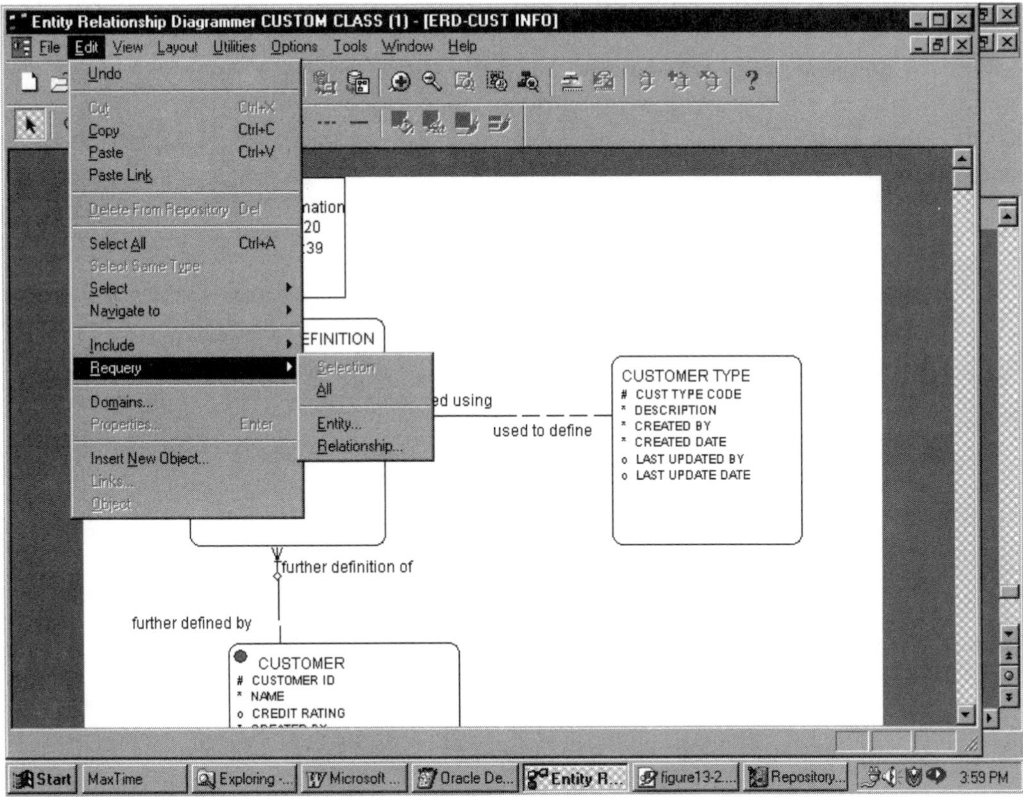

FIGURE 13.5 The ER Diagram requery options.

Delete Unneeded Diagrams

If a diagram is no longer needed, delete it from the Repository.

This practice may seem obvious, but many people create multiple versions of the same diagram and then forget which one is the most current (implementing a standard as mentioned above would help solve this problem). Once the diagrams have been opened, the dates in the legend will of course make this clear, but you may have to open several diagrams before you find the right one. So be sure to clean up after yourself (just make sure someone else did not need the other diagrams first).

Drawing Relationships to Subtypes

When drawing relationships to a sub-type entity, ensure that the line(s) between the sub-type and other entities are clearly connected to the sub-type and not its super-type.

Uses of sub-types imply that they will have attributes that are specific to them. If this is not the case, do not use sub-type constructs where simple examples will do. Instead, include examples as text on the drawing, where clarification is necessary.

This guideline is just a clarification on the use of sub-types and a caution about a common problem. In a complex diagram, it is possible to become confused about where the relationship really belongs, or if you have zoomed out too far, you may not attach the diagram properly. Be sure to double check your work.

COLOR CODING

As more people gain access to color printer and plotters, a new convention is emerging: people are color coding their diagrams. Colors (or even shading) of entities can be a nice way to visually distinguish among different types of entities or different subject areas. If this sounds like a useful convention to you, get your DA involved to determine specific colors or shading patterns to use (or avoid) and the detailed rules by which they should be applied.

To get you started, the template document includes the following guidelines:

Use color coding or shading to distinguish the following:

- ❑ Entities shared from other applications
- ❑ Entities that appear on more than one diagram
- ❑ Code type entities
- ❑ Subject area groupings

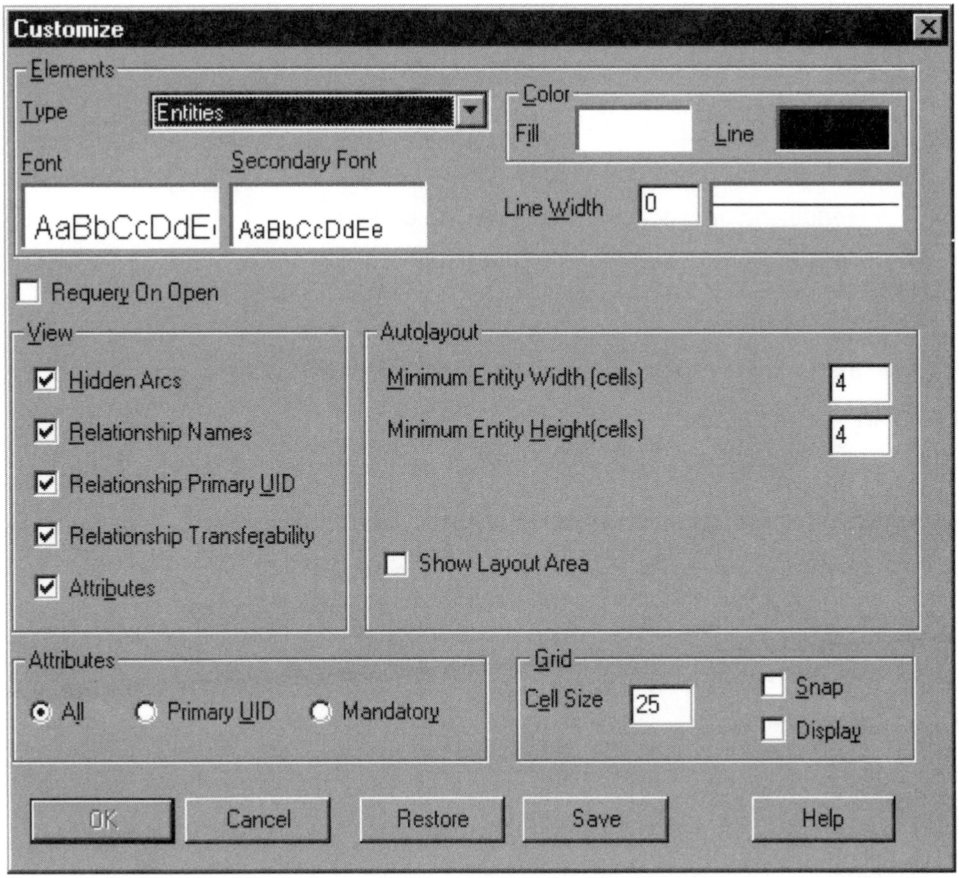

FIGURE 13.6 The Customize diagram dialog.

Selecting an entity (or entities) and then clicking on the SET FILL COLOR button on the diagrammer toolbar easily sets the color for the selected entity.

VIEW OPTIONS

Oracle Designer provides many options for what can be displayed on a diagram (Figure 13.6). These options are set by selecting *Options-> Customize* from the ER Diagrammer menu then checking or unchecking the various view options.

As a rule, when creating a diagram for detailed analysis, we use the default settings, which include all the view options (e.g., all attributes, arcs, relationship names). When building a diagram to be reviewed during the strategy phase, only the main entities and relationships are required. If they have been defined, primary unique identifiers (UID) may also be included.

Strategy phase diagrams should include:

- ❑ Fundamental and transaction entities (i.e., no codes)
- ❑ Relationship lines
- ❑ Relationship names

Strategy phase diagrams may also include (where defined):

- ❑ Primary UID attributes
- ❑ Primary UID relationship indicators

Analysis phase diagrams should include (where they exist):

- ❑ All entities including code types and intersection entities
- ❑ All attributes
- ❑ All relationships
- ❑ Relationship names
- ❑ Primary UID relationship indicators
- ❑ Relationship transferability indicators
- ❑ Hidden arcs

Chapter 14

Server Model Diagrams

This chapter presents some conventions for use when creating Server Model (SM) Diagrams in Oracle Designer. SM Diagrams present a picture of various physical structures in the Oracle database (e.g., tables, views, clusters, snapshots). As with conventions presented in other chapters, these conventions are also subjective. They will, however, be consistent with those presented for Entity Relationship (ER) Models, with only minor differences (consistent with differences in the tools). Even though what we are proposing here applies to physical database/server models, we felt there were enough similarities between the two diagramming tools (ER and SM) to warrant using similar conventions. The same two drawing conventions presented in the ER chapter are also applied to SM Diagrams in this chapter (again with minor changes). You ultimately have to decide which one you like the best and then include that one in your standards document. The template on the CD again contains both, so you will have to delete some sections once you decide.

We also present basic guidelines that should be applied regardless of the convention you ultimately choose.

MULTIPLE MODULAR DIAGRAMS

One of the goals of creating SM diagrams is to make it easier for developers and DBAs to understand the physical data structures being created and/or used. By walking through the diagram with these people you can help verify that database design is correct. Your diagrams must be well organized and easy to understand. You don't want your newbie developers to be overwhelmed by your diagrams! The first rule is to keep it simple. Don't try to put all the information in one picture. Break it up into smaller, more easily understood segments of the overall design. And remember, it is easier to maintain and manage smaller diagrams.

> Rather than creating one large diagram, create many smaller diagrams. This will eliminate the need to maintain one large diagram that will over time become unreadable, unmanageable, and overwhelming to non-technical users. If you need to answer questions such as, what tables have foreign keys to other tables, use the Design Editor (usages nodes) or the Table Definition report. Do not rely on one large diagram.

DIAGRAM CORRESPONDENCE TO BUSINESS MODEL

If you are going to break up the model into smaller diagrams, it helps to have some guidelines to determine what goes on each diagram.

> Each diagram should correspond to a logical section of the overall business model. They could represent a specific business area or logical data view. (In data warehousing terms these would be subject areas.) For example, If you have a high level function called "Capture Customer Information", create a diagram that will depict the data structures needed to support that business function.
>
> Do not include objects that are not needed to support that high level function. The table CONTRACTS should appear on a diagram called "Customer Contract" along with all the other tables and views to support the creation and administration of a Contract, but it may not be needed on a diagram showing customer invoicing.

As with the ER Diagrams, these really are just guidelines, not standards per se, so they are definitely open to interpretation. This is where the Application Administrator (or Database Administrator, DBA) can be invaluable in providing additional guidance for the development of specific diagrams.

AVOID OVERCROWDING

How many objects are too many? That depends on the complexity of the database design and the number of columns each table has. A diagram with simple master detail type relationships and few columns can have more tables and views than a diagram with multiple recursive foreign keys, arcs, and lots of columns. Building good, usable SM Diagrams can be as much an art as building ER Diagrams (although overall, most people don't worry about it too much).

> Do not crowd many objects onto a single diagram. In general, one diagram should contain no more than 15 to 20 tables and/or views.
>
> If a single diagram contains more than 15 objects, consider a logical refinement (e.g., the CUSTOMER INFO diagram would be subdivided into two diagrams: CUSTOMER INFO1 and CUSTOMER INFO2).

You need to use your own judgment when implementing or enforcing this standard. One factor to consider is the size of paper you will print the diagram on. If you have a plotter capable of printing larger diagrams, you can have many more than twenty objects and it will still be readable (of course, it may then be too large to manipulate on your monitor). If you only have a standard laser printer with 8.5 × 11 paper, and want the diagrams to print on one page, you are limited. That points to a second factor: the size of your monitor. If you have a small monitor, you will not be able to easily or clearly view a diagram with too many objects.

DISPLAY A LEGEND ON THE DIAGRAM

Since you will have more than one diagram, it will help to label them. Labeling allows you to go back to the tool, find the diagram (after having it "destroyed" in a review session), and then change it. If you have a large system with many diagrams, it could be hard to identify one in a list without some reference. The Design Editor offers a nice feature for identifying diagrams (Figure 14.1). We recommend you use the following guidelines:

> Under *File-> Summary Information,* check the following to be displayed: Title, Created, Last Modified, Author and Application.
>
> While the diagram name may be somewhat cryptic, the diagram title should be indicative of the business area being modeled and be understandable by business users.
>
> **Example:**
>
> Diagram Name = SMD-CUST INFO
>
> Title = Detailed Customer Data.

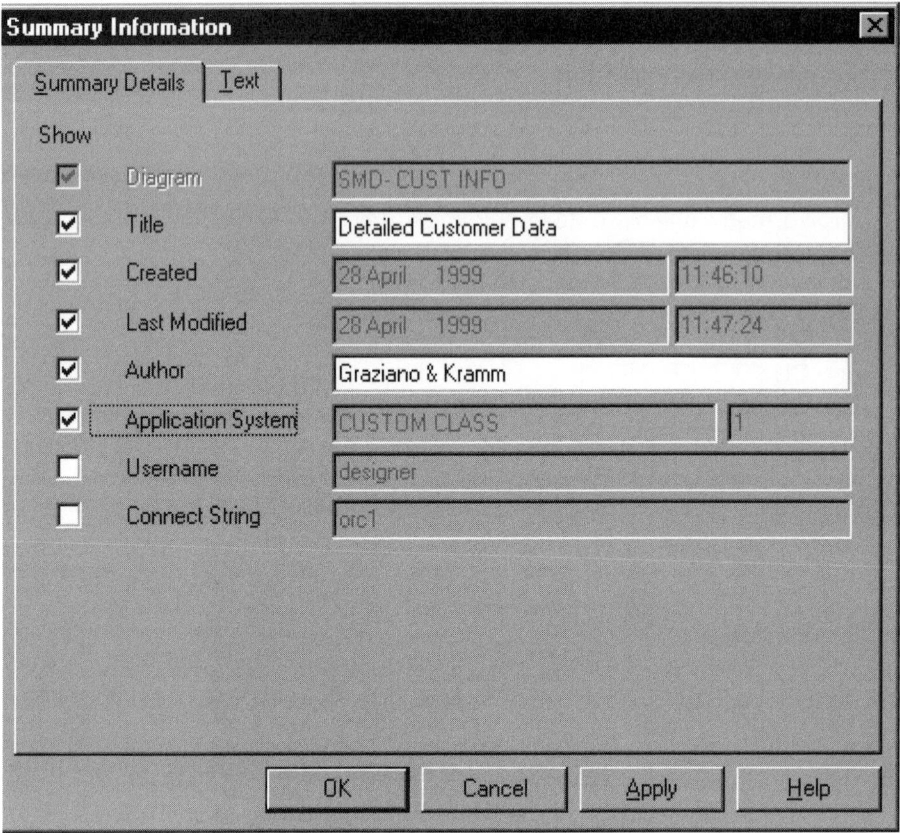

FIGURE 14.1 Summary information dialog in the Design Editor—Server Model Diagrammer.

Why display both the diagram name and title? The diagram name cannot be entered in mixed case, but the title can. You need the name to find it in the tool, but the title can be more explanative to the developers. If you don't care about the case of the title, just use the diagram name (assigned when you save the diagram). If you do this, be sure to give it an appropriate "name" since it will also then double as the diagram title.

Unlike the ER Diagrammer, the SM Diagrammer does *not* automatically show the summary information after you have selected the items to display. To display the summary information box, you must do a right mouse-click in white space on the diagram and then select the option SHOW DIAGRAM LEGEND. Then the box will appear (Figure 14.2). The summary box can be moved anywhere in the diagram, but we recommend you use the default location for simplicity.

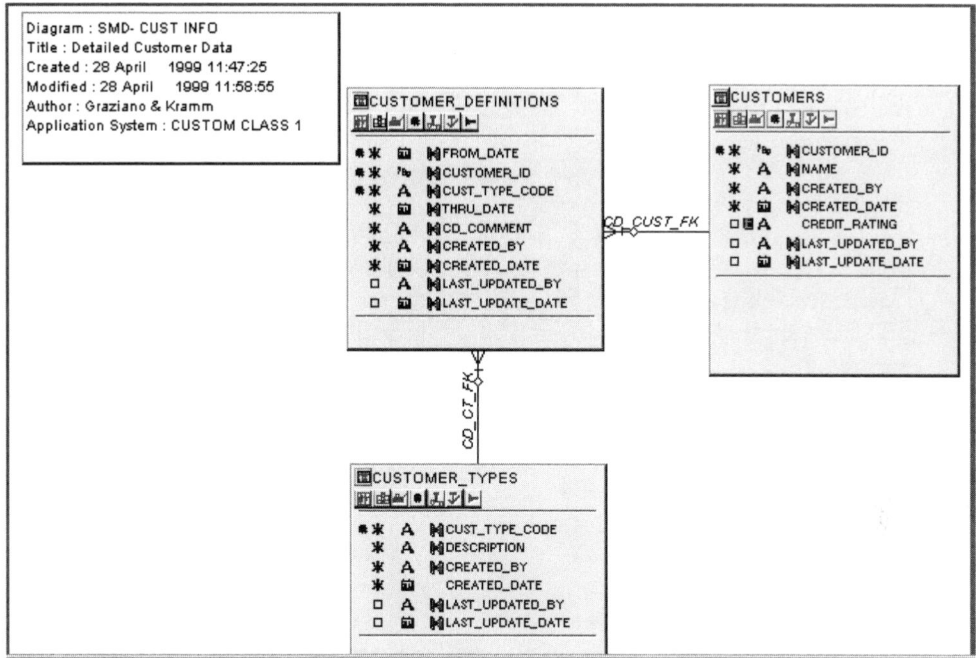

FIGURE 14.2 Sample Server Model Diagram with summary information displayed.

SERVER MODEL DIAGRAM LAYOUT CONVENTIONS

As mentioned at the beginning of the chapter, two conventions can be used. Both are presented along with some rationales for using each. Both are also included in the template document, so you will need to decided which you prefer and delete the other.

LAYOUT CONVENTION #1

Object Placement

- ❏ Place fundamental objects to the right of the diagram.
- ❏ Size objects so all columns can be seen and provide clear paths for foreign keys.
- ❏ Always use the *Edit->Include* facility first to prevent creating duplicate objects and constraints.

When this convention is followed, if all of the fundamental objects (primarily tables or views) are placed on the right side of the diagram, the crow's feet will naturally open to the left. Any object to the left of the fundamental objects will tend to be transactional (i.e., intersection tables and detail tables). As you move to the left, the objects become more transactional. To enforce this layout convention, you will likely have to experiment with the size (length and width) of the objects to make it work.

As a general practice, you should always use the Include facility before building a new object or constraint. When you invoke *Edit->Include*, a list of all tables, views, clusters, snapshots, and associations that are not included in the current diagram appears. By adhering to this practice, you will reduce the potential for creating a duplicate (actually the tool will not let you create two objects with the same name). In some cases, the same object exists in another application, but you are unaware of it. That's where peer reviews come in handy. If during a review you find that you have duplicated a table, delete your table and have the previously existing one shared into your application (with the permission of the Data/Application Administrator).

We have also found that it is a good practice to lay out all the tables and views to be included in the diagram first, before including their foreign key constraint lines. Once the lines are on the diagram, it can become quite confusing to sort out all the crossed lines as you try to rearrange the entities. If you do encounter this situation, simply cut the lines from the diagram, then include them again.

When drawing foreign key constraint lines, apply the following rules:

Drawing Foreign Key Constraints

- ❑ Face crow's feet to the left (West).
- ❑ Avoid line crossings if at all possible.
- ❑ Keep lines horizontal; do not angle them.
- ❑ Minimize the use of bent lines (straight lines are preferred).

The reason for these rules should be obvious: they keep the diagram easy to read. Crossing and bent lines only make it harder to trace the foreign keys when the diagram is being reviewed. If there are no bent lines and all crows' feet are to the left, all lines will be horizontal.

The last layout issue to consider is that of the placement of the constraint names.

Constraint name placement

Do not display foreign key constraint names.

Foreign key constraint names should not be displayed because they add little value to the diagram. These names are used only in generating the Data Definition Language (DDL). If you did not use the Database Design Transformer and need to check the names for standards compliance, use the Constraint Definition report to get a listing. See Figure 14.3 for an example of this convention.

LAYOUT CONVENTION #2

Object Placement

- ❑ Place fundamental objects to the right or the bottom of the diagram.
- ❑ Size objects so all columns can be seen and provide clear paths for foreign keys.
- ❑ Always use the *Edit->Include* facility first to prevent creation of duplicate objects and constraints.

When this convention is followed, if all of the fundamental objects (primarily tables or views) are placed on the right side or bottom of the diagram, then the crow's feet will naturally open up and/or to the left. Any object to the left or above of the fundamental objects will tend to be transactional. As you move to the upper left of the diagram, the objects tend to become more transactional. The result is that most transaction tables (and views) are in the upper left-hand corner of the diagram. To enforce this layout convention, you also have to experiment with the size (length and width) of the objects to make it work.

The use of the Include facility and other principles mentioned in the previous section also applies to this layout convention.

When drawing foreign keys, apply the following rules:

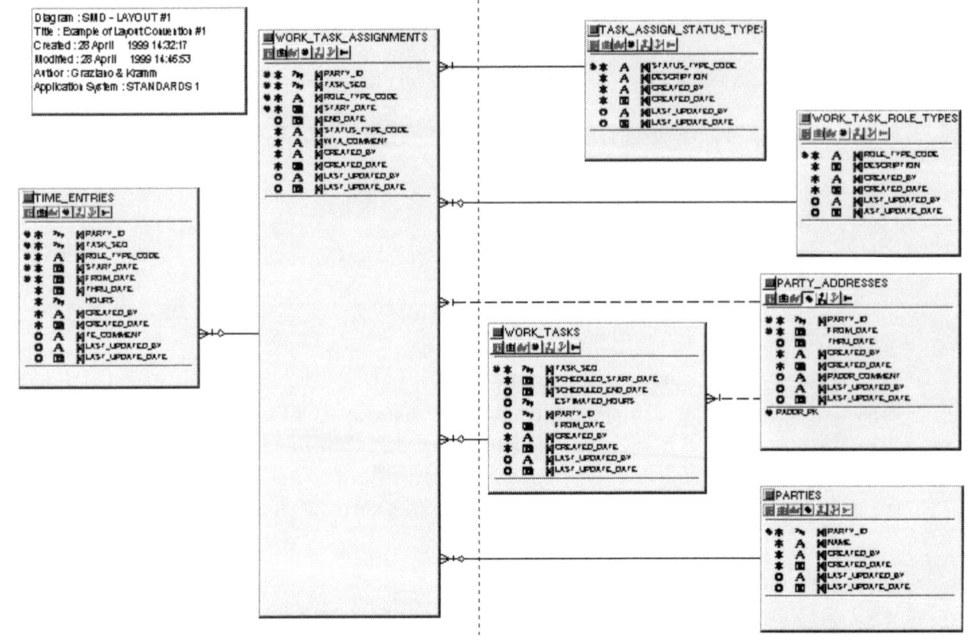

FIGURE 14.3 Example Server Model diagram using layout convention #1.

Drawing Foreign Key Constraints

- ❑ Face crow's feet to the left (West) or up (North).
- ❑ Avoid line crossings if at all possible.
- ❑ Keep lines horizontal or vertical; do not angle them.
- ❑ Minimize the use of bent lines (straight lines are more preferred).

The reason for these rules is the same as mentioned before: they keep the diagram easy to read. Crossing and bent lines only make it harder to trace a foreign key when the diagram is being reviewed, especially if there are both horizontal and vertical lines.

The last layout issue to consider is placement of constraint names.

Constraint name placement

Do not display foreign key constraint names.

This rule is the same regardless of the convention used. See Figure 14.4 for an example of this convention.

We have noticed that people sometimes interpret the standard as allowing them to have crows feet go up and to the left, as mentioned, or all go up or all go left. If you choose convention #2, you may want to refine it to specify which of those is allowed (or not allowed).

WHAT'S THE DIFFERENCE?

The main difference between these conventions is that in convention #1, all lines are horizontal, with the crow's feet facing left. In convention #2, lines may be ver-

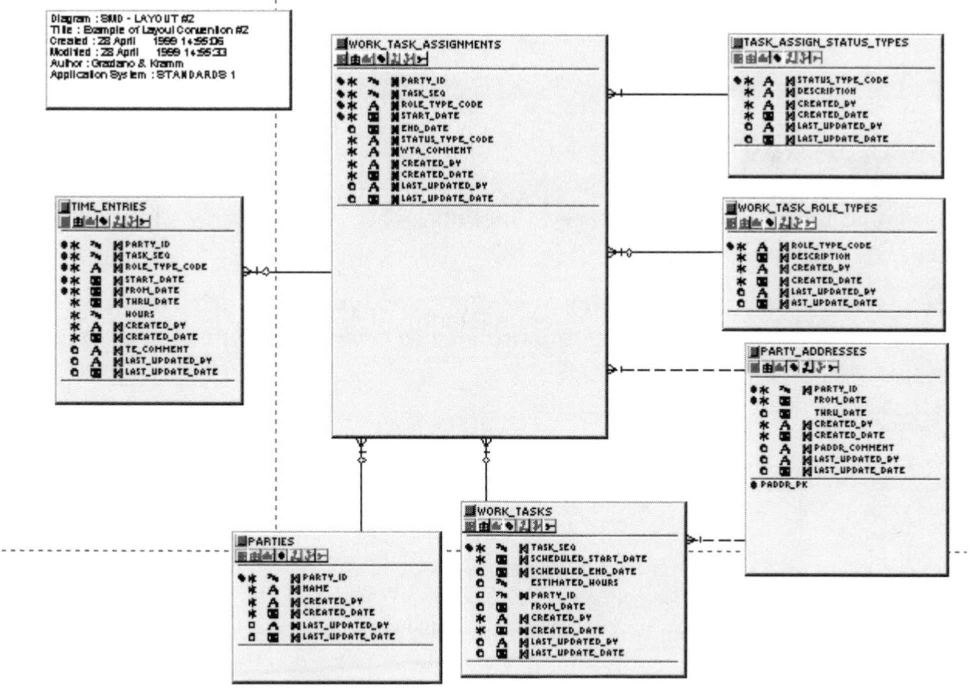

FIGURE 14.4 Example Server Model diagram using layout convention #2.

tical or horizontal, with crow's feet facing either up or left. The real question is which do you like better?

Convention #2 is based on the standard recommendation for ER modeling that was originally made by Richard Barker in *CASE*Method Entity Relationship Modelling*; it is used by many people in the industry. Convention #1 is a refinement of convention #2 and is preferred by some of our end users because it is simpler—the lines go in only one direction. Drawing diagrams with either convention can present challenges, but with time and practice, it can become nearly second nature. The benefit of following one of these conventions is that diagrams are easier to read and understand.

There is actually a third convention; it is the opposite of convention #2. The crows' feet point down and to the right. This convention makes master-detail (parent-child) associations more visible. It is an option you may want to consider.

OTHER CONSIDERATIONS

Once you have built all these diagrams, you need to maintain them. This can be quite a large task, so to help you, we have included a few other tips in the template that you should include as standard practices.

Consolidating Diagrams

There is no option to consolidate SM Diagrams. They are automatically consolidated upon opening.

If you wish to keep historical views of diagrams, you must print them on paper (before a change occurs) as there is no way to open one without seeing the underlying repository changes.

It is possible for someone to change the definition of a table, column, or constraint in the Design Editor (or RON) as well as in a diagram. If a change is made in the Design Editor while a diagram is open, any objects affected by the change will automatically be updated.

If changes were made while the diagram was closed, when you open it, the changes will be there already. If you then try to close the diagram, you will be asked to save changes. This means there is no easy way of keeping historical SM diagrams other than printing them out.

Delete Unneeded Diagrams

If a diagram is no longer needed, delete it from the Repository.

This practice may seem obvious, but many people create multiple versions of the same diagram and then forget which one is the most current. The only difference may be the arrangement of the objects. Once the diagrams have been opened, the dates in the legend will of course make the chronology clear, but you may have to open several diagrams before you find the right one. Be sure to clean up after yourself (just make sure someone else did not need the other diagrams first).

COLOR CODING

As more people gain access to color printer and plotters, a new convention is emerging: people are color coding their diagrams. Colors (or even shading) of objects can be a nice way to visually distinguish among different types of objects or different subject areas. If this sounds like a useful convention to you, get your Database Administrator or Application Administrator involved to determine specific colors or shading patterns to use (or avoid) and the detailed rules by which they should be applied.

To get you started, the template document includes the following guidelines:

Use color coding or shading to distinguish the following:

- ❑ Tables
- ❑ Views
- ❑ Snapshots
- ❑ Clusters
- ❑ Objects shared from other applications
- ❑ Objects that appear on more than one diagram
- ❑ Code type tables or views
- ❑ Subject area groupings

Selecting an object (or objects) and then clicking on the SET FILL COLOR button on the diagrammer toolbar easily sets colors for the selected object. By default, the SM Diagrammer uses different colors for the four main object types. You simple need to determine which colors to use. The default color selections are set using a dialog found under *Options -> Color/Font/Style* on the Design Editor menu (Figure 14.5).

As you can see, there are also options to set fonts (style and size) as well as line width and color. When you modify these settings, you can even choose whether to have them apply to new objects that are added to the diagram or to objects already on the diagram.

VIEW OPTIONS

The Design Editor also allows you to choose what can be displayed on a diagram (Figure 14.6). These options are set by selecting *Options-> Show/Hide* from the menu and then checking or unchecking the various view options.

As a rule, when creating a diagram for detailed design reviews we use the default settings, which include all the view options except the option for Associations Text. (This option turns off the foreign key constraint names.)

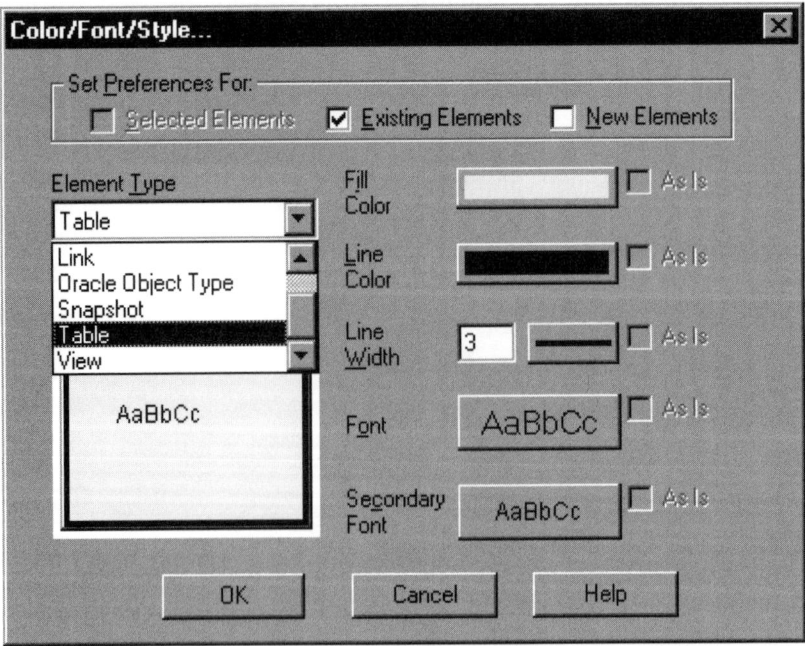

FIGURE 14.5 Dialog to establish default options for SM Diagrammer.

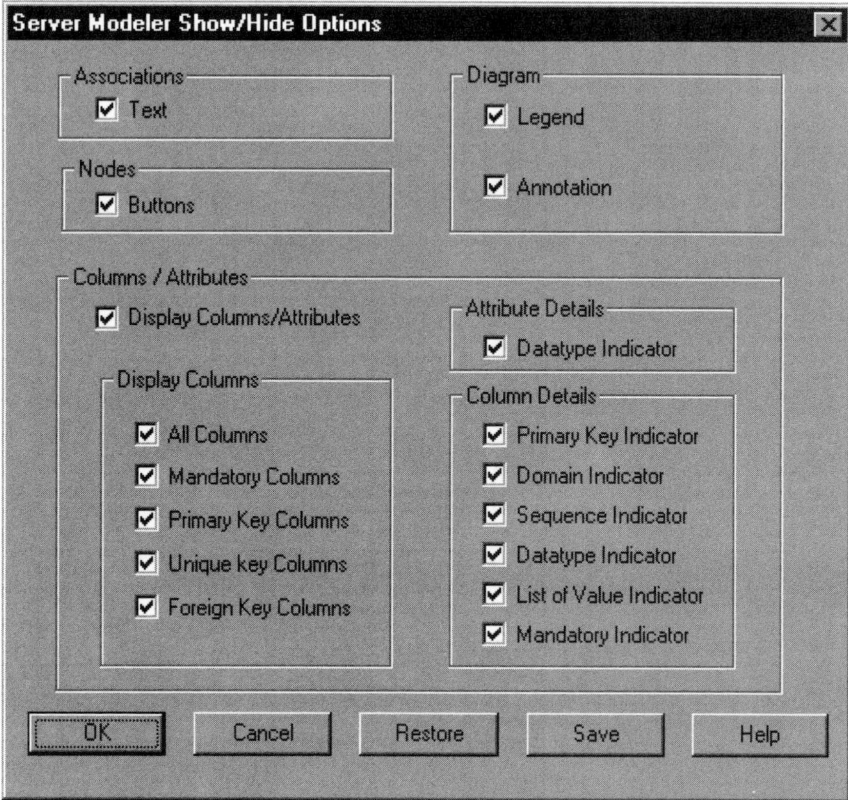

FIGURE 14.6 The Server Model Show/Hide Options dialog.

> Each Server Model diagram created for a logical area should include (where they exist):
>
> ❏ All tables and views within that logical area
>
> ❏ All columns
>
> ❏ All foreign key constraints
>
> ❏ All column detail indicators

The table displays in the SM Diagram also have iconic buttons on every table that allow you to control additional information that may be displayed (Figure 14.7). The buttons from left to right will display the names of:

- Database triggers
- Indexes
- Database synonyms
- Primary keys
- Unique keys
- Check constraints
- Foreign keys

You may chose to display some or all of these on a particular diagram, depending on the purpose of the diagram. For example, if you are reviewing the design for tuning considerations, you may want to display index names (Figure 14.7). If you are working on table API definitions, you may want to see database triggers and check constraints. There are many possibilities. Keep in mind, however, that the more you display, the more complex and larger your diagram will need to be in order to view all the information.

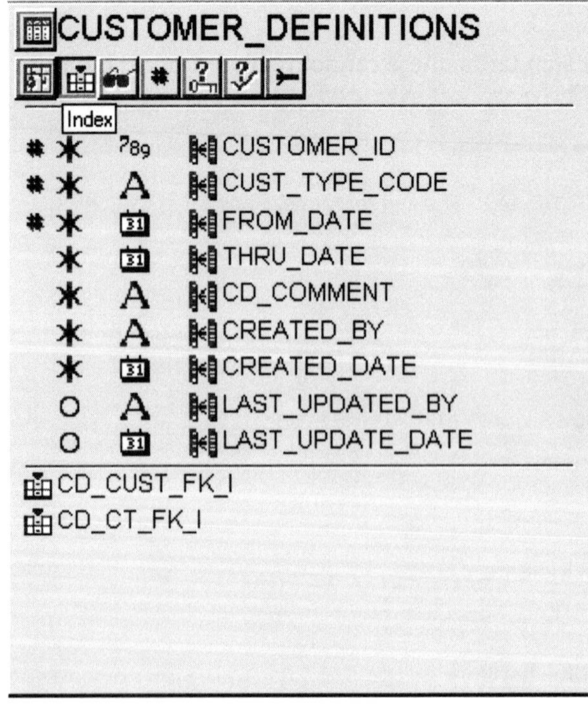

FIGURE 14.7 Table display with show indexes selected.

Appendix A

SAMPLE RELATIONSHIP NAMES

This appendix contains a table (Table A.1) showing some common and not so common relationship names for use in creating Entity Relationship Diagrams. These are not standards; there cannot really be any standards per se for relationship names. These are just examples we have used. A similar list appears in Appendix C of Richard Barker's book *CASE*Method Entity Relationship Modeling.*

TABLE A.1 Example Relationship Name Pairs

Crows Foot Side (many)	Single Side (one)
A condition for	Subject to
A modification of	Modified by
A usage of	Used for
Attached to	Inclusive of
Based on	The bases for
Based on	The originator of
Billed to	Billed for
Characterized by	The characteristics for
Classified by	The classification for
Copied from	The original for
Defined as	Used to define
Defined by	Used to define
Described by	The definition for
Described by	The description of
Described by	Used to describe
For	Subject to
Fulfilled by	Used to fulfill
Further defined by	A further definition of
Further described by	Used to describe
Further described by	A further description of
Included in	Comprised of
Located at	The location of
Made from	Composed of
Made by	The creator of
Manufactured by	The producer of
Part of	Composed of
Part of	Detailed by
Rated by	The rating for
Requested by	The requestor of
Returned from	Returned to
Shipped from	Shipped to
Shipped from	The source of
Shipped to	The destination of
Stored in	The storage for
The purpose for	Used for the purpose of
Used by	In need of

Appendix B

Object Format and Flow Down Chart

This appendix contains a set of tables showing most of the objects discussed in the standards document, their size, the source of the information, and how it is used throughout the tool.

A blank cell indicates no flow down usage or not applicable. Below are abbreviations used in the tables to represent the various Designer tools and utilities:

- ADT = Application Design Transformer
- AG = Application Generators
- BPM = Business Process Modeler
- DDT = Database Design Transformer
- DE = Design Editor
- DFD = Data Flow Diagrammer
- ERD = Entity Relationship Diagrammer
- FHD = Function Hierarchy Diagrammer
- LOV = List of Values
- MD = Matrix Diagrammer
- RON = Repository Object Navigator
- SG = Server Generator

TABLE B.1 Flow Down for Application Properties

INITIALIZATION

APPLICATION PROPERTIES

PROPERTY	MINIMUM LENGTH OF OBJECT NAME	MAXIMUM LENGTH OF OBJECT NAME	REQUIRED SUFFIX?	SOURCE	TOOL USED BY	FLOW-DOWN USAGE
Application Owner				Auto generated	All	Oracle user name of the Repository user who owns the application system
Name	1	14		RON	All	Used for tracking and access of all elements within this group
Version				Auto generated	Internal Processing	Maintenance of version group consistency
Version Date				Auto generated	All	
Parent				List of values	RON, Reporting	Collecting applications as a group—"versioning"
Title	1	40		RON	ADT, Generator	Top Title of a module of type "menu," which may be used in the menu area of a generated form
Status				Auto generated	All tools	Indicates whether application can currently be modified
Priority		240		RON		Repository reports
Constraints		240		RON		Repository reports
Comment		240		RON		Repository reports
Authority		10		RON		Repository reports
Latest Version				Auto generated		Repository reports
New Version Group				Auto generated		Indicates the group of applications that were versioned simultaneously with the current application system.
Summary		Multiline text		RON		Repository reports
Objectives		Multiline text		RON		Repository reports
Description		Multiline text		RON		Repository reports
Notes		Multiline text		RON		Repository reports

TABLE B.2 Flow Down for Business Unit Properties

PROPERTY	MINIMUM LENGTH OF OBJECT NAME	MAXIMUM LENGTH OF OBJECT NAME	REQUIRED SUFFIX?	SOURCE	TOOL USED BY	FLOW-DOWN USAGE
STRATEGY, ANALYSIS						
BUSINESS UNIT PROPERTIES						
Application system				Auto displayed	All tools	
Short Name	3	10		RON, BPM, MD		
Name	3	70		RON, BPM, MD	ADT	Menu name in Module Properties if default menu is used
Comment		240		RON		Repository reports
Decomposed				Auto displayed		
Parent				RON, BPM	BPM	Used for drill-up and drill-down in processes modeling
Sequence in Parent				RON, BPM	BPM	The position sequence of the business unit below the Parent
Description		Multiline text		RON, BPM		Repository reports
Notes		Multiline text		RON, BPM		Repository reports
Primary Location		100		RON, BPM		Repository reports
Primary Contact		240		RON		Repository reports
Head Count		10		RON, BPM		Repository reports
Role Cost Rate		23		RON		Repository reports
Role Cost Rate Unit		Not available		List of Values		Repository reports
Role Responsibilities		240		RON		Repository reports
Role Skill 1		240		RON		Repository reports
Role Skill 2		240		RON		Repository reports
Role Skill 3		240		RON		Repository reports
Role Skill 4		240		RON		Repository reports
Role?				RON, BPM		Repository reports
BPR multimedia Icon file Image file Sound file Video file Execution string				Text	RON	As of version 1.3.2, this information is not used for animation
BPR annotation Note type Note text Note picture file				RON	RON, BPM	As of version 1.3.2 this information is not used for animation

TABLE B.3 Flow Down for Entity Properties

STRATEGY, ANALYSIS

ENTITY PROPERTIES

PROPERTY	MINIMUM LENGTH OF OBJECT NAME	MAXIMUM LENGTH OF OBJECT NAME	REQUIRED SUFFIX?	SOURCE	TOOL USED BY	FLOW-DOWN USAGE
Name	3	23		RON, ERD MD (Text)	DDT	Is used in deriving the default Entity Plural
Short Name	4	7		RON, ERD MD (Text)	DDT	Used to generate Table Alias, part of FK column name to indicate source entity, part of table Unique Id name. May be used as Column Prefix if checked on DDT options tab. Can be modified.
Plural	3	26		RON, MD, ERD. Defaults as the plural from the Entity Name property (Text)	DDT	Used to generate the Table Name property. Refer to Table Journal for explanation of maximum object name limitation. Becomes the Display Title property for the table. Can be modified.
Type of				RON, ERD, MD (LOV)	DDT	Allows the choice of subtype implementation
Volumes: Initial				RON, ERD MD (Text)	DDT	Table Start Rows property. Volume information is used for the Database Sizing report.
Volumes: Average				RON, ERD MD (Text)		Repository reports
Volumes: Maximum				RON, ERD MD (Text)	DDT	Table End Rows property
Volumes: Annual Growth				RON, ERD MD (Text)		Repository reports
Volumes: Rate				RON, ERD MD(Text)		Repository reports
Description		Multiline text		RON, ERD MD (Text)	DDT	Table Description and User Help text Use as Block level Help in generated Form
Notes		Multiline text		RON, ERD MD (Text)	DDT	Table Notes

TABLE B.4 Flow Down for Attribute Properties

STRATEGY, ANALYSIS

ATTRIBUTE PROPERTIES

PROPERTY	MINIMUM LENGTH OF OBJECT NAME	MAXIMUM LENGTH OF OBJECT NAME	REQUIRED SUFFIX?	SOURCE	TOOL USED BY	FLOW-DOWN USAGE
Name	3	22		RON, ERD, MD	DDT	Used to generate Column Name and default Prompt property value. The DDT substitutes an underscore character for spaces. Refer to Column Prefix Property for Maximum Length limitation
Optional?				RON, MDatrix, ERD (LOV, Text)	DDT	Optionality of column in Column Properties. Generates NOT NULL constraint is 'Y'
Domain	3	30		RON, MD, ERD (LOV, Text)	DDT	Domain Format, length and precision flow down as Datatype, Maximum length and Decimal Places of column properties. Valid Values for Domain is used for LOV in generated Form and in-line column check constraints in (DDL Script)
Format				RON, MD, ERD (LOV)	DDT	Column Datatype property: Maps non-relational concepts e.g., VIDEO to relational datatypes like LONG RAW (LOB in ver. 8.x), or CHAR to VARCHAR2. Also maps down to the column Display Datatype
Maximum Length	1			RON, ERD, MD (Numeric)	DDT	Column Maximum Length and Display Length. Also used in DB sizing report.
Average Length				RON, ERD, MD (Numeric)	DDT	Column Average Length
Decimal Places				RON, ERD, MD (Numeric)	DDT	Column Decimal Places
Units		10		RON, ERD, MD (Text)		Repository reports
Comment		240		RON, ERD, MD (Text)	DDT	Column Comment and Hint properties
Default		40		RON, ERD, MD (Text)	DDT	Becomes Column Default Value property
Sequence in Entity				RON, ERD, MD (Number)	DDT	Becomes Column Display Sequence (default)

TABLE B.4 Flow Down for Attribute Properties (continued)

STRATEGY, ANALYSIS

ATTRIBUTE PROPERTIES

PROPERTY	MINIMUM LENGTH OF OBJECT NAME	MAXIMUM LENGTH OF OBJECT NAME	REQUIRED SUFFIX?	SOURCE	TOOL USED BY	FLOW-DOWN USAGE
Volumes: Percent Used: Initial Percent Used: Average				RON, ERD Matrix, (Number)	DDT	Column Initial and Average properties are derived from the attribute property values
On Condition		80		RON, ERD, MD (Text)		Repository reports
Authority		10		RON, ERD, MD (Text)		Repository reports
Responsible		10		RON, ERD, MD (Text)		Repository reports
Null Value		40		RON, ERD, MD (Text)		Used for databases other than Oracle
Derivation		240		RON, ERD, MD (Text)		Repository reports
Validation Rules		Multiline text		RON, ERD, MD		Repository reports
Text: Description		Multiline text		RON, ERD, MD (Text)	DDT	Column Description and User Help Text
Text: Notes		Multiline text		RON, ERD, MD		Column Notes

TABLE B.5 Flow Down for Attribute Allowable Value Properties

STRATEGY, ANALYSIS

ATTRIBUTE ALLOWABLE VALUE PROPERTIES

PROPERTY	MINIMUM LENGTH OF OBJECT NAME	MAXIMUM LENGTH OF OBJECT NAME	REQUIRED SUFFIX?	SOURCE	TOOL USED BY	FLOW-DOWN USAGE
For:				Auto displayed	DDT	Identifies which type of allowable values this is
Attribute						
Domain						
Column						
Module Argument						
Value		40		RON, ERD (Text)	DDT	Column Valid Value. If range of values, this is used for the low value
High Value		40		RON, ERD (Text)	DDT	Column Valid Value; High Value property if range is specified
Abbreviation		20		RON, ERD (Text)	DDT	Column Valid Value; Abbreviation property
Meaning		249		RON, ERD (Text)	DDT	Column Valid Value; Meaning property
Display Sequence				RON, ERD (Number)	DDT	Column Valid Value; Sequence property
Description		Multiline text		RON, ERD (Text)		Repository reports
Notes		Multiline text		RON, ERD (Text)		Repository reports

TABLE B.6 Flow Down for Domain Properties

ANALYSIS, DESIGN

DOMAIN PROPERTIES

Summary: Properties such as datatype and size information transfer to the attributes and columns to which they are assigned. If the domain is modified, the UPDATE ATTRIBUTES IN A DOMAIN or UPDATE COLUMNS IN A DOMAIN utility will cascade the changes through to the elements that are associated with that domain. In addition, the generators will use the Allowable Values for the domain to create validation code for the columns in that domain. Also, the GENERATE REFERENCE TABLES utility will load a CG_REF_CODES table with the values. The Forms, Reports and Table API generators will automatically create the code to look up the valid values.

PROPERTY	MINIMUM LENGTH OF OBJECT NAME	MAXIMUM LENGTH OF OBJECT NAME	REQUIRED SUFFIX?	SOURCE	TOOL USED BY	FLOW-DOWN USAGE
Name		40		RON, ERD (Text)	Update Attributes In A Domain and Update Columns In A Domain utilities, DDT	Attribute/Column Domain property. If Name modified, it will be reflected in its associations.
Subset Of				RON, ERD (LOV)		Repository reports
Authority		10		RON		Repository reports
Comment		240		RON, ERD (Text)	SG	Becomes default attribute or column comment when domain is assigned from pick list
Attributes in Domain:						
Format				RON, ERD (LOV)	Update Attributes In A Domain utility	Attribute Format property copied from domain
Ave Att Length				RON, ERD (Numeric)	Update Attributes In A Domain utility	Attribute Average Length property copied from domain
Max Att Length				RON, ERD (Numeric)	Update Attributes In A Domain utility	Attribute Maximum Length property copied from domain
Att Decimal Places				RON, ERD (Numeric)	Update Attributes In A Domain utility	Attribute Decimal Places property copied from domain

Att Unit of Measure	10	RON, ERD (Text)	Update Attributes In A Domain utility	Attribute Units property copied from domain
Derivation	240	RON, ERD		Repository reports
Validation rules	Multiline text	RON		Repository reports
Columns (Col) in Domain:				
Data type		RON, ERD (LOV)	Update Columns In A Domain utility	Column Datatype property copied from domain
Ave Col Length		RON, ERD (Numeric)	Update Columns In A Domain utility	Column Average Length property copied from domain
Max Col Length		RON, ERD (Numeric)	Update Columns In A Domain utility	Column Maximum Length property copied from domain
Col Decimal Places		RON, ERD (Numeric)	Update Columns In A Domain utility	Column Decimal Places property copied from domain
Default	60	RON, ERD (Text)	Update Attributes In A Domain and Update Columns In A Domain utilities	Attribute/Column Default Value property copied from domain
Null Value	40	RON, ERD (Text)	Update Attributes In A Domain and Update Columns In A Domain utilities	Attribute/Column Null Value property copied from domain
Dynamic List?		RON, ERD (LOV)	AG	When set to True and the display datatype for a column usage is Poplist or Text List, then the resulting list will be dynamic, i.e. based on a SELECT from CG_REF_CODES rather than hard coded values in the Form. Table API will use this information to SELECT values from CG_REF_CODES
Text: Description	Multiline text	RON, ERD (Text)		Repository reports
Text: Notes	Multiline text	RON, ERD (Text)		Repository reports

TABLE B.7 Flow Down for Domain Allowable Value Properties

ANALYSIS, DESIGN

DOMAIN ALLOWABLE VALUE PROPERTIES

PROPERTY	MINIMUM LENGTH OF OBJECT NAME	MAXIMUM LENGTH OF OBJECT NAME	REQUIRED SUFFIX?	SOURCE	TOOL USED BY	FLOW-DOWN USAGE
For: Attribute Domain Column Module Argument				Auto displayed	DDT	Identifies which type of allowable values this is
Value		40		RON, ERD (Text)	SG,AG	In-line check constraint in DDL, field validation in generated Form, LOV in generated Forms
High Value		40		RON, ERD (Text)	SG,AG	In-line check constraint in DDL, field validation in generated Form, LOV in generated Forms
Abbreviation		20		RON, ERD (Text)	AG	Creates the code to allow entry of an abbreviation of a value in a generated field, label of GUI display types in Forms
Meaning		249		RON, ERD (Text)	AG	LOV Description in Forms, Labels for GUI display types in forms
Display Sequence				RON, ERD (Number)	AG	Display Sequence in LOV for generated application
Description		Multiline text		RON, ERD (Text)		Repository reports
Notes		Multiline text		RON, ERD (Text)		Repository reports

TABLE B.8 Flow Down for UID Properties

ANALYSIS, DESIGN

UNIQUE IDENTIFIER PROPERTIES

PROPERTY	MINIMUM LENGTH OF OBJECT NAME	MAXIMUM LENGTH OF OBJECT NAME	REQUIRED SUFFIX?	SOURCE	TOOL USED BY	FLOW-DOWN USAGE
Entity				RON, ERD, (Auto displayed)	DDT	The plural of the entity becomes the Table Name property for the PK and unique key (UK) Constraints
UID				RON, ERD, (Auto displayed)	DDT	Table primary key (PK) and UK Constraint Name is derived from this
For: Attribute				RON, ERD (POP List)	DDT	These identify columns that participate in the PK or UK constraint. If *PK*: Table PK Key Component (columns used as foreign key (FK) in referring tables) If *UK*: Table UK Key Component
For: Relationship				RON, ERD (POP List)	DDT	These become FK columns that participate in the PK or UK constraint. If *PK*: Table PK, FK Component If *UK*: Table UK, FK Component
Primary?				RON, ERD (numeric)	DDT	PK versus UK flag. A check (in ERD) or a 'YES' (in RON) denotes its use as a primary unique identifier (which becomes a PK), otherwise it is a secondary key (which becomes a UK constraint)

TABLE B.9 Flow Down for Synonym Properties

ANALYSIS, DESIGN

SYNONYM PROPERTIES

PROPERTY	MINIMUM LENGTH OF OBJECT NAME	MAXIMUM LENGTH OF OBJECT NAME	REQUIRED SUFFIX?	SOURCE	TOOL USED BY	FLOW-DOWN USAGE
Name		40		RON, ERD (Text)	SG	If for: Entity; AKA, repository reports Term; AKA, repository reports Table, View, Snapshot, Sequence or Module; Name used for Synonym created in DDL
For: Entity Term Table View Snapshot Sequence Module				RON, ERD (Auto displayed)	SG	Identifies the object type that the Synonym is for in the DDL statement
Scope				RON (LOV)	SG	Indicates ID synonym is public or private
Complete?				RON (LOV)	SG	Indicates whether this synonym is finished and will be available for the server generator
Text: Description		Multiline text		RON (Text)		Repository reports
Text: Notes		Multiline text		RON (Text)		Repository reports

TABLE B.10 Flow Down for Relationship Properties

ANALYSIS, DESIGN

RELATIONSHIP PROPERTIES

PROPERTY	MINIMUM LENGTH OF OBJECT NAME	MAXIMUM LENGTH OF OBJECT NAME	REQUIRED SUFFIX?	SOURCE	TOOL USED BY	FLOW-DOWN USAGE
Application Name				RON (Auto displayed)	RON, ERD	Repository reports
From: Entity				RON, ERD	DDT	Identifies either the source or destination of a foreign key (FK) in the Column Properties and FK Constraint Properties. By default, FK Index as well as Constraint properties are automatically created by the DDT
Relationship Name		60		RON, ERD (Text)	DDT	May be used as part of the FK Constraint Name (if necessary) to ensure uniqueness of name
Minimum Cardinality				RON, ERD	DDT	If set to 1, Column Property "Optional?" will be set to "False"(column is not null) and FK Constraint Property "Mandatory?" is set to "True" (mandatory FK constraint). If set to 0, Column properties will be nullable and FK constraint will be optional
Maximum Cardinality				RON, ERD	DDT	Determines where the FK goes. If set to null FK on other end, if set to 1, FK column will be created in this table. If one to one relationship, an intersection table will be created automatically by DDT

Note: The location of the FK for 1:1 optional relationship depends on the entity volumetric information. If volume information matches or is absent, the FK will be placed alphabetically.

TABLE B.11 Flow Down for Other Object Properties

ANALYSIS, DESIGN

OTHER OBJECT PROPERTIES

PROPERTY	MINIMUM LENGTH OF OBJECT NAME	MAXIMUM LENGTH OF OBJECT NAME	REQUIRED SUFFIX?	SOURCE	TOOL USED BY	FLOW-DOWN USAGE
Business Function	6	70		FHD, BPM, RON, MD, DFD		Repository reports
Business Function Short Name	1	10		FHD, BPM, RON, MD, DFD		See discussion of format in Chapter 5
Business Process	6	70		BPM, RON, MD, DFD		Repository reports
Business Process Short Name	1	10		BPM, RON, MD, DFD		Same as Business Function Short Name
Business Term	3	70		RON		Repository reports
Datastore	6	70		BPM, RON		Repository reports
Datastore ID	3	10		BPM, RON		Repository reports
Diagrams	10	40		DE, ERD, FHD, DFD		Repository reports
Foreign Key Constraint	n/a	30	_FK	DE, RON	SG, AG	CASE generated. Becomes generated database object name.
Foreign Key Index	n/a	30	_FK_I	DE, RON	SG, AG	CASE generated. Becomes generated database object name
Library	8 + suffix	8 + suffix	.PLL	DE, RON	AG	Becomes generated library name
Module Name	8	40		DE, RON	AG	Becomes generated application module title
Module Short Name		8		DE, RON	AG	Becomes generated module name
Cursor		40		DE, RON	SG	Becomes generated database object name
Function		40		DE, RON	SG	Becomes generated database object name
Package		24		DE, RON	SG, AG	Becomes generated database object name. May be referenced in a generated application.
Procedure		40		DE, RON	SG, AG	Becomes generated database object name. May be referenced in a generated application.
Trg-Logic		40		DE, RON	SG	Becomes generated database object name. May be referenced in a generated application or table API script.
Module Implementation Name		8		DE, RON	AG	Must Equal Module Short Name. Defaults from Module Short Name. Will override Short Name if entered

TABLE B.12 Special Requirements for Certain Physical Objects

DESIGN, BUILD

PHYSICAL OBJECT	MINIMUM LENGTH OF OBJECT NAME	MAXIMUM LENGTH OF OBJECT NAME	REQUIRED SUFFIX?	SOURCE	TOOL USED BY	SPECIAL REQUIREMENTS AND FLOW-DOWN USE
Primary Key Constraint	n/a	30	_PK	DDT, DE, RON	SG, AG	Becomes generated database object name. May be referenced in a generated application.
Sequence (for ID)	8	30	_SEQ	DDT, DE, RON	SG, AG	Becomes generated database object name. May be referenced in a generated application or table API.
Table	3	26		DDT, DE, RON	SG, AG	Should be plural of entity name. Becomes generated database object name. May be referenced in a generated application.
Table Alias (Short Name)	4	6		DDT, DE, RON	AG	Must equal Entity Short Name. May be referenced in a generated application.
Journal Table	3	30	_JN	DE, RON	SG, AG	CASE generated. Suffix included in length. Becomes generated database object name. May be referenced in a generated application or table API
Triggers	8	30	_T	DE, RON	SG, AG	Becomes generated database object name. May be referenced in a generated application.
Check Constraint	10	30	_CHKnn	DE, RON	SG	Not CASE generated. Becomes generated database object name.
Unique Key Constraint	n/a	30	_UK	DDT, DE, RON	SG, AG	CASE generated. Becomes generated database object name. May be referenced in a generated application or table API
View	8	30	V_ (prefix)	DE, RON	SG, AG	Prefix included in length. Becomes generated database object name. May be referenced in a generated application.
Non-unique Index on Table	6	30	_NU_I	DE, RON	SG, AG	Becomes generated database object name
PL/SQL local variable	3	30	V_ (prefix)	DE, RON	SG, AG	Prefix included in length.
PL/SQL program unit	8	30		DE, RON	AG	Same as Procedures. May be referenced in generated application logic.

Appendix C

Relationship between the Process Modeler and the Functional Hierarchy Diagrammer

This appendix details the interaction between the Business Process Diagrammer and the Function Hierarchy Diagrammer as they both coexist within an application system defined in Oracle Designer.

BUSINESS PROCESS MODELER

Oracle CASE*Method now includes the use of the latest addition to Oracle's suite of diagramming tools for CASE development, the Business Process Modeler (BPM).

The new suggested approach for enterprise modeling is to create diagrams that pictorially document the flow of information between functions and the business units that use them. In fact, if you were to enroll in Oracle's Enterprise Modeling course you would notice the absence of the use of the Function Hierarchy Diagrammer (FHD). Pre-Designer/2000 Oracle CASE users will remember that the FHD was the only diagramming tool available to model functions.

Let's take a high level look at process modeling. You start by creating a root process. This will become the basis or parent for all additional processes that you create while in this diagram. The following are two approaches to using the Business Process Diagrammer.

EXAMPLE 1: MANY PROCESSES IN SAME PROCESS MODEL

Root Process: **"ABC Video Rental Store"**

In Figure C.1, I have created one large process model that contains some of the processes and the business areas or roles that perform them for ABC Video Rental. This approach allows the analyst to view the processes of ABC Rental Video from a glance. However, there are unrelated processes on this diagram. The processes for managing inventory and employees are unrelated to the process of returning a video. A better method would be to use a drill down approach as described in the following.

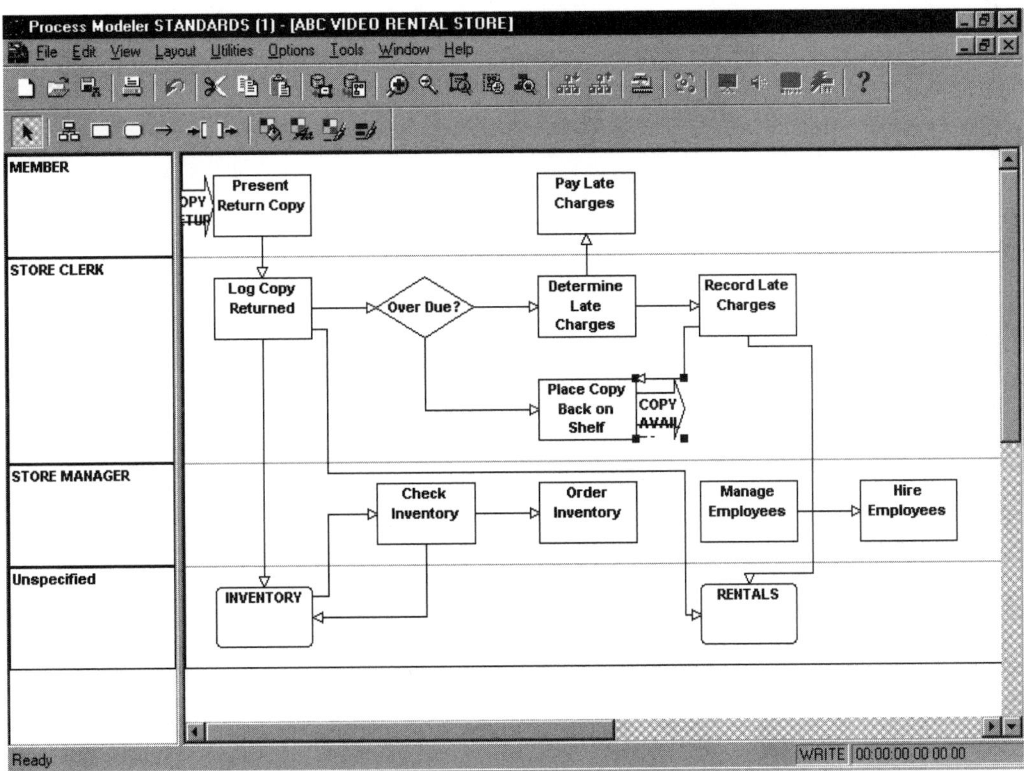

FIGURE C.1 Process model example #1.

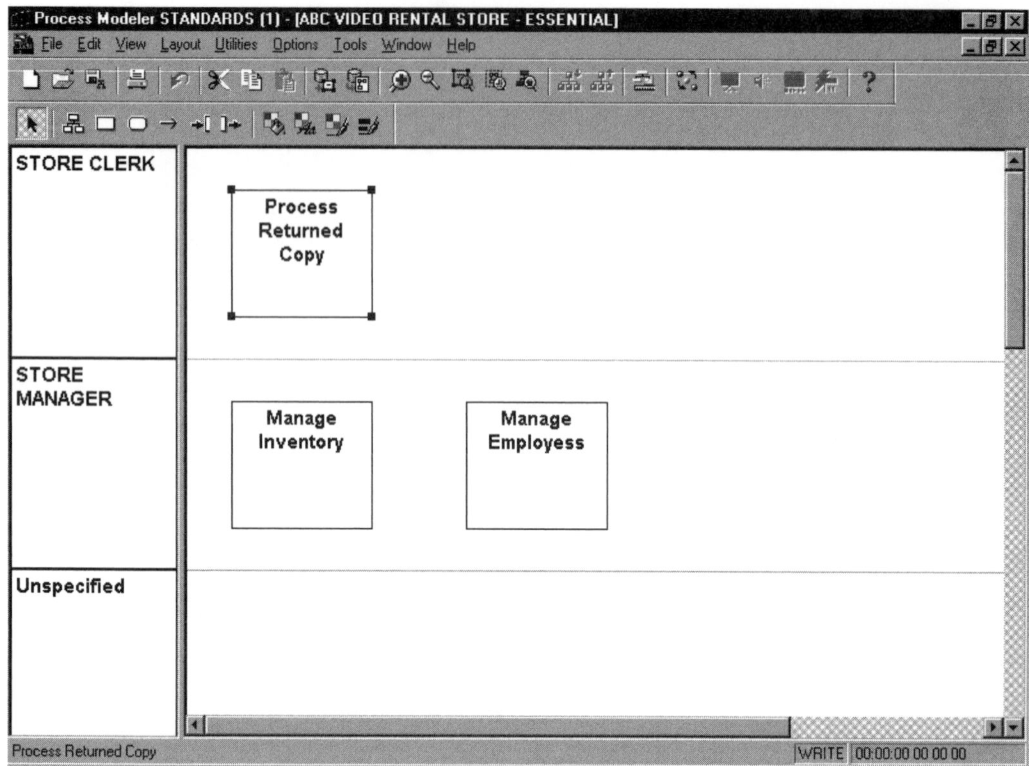

FIGURE C.2 Process model Example 2a.

EXAMPLE 2A: ESSENTIAL PROCESSES

In the example Figure C.2, I have created a high-level process model that contains a sample of the essential processes for ABC Rental Video. It is a rollup of the supporting processes performed at ABC Video Rental.

Root Process: **"ABC Video Rental Store"**

Each essential process can be viewed in detail by using the methods described in Example 2b.

EXAMPLE 2B: DRILL DOWN APPROACH (USING FILE-> OPEN DOWN)

In examples 2b, 2c and 2d (Figures C.3, C.4, C.5), I have drilled down the essential processes "Process Returned Copy," "Manage Inventory," and "Manage Employees, " resulting in the following business process diagrams. (Done by selecting a process and clicking on the menu options *File-> Open Down*).

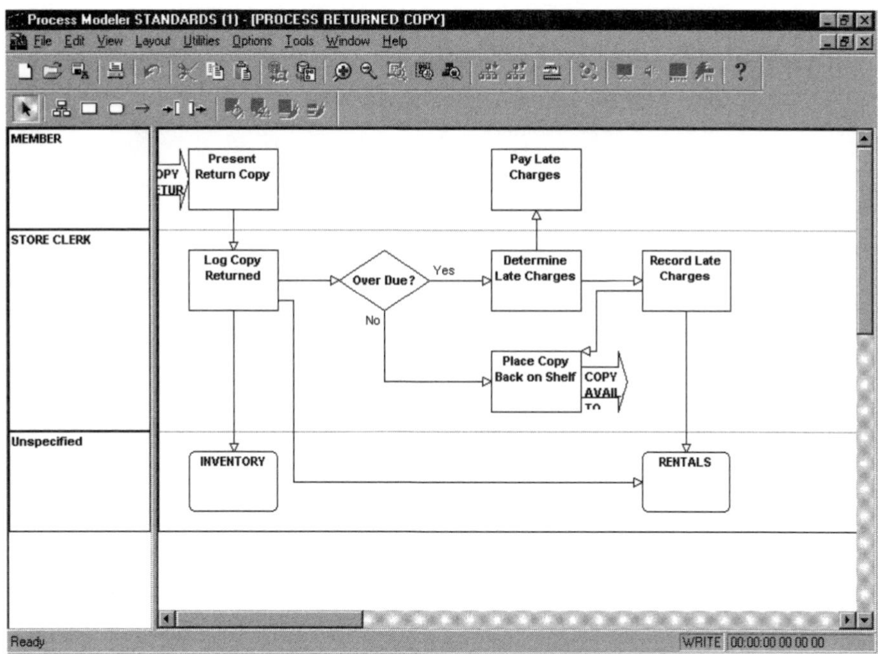

FIGURE C.3 Process model Example 2b.

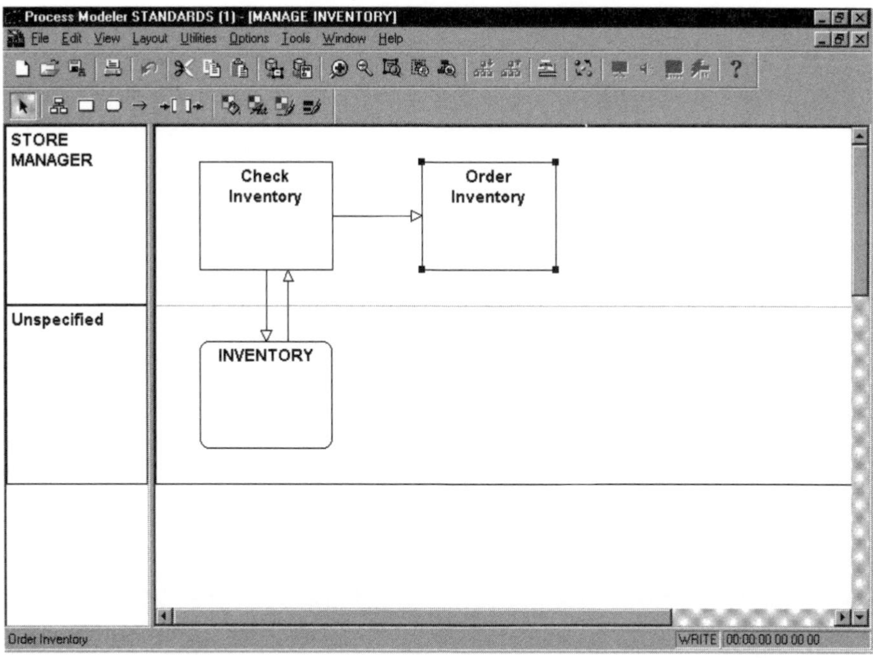

FIGURE C.4 Process model Example 2c.

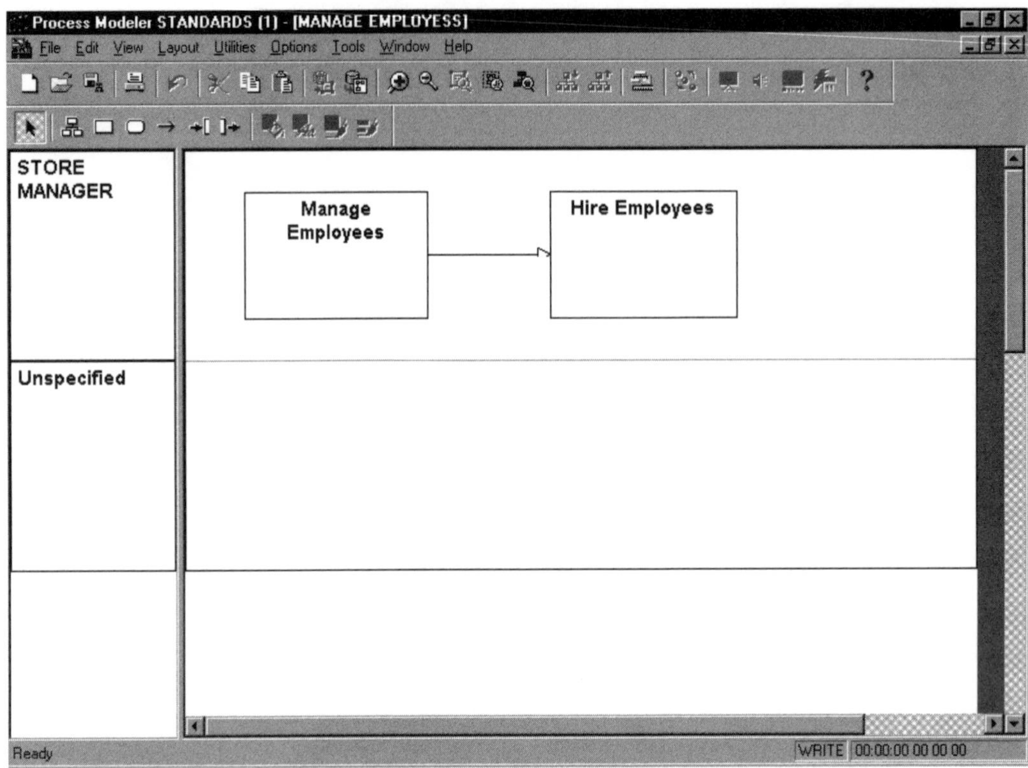

FIGURE C.5 Process model Example 2d.

Root Process: **"Process Returned Copy"**

Each of the processes in Example 2b (Figure C.3) are examples of support processes for the essential process "**Process Returned Copy**."

Root Process: **"Manage Inventory"**

Each of the processes in Example 2c (Figure C.4) are examples of support processes for the essential process "**Manage Inventory**."

Root Process: **"Manage Employees"**

Each of the processes in Example 2d (Figure C.5) are support processes for the essential process "**Manage Employees**."

FUNCTION HIERARCHY DIAGRAM

While performing business process modeling, you will create objects such as processes, decisions, triggers, and outcomes to support a root process.

When you open a new Function Hierarchy Diagram (FHD) and use an existing root Function that was created via the BPM, you will soon find out that objects created during business process modeling for the root process that you selected will also be included in the FHD automatically by default. Depending on the approach used during business process modeling as mentioned previously, this may or may not be the result you desired.

Figure C.6 is an example of the default FHD created when using the root function "ABC Video Rental Store" that was initially created using the business process modeling approach in "Example 1: Many processes in same process model".

All of the processes that comprise ABC Video Rental Store are grouped under the essential process "ABC Video Rental Store" as level 1 of the function Hierarchy. No distinction is made between essential and supporting processes.

Alternatively, notice the level of organization and structure with the following examples shown in Figure C.7 through Figure C.9. These are the default FHDs created from the BPMs in Examples 2a through 2d.

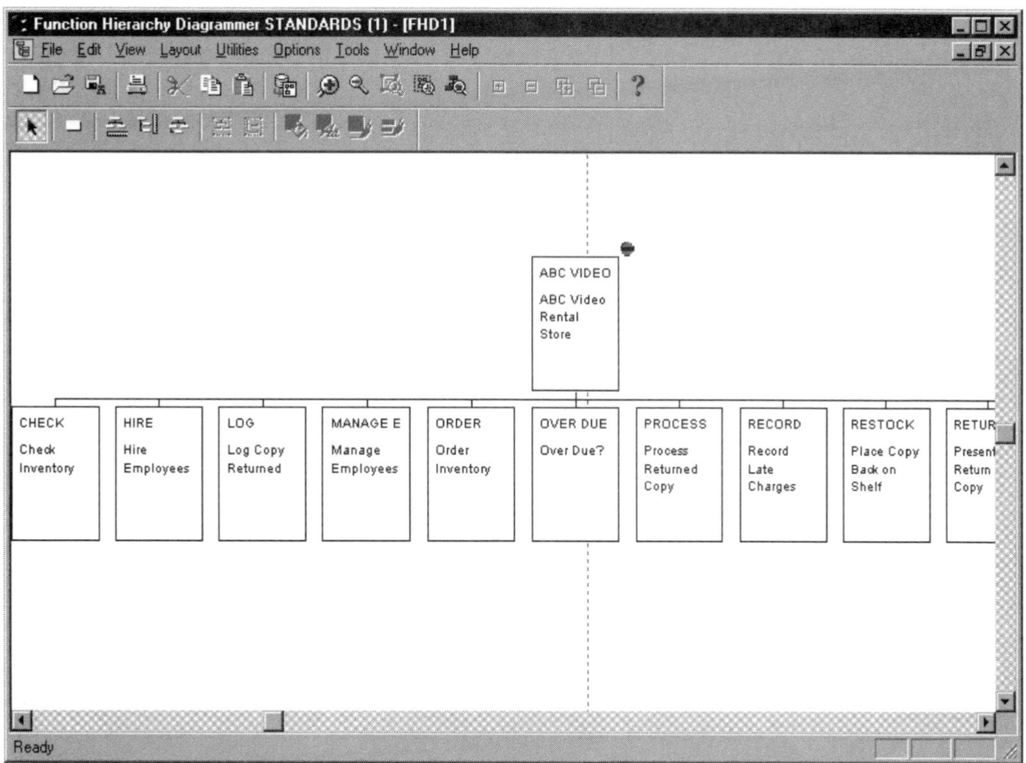

FIGURE C.6 Function Hierarchy Diagram Example 1.

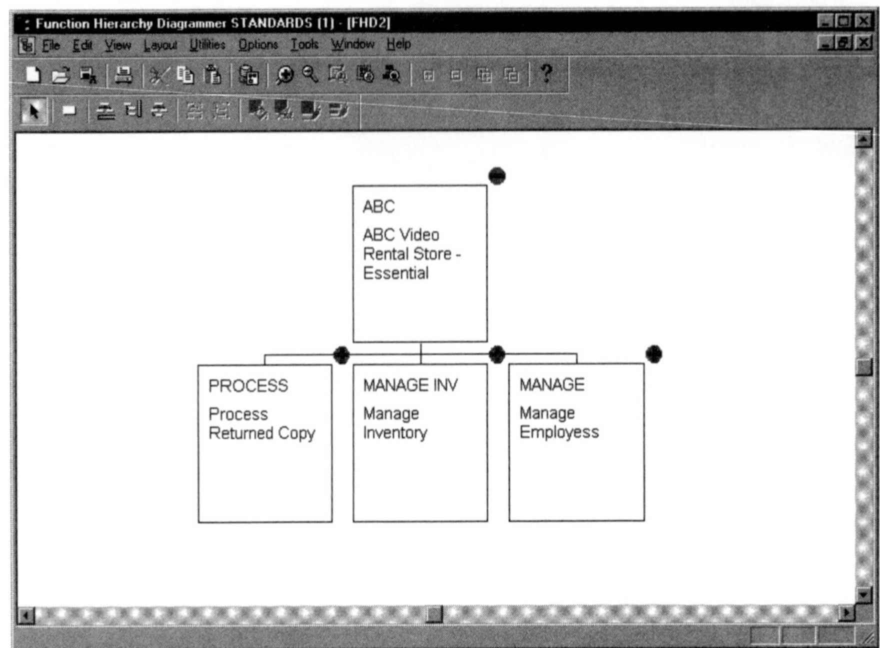

FIGURE C.7 Function Hierarchy Diagram Example 2a.

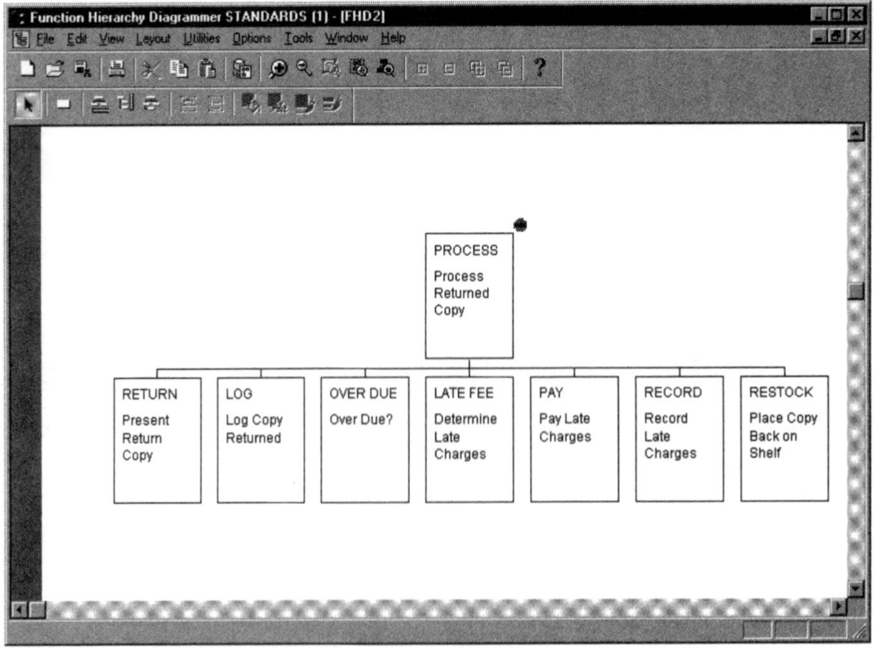

FIGURE C.8 Function Hierarchy Diagram Example 2b.

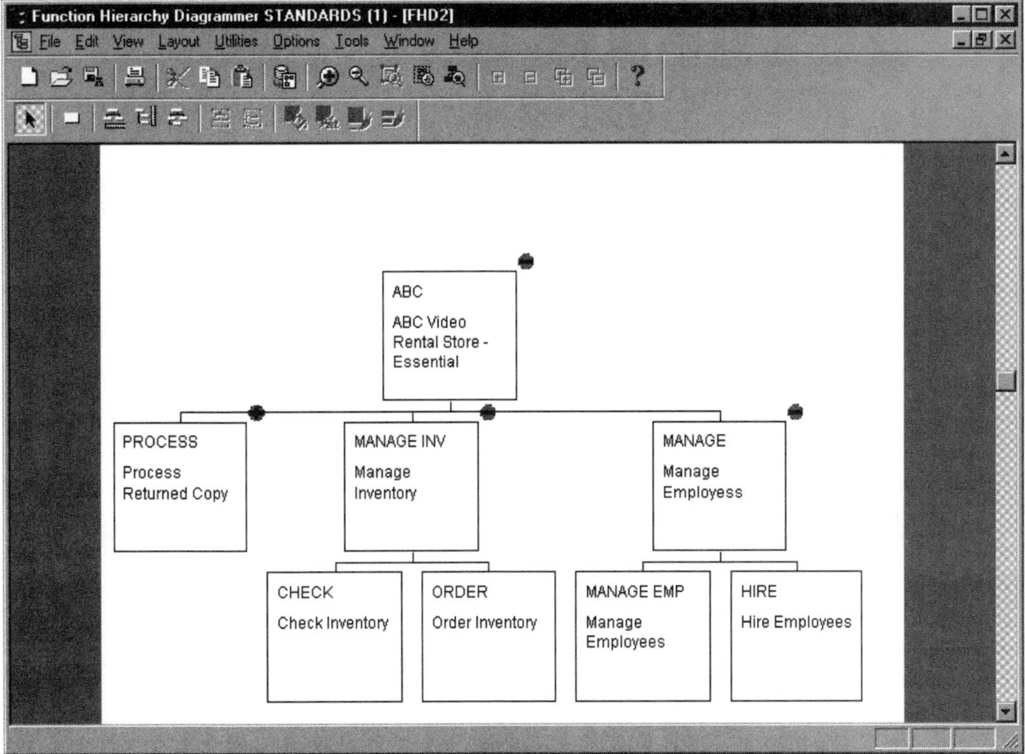

FIGURE C.9 Function Hierarchy Diagram Example 2c.

The essential processes and their supporting functions are grouped in a structured hierarchically rather than in a flat, less organized structure.

WHAT BECOMES OF THE OBJECTS CREATED DURING BUSINESS PROCESS MODELING?

Below is a list of various objects created in Designer by the BPM along with a listing of other places in the tool that can reference those objects.

Triggers: Triggers created during business process modeling are documented as Events when viewed in the Repository Object Navigator (RON) and do not show up in the FHD.

Outcomes: Outcomes created during business process modeling are documented as Events when viewed in the RON and do not show up in the FHD.

Processes: A process can be categorized as Data Entry, Decision Point, Process Step, or a Report. All of these types of processes show up in the FHD. If you do not want the Decision Points to show up in your FHD (for example "Over due?" in Figure C.5 and Figure C.7), you can create a new root process called decision points and reparent them to that process. Later I discuss how this approach will not affect your existing business process models.

Flows: A flow can be categorized as a Data Flow, Flow, Material Flow or a Temporal Flow. They are documented as Data Flows (under Business Functions) when viewed in the RON and do not show up in the FHD.

Stores: A store can be categorized as a Datastore, Material Store or a Store. They are documented as Stores when viewed in the RON and do not show up in the FHD.

REPARENTING OF FUNCTIONS AND HOW IT AFFECTS THE BPM, FHD, AND RON

If you were to reparent a function in an FHD, it would not have any effect on the BPM Diagram; however, it will show as being reparented when viewed in RON. Therefore, your business process model diagram may not reflect what is currently defined in the repository.

Conversely, if you were to reparent a function in a Business Process Diagram (by cutting it from the diagram and including it in a new diagram that has a different base or root function), it will not have any effect on the FHD or the RON. In other words it will not be documented in the FHD or RON as having been reparented in the process model.

The RON and the FHD work closely with each other, but the BPM tool is not as closely associated.

REASSOCIATING BUSINESS UNITS TO PROCESSES AND FUNCTIONS, AND HOW IT AFFECTS THE BPM AND RON

In the Business Process Modeler, if you have a process associated to a business unit called "Manager," it will show up in RON as being associated to that business unit with the element "Single BPR Business Unit?" set to "True." This is done to designate the primary business unit responsible for that process. If you were to drag the process to another business unit swim lane, for example, "Sales Clerk," it will show up in RON as being associated to the new business unit "Sales Clerk" with its "Single BPR Business Unit?" set to "True." Therefore, by dragging a process between swim lanes you are updating the primary business unit responsible for that process.

COMMON FUNCTIONS

In a business process model diagram, you can only show a process being performed by one business unit. However, in the RON, you can associate zero to many business units to processes and functions. You are not allowed to change the setting of "Single BPR Business Unit?" this is read only. *Therefore, if you do not use the Business Process Modeler, you will not be able to identify the primary business unit responsible for a given process.*

How do you show a process, for example "Order Inventory," as being performed by multiple business units within a Business Process Model diagram? Within the FHD, create a new root process called COMMON FUNCTIONS. This will be used to document common functions used while performing business process modeling. Under this process, create a new function (name it TEMP with a label of COMM1). Then, using the common function tab, designate "Order Inventory" as its master function. Include this new common function in your BPM

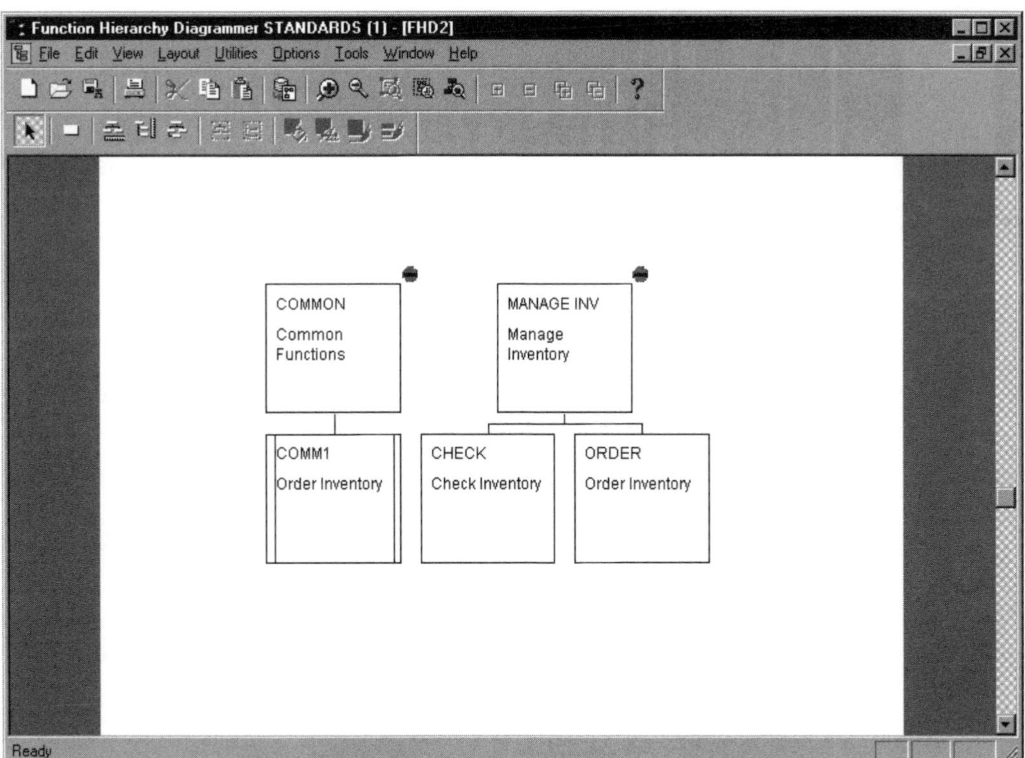

FIGURE C.10 Function Hierarchy Diagram Example 3a.

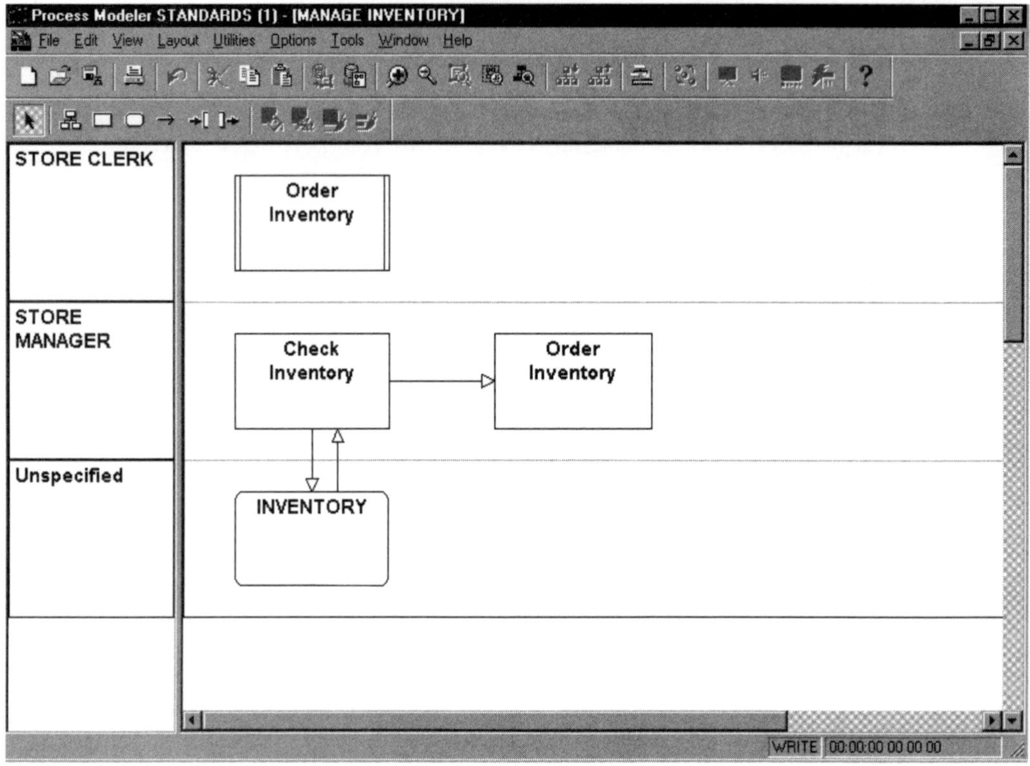

FIGURE C.11 Process Model Example 3b.

in the swim lane of the business unit "Store Clerk" (in release 2.x use *Edit -> Include -> Global Process Step*). Remember that the master function "Order Inventory" is still diagrammed in the swim lane of the business unit "Store Manager." The two diagrams Figures C.10 and C.11 show the final results.

Root Process: **"Manage Inventory"**

One other way to show multiple Business Units performing the same process is to create a Parent Business Unit (AKA Organization Unit) for "Store Clerk" and "Store Manager." In Figure C.12, I called the Parent Business Unit "Store." Since the function "Check Inventory" can now be moved to the swim lane of the Parent Business Unit "Store," both subordinate Business Units will be able to perform that function. Hence there is no need to create a common function with this method.

Root Process: **"Manage Inventory"**

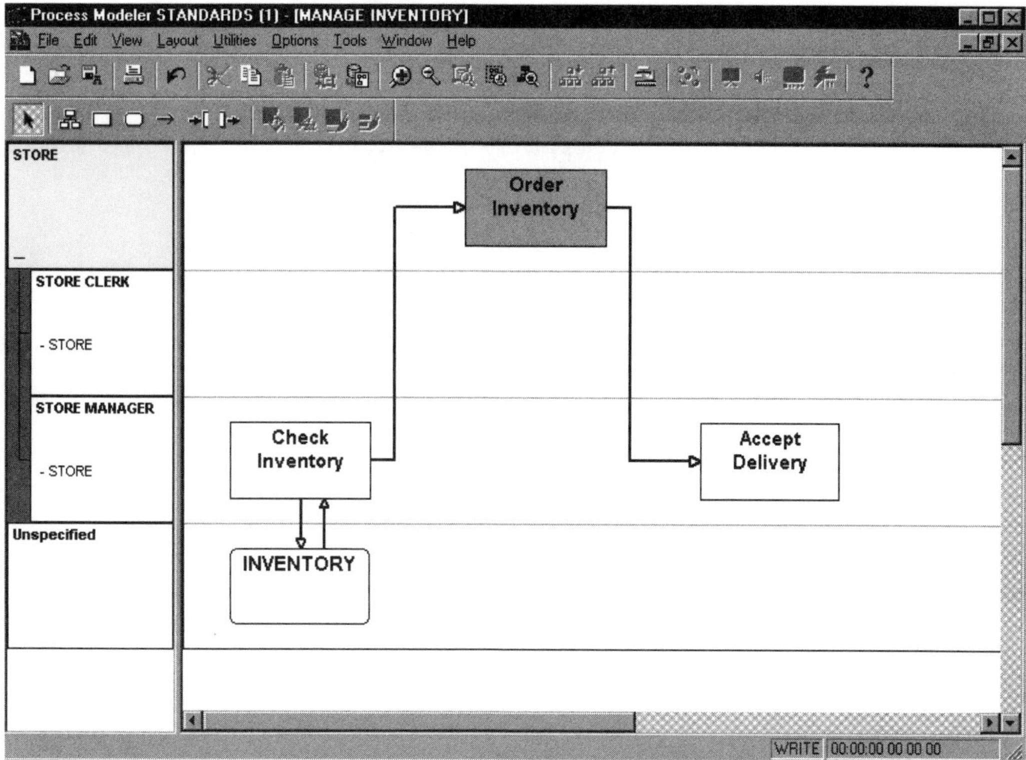

FIGURE C.12 Process Model Example 3c.

SUMMARY

Business Process Modeling and Function Hierarchy Decomposition are two different methods of business process modeling that can be done in Oracle Designer. Business Process Modeling allows the analyst to document the flow between business processes and the interaction of the business units that perform them. Function Hierarchy Decomposition entails the capturing of business processes and their lower level supporting functions without identifying the business units that performs them. Both methods can coexist during the same business engineering/re-engineering effort. However, you need to be made aware of and understand the interaction between the two methods and approaches and how they interact with the RON.

ABOUT THE APPENDIX

The preceding text was previously published by Mark Kramm in the proceedings for the Oracle Development Tools User Group 1998 Conference (www.odtug.com).

Appendix D

The Template Standards Document

The following pages contain the template standards document in its entirety. The document can also be found in Word 97 format on the CD-ROM.

Oracle Designer OBJECT NAMING STANDARDS & DIAGRAMING CONVENTIONS

Company-Name

Version 1.0

Author: *Company-Name* Information Resources Standards Team
Creation Date: Sept. 18, 1998
Last Updated: Sept. 18, 1998
Control Number: The Book.doc

This document is based on the template document provided with the book *Oracle Designer: A Template for Developing an Enterprise Standards Document* by Mark Kramm (kramm@palindrome-solutions.com) and Kent Graziano (graziano@bewellnet.com).

Approvals:

Project Manager ______________________________
Project Team Representative ______________________________

Change Record

Date	Author	Version	Change Reference

Reviewers

Name	Position

Distribution

Copy No	Name	Location
1		

Table of Contents

GENERAL

INTRODUCTION

This document establishes naming conventions for *Company-Name* for logical and physical objects generated from the Oracle Designer CASE tool. It also establishes diagramming conventions to be used with the various diagramming tools provided with Oracle Designer. These standards are based on the functionality available with Oracle Designer 2.1.2 but may be applicable to both earlier and later versions.

OBJECTIVES

The purpose of this document is to provide a common basis for analysis and development of business systems at *Company-Name*. The standards and conventions established by this document are intended to assist in the integration of methodologies and applications across all business areas within the company. Standardization is critical to the successful achievement of quality in the system engineering process.

This document establishes standards for system development and sets naming conventions for logical and physical objects as well as for data and process elements. It is expected that the standards contained herein will continue to evolve to support the changing needs of *Company-Name.*

The initial version of this document establishes the standards and conventions needed to support the processes of business reengineering and documentation of the corporate Enterprise using Oracle Designer. Subsequent efforts will focus on expanding the contents to incorporate standards for all automated systems and tools purchased and/or developed at *Company-Name.* Appropriate subject areas have been named in paragraph headings in this document to indicate future additions. These are marked *'(TBD)'* to indicate that the content is to be developed at some future time.

APPLICABILITY

This document applies to all custom development efforts that will be developed using Oracle Designer.

REFERENCES

This document includes and adopts selected standards that were developed as a result of *Company-Name's* Enterprise Standardization Efforts.

AUTHORIZATION

The System Architecture Committee is responsible for the establishment of these Standards and Naming Conventions. This committee will consist at a minimum of the Lead Data Architect, the Lead Application Architect, and the Lead Database Administrator (when appropriate). All future additions and amendments to this document will be controlled by this committee.

Changes to these standards will go through the following process:

1. Requests for change(s) must be submitted, in writing, to this committee.
2. The committee will review the requested changes, and either accept or reject them. If the requested changes are rejected, the committee will inform the requestor and tell them the reasons for rejection.
3. If the changes are accepted, the standards document will be updated, and all of the analysts, designers, and developers will be informed that the standards have changed, and given a brief summary of the changes. This step can be done on a periodic basis if there are many changes in progress.

Deviations from the standards must be reviewed and approved by the committee prior to implementation.

ACCESS

This document can be accessed by any system user on a read-only basis via the *Company-Name* Intranet or internal file system.

DOCUMENT ORGANIZATION

This document is organized into six distinct sections:

- ❑ Oracle Objects
- ❑ Strategy/Analysis
- ❑ Design
- ❑ Build
- ❑ Diagramming Conventions
- ❑ Appendices

NAMING ORACLE OBJECTS: GENERAL RULES

All rules established in this section must be followed when naming objects, unless **specifically** excepted by individual object descriptions in later sections.

The individual sections contain any additional rules specific to an object and one or more examples to illustrate usage.

LENGTH OF LABELS

ORACLE database object names are restricted to no more than thirty (30) characters and include entities, attributes, tables, columns, views, sequence generators, and domains. However, some Designer utilities may add a suffix of 4 additional characters for example "_JNL". For this reason, the recommended length is 26 characters. The words' 'alias' and 'short name' are used to describe a codified label of two (2) to four (4) characters. The word 'name' will signify a descriptive label of three (3) to twenty-six (26) characters. Names should be meaningful, and should accurately describe the object to which they are assigned. Oracle Applications' data names for entity and attributes should be used if possible. The consistent use of abbreviations and standard acronyms will assist in this endeavor.

Specific formats and lengths (where appropriate) are detailed by object in **Appendix B Object Format & Flow Down Charts** in the book *Oracle Designer: A Template for Developing an Enterprise Standards Document*. These specifications are the basis of all object names and must be followed. These limits are established to promote consistency and to ensure that all objects used in module generation are of appropriate length.

ACRONYMS/ABBREVIATIONS

Full words should always be used, unless an approved acronym can be substituted or an abbreviation is required for length considerations. In other words, always substitute an acronym if an appropriate one exists, and only abbreviate when necessary because of name length considerations. (An acronym is a word formed from the initial letter or letters of each of the successive or major parts of a compound term.)

If name length considerations mandate abbreviation of words, begin the abbreviation process from the right. If the word has an approved abbreviation, substitute the abbreviation. If, after all appropriate acronyms and abbreviations have been substituted, it is still necessary to reduce the length of a label, begin to abbreviate the last word in the label and continue to reduce one word at a time until the total length of the label is acceptable. Apply the following techniques, in the order given, to create a unique abbreviation of appropriate length.

- Remove internal vowels and final 'e'.

  Example: country is abbreviated 'cntry', object is abbreviated 'objct'.

- Sequentially remove consonants beginning at the end of the word.

  Example: address is abbreviated 'addr', abbreviation is abbreviated 'abbr'.

An abbreviation should be no less than three and no more than five characters. In some instances, an abbreviation of two (2) characters is allowable if the meaning of the abbreviation is clear and/or it is in common usage such as 'oz', 'ft', or 'lb'. If the qualifying word is four or fewer characters long, it should not be abbreviated.

Tables of standard abbreviations and acronyms are provided in Appendix A (Approved Acronyms) and Appendix B (Approved Abbreviations).

If further assistance is required, contact the Data Administrator to determine the acronym(s) or abbreviation(s) required. If you have created a new abbreviation using the rules above, contact your Data Architect to update the approved abbreviation, codes and acronyms list.

USE OF SIGNIFICANT WORDS

Use root words wherever possible. Dropping the suffix (-age, -ence, -ance, -ing, -ant, -ity, -any, -ive, -ary, -ony, -aty, -ory, -ation, -ment, -ed, -tion) will generally leave the root word. Do this only if the remaining root word is meaningful as is.

Words such as who, what, when, or where are *not* allowed.

The use of articles and prepositions (such as **the** or **of**), adjoining words or conjunctions (such as **and** or **or**), qualifying words such as **new** or **old**, and numbers should be on an exception basis.

USE OF SPECIAL CHARACTERS

Special characters, including brackets, quotation marks, question marks, and slashes are *not* permitted. Dashes are allowed only in legitimately hyphenated words.

Underscores will not be used except where needed to separate words in physical implementation objects (like tables, columns, and modules). The Designer tool will insert underscores, when required, during transformation from logical to physical repository objects.

STRATEGY / ANALYSIS

This section describes naming standards for objects that will be encountered or defined in the Strategy or Analysis phase of application development. All rules established in the Oracle Objects General Rules section must be followed when naming Designer Repository objects, unless specifically excepted by individual object descriptions in this section.

APPLICATION NAME

Application names will be representative of the Master Development Project it is associated with.

Application names will have a maximum of 10 characters.
Valid application abbreviations include:

1. LO	Logistics
2. PM	Product Marketing
3. ER	Employee Relations
4. FN	Financials
5. PR	Production
6. AC	Acquisitions
7. VP	Vendor Packages

BUSINESS OBJECTIVES

Business Objectives will be extracted from the Corporate Strategic Plan and maintained in the Corporate Level Enterprise Model. Business Objective names can be up to forty (40) characters in length.

Example: EXPAND TO BE RECOGNIZED NATIONALLY.

CRITICAL SUCCESS FACTORS

The resources, events and conditions required to meet each Business Objective will be identified and cataloged as Critical Success Factors (CSF's). CSF names are nouns or nominative phrases of up to forty (40) characters.

Examples: AGGRESSIVE MARKETING STRATEGIES,
HANDLE NEW GOVERNMENT REGS QUICKLY

KEY PERFORMANCE INDICATORS

Deliverables, schedules, milestones and other tracking mechanisms will be assigned to each Critical Success Factor and will be used to determine progress. Key Performance Indicator (KPI) names are nouns or nominative phrases of up to forty (40) characters.

Example: OPEN 5 NEW OFFICES IN NEW STATES.

BUSINESS EVENTS

An **Event** is a named action, which initiates the execution of a business process. Event names must consist of a verb and an object and are restricted to thirty (30) characters.

Examples:

RECEIVE INVOICE is an example of a trigger that is an initiating event for an Accounts Payable process.

VENDOR PAYED is an example of an outcome event for an Accounts Payable process.

BUSINESS TERMINOLOGY

Business Terminology should be additional terms and associated definitions useful for understanding the enterprise being modeled.

Terms entered must not duplicate entity names.

Terminology names can be up to (40) characters in length

BUSINESS UNITS

A Business Unit definition will contain a long descriptive name and a short name.

Business Unit short names will have a minimum of two (2) characters and a maximum of four (4) characters, two characters is preferred.

Business Unit short names are codes which will be derived from the longer, descriptive name of the Business Unit.

Example:

Long name = Database Services

Short name = DBSV

BUSINESS POLICIES & RULES

A convention of storing Business Policies and Rules as functions under A separate RULES ROOT FUNCTION will be used at *Company-Name.*

All the highest-level **Business Area Policies and Rules (BAPR)** have been identified and entered into the Enterprise model. These BAPRs detail the highest levels of the major process areas in the Enterprise and have been modeled to establish a common environment for recording business policies and rules for the corporation. In most cases, standard industry descriptions have been used to identify BAPRs. In a changing business environment, the use of standard names and descriptions provides the flexibility needed to support a dynamic environment.

As business policies are identified, they will be appended to the appropriate higher level BAPR in the Enterprise Model. These extensions of the BAPR Enterprise Model may be only one level deep before business rule decompositions begins.

If additional levels are required for a very complex model, the extension must be approved by the System Architecture Committee.

Business Policy Short Definition

Business Policies are high level statements of desired constraints and may imply one or more business rules.

The short definition of a business policy is usually a statement or phrase and can be up to (70) characters.

Business Policies *must* not be "Atomic" and *must not* be "Elementary" when defined in the Oracle Designer Repository

Example: Employees will be billed using the lowest published price.

Business Policy Label

At the third level of the model, the business policy label will be composed of seven (7) alpha characters where the *first* of the six characters is the name of the level two parent and the seventh is a single number character. This digit is positional and begins with one (1).

Use of alpha characters in the positional parameter will be permitted only on an exception basis with approval of the System Architecture Committee.

Note: Level two labels are composed of six (6) alpha characters where the *first two* characters are "Z_" and the next four (4) is an acronym of the short definition. These have already been established.

Example:

Z_BILL1 is the label for the Billing Business Policy which is a child of the level two BAPR 'Z_BILL Billing Business Policies and Rules.

Business Rule Short Definition

A Business Rule is an elementary (single action) statement of a constraint on data that is enforced by processes.

The short definition of a business rule is usually a single statement containing actions and verbs and can be up to (70) characters.

Business Rules *must* be "Atomic", and must be defined as "Elementary" in the Oracle Designer Repository

Example 1:

Business Policy:

Employees will be billed using the lowest published price.

Business Rules:

1. If time of service was prior to employment with company, bill for the service(s).
2. If service is within 2 weeks of employee termination, do not bill for service(s).

Example 2:

Business Policy:

Federal and State Environmental Regulations govern the disposal of hazardous materials.

Business Rules:

1. Biological waste must be incinerated with a temperature of at least 1000 degrees.
2. Transfer of hazardous material must be via an authorized carrier with a DOT Number.

Business Rule Label

All business rule labels are limited to ten (10) characters.

Labels are a concatenation of the label from the parent business policy, and from one (1) to three (3) numeric characters. The digits, which identify the level of decomposition within the business policy are positional and begin with the number one (1).

The examples in this section show how business rule labels are built.

Z_BILL1: Employees will be billed using the lowest published price (policy)

Where:

Z_BILL = Billing Business Policies and Rules (Business Area Policies and Rules (BAPR))

1 = Employees will be billed using the lowest published price (which is a Policy, of the Business Area Policies and Rules; Z_BILL Billing Business Policies Rules)

Z_BILL11: If time of service was prior to employment with company, bill for the service(s).

Where:

Z_BILL = Billing Business Policies and Rules (Business Area Policies and Rules (BOPR))

1 = Employees will be billed using the lowest published price (which is a Policy, of the Business Area Policies and Rules; Z_BILL Billing Business Policies and Rules)

1 = If time of service was prior to employment with company, bill for the service(s) (left most, Business Rule, of the Policy; Z_BILL1 Employees will be billed using the lowest published price).

Z_BILL12: If service is within 2 weeks of employee termination, do not bill for service(s).

Where:

Z_BILL = Billing Business Policies and Rules (Business Area Policies and Rules (BAPR))

1 = Employees will be billed using the lowest published price (which is a Policy, of the Business Area Policies and Rules; Z_BILL Billing Business Policies and Rules).

1 = If service is within 2 weeks of employee termination, do not bill for service(s).

Linking Business Rules to Business Functions

All Business Rules must be linked to at least one Business Function.

(Refer to Chapter 4 Business Rules and Policies in the Handbook for illustrated details on how to accomplish this task.)

BUSINESS PROCESS

Business processes will be captured using the Process Modeler and the Function Hierarchy Diagrammer

All the highest level Business Processes have been identified and entered into the process model. Standard industry descriptions have been, and will continue to be used to identify business processes.

As additional process models are developed, they will be appended to the appropriate higher level process in the Enterprise Model. These extensions of the Enterprise Model may not exceed two additional levels of business processes before functional decomposition begins.

If additional levels are required for a very complex model, the extension must be approved by the System Architecture Committee.

Business Process Label

At the highest two levels of the enterprise, the business process labels have a single alpha character and have already been established. All subsequent levels of business processes will be composed of three (3) alpha characters where the *first* of the three characters is the name of the level two parent.

Example:

CAM is the label for the Customer Account Maintenance process, which is a child of the level two process 'C' Customer Services.

Labels are automatically displayed in FHD's to help identify processes and functions hierarchic relationships.

Refer to the illustrations in the handbook in Chapter 5 Business Processes & Functions.

Business Process Short Definition

The short definition of a business process is always a noun or nominative phrase.

Example 1:

Accounting and Fixed Assets are standard high level processes;

Accounts Payable, Accounts Receivable and General Ledger are processes which are functions of the higher level process, Accounting;

Asset Acquisition, Asset Capitalization, Asset Depreciation and Asset Retirement are processes, which are functions of the higher level process, Fixed Assets.

Example 2:

Planning, Customer Service and Marketing are standard high level processes;

Customer Account Maintenance and Collections are processes, which are functions of the higher level process, Customer Service.

BUSINESS FUNCTIONS

A business function is a named action performed by one or more business units as part of a business process.

Business Function Label

All business function labels are limited to ten (10) characters.

Labels are a concatenation of the label from the parent business process, and from one (1) to seven (7) numeric characters. The digits, which identify the level of functional decomposition within the business process are positional and begin with one (1). This scheme supports a maximum of seven (7) levels of functional decomposition of a business process.

Use of alpha characters in the positional parameters will be permitted only on an exception basis with approval of the System Architecture Committee.

Examples:

CAM1: Establish New Account

Where:

C = Customer Service (*primary* Business Process)

CAM = Account Maintenance (Business Process which is also a function of the *primary* business process Customer Service)

CAM1 = Establish New Account (First, First Level Function of the process CAM Account Maintenance)

CAM11: Conduct interview

Where:

C = Customer Service (*primary* Business Process)

CAM = Account Maintenance (Business Process which is also a function of the *primary* business process Customer Service)

CAM1 = Establish New Account (First, First Level Function in the process CAM Account Maintenance)

CAM11 = Conduct interview (First, Second Level Function in the process CAM1 Establish New Account)

CAM12: Record applicant data

Where:

C = Customer Service (*primary* Business Process)

CAM = Customer Account Maintenance (Business Process which is also a function of the *primary* business process Customer Service)

CAM1 = Establish New Account (First, First Level Function in the process CAM Account Maintenance)

CAM12 = Record applicant data (Second, Second Level Function in the process CAM1 Establish New Account)

Business Function Short Definition

Business Functions will have a short definition consisting of a verb and an object. Always describe the function starting with a verb. If you don't it will be confused with a process. The short definition can consist of as few as two words, or it can be as long as a sentence. It should clearly describe the complete activity carried out within the scope of that function.

Examples: Establish New Account, Revise Existing Contract

COMMON FUNCTIONS

All Common Functions must include the master function label as part of the short definition.

Example:

Label: M11

Definition: Interview the customer (CAM11)

Where CAM11 is the master function "Conduct Interview".

DATA STORES

A datastore must have a name and an id.

Datastore names describe the contents of the datastore and are restricted to thirty (30) characters. Datastore IDs are limited to ten (10) characters.

Example:

CUSTOMER SERVICE INFORMATION is the name of a data store that contains files, tables, paper forms, etc. related to Customer Service.

CSI is the ID for the datastore.

Data is the type for the datastore.

DATA FLOWS

Data flows do not have to be named.

Flow names describe the contents of the flow and are restricted to thirty (30) characters.

Data is the type for the data flow.

Example:

CUSTOMER ACCOUNT INFO is the name of a data flow that contains information related to Customer Service Information datastore. **As Customer Account Information may just be a subset of the information defined by the data store Customer Account Information.**

DIAGRAMS

The names of all diagrams stored in the Designer/2000 repository will conform to these conventions.

Generally, the name of a diagram should describe the functional area or business area view of the Enterprise Model.

Diagram names will begin with the appropriate Diagram Type Code (shown in the table below) followed by a colon (:), a blank space, and a meaningful description of up to thirty-six (36) additional characters. This will allow you to distinguish the types of diagrams when viewing them from the Repository Object Navigator.

Diagram Type	Tool Used to Generate Diagrams
BP	Business Process Modeller
DD	Data Diagrammer
DF	Data Flow Diagrammer
ER	Entity Relationship Diagrammer

FH	Functional Hierarchy Diagrammer
MD	Module Data Diagrammer
MX	Matrix Diagrammer

The following sample diagram names illustrate usage of the convention.

BP: Accounting

ER: Customer Services Information

ER: Order Entry Information

FH: Enterprise Model

ENTITIES

Entity Names

Entity Names should be singular nouns or nominative phrases. They must be business-oriented, and will contain one blank space between each word. Use single or multiple full-word descriptive names, but allow exceptions for approved acronyms and/or abbreviations (e.g., CUST or ADDR) when the name exceeds 24 characters.

- ❑ Entity names may not contain the names of *physical* constructs such as "file" or "table" as a qualifier.

Example: Use **Customer** *not Customer File* or *Customer Table.*

- ❑ Entities must not exceed 24 characters including spaces. See the section on use of abbreviations if your entity name exceeds this limit.

Example: CUSTOMER ADDRESS, ORDER HEADER, MAX UNIT OF MEASURE.

If you maybe sharing entities from other vendor applications (e.g. Oracle Applications) with the same name as your entities, for example, CUSTOMER, you may want to prefix your entities with a two or three character application identifier. For example, if your application name is ANY COMPANY, then prefix your entities with "AC" (e.g. AC_CUSTOMER).

Entity Plural

At *Company-Name*, it has been decided that all tables will be the plural form of the entity name.

Thus the plural for each entity must also be defined at the time an entity is named (since the DDT will use this to create the table name). Some utilities impose a restriction on the length of the entity plural name. For example if you decide to create journal tables using Designer, the tool will generate a three-character suffix "_JN".

- ❑ Entity Plural must not exceed 26 characters including spaces.

Entity Short Name (Alias)

An entity short name is composed of a distinct word or words (10 characters or less) or a concatenation of Entity word fragments. Oracle Designer uses the short name in the generation of names for constraints, foreign keys, and sequences. A user should be able to look at an entity short name and know to which entity it refers. Since the entity short name may be used to create any migrated foreign-key column name, it is important that the short name indicate the entity from which it came from. Use a standard abbreviation if one exists. Short names should be a minimum of 3 characters and a maximum of 10.

If an entity name consists of one word, the short name should be the first 3 to 6 characters or it can be an approved acronym or abbreviation. If the entity name consists of two or more words, the short name should be the first letter of each of the words in the name not to exceed 6 characters, or each word can be an approved acronym or abbreviation with no space between them.. If more characters are needed for readability, contact the data administrator for approval. Resolve vulgar or objectionable words with your data administrator as well.

Example: CUST is the short name for the entity CUSTOMER;

ADDR is the short name for the entity ADDRESS;

PHNUM is a possible short name for the entity PHONE NUMBER. PN will be the short name automatically created

ORDHDR is the short name for the entity ORDER HEADER. OH will be the short name automatically created.

Intersection Entities

An intersection entity associates two different entities and resolves a many-to-many relationship. It is named according to its business functionality.

Example:

If entity one is named ORDER and entity two is named PRODUCT, an intersection entity may be created called ORDER ITEM.

If there are no business terms that will work, the name is simply formed from the names of the entities which are associated.

Example:

CUSTOMER ADDRESS describes the connection of the CUSTOMER and ADDRESS entities.

Association Entities

An association entity is used to resolve a many to many **recursive** relationship between an entity and itself. It is named for its parent entity with the word ASSOCIATION appended.

Example: CUSTOMER ASSOCIATION

Validation Entities

A validation entity is one that contains "lookup" or code information. Validation entities should be suffixed with a blank space and the word "TYPE" to distinguish them from other types of entities.

Example:

COUNTRY OF ORIGIN TYPE

ORDER TYPE

CUSTOMER TYPE

VEHICLE TYPE

DOMAINS

It is suggested that an initial set of domains be established in a separate application and then shared into other application systems. Subsequent additions to domains will be created in the domain application and then shared into the appropriate applications. This will add a level of security to safeguard the deletion or modification of domains by users.

An initial set of domains has been developed for the enterprise by the Data Administrator (DA) and resides in the Oracle Designer repository (see Appendix C for a list).

Domain names may be up to (30) characters and should indicate the scope or contents of the domain. Do not place underscores between words in a domain name. If the name becomes too long, refer to the list of approved abbreviations and acronyms in the appendices of this document.

Examples:

Address

Amount

Id

Long Text (1000)

Very Long Text (2000)

Name

Standard uses for domains

There are several things that domains should be commonly used to provide. They are:

- ❑ A list of values
- ❑ A range of values

- ❑ A specified data type and size
- ❑ Any combination of these.

The following properties are mandatory for all domains created for the enterprise:

- ❑ Name
- ❑ Attribute Format
- ❑ Column Datatype
- ❑ Maximum Length (both attribute and column)
- ❑ Comment (describes domain purpose, suggested uses, etc.).

Default initial values will also be specified, when appropriate.

Domains will also be used, as required, to provide lists of values (LOV's) when generating forms from Designer. For such a domain, known as a reference domain, the domain name will be the plural of the attribute referenced.

Example: **STATES** is the reference domain for the attribute **STATE**.

In general, domains will be used only if the values are relatively static and encompass fifty (50) or fewer discrete values.

Examples: **STATES** is an approved LOV domain because the values are static and limited.

AREA CODES is *not* an approved domain. The values are not sufficiently limited.

The DA will construct additional domains as they become required and will be generated for the enterprise.

ATTRIBUTES

An attribute is any detail, which serves to identify, qualify, quantify, classify, express the state of, or otherwise describe properties of an entity. Each occurrence of an attribute within an entity has one and only one value.

Attributes are classified in the repository by functionality and depicted on Entity Relationship Diagrams with the following symbols:

Symbol	*Description*
#	Primary Unique Identifier (UID)
*	Mandatory Attribute (may not be null)
o	Optional Attribute (may be null)

Attribute names may be up to 30 characters long. Since attributes are always shown in the context of an owning entity, do not repeat the name of the entity as part of the attribute name, unless it participates in the unique identifier (UID). Attributes can have multi-part names and should not have underscores between the words. Attribute names should be as descriptive as possible without being overly convoluted. They should be named using terms an end-user will recognize as much as possible. If necessary, abbreviations and acronyms may be used to meet length requirements.

Examples:

Start Date

End Date

Description

Primary UID Attributes

When naming an attribute that participates in the UID, use the entity name (if it is relatively short) or the entity short name plus one of the following words as a suffix:

ID is used for a UID that contains a system-generated number and is used internally during processing to access or link data. The values are meaningful only as pointers or keys, and usually do not show on end user reports or screens. *The domain for IDs is 'UID'.*

NUMBER is used for a UID that contains a number by which the end user recognizes the entity. NUMBERs **are** displayed on reports or screens to provide information to an end user. The number may be system generated but is usually determined by the user or has been provided from a legacy system. *The domain for NUMBERs in a UID is 'UID'.*

CODE is used for a UID that contains an alphanumeric value by which the end user recognizes the entity. CODEs are displayed on reports or screens to provide information to an end user. The value of the code is usually representative of the entity it identifies. *The domain for CODEs is 'CODE'.*

TYPE is used for an attribute that contains an alphanumeric value to represent a categorization of an entity (i.e., a sub-type). *The domain for TYPEs is 'TYPE'.*

Examples:

CUSTOMER ID: If the entity CUSTOMER has a system generated internal use UID, the attribute will be designated **CUSTOMER ID.**

CUSTOMER NUMBER: If the entity CUSTOMER has a system generated or user generated UID which is significant to the end user, the attribute will be designated **CUSTOMER NUMBER**.

CUSTOMER CODE: If the entity CUSTOMER were identified by an alphanumeric UID (e.g., GRAZ1), it would be called **CUSTOMER CODE.**

CUSTOMER TYPE: Account management recognizes several categories for Customers, such as commercial or residential. Each grouping is identified by an alphanumeric value called **CUSTOMER TYPE**.

Except for these specific rules, attribute names should be determined by the same rules used for data entities in **Section Entities.**

Audit Attributes

Audit capabilities are required in all systems developed for the enterprise. Every entity **must** contain the following four audit attributes:

CREATED BY

CREATION DATE

LAST UPDATED BY

LAST UPDATE DATE

These audit attributes are to be detailed in the logical models for any entity. When tables and columns are later generated from entities and attributes, the Database Design Transformer will create the appropriate columns.

Required Domains

Whenever possible, each attribute should have a **domain type**. In some situations it is possible that an attribute may have unique characteristics that are not repeated elsewhere, in this case use of a domain would be of little value.

If the domain associated with an attribute contains allowed values, the attribute name will be the same as the domain name, only singular.

See **Appendix C** for a list of approved domains.

RELATIONSHIPS

Relationships should be named so that the diagram can be easily read. To read any relationship simply and definitively, the following syntax is used:

Each (and every) ENTITY-A {must be, may be} relationship-name {ONE AND ONLY ONE ENTITY-B (singular), ONE OR MORE ENTITY-B plural}

Where *ENTITY-A* is the source entity of the relationship, *ENTITY-B* is the destination end of the relationship, and *relationship-name* is the name applied to the relationship in the direction the relationship is being read. Note the following rules:

- The choice between *must be* and *may be* is determined by the modality (optionality) of the relationship emanating from the source entity. A solid line represents *must be* (mandatory) and a dashed line represents *may be* (optional).
- The choice between *ONE AND ONLY ONE ENTITY-B (singular)* and *ONE OR MORE ENTITY-B plural* is determined, respectively, by the absence or presence of the "crows feet" at the ENTITY-B end. This is also known as the cardinality of the relationship.

Since relationships are always bi-directional, naming a relationship requires two relationship names be supplied. Hence, the relationship must be readable using the above syntactic structure in both directions.

Examples:

Each (and every) PERSON *may be* **located at** ONE OR MORE ADDRESSES.

Each (and every) ADDRESS *must be* **the location for** ONE AND ONLY ONE PERSON.

Each (and every) DEPARTMENT *may be* **responsible for** ONE OR MORE EMPLOYEES.

Each (and every) EMPLOYEE *must be* **assigned to** ONE AND ONLY ONE DEPARTMENT.

Whenever multiple relationships are created into a single entity, from the same parent entity, the relationship labels **must be** unique to prevent duplicate index names from being created by the Database Transformer. Otherwise, the indexes will not be generated during "DDL Generation"

Do not use weak relationship names, such as "associated with", or "related to". Remember that relationships are documenting business rules and will be used to explain the model to end users. Whenever possible, use business terminology. For example, the correct way to document a person and their address would be:

A PERSON *may be* **located at** one or more ADDRESSes, ***not*** a PERSON *may be* **associated with** one or more ADDRESSes.

UNIQUE IDENTIFIERS

Every entity must have at least one unique identifier that will eventually serve as the primary key. This will insure the uniqueness of the data to be entered. It is also possible for an entity to have additional unique identifiers.

If the primary UID of a "fundamental" entity is based on a surrogate key, then the entity must also have a secondary UID, which represents the natural key for the entity.

Designer will automatically name the primary unique identifier with the Entity Short name. Any additional UIDs created against the entity should be named:

<Entity Short Name>#

Where '#' is a number indicating the sequence of the UID.

Example:

The entity PERSON has the short name PER. The primary UID will be named PER.

A secondary UID on the attribute NAME should then be named PER2.

DESIGN

This section describes naming standards for objects that will be encountered or defined in the Design phase of application development.

MODULES SCOPE

The names of all modules developed with and generated from Oracle Designer will conform to these conventions. This includes all menus, reports, screens, libraries, webserver modules, and Visual Basic programs. In addition, all SQL*Plus reports (where documented) developed at *COMPANY-NAME* will also conform to these conventions. Changes to these standards must be approved by the lead Application Architect.

The following distinctions between modules developed for or associated with Legacy systems and Vendor-supplied software and those to be developed for new or replacement systems are recognized:

All new or replacement systems developed for *Company-Name* will be developed using the Designer tool set. All modules, whether custom designed or generated from Designer, will adhere to standards without exception.

Legacy modules' names will not be changed. After Legacy software is recovered into the Designer repository, any future modules created to augment the legacy system must conform to these standards.

Vendor's modules' names will not be changed. If objects from a purchased package are recovered into the Designer repository, and any modules are generated in-house to use those vendor objects, the new modules will be developed according to this standard.

FORMAT

Module names should consist of:

- ❑ a two character prefix representing the application
- ❑ two characters representing the Functional Area within the application
- ❑ one character identifying the type of module
- ❑ a sequence number

The following table lists the valid module identifiers for applications under development at *Company-Name*:

Application System	Value
Logistics	LO
Acquisitions	AC
Financials	FN
Product Marketing	PM
Production	PR
Employee Relations	ER
Multiple Application Systems (common module)	CM

The third and fourth characters of the name indicate the Functional Area (within an Application System) for which the module is developed.

Functional Area	Value
Accounts Payable	AP
Accounts Receivable	AR
Collections	CL
Cost Accounting	CA
Employee Benefits	BE
General Ledger	GL
Planning	PL
Order Entry	OE
Shared Module (common modules)	SH

The fifth character of the name indicates the Type of the Module.

Type of Module	Value
Oracle Forms	F
Oracle Forms – Query Only	Q
Oracle Reports	R
Oracle WebServer	W
Menu	M
Developer Library (pll)	L
Object Library	O
Template Form	T
Reference Form	R
Visual Basic	B
SQL*Plus Report (doc only)	P

The last component of the module name, the sequence number, is simply three digits, which are incremented by 10. The increment may be modified to five (5) if the number of modules per subsystem becomes extremely large.

Following are some example module names using this standard:

Screens Examples:

Name: FNAPF010

Translation: Financials applications, Accounts Payable subsystem, Oracle Form

Name: ERBEF010

Translation: Employee Relations application, Employee Benefits subsystem, Oracle Form

Reports Examples:

Name: FNAPR010

Translation: Financials applications, Accounts Payable subsystem, Oracle Report

Name: ERBER0010

Translation: Employee Relations application, Employee Benefits subsystem, Oracle Report

Menus Examples:

Name: FNAPM010

Translation: Menu for the Financials applications, Accounts Payable subsystem

Name: ERBEM010

Translation: Menu for Employee Relations application, Employee Benefits subsystem

Libraries Examples:

Name: FNAPL010

Translation: Oracle Developer library for Financials applications, Accounts Payable subsystem

Name: ERSHL010

Translation: Oracle Developer library containing shared program units for the Employee Relations application

MODULE COMPONENTS

All Module Components (MC) must adhere to the following naming convention:

- ❑ The name must include the alias of the base table name upon which the module is based.

Example: INV is the MC name for a component based on the Invoices table

- ❑ If there will be multiple components within a module using the same base table, then the name will include an underscore followed by an abbreviation of the purpose.

Example: INV_QRY is the MC name for a second component based on the Invoices table that will be query only

REUSABLE MODULE COMPONENTS

All Reusable Module Components (RMC) must adhere to the following naming convention:

- ❑ The name must include the base table name and a prefix of R_

Example: R_Invoice

- ❑ If there will be multiple reusable components with different layout styles, then the name will include an underscore followed by one of these abbreviations:

  ST = Spread table

  OB = Overflow area below

  OR = Overflow area right

  WL = Wrap line

Example: R_Invoice_ST

- ❑ If the display characteristics specify a number of rows, the name will include an underscore followed by that number, otherwise the word "MAX" will be included

Example: R_Invoice_ST_MAX or R_Invoice_ST_6

- ❑ If a RMC is "query only" then the name will include an underscore followed by the letter "Q" (_Q), if it allows insert then use "I", if update use U, if delete then D. If all of these are used then add nothing.

Examples: R_Invoice_ST_MAX_Q, R_Invoice_ST_MAX_QIU

- ❑ If there are multiple RMCs with the same base table and some contain all the possible enterable columns, these RMC's will include and underscore and the word ALL. If there is only one RMC for a base table, no notation is required.

Example: R_Invoice_ST_MAX_ALL

- ❑ If the RMC name becomes too long (over 20 characters), then use the table alias instead

Example: R_Invoice_line_items_ST_MAX_ALL becomes R_ILI_ST_MAX_ALL

- ❑ If the RMC is not based on a table (i.e., a control block) it will be named with the prefix CTL followed by a string that represents its basic functionality or usage.

Example: R_CTL_calc_totals

- ❑ If the RMC is based on a PL/SQL package then it will be named with PLSQL followed by the name of the package.
  Example: R_PLSQL_MyPackage

MODULE COMPONENT ELEMENTS

All Module Components Elements must adhere to the following naming conventions:

Item Groups

- ❑ Item groups may be named to represent a functional grouping of data. The name may be multiple words with no underscores between them.

Example: The item group encompasses columns that make up the information for a mailing address so the item group is named MAILING ADDRESS

- ❑ If the layout item group is a horizontal item group, the name will prefixed with an "H". If it is a vertical item group, it will be prefixed with a 'V'. (Additional prefixes may be developed to represent the additional functions for which item groups are used in reports generation.)

Example: H MAILING ADDRESS is a horizontal item group containing columns for a mailing address

- ❑ If the purpose of the item group is to enable the generation of a specific layout then the name will be LAYOUT #, where # represents an integer.

Example: V LAYOUT 1 is a vertical item group used specifically for layout generation

- If nested item groups are used to achieve a complex layout then the name of the nested item groups will be NESTED LAYOUT #-#, where the first # represents the number associated with the parent layout group and the second # is a sequential integer within that group

Example: H NESTED LAYOUT 1-2 represents the 2nd nested item group within the item group named LAYOUT 1. It is a horizontal item group.

Example: V NESTED LAYOUT 1-2-1 represents the 1st nested item group within the 2nd nested item group within the item group named LAYOUT 1. It is a vertical item group.

Unbound Items

- All unbound items will be prefixed with UB and an underscore followed by text that describes its function. Approved abbreviations and acronyms may be used as necessary.

Example: UB_TOTAL_PRICE is an unbound item that will contain the results of a calculation for total price

SQL Query Sets

- All SQL Query sets will be named with the word UNION and the table alias of the base table usage in the module component.

Example: UNOIN EMP is the name of the query set containing a reference to the EMPLOYEES base table usage

Navigation Action Items (Buttons)

- Navigation action items will be named using a prefix of NA followed by the module component name followed by the target module component or module name with an underscore in between

Example: NA_CUST_FNAPF010 indicates a button to navigate from the CUST component in the current module to the module FNAPF010

Custom Action Items (Buttons)

- Custom action items will be named using the prefix CA followed by text that describes the function of the action item. Approved abbreviations and acronyms may be used as necessary.

Example: CA_CALC_TOTAL indicates a button that when pressed will cause a total to be calculated

Application Logic Event Code Segments

- ❑ All code segments entered to implement custom application logic will be named using a text string that defines the purpose of the code. Approved abbreviations and acronyms may be used as necessary.

Example: Use parameter value when present

Application Logic Named Routines

- ❑ Named routines will conform to the same standard set forth for PL/SQL procedures

API Logic Code Segments

- ❑ API Logic code segments will conform to the same standard set forth for Application Logic code segments

NAMED PREFERENCE SETS

All preference sets will be named with one of the following prefixes that indicate at what level the preference set is intended to be used:

AP_ = Application

MD_ = Module

MC_ = Module Component

IG = Item Group

IT = Item

The rest of the preference set name should use abbreviations to describe the purpose of the set or the major preference settings for the preference set.

For example, if you have an *item group* (IG) preference set that sets the preferences to create a horizontal item group, allowing 2 items in each row, with a rectangle decoration and left justified title, you could name it "IG_H_2_REC_LEFT".

If you have a preference set that is intended to be used for *modules* (MD) that consist of only tab canvases, you could name it "MD_TAB_ONLY".

TABLES

Table Names

Table names must be the plural of the Entity names, with the spaces translated to underscores. If the resulting name has more than 26 characters, see **Appendix A** and **Appendix B** for a list you can use to acceptably shorten the table name.

Table names will not be prefixed with an application abbreviation unless that prefix is inherited as part of the original entity name.

Table Alias

All tables must have an alias. The alias must conform to the same standard set forth for entity short names. If the table is based on an entity, then the alias must be the same as the entity short name.

Table Comment

To insure that appropriate meta-data is included in the Oracle data dictionary, all tables must have a comment entered into Designer. This comment should describe the basic information stored in the table.

COLUMNS

A column name must be the same as the name of the attribute from which the column was mapped, with the spaces translated to underscores. The column name must not be a plural. If the resulting name has more than 30 characters, use the approved acronyms and abbreviations in the appendices to shorten it.

If the column is not based on an attribute, then it should be named using the naming standard set forth for attributes with the exception that an underscore is used instead of a space between segments.

Column names will **not** be prefixed with the table short name. This can be controlled via a checkbox in the 'Setting' dialog on the Database Design Transformer.

The Database Design Transformer will also prefix foreign key column names with the parent entity's short name by default ***unless the check box for this option is unchecked*** in the 'Settings' dialog. Since the standard for naming primary UID attributes already includes using the entity name or entity short name, this option must be de-selected or the resulting foreign key column will be redundantly prefixed.

CONSTRAINTS

Constraint names will conform to the default Designer constraint naming conventions that are automatically created when using the Database Design Transformer. Any manually created constraints must conform to this standard.

Primary Key Constraints

The naming convention used by Designer is:

Primary key = <table alias>_PK

Example: For the table CUSTOMER with the alias CUST the primary key will be:

CUST_PK

Unique Key Constraints

As for unique key constraints, the naming convention used by Designer is:

Unique key = <table alias>_<UID Name>_UK

where the UID Name is the name specified for a secondary unique identifier on the entity.

Example: The table called ORDERS (ORD) has two unique identifiers named ORD2 and ORD3. The unique key constraints will be named:

ORD_ORD2_UK

ORD_ORD3_UK

Foreign Key Constraints

Designer will generate one of two possible names depending on the number of relationships between two entities. Foreign key names are usually generated with the following algorithm:

Foreign key = <table alias of the target table>_<table alias of the originating key>_FK

Example:

ORDER _LINES (ORDLIN) >------------------------ ORDERS (ORD)

The foreign key constraint on ORDER_LINES will have the foreign key constraint name generated as ORDLIN_ORD_FK.

However, if a table has multiple foreign keys to one other single table, then the algorithm for the first foreign key constraint will be the same as above. However, the second constraint with be generated as follows:

Foreign key = <table alias of the target table>_<table alias of the originating key>_relationship name_FK

Where 'relationship name' is the text associated with the relationship as depicted on the logical model.

Example:

```
              shipped from
ORDERS >------------------------ LOCATIONS (LOC)
   (ORD) >------------------------ LOCATIONS
               returned to
```

The foreign key constraints on ORDERS will have the foreign key constraint names generated as:

ORD_LOC_FK

ORD_LOC_RETURNED_TO_FK

For the sake of clarity, in this case the first FK constraint should be renamed to:

ORD_LOC_SHIPPED_FROM_FK

Check Constraints

This standard applies to table level check constraints as defined in the Design Editor.. The naming convention is:

Check constraint = <table alias> _ *what is being checked_CHK*

Where 'what is being checked' is either a column name or some abbreviated text to describe the condition being validated.

Example: The table called Location_History (LOCHIST) has a check constraint to enforce an arc relationship. The check constraint will be named:

LOCHIST_ ARC_ CHK

Example: The table called CP_X_Competitors (COMPET) has a check constraint on the column END_DATE to insure it is greater than the start date. The check constraint will be named:

COMPET_ END_DATE_CHK

INDEXES

Primary and UniqueKey Indexes

Designer does not create primary or unique key indexes. Oracle7 and newer versions implicitly create the index when creating primary and unique key constraints in the database. Do not create primary key indexes in the repository as this will result in problems when running the DDL scripts generated from Designer.

Foreign Key Indexes

The Oracle Designer naming convention for foreign key indexes is the foreign key constraint name with "_I" appended at the end. Designer will automatically create foreign key indexes through the Database Design Transformer if it is specified in the run options.

Foreign key index = <foreign key constraint name>_I

Example: For the foreign key ORDLIN_ORD_FK, the resulting foreign key index name would be ORDLIN_ORD_FK_I

In the case where multiple foreign keys were generated, and one was subsequently changed, it will be necessary to manually modify the associated index name so that it matches the renamed constraint.

Example:
Designer created:

ORD_LOC_FK with index ORD_LOC_FK_I

You modified the constraint to:

ORD_LOC_SHIPPED_FROM_FK

So you will need to modify the index to be:

ORD_LOC_SHIPPED_FROM_FK_I

Non-Key Indexes

For indexes created manually that are not related to any keys, the naming convention will be:

Non-key index = <table alias>_<column name>_NU_I

Where 'NU' stands for non-unique.

If the index to be created is a bit-mapped index then the standard is:

Non-key index = <table alias>_<column name>_BM_I

Where 'BM' stands for bit-mapped.

If the index is on multiple columns, then <column name> will be the first column in the series.

Example: To improve query performance, an index on the column Employee Name in table Employee (EMP) is created. The index name will be:

EMP_Employee_Name_NU_I

SEQUENCE GENERATORS

In most cases sequence names will be created as follows:

Sequence = <table name>_SEQ

Where <table name> is the table for which the sequence will provide values to the primary key.

Example: CUSTOMERS_SEQ

Additionally, sequences may need to reflect functionality because a single sequence may be used with multiple tables. In this case, the standard is:

Sequence = <common functionality>_SEQ

Example:

Three tables are generated from sub-types of the entity MODEL. They each represent a different type of model but to avoid potential key conflicts, the decision is to use one sequence for all the primary keys because they will all be mapped to a common cross-reference table. So the sequence name is MODEL_ID_SEQ since the sequence will generically represent a model identifier.

VIEWS

All views must be named as follows:

View name = V_<table name>_<criteria>

Where the table name is the name of the root (or 'master') table the view is based on. The *criteria* qualifier is optional .

The maximum length for a view name will be 26. If the name of the view exceeds 26, then use the table alias, abbreviations and acronyms as needed. View names must be plural just like tables.

Example:

V_EMPLOYEES is a view on the EMPLOYEES table

The qualifier, if used, should give the end users a clear idea of the purpose and contents of the view. Use the *criteria* qualifier if

1. Using the table name alone is not unique
2. The view is based on a join of 2 or more tables
3. The view contains a where clause
4. The view is unusually complex.
5. The view is a summary.

Examples:

V_ACTIVE_CUSTOMERS provides information on only active CUSTOMERS.

V_EMPLOYEES_DEPARTMENTS is a view joining the EMPLOYEES table to the DEPARTMENTS table.

V_CUSTOMER_COMPLAINTS provides information about CUSTOMERS and their NOTES of type 'complaint'.

V_TOTAL_CUSTOMER_SALES provides summary information on customer sales activity

PL/SQL PACKAGES

Packages will be named according to this standard:

Package name = <app>_<description >

Where <app> is the Designer application abbreviation and <description> is a one or two word explanation of the purpose. Select a description that will help simplify the naming of procedures stored within the package.

Additional restrictions are:

1. **Stored Package** (i.e. Packages stored in the database) names must be 24 characters or less.
2. **Library Packages**, (i.e. Packages stored within a Oracle Developer library file) the package name must be unique within 27 characters.

Example: FN_CALC is a package containing various calculation routines for the Financial application system

PL/SQL PROCEDURES

Packaged Procedures

Packaged Procedures will be named using the following standard:

Procedure name = verb or noun or both

Where the verb or noun is a brief explanation of the purpose of the procedure. Do not reuse the application abbreviation or any part of the package name in the procedure name.

Example: GROSS_PROFIT is a procedure to calculate the companies gross profit.

Stand-Alone Procedures

Stand-alone procedures will be named using the following standard:

Procedure name = <app>_<verb or noun or both>

Where the verb or noun is a brief explanation of the purpose of the procedure. The <app> is the application abbreviation of the owning Designer application.

Example: ER_TERMINATE_EMPLOYEE is a stand-alone procedure for the Employee Relations applications that processes an employee termination.

PL/SQL FUNCTIONS

All PL/SQL functions must be sub-programs within a PL/SQL package.

All PL/SQL function names will conform to the following standard:

Function = f_<noun or verb phrase>

Where the verb or noun phrase is a brief explanation of the purpose of the function. Do not reuse the application abbreviation or any part of the package name in the procedure name.

Precede the <noun or verb phrase> with "f" so that there are no conflicts with other PL/SQL program units (like procedures).

Example: f_get_header_id is a function that returns the header id column

Example: f_check_total_units is a function that returns TRUE if the total unit count is greater than zero.

CURSORS

All cursors defined for PL/SQL programs will conform to the following standard:

Cursor = c_<cursor name>

Where <cursor name> is a logical, meaningful, and concise name representing the function the cursor serves.

Precede the <cursor name> with "c" so that there are no conflicts with other PL/SQL program units (like functions).

Example: c_get_header_id is a cursor that selects the header id column into a variable

Example: c_check_total_units is a cursor that checks to insure the total count is greater than zero.

PL/SQL PROGRAM DATA

Arguments

All arguments for PL/SQL packages and procedures will conform to the following standard:

Argument = P_<argument name>

Where <argument name> is a logical, meaningful, and concise name representing the value that will be passed to the program unit. Where the argument will be used to hold the value of a column in a SQL statement, then <argument name> must be the same as the column name.

Precede the <argument name> with "P" so that there are no conflicts with database object names or confusion as to which are PL/SQL arguments and which are database objects. All arguments must be in lower case, excluding the prefix.

Example: P_header_id

Variables

All PL/SQL program variables will conform to the following standard:

Variable = v_<variable name>

Where <variable name> should be a logical, meaningful, and concise name representing the value the variable will hold. Where the variable will be used to hold the value of a column in a SQL statement, then <variable name> must be the same as the column name.

Precede the <variable name> with "v" so that there are no conflicts with database object names or confusion as to which are PL/SQL variables and which are database objects. All variables must be in lower case, including the prefix.

Example: v_header_id

Constants

All PL/SQL program constants will conform to the following standard:

Constant = c_<constant name>

Where <constant name> should be a logical, meaningful, and concise name representing the use of the value the constant will hold. Where the constant will be used to hold a value to be assigned to a column in a SQL statement, then <constant name> must be the same as the column name.

Precede the <constant name> with "c" so that there are no conflicts with database object names or confusion as to which are PL/SQL constants and which are database objects or variables. All constants must be in lower case, including the prefix.

Example: c_header_id

Global Variables (forms only)

All Oracle Forms global variables will conform to the following standard:

Variable = global.<variable name>

Where <variable name> should be a logical, meaningful, and concise name representing the value the variable will hold. Where the variable will be used to hold the value of a field in the data block, then <variable name> must be the same as the field name.

Global variables must always be referenced with ':GLOBAL.' preceding the variable name. Therefore, no additional prefix is required to distinguish global variables from local or standard variables. In order to avoid confusion, do not use the same name for both a global and a local variable.

Example: header_id (i.e., :global.header_id)

DATABASE TRIGGERS

All database trigger names and trigger logic definitions will conform to the following standard:

Trigger = <table alias>_ <when><type><level>_<further description>_T

Where <table alias> is the alias of the table on which the trigger is based and <type> is the action performed by the trigger. Valid types are: Insert, Update, and Delete. <Level> indicates if the trigger is fired for every row in the table or once for every DML executed. <When> refers to whether the trigger is executed before or after an insert, update, or delete. The rest of the name, which must end with an underscore and a "T", is to describe the purpose of the trigger.

Types should be abbreviated:

- Insert = I
- Update = U
- Delete = D

When should be abbreviated:

- Before = B
- After = A

Level should be abbreviated:

- Row = R
- Statement = S

Examples:

CPCAI_BUR_SAVE_LOC_T = A before update trigger to save previous location information for every row updated

CPCAI_AIUDS_CHG_STATUS_T = An after insert, update or delete trigger to change the status code in an audit table after each DML statement

BUILD

This section describes naming standards for objects that will be encountered or defined in the "Build" phase of application development. These objects are primarily database objects therefore the naming of these objects was developed with the cooperation of *company-name's* lead Database Administrator (DBA). Any deviations from these standards must be approved by the DBA

DATABASE

The database name should reflect the very broad domain of the database. Examples would be PROD, DEV, and TEST.

- ❑ Database names should not indicate version (of application/domain/software).
- ❑ Database names should refer to the domain of the data rather than the application or project. Databases are generally shared by multiple projects and, if they are not, application/project names are likely to change over time.

TABLESPACE

A tablespace name should reflect the contents of the tablespace. Some standard tablespace names are USER_DATA, TEMP, SYSTEM, RBS, and TOOLS. These are usually named during a standard Oracle installation and should not be changed.

Tablespace names that are reserved for application specific table data and indexes should reflect the following information:

- ❑ Ownership
- ❑ The growth pattern of the database objects
- ❑ The type of database objects it contains (i.e. data or index)

Tablespaces can be in one of many ranges of growth patterns. For tables/indexes which have a limited range of growth patterns, the range can be (s)mall, (m)edium, and (l)arge. For tables/indexes needing a wider range of growth patterns, the range can be 1–9, with "1" being the smallest growth. A decision must be made on which range of growth patterns is needed for the database. This decision should be based on detailed analysis of the growth patterns of the tables and indexes. Once the growth pattern range has been decided, then the growth pattern range and size should be indicated in the tablespace name. The tablespace name should also indicate whether it contains table data or index data. The tablespace name should be constructed as follows:

<3-char abbr. of THE OWNER ACCOUNT NAME>_<growth pattern range/size>_<object type>

Where <object type> is DATA or IDX

Example 1:

Tables are owned by PERSONNEL

Growth pattern range is limited and contains S, M, L

Object type is Table Data

TABLESPACE NAME

PER_S_DATA

PER_M_DATA

PER_L_DATA

Tables are owned by PERSONNEL

Growth pattern range is limited and contains S, M, L

Object type is Index data

TABLESPACE NAME

PER_S_IDX

PER_M_IDX

PER_L_IDX

Example 2:

Tables are owned by PERSONNEL

Growth pattern range is wide and contains 1,2,3,4,5,6,7,8,9

Object type is Table Data

TABLESPACE NAME

PER_1_DATA

PER_2_DATA

PER_5_DATA

PER_9_DATA

Tables are owned by PERSONNEL

Growth pattern range is wide and contains 1,2,3,4,5,6,7,8,9

Object type is Index Data

TABLESPACE NAME

PER_2_IDX

PER_3_ID

PER_9_IDX

Single Table Tablespace

In a very large database (VLDB), such as a data warehouse, it may be necessary to assign certain tables to their own tablespace. **This is a decision that should be made by the DBA.**

In this case the naming standard will be:

<Table alias>_DATA

Example: Table name: ORDER_SUMMARIES

Alias: OS

Tablespace name: OS_DATA

In the case where table partitioning is being used and the system requirements indicate that each partition should have its own tablespace, then the standard is modified to include a suffix on the table alias to indicate the partitioned data that is included.

Example: Table name: ORDER_SUMMARIES

Alias: OS

Partitioned by: Month and year

Tablespace name: OS_JAN98_DATA

Single Index Tablespace

In the same manner, it may be necessary to create a tablespace for a very large index. Again this is a call for the DBA to make. In this case the naming standard will be:

<Index name>_IDX

Where <index name> is the actual name of the index being stored.

Example: Index name: ORD_LOC_FK_I

Tablespace name:ORD_LOC_FK_IDX

TABLESPACE DATAFILE NAME

Tablespaces can contain anywhere from 1 to many data files. The names for the data files should reflect the tablespace name, an incremented number, the instance name, and the database file extension (.dbf or .ora). The tablespace data file name should be constructed as follows:

<Tablespace name>_<n><SID>.dbf

Where <n> is an integer, starting from 1 and <SID> is the database instance name.

Example 1:

Tablespace name = PER_S_DATA
Number of data files = 3
Instance name = ORCL

Data file names:

per_s_data01orcl.dbf
per_s_data02orcl.dbf
per_s_data03orcl.dbf

Example 2:

Tablespace name = PER_3_IDX
Number of data files = 2

Data file names:

per_3_idx01orcl.dbf
per_3_idx02orcl.dbf

ROLLBACK SEGMENTS

The naming convention for rollback segments is:

Rollback = <size>_RBS<number>

Where:

- <number> is a sequentially increasing integer, starting at 01. The sequence is specific to the "size" type of the rollback segment
- <size> is one of: SM(all), MED(ium), LA(rge), and VL(very large)

Examples:

SM_RBS01
SM_RBS02

MED_RBS01
VL_RBS02

CLUSTER

Clusters should follow this naming convention:

Cluster = <Table1 alias>_<Table2 alias>_<Common Column>_C

Where 'C' is for cluster and <common column> is the name of the column the cluster is built on.

Example:

Table 1 name = EMPLOYEES

Alias = EMP

Table 2 name = DEPARTMENT

Alias = DEPT

Common Column = DEPTNO

Cluster name = EMP_DEPT_DEPTNO_C

SNAPSHOTS

There are two kinds of snapshots that can be defined in Designer; simple and complex. Simple snapshots (ones accessing only one table) will be named in this way:

Snapshot name = SS_<table name>

Where 'SS' represents 'snapshot' and the table name is the name of the table or view the snapshot is based on.

The maximum length for a snapshot name will be 26. If the name exceeds 26, then use the table alias, abbreviations and acronyms as needed. Snapshot names must be plural just like tables.

Example:

SS_EMPLOYEES is a snapshot of the EMPLOYEES table

Complex snapshots will be named in this way:

Snapshot name = SS_<table name>_<criteria>

The qualifier, if used, should give the end users a clear idea of the purpose and contents of the snapshot. Use the *criteria* qualifier if

1. Using the table name alone is not unique
2. The snapshot is based on a join of 2 or more tables

3. The snapshot contains a where clause
4. The snapshot is unusually complex.
5. The snapshot is a summary

Examples:

SS_ACTIVE_CUSTOMERS provides information on only active CUSTOMERS.

SS_EMPLOYEES_DEPARTMENTS is a snapshot joining the EMPLOYEES tables and the DEPARTMENTS table.

SS_CUSTOMER_COMPLAINTS provides information about CUSTOMERS and their NOTES of type 'complaint'.

SS_TOTAL_CUSTOMER_SALES provides summary information on customer sales activity.

USERS

ORACLE usernames will consist of the user's first initial and last name, with no space between.

Examples: LPHILLIP, RJAHR, BJOHNSON

ROLES

Application specific roles should be named in this manner:

Role = <Application abbreviation>_<Access level>

The access levels must be determined by the Application Administrator.

Examples of access levels might be ADMIN, USER, and REPORT. So examples of role names might be:

PM_ADMIN
PM_USER
ER_REPORT
AC_USER

PROFILE

Profile names should describe the interaction of the ORACLE user with the database. The DBA and the Application Administrator should determine profile definitions together.

Some recommended profile names are:

- USER — Profile for end users. May be broken into multiple profiles if application warrants different resource limits for different types of users.
- SUPPORT — Profile for developers supporting the application.
- DBA— Profile for DBAs.

If the profile is application specific, then it should be prefixed with the application abbreviation.

Example: FN_USER

SYNONYMS

The naming convention for synonyms is:

Synonym name = *table or view* name

Synonyms, whether public or private should always match the underlying object which the synonym is referencing.

CONTROL FILE

The convention for a control file name is:

Control file = CTL<n><SID>.ora

Where <n> is an integer, starting from 1 and <SID> is the database instance name.

Examples:

CTL1ORCL.ORA
CTL2ORCL.ORA

DATABASE LINKS

A database link should be the same as the name of the remote database to which it points. The naming convention for a database link is:

Link = <remote database>

Where:

<remote database> is the name of the remote database

Example: ORCL_DEN

SCHEMA

In Oracle Designer a schema is represented as a set of objects owned by a user within a database. As such no additional naming convention is required.

DIAGRAMMING GUIDELINES

GENERAL

Introduction

This section of the standards document specifies standard practices for elements and characteristics of Diagramming. By implementing consistent diagramming practices confusion will be minimized when interpreting diagrams and attempting to understand business rules.

Objectives

The intent of this section is to establish Diagramming standards and guidelines that will accomplish the following:

- Increase consistency
- Improve readability
- Improve pattern recognition.

Applicability

This document applies to all Custom development.

References

Some layout methodologies presented here are based on information from the Oracle book *CASE*Method Entity Relationship Modelling* by Richard Barker.

Document Organization

This document is organized into six distinct sections:

- Process Model Diagrams
- Function Hierarchy Diagrams
- Entity Relationship Diagrams
- Data Flow Diagrams
- Matrix Diagrams
- Server Model Diagrams

BUSINESS PROCESS MODEL (BPM) DIAGRAMS

These guidelines should be implemented when creating BPM Diagrams via the Oracle Designer Business Process Modeler Diagrammer.

Multiple Modular Diagrams

Rather then creating one large business process diagram, create many sub diagrams. This will eliminate the need to maintain one large diagram that will over time become unreadable and unmanageable. Also, each process step of a business process diagram will appear as a function on a function hierarchy diagram.

Avoid Overcrowding

Do not crowd many processes onto a single business process diagram. In general, one diagram should contain no more than six to nine process steps.

If a single diagram contains more than nine process steps, consider drilling down on one of the more complex process steps into a new diagram.

Display a Legend on the Diagram

Under *File-> Summary Information*, check the following to be displayed:

- ❏ Title
- ❏ Created
- ❏ Last Modified
- ❏ Author
- ❏ Application.

The legend must appear under and to the right of the Unspecified business unit.

While the diagram name may be somewhat cryptic, the diagram title should be indicative of the business area being modeled and be understandable by business users.

Example:

Diagram Name = INTERVIEW APPLICANTS

Title = Interview Applicants Process

BPM Diagram Layout Convention

In this section, please refer to the example diagram; Figure BPM-1 Example of correct use of standards.

Following are the guidelines to be used for determining the layout of a BPM diagram:

Diagrams should include:

- ❑ Major process steps (i.e., no functions)
- ❑ Flows (i.e., data, material or temporal)
- ❑ Flow names
- ❑ Process labels
- ❑ Triggers and outcomes
- ❑ Stores (data and material)

Process Step Placement

- ❑ Place process steps in the business unit's swim lane that performs it.
- ❑ When possible, place process steps to the right of a dependent process step rather than under it. This will reduce the swim lane height.
- ❑ Place process steps that are associated with a trigger one extra grid-snap to the right of the business unit. This will make the printout more readable.
- ❑ Before creating a new process step, always use the *Edit->Include* facility first to prevent duplicate processes.

Drawing Flows

- ❑ Face arrowheads to the right if at all possible.
- ❑ Avoid line crossings if at all possible.
- ❑ Before creating a new flow, always use the *Edit->Include* facility first to prevent creation of duplicate flows.

Flow name placement

- ❑ When flow names are used, place flow names in the middle of the flow.

Label placement

Place the label of the process above and to the left of the process step using this method:

1. Copy label to the annotation text field, set annotation type to 'TEXT' in multimedia tab.
2. Check Display Annotation in *Options->Custimize->Graghics* menu item.

Material Store placement

- ❑ Before creating a new material store, always use the *Edit->Include* facility first to prevent creation of duplicate material stores.
- ❑ Place material stores in the Business Units swim lane to show that they are responsible for the material.

Data Store placement

- ❑ Before creating a new data store, always use the *Edit->Include* facility first to prevent creation of duplicate data stores.
- ❑ Place data stores in the Unspecified swim lane.

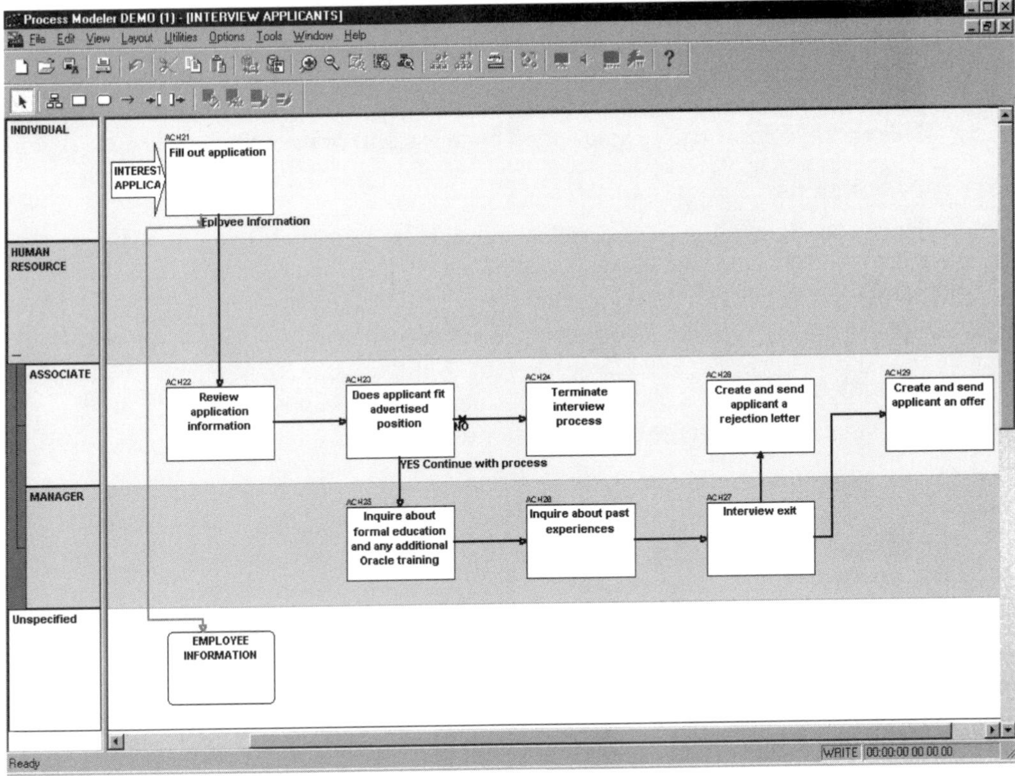

FIGURE BPM.1 Example of correct use of standards.

Consolidating Diagrams

Consolidate Diagrams frequently using *Edit->Requery*

In general, it is a good practice to consolidate a diagram each time you open it to ensure that you are working with current information. At a minimum, diagrams should be consolidated when there is a change to the Designer Repository relative to business functions, flows, stores, events (triggers) and business units. **If you wish to keep historical views of diagrams, save them under another name and do not consolidate them.**

Delete Unneeded Diagrams

If a diagram is no longer needed, delete it from the Repository.

Color Coding Diagrams

Use color coding or shading to distinguish the following:

- ❑ Process steps that are drilled down (open down) into sub diagrams.
- ❑ Different type of flows (Data flows from material flows)
- ❑ Alternating business units and/or swim lanes

Do not use colors on the Unspecified business unit or its swim lane.

Annotations

Use annotation in the form of notes or graphics to facilitate communication.

Specific Types

Set the specific type for all objects in the BPM whenever the type is known.

Display Modes

Display Diagrams in the following modes:

- ❑ **Symbol Mode:** Use Symbol mode for simple diagramming. This mode is appropriate for presentations to the non-technical business community
- ❑ **Enhanced Symbol Mode:** Use Enhanced Symbol mode for flowcharting. This mode is appropriate for presentations to a more technical audience
- ❑ **Iconic Mode:** Use Iconic mode to display associated icons for process steps, stores, and flows. This mode is appropriate for upper management and end-user presentations

Visualizing a Process

The BPM Diagrammer in Designer has a number of other options that can be used to enhance the presentation of a diagram. Below are some additional recommendations on the use of these features.

Images
Use images only if it facilitates in communication.

Video
Use video clips only when it facilitates in communication.

Sound
Use sound (digital recordings) only when it facilitates in communication.

Animation
Use animation only when it facilitates in communication.

FUNCTION HIERARCHY DIAGRAMS (FHD)

These guidelines should be implemented when creating Function Hierarchy Diagrams via the Oracle Designer Function Hierarchy Diagrammer.

Multiple Modular Diagrams

Rather then creating just one function hierarchy diagram, create many sub diagrams.

- ❑ Create one diagram that will function as a view of the entire enterprise.
- ❑ Create a diagram for each of the major processes that are sub-function of the root function.

Avoid Overcrowding

Do not crowd many processes onto a single function hierarchy diagram. In general, one diagram should contain no more than twenty functions.

If a single diagram contains more than twenty functions, consider drilling down on one of the more complex process steps into a new diagram.

Display a Legend on the Diagram

Under *File-> Summary Information,* check the following to be displayed:

- ❑ Diagram
- ❑ Title
- ❑ Created
- ❑ Last Modified
- ❑ Author
- ❑ Application System

Display the legend in the upper left-hand corner of the diagram.

While the diagram name should be the same as the context function label, the diagram title should be indicative of the functional area being modeled and be understandable by business users.

Example:

Diagram Name = ANY COMPANY

Title = "Any Company" Enterprise Function Model

FHD Layout Conventions

This section lists some layout conventions that are helpful when creating diagrams. These conventions aid in making the diagrams easier for you to print and the business community to understand. The three layout styles are shown in figures FHD-1 through FHD-3.

Horizontal Layout is the default layout. This style shows each level of the hierarchy in a horizontal row

Vertical Layout displays each level of the hierarchy in a vertical line, with each level indented slightly to the right of the one above it.

Hybrid Layout is a combination of vertical and horizontal layouts that show parent functions in a horizontal layout and elementary (childless) functions in a vertical layout. This style is the best of the three options for reading and printing multilevel hierarchies

In most cases, use the hybrid option as it uses the diagram space most efficiently. But this is really most dependent on how deep your function model is. If it is shallow and wide, often the horizontal layout will also look good. In general the vertical style should be avoided unless the model (or model segment) is very small.

Consolidating Diagrams

Consolidate Diagrams frequently using *Edit->Requery*

In general, it is a good practice to consolidate a diagram each time you open it to ensure that you only work with current information. At a minimum, diagrams should be consolidated when there is a change to the Designer Repository relative to business functions. **If you wish to keep historical views of diagrams, save them under another name and do not consolidate them.**

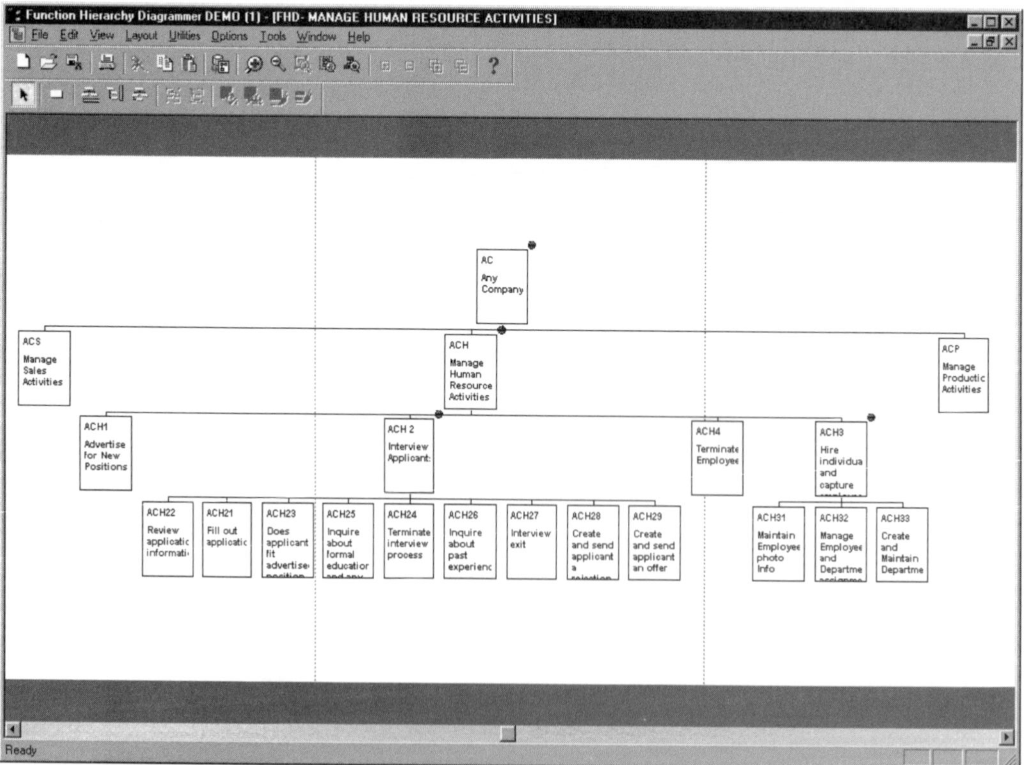

FIGURE FHD.1 Example FHD displayed in horizontal layout style.

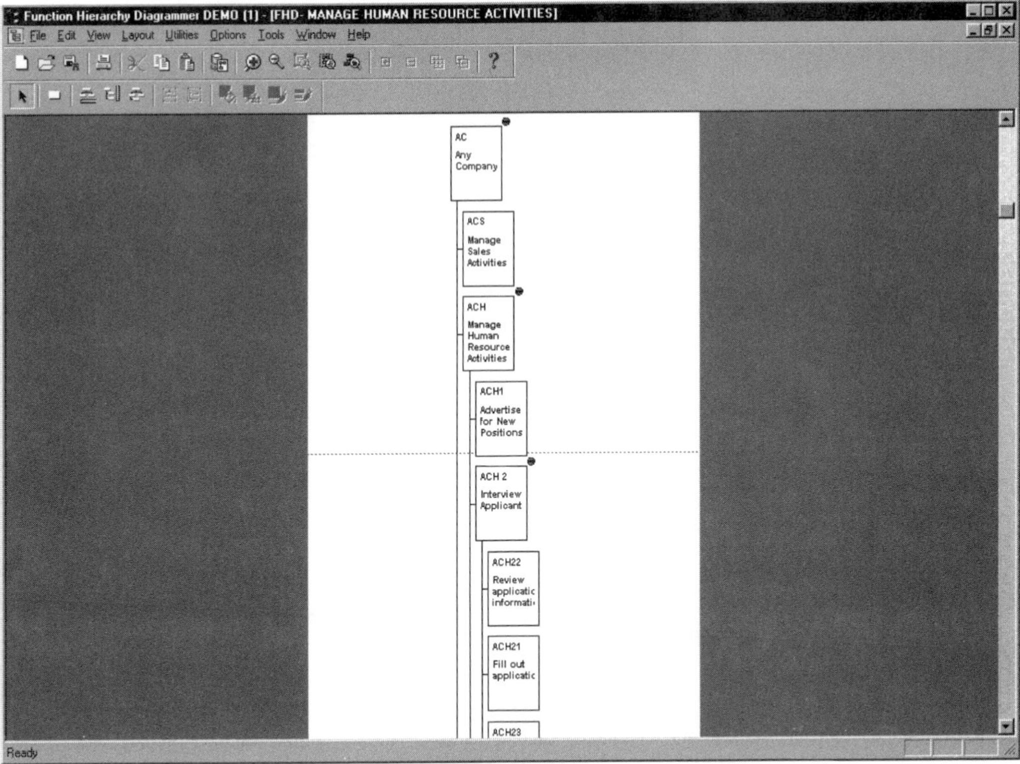

FIGURE FHD.2 Example FHD displayed in vertical layout style.

Delete Unneeded Diagrams

If a diagram is no longer needed, delete it from the Repository.

Color Coding Diagrams

Use color coding or shading to distinguish the following:

- ❑ Elementary functions, functions that have been decomposed to their lowest level
- ❑ External functions, functions that are performed by external organizations but may have an effect on our organizations processes
- ❑ Functions which are the basis of other diagrams (i.e., indicate the ability to open down)

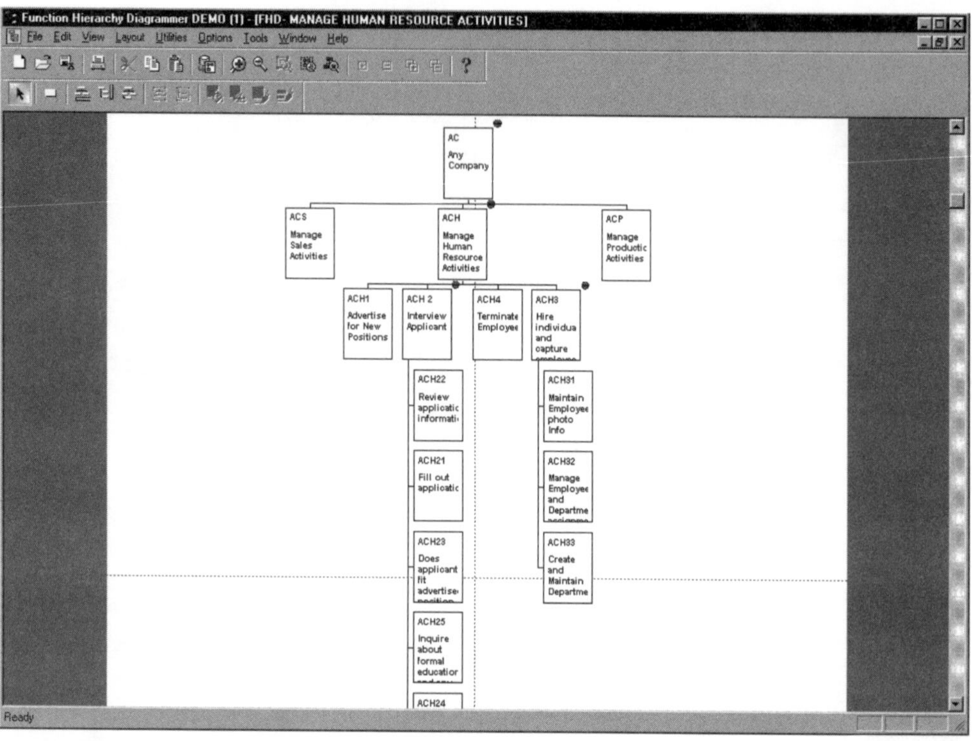

FIGURE FHD.3 Example FHD displayed in hybrid layout style.

ENTITY RELATIONSHIP (ER) DIAGRAMS

These guidelines should be implemented when creating ER Diagrams via the Oracle Designer Entity Relationship Diagrammer.

Multiple Modular Diagrams

Rather than creating one large diagram, create many smaller diagrams. This will eliminate the need to maintain one large diagram that will over time become unreadable, unmanageable, and overwhelming to non-technical users. If you need to answer questions such as, what entities are related to other entities, use the Repository Object Navigator or the Entity Definition report. Do not rely on one large diagram.

Diagram Correspondence to Business Model

Each diagram should correspond to a logical section of the overall business model. They could represent a specific business area or logical data view (In data warehousing terms these would be subject areas. For example; If you have a high level function called "Capture Customer Information", create a diagram that will depict the data needed to support that business function.

Do not include entities that are not needed to support that high level function. The entity CONTRACT should appear on a diagram called "Customer Contract" along with all the other entities to support the creation and administration of a Contract, but it may not be needed on a diagram showing customer invoicing.

Avoid Overcrowding

Do not crowd many entities onto a single diagram. In general, one diagram should contain no more than 15 to 20 entities.

If a single diagram contains more than 15 entities, consider a logical refinement (e.g., the CUSTOMER INFO diagram would be subdivided into two diagrams: CUSTOMER INFO1 and CUSTOMER INFO2).

Display a Legend on the Diagram

Under *File-> Summary Information,* check the following to be displayed Diagram, Title, Created, Last Modified, Author and Application.

While the diagram name may be somewhat cryptic, the diagram title should be indicative of the business area being modeled and be understandable by business users.

Example:

Diagram Name = ERD-CUST INFO

Title = Customer Definition Information.

ER Diagram Layout Convention #1

In this section, please refer to the example diagram; Figure ERD- Example of correct use of standards.

Following are the guidelines for to be used for determining the layout of an ER diagram:

Entity Placement

- ❑ Place fundamental entities to the right of the diagram
- ❑ Size entities to reduce clutter and provide clear paths for relationships.
- ❑ Always use the Edit->Include facility first to prevent duplicate entities and relationships.

Drawing Relationships

- ❑ Face crow's feet to the left (West).
- ❑ Avoid line crossings if at all possible.

- ❑ Keep relationship lines horizontal; do not angle them.
- ❑ Minimize the use of bent lines (straight lines are preferred).

Relationship name placement

Place relationship names in a clockwise pattern.

Tip: In release 2.1.2, if you select a relationship and click on Autolayout, it will place the relationship name in the pattern mentioned above.

ER Diagram Layout Convention #2

In this section, please refer to the example diagram; Figure ERD-2 Example of correct use of standards.

Following are the guidelines for to be used for determining the layout of an ER diagram:

Entity Placement

- ❑ Place fundamental entities to the right or bottom of the diagram.
- ❑ Size entities to reduce clutter and provide clear paths for relationships.
- ❑ Always use the Edit->Include facility first to prevent duplicate entities and relationships.

Drawing Relationships

- ❑ Face crow's feet to the left (West) or up (North).
- ❑ Avoid line crossings if at all possible.

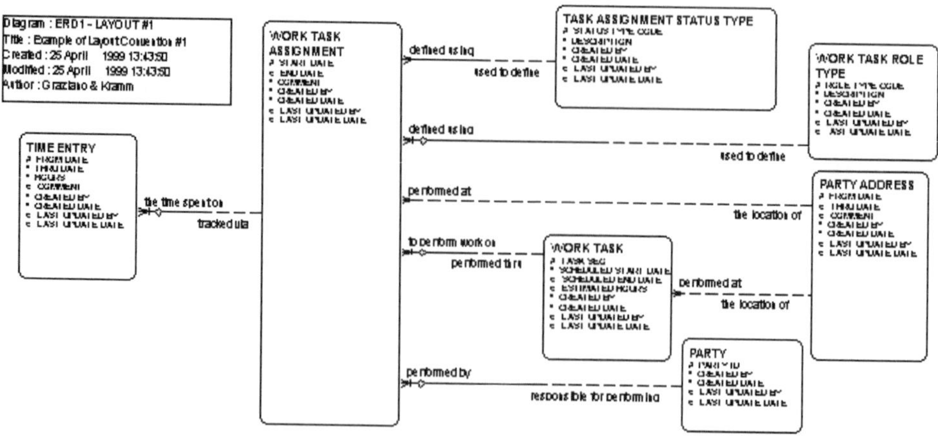

FIGURE ERD.1 Example of correct use of standards.

- ❑ Keep relationship lines horizontal or vertical; do not angle them.
- ❑ Minimize the use of bent lines (straight lines are preferred).

Relationship name placement
Place relationship names in a clockwise pattern.

Tip: In release 2.1.2, if you select a relationship and click on Autolayout, it will place the relationship name in the pattern mentioned above.

Consolidating Diagrams

Consolidate Diagrams frequently using *Edit ->Requery*.

In general, it is a good practice to consolidate a diagram each time you open it to ensure that you only work with current information. At a minimum, diagrams should be consolidated when there is a change to the Designer Repository relative to entities or relationships. **If you wish to keep historical views of diagrams, save them under another name and do not consolidate them.**

Delete Unneeded Diagrams

If a diagram is no longer needed, delete it from the Repository.

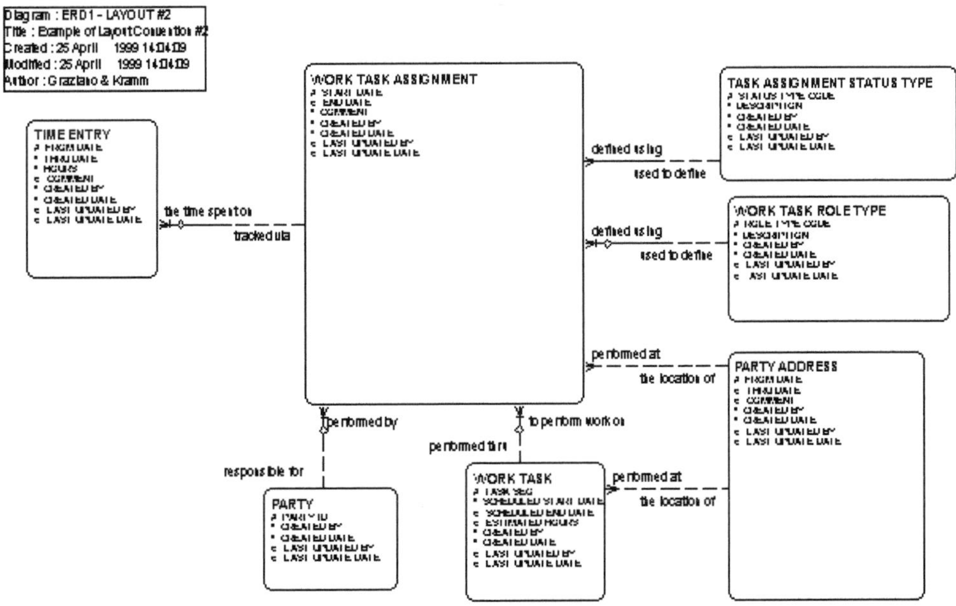

FIGURE ERD.2 Example of correct use of standards.

Drawing Relationships to Subtypes

When drawing relationships to a sub-type entity, insure that the line(s) between the sub-type and other entities are clearly connected to the sub-type and not its super-type.

Uses of sub-types imply that they will have attributes that are specific to them. If this is not the case, do not use sub-type constructs where simple examples will do. Instead, include examples as text on the drawing, where clarification is necessary.

Color Coding Diagrams

Use color coding or shading to distinguish the following:

- ❑ Entities shared from other applications
- ❑ Entities that appear on more than one diagram
- ❑ Code type entities
- ❑ Subject area groupings

View Options

Strategy phase diagrams should include:

- ❑ Fundamental and transaction entities (i.e., no codes)
- ❑ Relationship lines
- ❑ Relationship names

Strategy phase diagrams may also include (where defined):

- ❑ Primary UID attributes
- ❑ Primary UID relationship indicators

Analysis phase diagrams should include (where they exist):

- ❑ All entities including code types and intersection entities
- ❑ All attributes
- ❑ All relationships
- ❑ Relationship names
- ❑ Primary UID relationship indicators
- ❑ Relationship transferability indicators
- ❑ Hidden arcs

SERVER MODEL DIAGRAMS

These guidelines should be implemented when creating SM Diagrams via the Oracle Designer Design Editor.

Multiple Modular Diagrams

Rather than creating one large diagram, create many smaller diagrams. This will eliminate the need to maintain one large diagram that will over time become unreadable, unmanageable, and overwhelming to non-technical users. If you need to answer questions such as, what tables have foreign keys to other tables, use the Design Editor (usages nodes) or the Table Definition report. Do not rely on one large diagram.

Diagram Correspondence to Business Model

Each diagram should correspond to a logical section of the overall business model. They could represent a specific business area or logical data view (In data warehousing terms these would be subject areas. For example; If you have a high level function called "Capture Customer Information", create a diagram that will depict the data structures needed to support that business function.

Do not include entities that are not needed to support that high level function. The table CONTRACTS should appear on a diagram called "Customer Contract" along with all the other tables and views to support the creation and administration of a Contract, but it may not be needed on a diagram showing customer invoicing.

Avoid Overcrowding

Do not crowd many objects onto a single diagram. In general, one diagram should contain no more than 15 to 20 tables of views.

If a single diagram contains more than 15 objects, consider a logical refinement (e.g., the CUSTOMER INFO diagram would be subdivided into two diagrams: CUSTOMER INFO1 and CUSTOMER INFO2).

Display a Legend on the Diagram

Under *File-> Summary Information,* check the following to be displayed Diagram, Title, Created, Last Modified, Author and Application.

While the diagram name may be somewhat cryptic, the diagram title should be indicative of the business area being modeled and be understandable by business users.

Example:

Diagram Name = SMD-CUST INFO

Title = Detailed Customer Data.

Server Model Diagram Layout Convention #1

In this section, please refer to the example diagram: Figure SMD-1Example of correct use of standards.

Following are the guidelines for to be used for determining the layout of a SM diagram:

Object Placement

- Place fundamental objects to the right of the diagram.
- Size objects so all columns can be seen and provide clear paths for foreign keys.
- Always use the Edit->Include facility first to prevent creation of duplicate objects and constraints.

Drawing Foreign Key Constraints

- Face crow's feet to the left (West).
- Avoid line crossings if at all possible.
- Keep lines horizontal; do not angle them.
- Minimize the use of bent lines (straight lines are preferred).

Constraint name placement

Do not display foreign key constraint names.

Server Model Diagram Layout Convention #2

In this section, please refer to the example diagram; Figure SMD-2 Example of correct use of standards.

Following are the guidelines for to be used for determining the layout of a SM diagram:

Object Placement

- Place fundamental objects to the right of the diagram.
- Size objects so all columns can be seen and provide clear paths for foreign keys.
- Always use the Edit->Include facility first to prevent creation of duplicate objects and constraints.

Drawing Foreign Key Constraints

- Face crow's feet to the left (West) or up (North).
- Avoid line crossings if at all possible.
- Keep lines horizontal or vertical; do not angle them.
- Minimize the use of bent lines (straight lines are preferred).

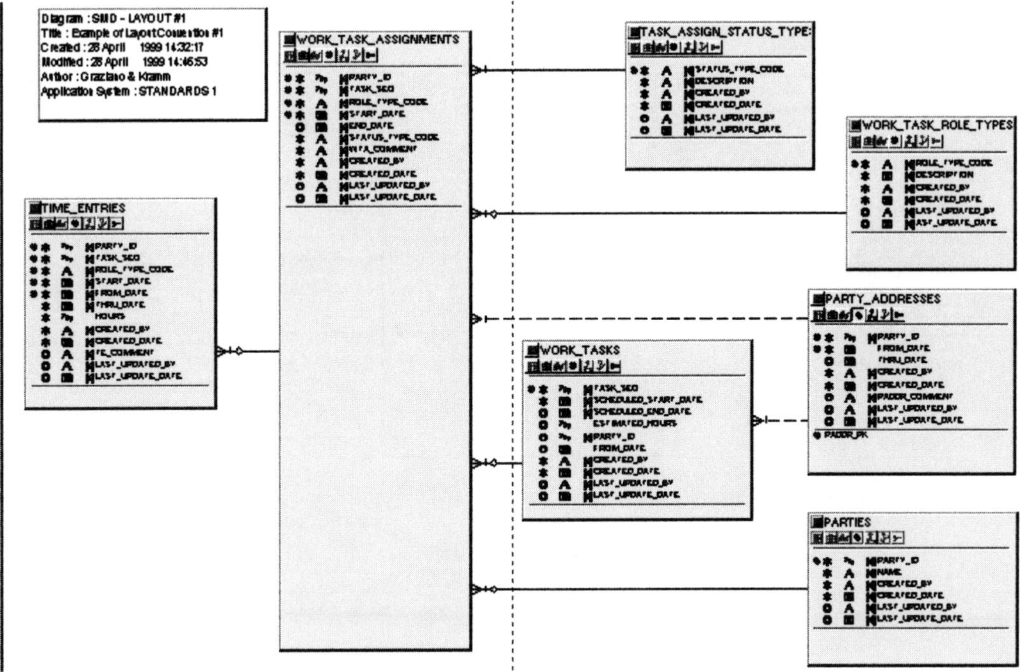

FIGURE SMD.1 Example of correct use of standards.

Constraint name placement

Do not display foreign key constraint names.

Consolidating Diagrams

There is no option to consolidate SM Diagrams. They are automatically consolidated upon opening.

If you wish to keep historical views of diagrams, you must print them on paper (before a change occurs) as there is no way to open one without seeing the underlying repository changes.

Delete Unneeded Diagrams

If a diagram is no longer needed, delete it from the Repository.

Color Coding Diagrams

Use color coding or shading to distinguish the following:

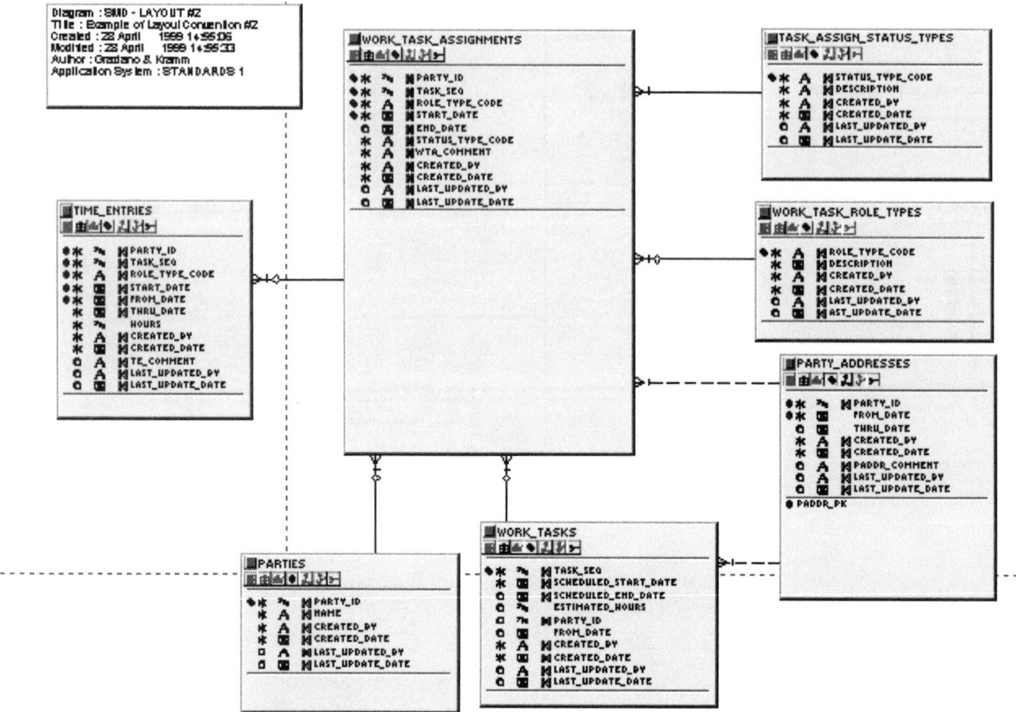

FIGURE SMD.2 Example of correct use of standards.

- ❑ Tables
- ❑ Views
- ❑ Snapshots
- ❑ Clusters
- ❑ Objects shared from other applications
- ❑ Objects that appear on more than one diagram
- ❑ Code type tables or views
- ❑ Subject area groupings

View Options

Each Server Model diagram created for a logical area should include (where they exist):

- All tables and views within that logical area
- All columns
- All foreign key constraints
- All column detail indicators

APPROVED ABBREVIATION LIST

ABBREVIATION	FULL WORD
ACCT	Account
ACCUM	Accumulative
ADDR	Address
ADDTL	Additional
AGRMNT	Agreement
AMT	Amount
APR	April
AUG	August
AVG	Average
BEG	Beginning
BLDG	Building
CDE	Code
CNT	Count
COMP	Company
CONF	Conference
CPTL	Capital

ABBREVIATION	FULL WORD
CRED	Credit
CURR	Current
CUST	Customer
DTE	Date
DEC	December
DEPT	Department
DFLT	Default
DOC	Document
EMPL	Employee
FEB	February
FLG	Flag
FREQ	Frequency
FRI	Friday
GAL	Gallon
GOVT	Government
HIST	History
ID	Identifier
IDX	Index
INFO	Information
JAN	January
JUL	July
JUN	June
LIQ	Liquid
LOC	Location
MAR	March
MAX	Maximum
MFG	Manufacturing
MGR	Manager
MIN	Minimum
MISC	Miscellaneous
MON	Monday

ABBREVIATION	FULL WORD
NAM	Name
NOV	November
NUM	Number
OCT	October
PCT	Percent
PR	Payroll
PREV	Previous
PROD	Product
PROJ	Project
QTY	Quantity
SAT	Saturday
SEP	September
ST	State
STAT	Status
STD	Standard
STMT	Statement
STRT	Street
SUN	Sunday
TIM	Time
TMSTP	Timestamp
TXT	Text
TUE	Tuesday
THUR	Thursday
WED	Wednesday

Template—Appendix B

Approved Acronym List

ACROYNYM	DEFINITION
AP	Accounts Payable
AR	Accounts Receivable
ASU	Air Separation Unit
BSP	Business System Planning
BTU	British Thermal Unit
CAS	Chemical
CEU	Continuing Education Unit
DBS	Dun and Bradstreet
DOT	Department of Transportation
DTD	Day To Date
ECN	Equipment Completion Notification
EDI	Electronic Data Interchange
EEO	Equal Employment Opportunity
FCC	Federal Communications Commission
FDA	Federal Drug Administration
FOB	Freight On Board
FUI	Federal Unemployment Insurance
GL	General Ledger
HRS	Human Resources

ACROYNYM	DEFINITION
IBM	International Business Machines
ICOPS	Inventory Control and Order Processing
IRA	Investment Retirement Account
ITC	Investment Tax Credit
KWH	Kilowatt Hours
LB	Pounds
LOA	Leave of Absence
LOB	Line of Business
LTD	Long Term Disability
MBTU	Thousands of Thermal Units
MMBTU	Millions of Thermal Units
MCF	Thousands of Cubic Feet
MMCF	Millions of Cubic Feet
MGAL	Thousands of Gallons
MMGAL	Millions of Gallons
MLBS	Thousands of Pounds
MMLBS	Millions of Pounds
MTON	Thousands of Tons
MMTON	Millions of Tons
MTD	Month To Date
MSDS	Material Safety Data Sheet
PSI	Pounds Per Square Inch
RFQ	Request For Quote
SCF	Standard Cubic Feet
SIC	Standard Industry Classification
SUI	State Unemployment Insurance
SKU	Stock Keeping Unit
TBS	Tonnage Billing System
UOM	Unit of Measure
VAN	Value Added Network
VAT	Value Added Tax
WTD	Week To Date
YTD	Year To Date

Template—Appendix C

APPROVED DOMAIN LIST

DOMAIN NAME	FORMAT	SIZE	DESCRIPTION
Address	Varchar2	35	The first line of an address.
Amount	Number	9,2	Money amounts. (Formatted for US dollars).
Code	Varchar2	10	Character id for alphanumeric unique identifiers by which the users recognize the entity.
Created by	Varchar2	30	Oracle user id of the person who created this record.
Creation date	Date	N/A	Date this record was created.
Date	Date	N/A	Generic date domain.
Description	Varchar2	40	Description text for a code.
Ind	Varchar2	1	Yes/no indicator.
Last updated by	Varchar2	30	Oracle user id of the person who last updated this record.
Last update date	Date	N/A	Date this record was last updated.
Long text	Varchar2	1000	A long string of text.
Name	Varchar2	40	A text string to indicate the formal name for a person, place or thing.
Rate	Number	6,2	Used for dollar value rates—includes a min and max rate.
Seq Id	Number	4,0	Integer identifier for use as a line item (sequence within parent).
Small text	Varchar2	30	Small string of text.
States	Varchar2	2	Valid state abbreviations.

DOMAIN NAME	FORMAT	SIZE	DESCRIPTION
Text	Varchar2	240	Generic mid-length text string. Size based on legacy Oracle restrictions.
Type	Varchar2	10	An attribute that contains an alphanumeric value to represent a categorization of an entity (i.e., a sub-type).
UID	Number		System generated unique identifier.
Very long text	Varchar2	2000	A very long string of text.

Appendix E

Database Design Capture

Oracle Designer gives the system engineer and database analyst some nice tools for reverse engineering existing database designs into the Designer repository. By combining the server design capture facility with the table-to-entity retrofit utility, it is even possible to develop a logical model from an existing database system and then build an Entity Relationship diagram. This appendix outlines the exact steps required to allow you to effectively use the design capture features of Oracle Designer with a minimum of wasted time and effort.

PHASE I: REVERSE ENGINEERING THE PHYSICAL OBJECTS

First note as of Designer 2.1 this process is now called "Design Capture" rather than reverse engineering. Next, I am assuming that you have created an application to capture the objects into. (**Note:** It is perfectly acceptable to reverse engineer into an existing Designer application; just be aware of any potential conflicts with previously defined objects. Designer will do iterative reverse engineering. If the object name already exists, the capture will be merged.)

Using the Design Capture utility, you can capture all database objects of interest into Designer. In 2.1 you have two options for launching this utility. First, you need to start the Design Editor. Select the *Server Model* radio button and press *OK*. Next you will see the Server Model Guide (a new feature in 2.1). On this guide you can press the button labeled *Run the Design Capture*. This will start the process. If you do not want to use the guide, you can also start the utility by selecting *Generate -> Capture Design of -> Server Model From Database* from the menu.

As in previous releases, you must have a database definition to associate the objects with. In the new tool, you now must also have a user/schema as well. If you have not previously defined a database and user, the *Create Database User* dialog will appear (Figure E.1).

In this dialog you can enter the name for a database, pick the Oracle version, and enter the name for a default user. When you press *OK,* these objects will be created in the repository and be set as the target for the design capture.

Once this step is completed, the design capture dialog appears (Figure E.2). In the first tab of the dialog you will be asked to specify the username, password, and connect string for the owner of the database objects to be reverse engineered. Notice that there are several additional options on this screen as well. You now can choose to capture the definitions from DDL files or through an ODBC connection. Both of these options include several non-Oracle sources (e.g., SQL Server, Sybase, DB2).

Another new feature is the ability to direct the object definitions to a particular schema. The *Capture Objects Into* pull-down list gives you this control. The list will contain all database and user definitions in the current application. If you had to use the *Create Database User* dialog to build one, then what you input will default into this field. Note also the additional check box options on the bottom of this dialog that give you further control on what is automatically captured and how it is processed.

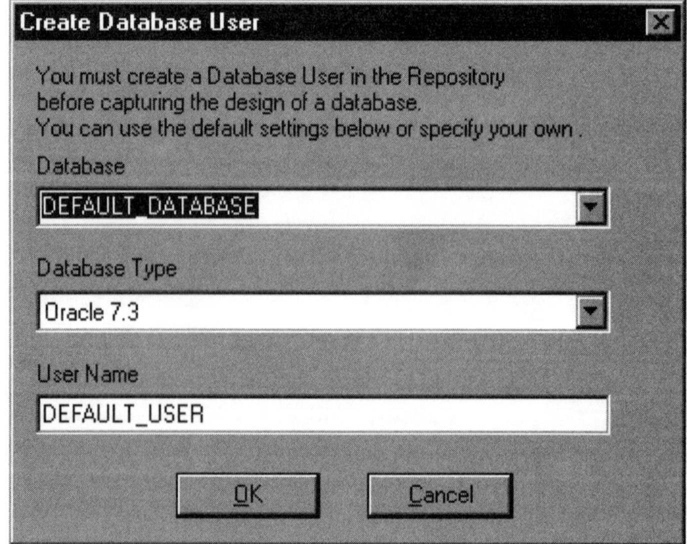

FIGURE E.1 Create database user dialog.

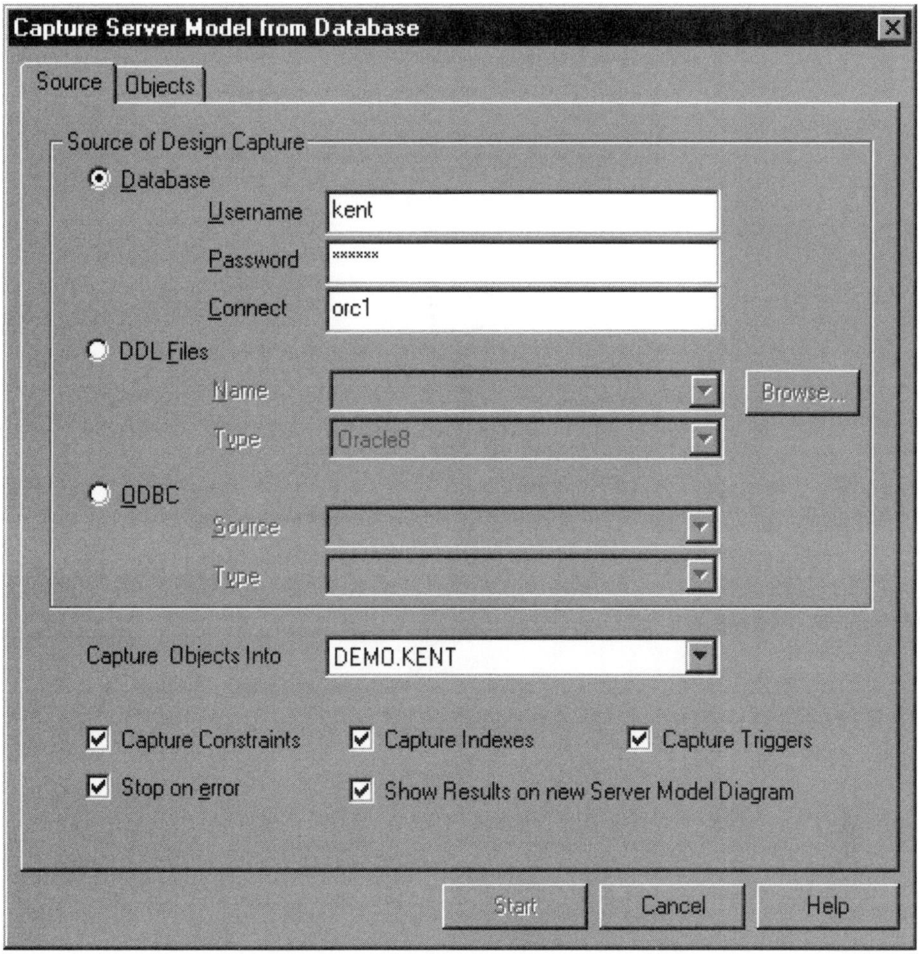

FIGURE E.2 Capture server model dialog.

In the second tab (Figure E.3), you can select the object type followed by the object names that are to be reverse engineered. A simple point and click interface is provided for easy selection. Expand the object node, then click on the object to capture. Next press the single right arrow icon. Multiple object names can be selected by using <shift> or <ctrl> as in most windows applications. Selecting **all** objects of one type can be accomplished by clicking on the type name then pressing the right arrow icon. Pressing the double arrow icon will move ***all objects in the schema*** into the *Capture* window.

Designer allows you to capture the design of 16 types of database objects from an Oracle database. Included are tables, indexes, sequences, views, clusters,

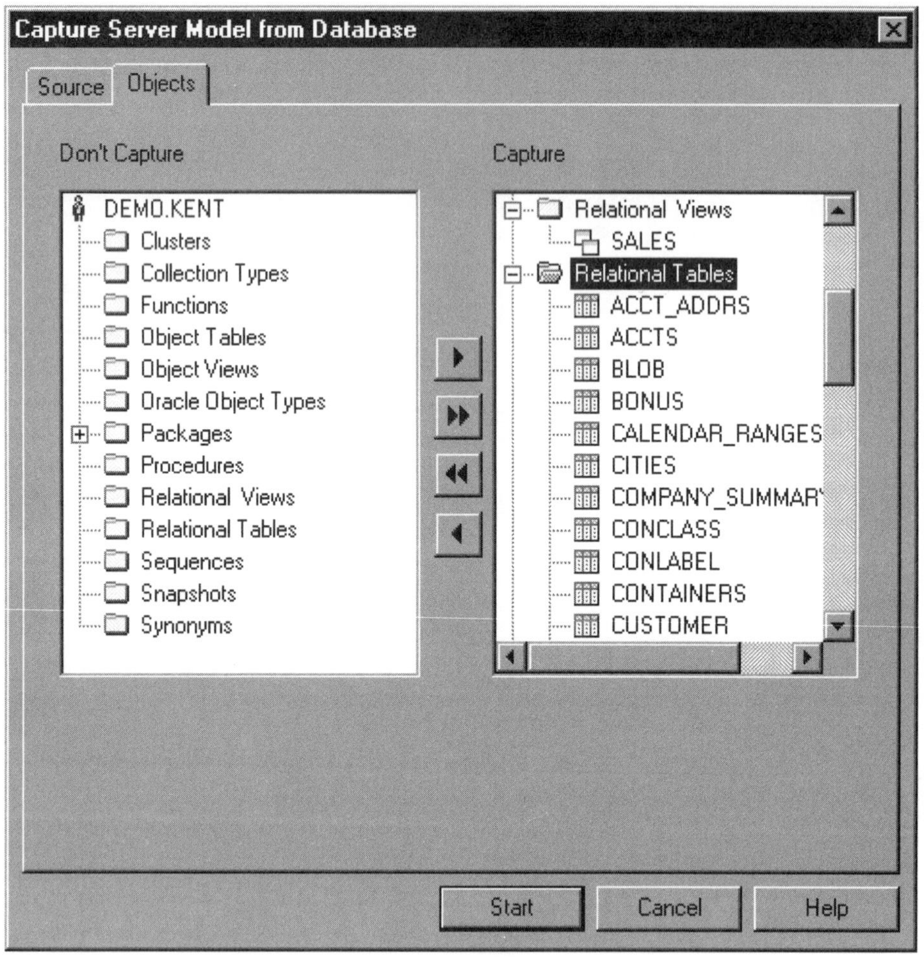

FIGURE E.3 Object tab in the design capture dialog.

functions, packages, procedures, snapshots, and triggers. The current version also has options for capturing object tables and views. When a relational table is captured, the tool brings with it the columns, column comments, check constraints, and key constraints associated with that table.

Feature alert: The new release of Designer no longer supports reverse engineering of tablespace definitions *unless* you have database administrator (DBA) privileges (then you can get all kinds of stuff!). As a result you will always get a warning when tables and indexes are captured that the tablespace definition does not exist. You can ignore the warning.

Once all the objects of interest have been selected, press the *Start* button to fire the utility. A message window will pop up for the utility and present various messages tracking the process. Once the process is done, a dialog box with the message *Design Capture is complete* will appear. The dialog gives you the option to save the results of the operation, *revert* or rollback the operation, or browse and edit the results in the Design Editor before saving. I would recommend you simply save the results, then do your editing. At this point you should see that the Server Model tab now includes the captured definitions.

PHASE II: BUILDING THE SCHEMA DIAGRAM

One of the nice additions to Designer 2.1 is the option to have a diagram (now called Server Model Diagram) automatically built as part of the design capture process. This tool provides the capability to diagram a physical database design

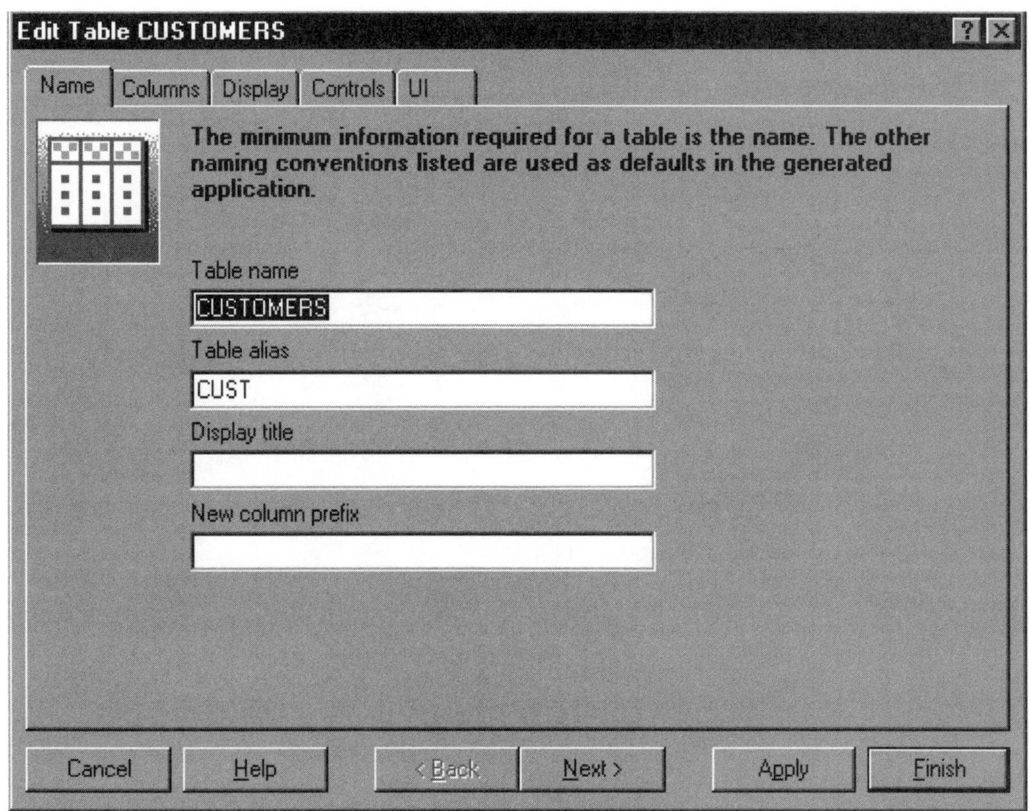

FIGURE E.4 Edit table dialog.

separate from a logical design. In addition, it has provided analysts and designers with the ability to visually assess the state of a reverse engineered database and then easily modify it if needed.

Often when reverse engineering, I find that the database is old and incomplete by current relational design standards. So it may be necessary to modify the captured design to bring it up to par.

First, double click on a table. If you are in *dialog mode,* the Edit Table wizard will appear. Then using the Name tab, add a table alias, and display title (Figure E.4). The application generators will use these later.

Unfortunately this new interface has made it harder to do some things that Designer veterans are used to doing. One important item for documentation is the table comment, which is used in DDL generation and in user help. It no longer appears in this wizard. To edit it, you need to exit the wizard, click the *Switch to Palette* button (on the top tool bar), then double click the table again. This brings up the table definition property sheet. If there was no table comment

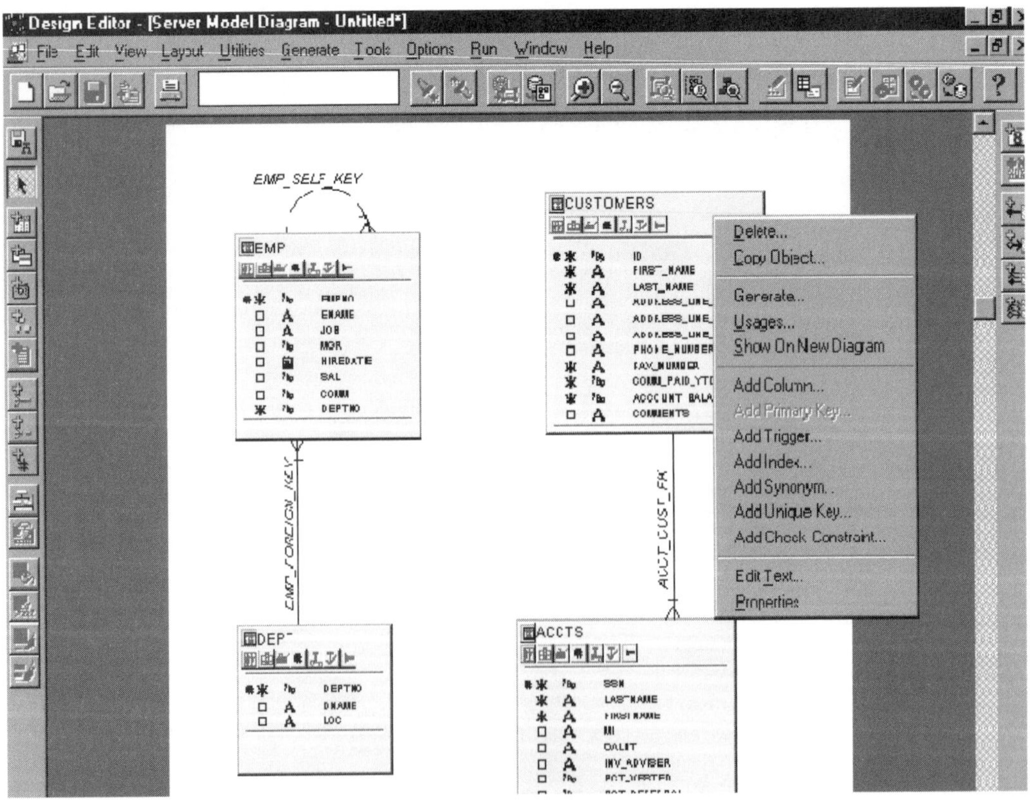

FIGURE E.5 Server model diagram with edit table menu.

in the database, this field will be blank. The alias and display title can also be accessed here.

To add primary or unique keys to a table, simply right click on a table to bring up the mouse menu (Figure E.5), then select *Add Primary Key.* Or you can right mouse click on the primary key icon (#) in the table header on the diagram.

Either will bring up the *Create Primary Key* wizard (Figure E.6). On the left will be a list of candidate columns (defined as any mandatory column). Select the column or columns to include in the key then press the right arrow icon. A default constraint name is provided. This is a *critical* step since this information will be used later in determining relationships and unique identifiers for the logical model.

To add foreign keys between the tables, right click on the foreign key icon in the table header. This will bring up the Create Foreign Key wizard (Figure E.7). The drop down list allows you to select the join table, and then a constraint name will automatically be created.

To add columns to the constraint, press the *Next* button. Here you have the option to use the primary key in the join table or choose the columns. If you choose to use the primary key, you again have to choose to either create a new join column or use an existing column. Given you are trying to add referential in-

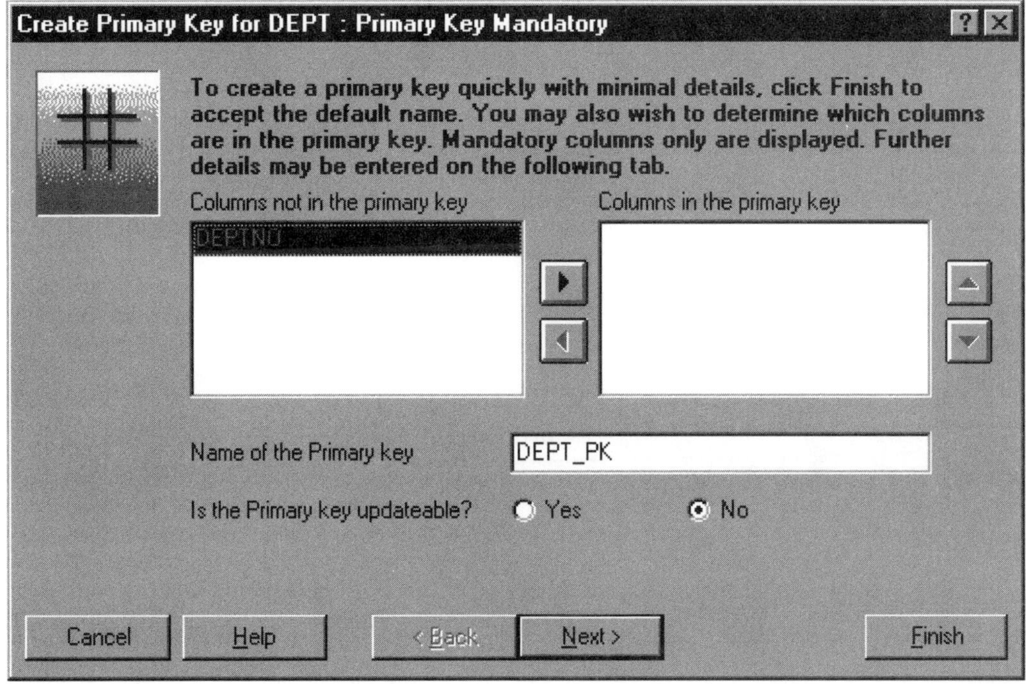

FIGURE E.6 Create primary key wizard.

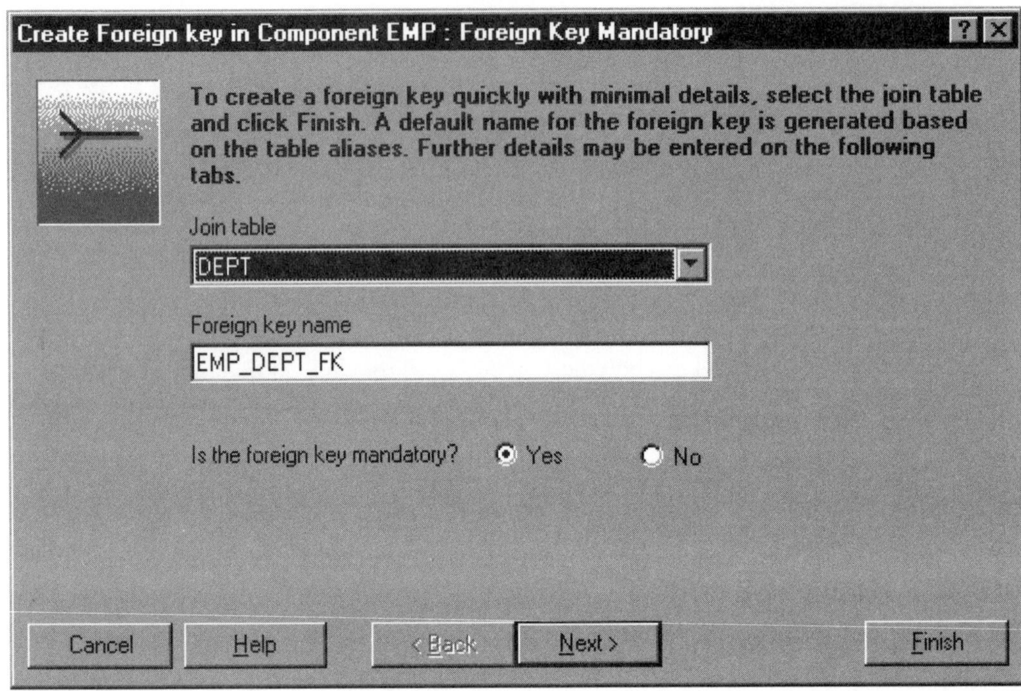

FIGURE E.7 Create foreign key wizard.

tegrity to an existing table, you should be able to simply select the columns to be used in the foreign key. Continue through the wizard filling in the other options as appropriate. Again, this is *critical* information that will be used in the next phase for generating the entity relationships.

Continue this process until all constraints have been added. Note that changes to the table definitions and the addition of the various key constraints can also be done through the property palette interface as well.

PHASE III: REVERSE ENGINEERING THE LOGICAL OBJECTS

To move the reverse engineered (and modified) physical design to the logical level in Designer, the Table-to-Entity Retrofit utility is used. It is found in the Repository Object Navigator (RON) (the Navigator button on the launch pad) under *Utilities->Table to Entity Retrofit*. This utility will convert all tables, columns, and constraints into entities, attributes, relationships, and unique identifiers. *Again note that if you have no primary or foreign key constraints defined, there will be no unique identifiers or relationships created.*

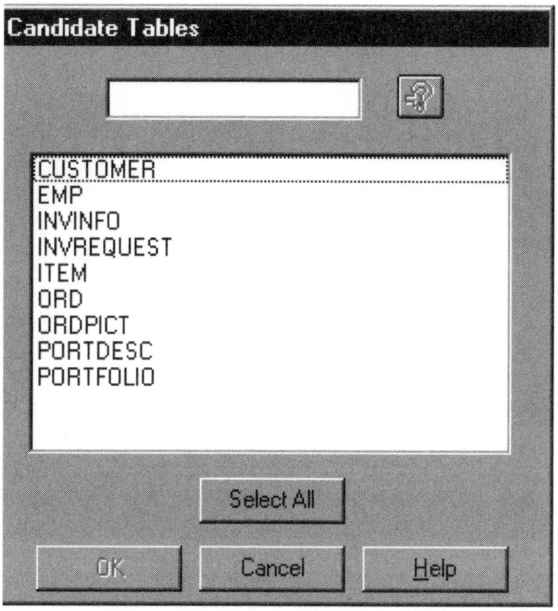

Candidate Tables

CUSTOMER
EMP
INVINFO
INVREQUEST
ITEM
ORD
ORDPICT
PORTDESC
PORTFOLIO

Select All

OK Cancel Help

FIGURE E.8 Candidate table dialog.

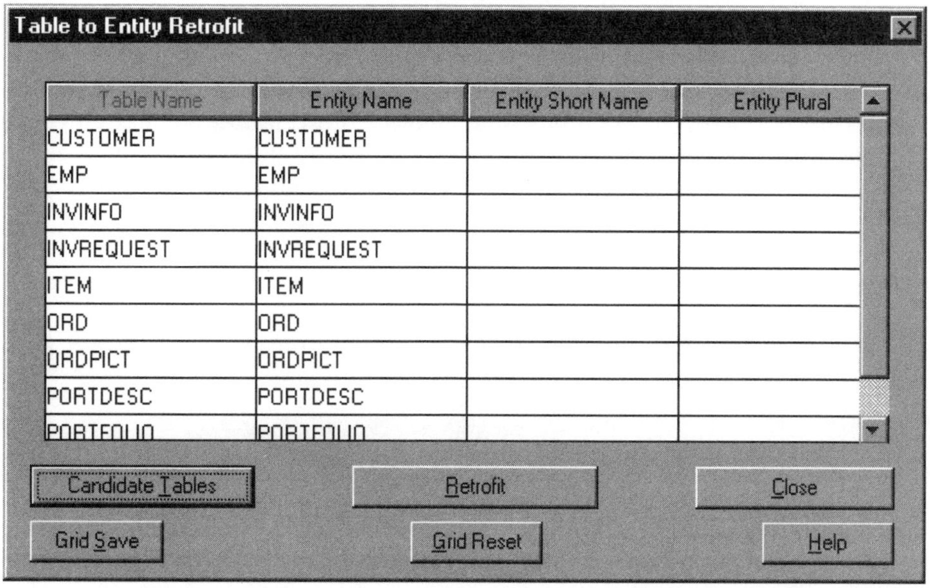

Table to Entity Retrofit

Table Name	Entity Name	Entity Short Name	Entity Plural
CUSTOMER	CUSTOMER		
EMP	EMP		
INVINFO	INVINFO		
INVREQUEST	INVREQUEST		
ITEM	ITEM		
ORD	ORD		
ORDPICT	ORDPICT		
PORTDESC	PORTDESC		
PORTFOLIO	PORTFOLIO		

Candidate Tables Retrofit Close

Grid Save Grid Reset Help

FIGURE E.9 Table to entity retrofit dialog, populated with candidates

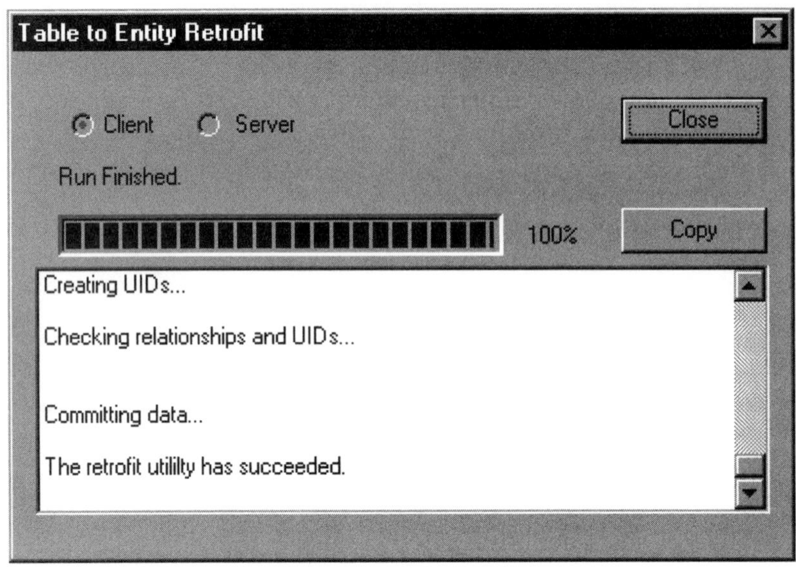

FIGURE E.10 Table to entity retrofit tracking dialog showing progress.

In the dialog that appears, first press the *Candidate Tables* button to get a list of tables that have no logical counterparts. The dialog for candidate tables will appear (Figure E.8). Press the *Select All* button, then the *OK* button.

This will populate the retrofit dialog with table and entity names (Figure E.9).

Notice in the figure that the entity names are the same as the table names. If your table names are plural, you should edit the entity names to be singular. If you do not, and let the utility derive the entity plurals, some strange plural names will be generated. Also you can add an entity short name. If you do not fill this in, the utility will generate a short name for you. *It will not automatically use the table alias assigned in the Edit Table dialog!*

When all data have been updated, press the *Retrofit* button. This will bring up a message dialog that tracks the progress of the utility. When the process is done the message *The retrofit utility has succeeded* will appear (Figure E.10). Press the *Close* button on the message box, then the *Close* button on the retrofit dialog.

PHASE IV: BUILDING THE ENTITY RELATIONSHIP DIAGRAM

To prepare to build the ER model using the diagrammer, it helps to have on hand an old ER diagram of the system (if one existed), or sketch a rough model on paper. The diagrammer has limited automated, intelligent formatting capabilities to help you make a nice picture, so some advance preparation is worth the effort.

Next, bring up the ER Diagrammer and select the application to work on. Once it is open, create a new diagram by pressing the *New* icon or selecting *new* from the *File* menu. Using the Include Entity dialog from *Edit->Include-> Entity*, select all the reverse engineered entities onto the diagram area. Be sure to uncheck the box *with relationships* so that you get the entities only on the canvas. Then, try to arrange them in a reasonable manner that will look good once the relationships are in place (using the sketch as a guide).

After all the entities have been copied in and arranged, use *Edit->Include-> Relationship* to bring in the relationships. Depending on how well the entities were arranged, this operation could result in a mess. Unless you really know all the relationships well, your diagram may look like tangled fishing line.

In previous versions, it was very useful to build and save several diagrams. The initial layout was usually such a mess that it was easier to start over, having gotten a better idea of a reasonable layout. With the advent of Designer, it is much easier to select all the relationships, *cut* them, re-arrange the entities, then

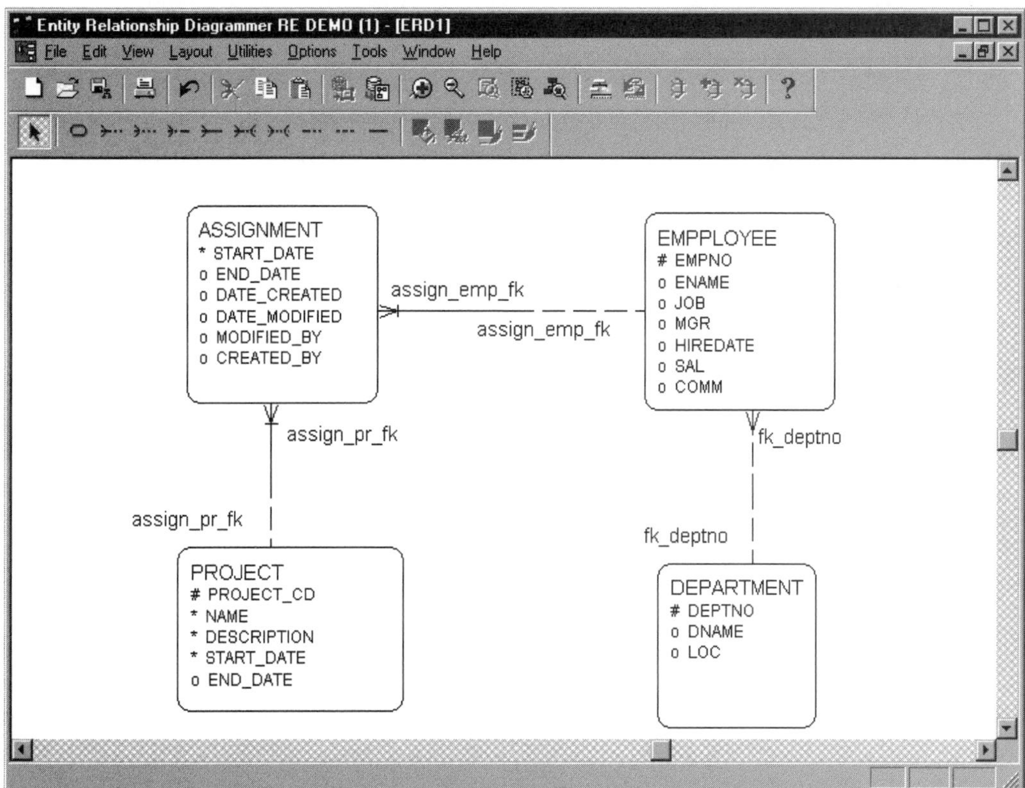

FIGURE E.11 ER Diagrammer showing retrofitted data model.

include them again. To cut all the relationships at once, select one relationship then go to *Edit->Select Same Type* then select *Edit->Cut* or press the *cut* icon (looks like scissors). Note that a *cut* simply removes things from the diagram, while a *delete* removes them from the repository. Next rearrange the entities and reinclude the relationships. Once all the pieces are in place, save the diagram.

As a side note, if you wish to put a title on the diagram itself, look under *File->Summary Information*. This allows you to place a title, author, create, and modified date label on the diagram.

Now take a closer look at the diagram (Figure E.11). The Retrofit utility creates relationship names by using the foreign key constraint name at both ends of a relationship. This will not usually provide good names for your relationships, so it will be necessary to edit them. To do this in the diagrammer, double click on the *relationship line* (clicking on the text will not work in this diagrammer). This

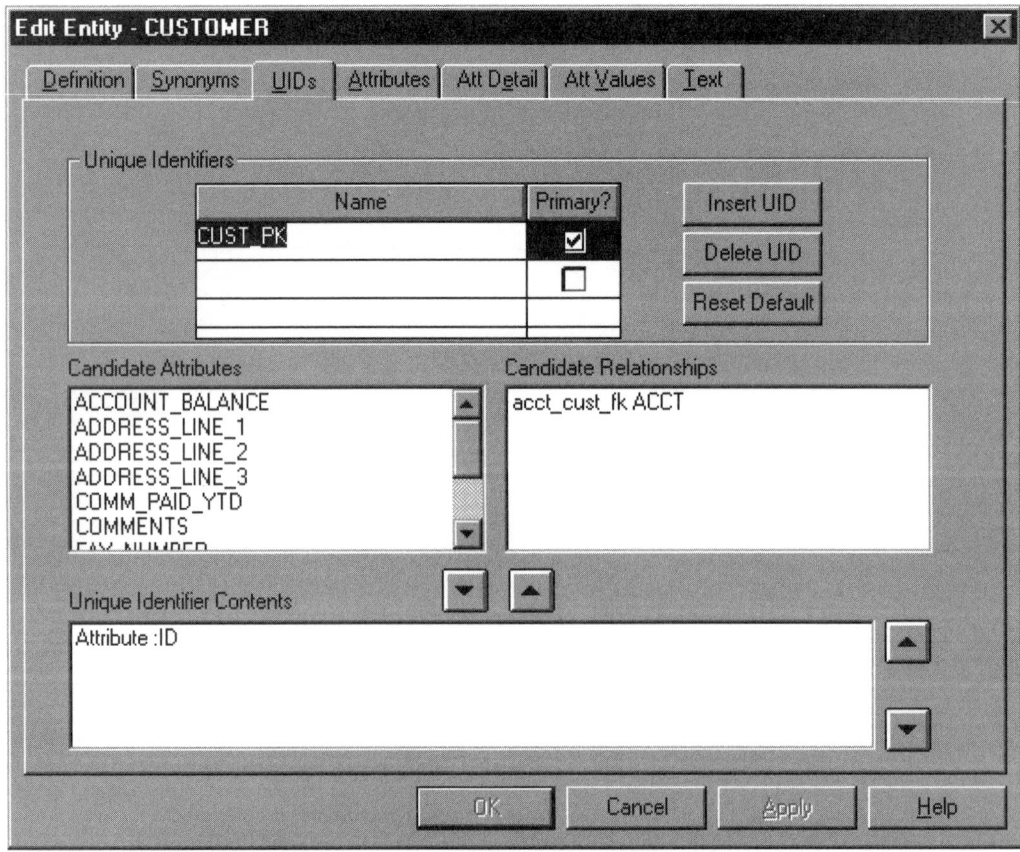

FIGURE E.12 Edit entity dialog, UID tab for checking UID definitions.

will bring up the *Edit Relationship dialog*. Here you can change all the information about a relationship, including the *from name* and *to name* text. Do so, and then press *OK* to save the changes.

After modifying the relationship names, verify that all the unique identifiers and the primary key are properly defined. The primary key is identified in two ways. One way is by going to the unique identifier (UIDs) tab in the Edit Entity dialog (Figure E.12). In this tab it is the unique identifier with the Primary box checked. If the box was not checked, that would indicate a secondary unique identifier. Note that only with this tab can a relationship be added to the primary key.

The other way to check for primary key attributes is to go to the *Attributes* tab (Figure E.13). The check box *primary* will be marked for an attribute that is included in the primary key.

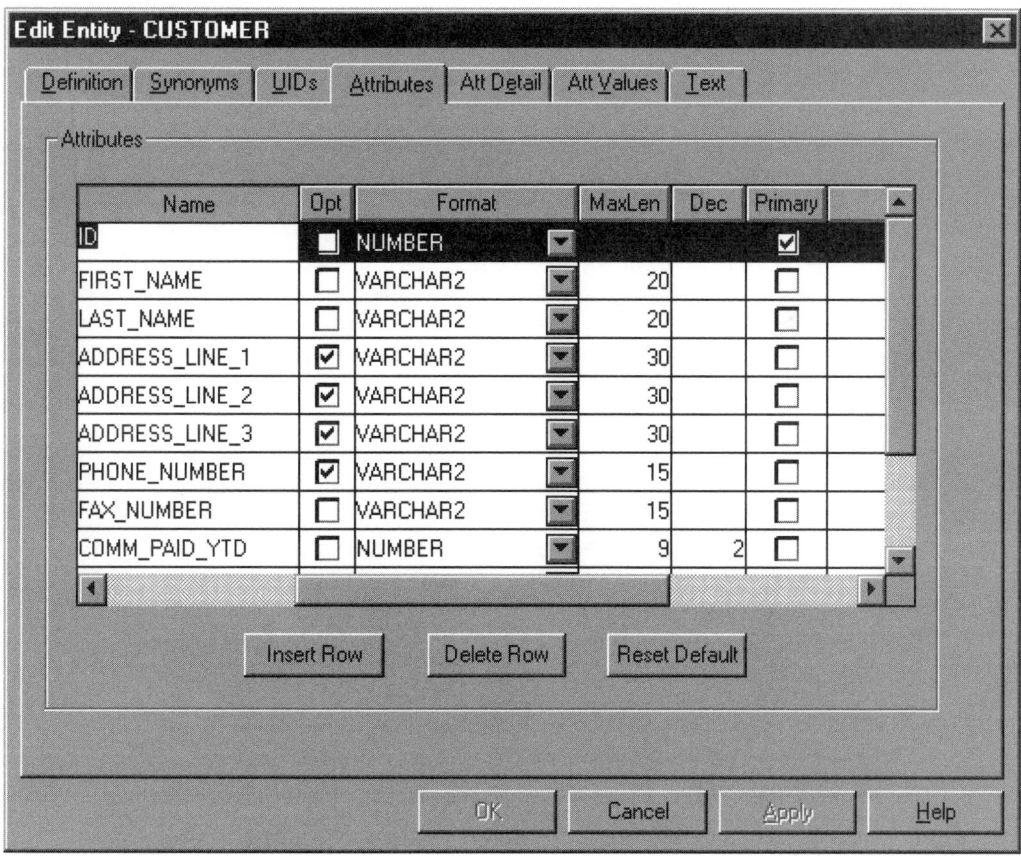

FIGURE E.13 Edit entity dialog, attributes tab can also be used to check primary UIDs.

When you are finished with the changes, press *OK* to return to the diagrammer. If you are satisfied with the diagram, save it and print it.

At this point you essentially have a *logical view of a physical design*. It may be necessary to add or remove objects and relationships to get a true logical model. How much of this you need to do will be determined by your objectives in reverse engineering. If the goal was simply to document an existing system, you may be finished. However, if you want to re-engineer the existing system, there could be a lot more work ahead.

PHASE V: FILLING IN THE BLANKS

WARNING AND DISCLAIMER

The utilities presented in this section directly update the Oracle Designer repository. No error checking of any kind is included. Use at your own risk. Always back up your Designer repository before running any update scripts against the underlying tables! These scripts were tested using Designer 2.1.2.

To get the most out of the Designer tools after going to all this effort, there are a few holes that were left during the reverse engineering process that need to be filled. First are the attribute comments. To get to them, double click on the entity (in an ER diagram) and go again to the Attributes tab (or click on the attribute name in the object navigator in RON and look at the property sheet).

You will see in some cases that the *comment* field is blank. If there was a comment in the database (or one was added in the Server Model), then there will be a corresponding attribute comment. One of the reasons to do design capture is documentation, so at this point you may want to start entering valid definitions for this information. To remedy this the only option is to start typing in the attribute comments (or get someone else to).

To help this process, I wrote the following script that will add a user-defined comment to each appearance of a selected attribute *name*. Use this script if you have any standard attributes that may occur in multiple entities within an application (otherwise, just use the screens). Notice that the script will not overwrite any existing text:

```
update ci_attributes att
set att.notes = '&note'
where att.name = UPPER('&attname')
and att.notes is null
and EXISTS
(select 'x'
  from ci_entities ent,
         ci_application_systems app
   where ent.id = att.entity_reference
```

```
and ent.application_system_owned_by
    = app.id
and app.name = UPPER('&application')
and app.version = &version);
```

This is especially useful if there are standard audit attributes (e.g., user created, date created) added to every entity or other standard attributes used through out an application. The script should be run as the Designer *repository owner*.

Another of these holes is the column comments. If there are no column comments stored in the database (the most likely situation for non-CASE generated tables), the tool leaves these blank. If there were comments in the database, they will be filled in.

In addition, if a column comment was captured, the column hint text is still left blank. This field is of critical importance if you plan to generate forms, since it becomes the hint line for a field. This is an easy fix—simply run the Database Transformer with the column modify options checked (Figure E.14). This will cause the attribute/column comment to be written into the column hint.

In addition, if the attribute description has been modified, the column description and user help text will also be modified. (Note that the column display data type and size is also affected by this option. If you choose the *Modify* option under *Tables* as well, the description and user help text for the selected table will also be updated.)

The bad news is that this tool will *not* copy newly entered attribute comments into the comment property of an existing column. I have been assured by Oracle support that *this is a feature, not a bug!* It only works when creating a column for the first time.

So what do you do? There were three options:

1. Use the RON or the Design Editor and the delete option to remove the table, its columns, indexes, and associated constraints. Then run the Database Transformer to rebuild the definitions (i.e., forward engineer the retrofitted entity).
2. Write a utility script to do the updates.
3. Edit the comments manually.

I chose option #2 since I had written similar utilities against the CASE repository in the past. In addition, I did not want to risk the chance that the Database Transformer might come up with a different physical design than what I already had.

The script below takes all the attribute notes for an entire application and copies them to the matching column comment based on the source attribute id:

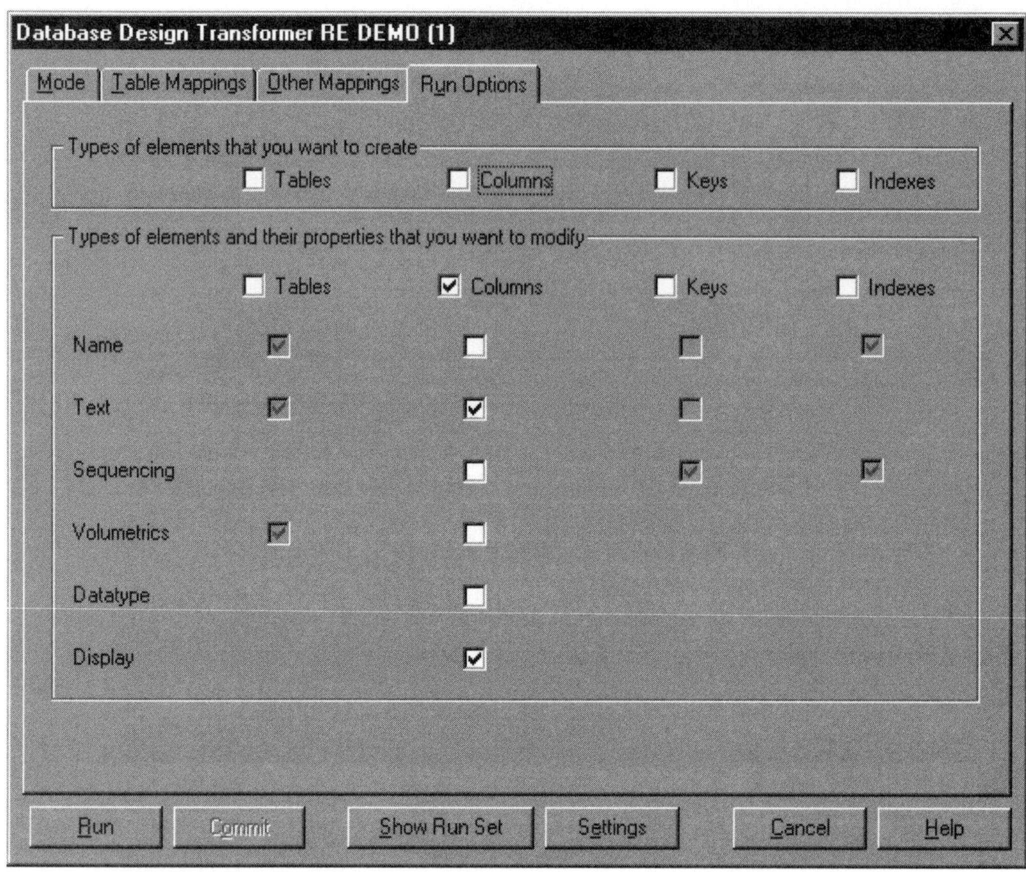

FIGURE E.14 Database design transformer. *Run options* tab set to move text.

```
update ci_columns col
set col.remark =
    (select att.notes
     from ci_attributes att
     where col.source_attribute_reference
           = att.id)
WHERE exists
(select 'x'
 from ci_attributes att,
      ci_entities ent,
      ci_application_systems app
 where col.source_attribute_reference = att.id
   and ent.id = att.entity_reference
```

```
and ent.application_system_owned_by
    = app.id
and app.name = UPPER('&application')
and app.version = &version);
```

Again, remember that the Designer repository owner should run these scripts.

CONCLUSION

Proper use of Oracle Designer can greatly enhance productivity in most software development projects. The many options provided in Designer add to this productivity. The ability to reverse engineer to both the physical and logical level can benefit any project that needs to work with an existing application system that was not built from Designer or Oracle CASE originally. Once the steps presented here are completed, the system engineer can use Designer to produce structured documentation with the wide variety of reports available. In addition, the engineer can leverage the power of the entire suite of Designer tools to enhance or re-engineer an application.

ABOUT THIS APPENDIX

The preceding text was previously published by Kent Graziano under the title *Using Design Capture to Reverse Engineer an Existing Database with Oracle Designer 2.1* in the proceedings of the Rocky Mountain Oracle Users Group Training Days 1999 (*www.rmoug.org*), the proceedings for IOUG-A Live! 99 (*www.ioug.org*), the proceedings for the Oracle Development Tools User Group 1999 Conference (*www.odtug.com*), and the proceedings for the European Oracle Users Group 1999 conference (www.eoug.org).

INDEX

A

B

C

G

I

K

L

M

N

T

LICENSE AGREEMENT AND LIMITED WARRANTY

READ THE FOLLOWING TERMS AND CONDITIONS CAREFULLY BEFORE OPENING THIS DISK PACKAGE. THIS LEGAL DOCUMENT IS AN AGREEMENT BETWEEN YOU AND PRENTICE-HALL, INC. (THE "COMPANY"). BY OPENING THIS SEALED DISK PACKAGE, YOU ARE AGREEING TO BE BOUND BY THESE TERMS AND CONDITIONS. IF YOU DO NOT AGREE WITH THESE TERMS AND CONDITIONS, DO NOT OPEN THE DISK PACKAGE. PROMPTLY RETURN THE UNOPENED DISK PACKAGE AND ALL ACCOMPANYING ITEMS TO THE PLACE YOU OBTAINED THEM FOR A FULL REFUND OF ANY SUMS YOU HAVE PAID.

1. **GRANT OF LICENSE:** In consideration of your payment of the license fee, which is part of the price you paid for this product, and your agreement to abide by the terms and conditions of this Agreement, the Company grants to you a nonexclusive right to use and display the copy of the enclosed software program (hereinafter the "SOFTWARE") on a single computer (i.e., with a single CPU) at a single location so long as you comply with the terms of this Agreement. The Company reserves all rights not expressly granted to you under this Agreement.

2. **OWNERSHIP OF SOFTWARE:** You own only the magnetic or physical media (the enclosed disks) on which the SOFTWARE is recorded or fixed, but the Company retains all the rights, title, and ownership to the SOFTWARE recorded on the original disk copy(ies) and all subsequent copies of the SOFTWARE, regardless of the form or media on which the original or other copies may exist. This license is not a sale of the original SOFTWARE or any copy to you.

3. **COPY RESTRICTIONS:** This SOFTWARE and the accompanying printed materials and user manual (the "Documentation") are the subject of copyright. You may not copy the Documentation or the SOFTWARE, except that you may make a single copy of the SOFTWARE for backup or archival purposes only. You may be held legally responsible for any copying or copyright infringement which is caused or encouraged by your failure to abide by the terms of this restriction.

4. **USE RESTRICTIONS:** You may not network the SOFTWARE or otherwise use it on more than one computer or computer terminal at the same time. You may physically transfer the SOFTWARE from one computer to another provided that the SOFTWARE is used on only one computer at a time. You may not distribute copies of the SOFTWARE or Documentation to others. You may not reverse engineer, disassemble, decompile, modify, adapt, translate, or create derivative works based on the SOFTWARE or the Documentation without the prior written consent of the Company.

5. **TRANSFER RESTRICTIONS:** The enclosed SOFTWARE is licensed only to you and may not be transferred to any one else without the prior written consent of the Company. Any unauthorized transfer of the SOFTWARE shall result in the immediate termination of this Agreement.

6. **TERMINATION:** This license is effective until terminated. This license will terminate automatically without notice from the Company and become null and void if you fail to comply with any provisions or limitations of this license. Upon termination, you shall destroy the Documentation and all copies of the SOFTWARE. All provisions of this Agreement as to warranties, limitation of liability, remedies or damages, and our ownership rights shall survive termination.

7. **MISCELLANEOUS:** This Agreement shall be construed in accordance with the laws of the United States of America and the State of New York and shall benefit the Company, its affiliates, and assignees.

8. **LIMITED WARRANTY AND DISCLAIMER OF WARRANTY:** The Company warrants that the SOFTWARE, when properly used in accordance with the Documentation, will operate in substantial conformity with the description of the SOFTWARE set forth in the Documentation. The Company does not warrant that the SOFT-

WARE will meet your requirements or that the operation of the SOFTWARE will be uninterrupted or error-free. The Company warrants that the media on which the SOFTWARE is delivered shall be free from defects in materials and workmanship under normal use for a period of thirty (30) days from the date of your purchase. Your only remedy and the Company's only obligation under these limited warranties is, at the Company's option, return of the warranted item for a refund of any amounts paid by you or replacement of the item. Any replacement of SOFTWARE or media under the warranties shall not extend the original warranty period. The limited warranty set forth above shall not apply to any SOFTWARE which the Company determines in good faith has been subject to misuse, neglect, improper installation, repair, alteration, or damage by you. EXCEPT FOR THE EXPRESSED WARRANTIES SET FORTH ABOVE, THE COMPANY DISCLAIMS ALL WARRANTIES, EXPRESS OR IMPLIED, INCLUDING WITHOUT LIMITATION, THE IMPLIED WARRANTIES OF MERCHANTABILITY AND FITNESS FOR A PARTICULAR PURPOSE. EXCEPT FOR THE EXPRESS WARRANTY SET FORTH ABOVE, THE COMPANY DOES NOT WARRANT, GUARANTEE, OR MAKE ANY REPRESENTATION REGARDING THE USE OR THE RESULTS OF THE USE OF THE SOFTWARE IN TERMS OF ITS CORRECTNESS, ACCURACY, RELIABILITY, CURRENTNESS, OR OTHERWISE.

IN NO EVENT, SHALL THE COMPANY OR ITS EMPLOYEES, AGENTS, SUPPLIERS, OR CONTRACTORS BE LIABLE FOR ANY INCIDENTAL, INDIRECT, SPECIAL, OR CONSEQUENTIAL DAMAGES ARISING OUT OF OR IN CONNECTION WITH THE LICENSE GRANTED UNDER THIS AGREEMENT, OR FOR LOSS OF USE, LOSS OF DATA, LOSS OF INCOME OR PROFIT, OR OTHER LOSSES, SUSTAINED AS A RESULT OF INJURY TO ANY PERSON, OR LOSS OF OR DAMAGE TO PROPERTY, OR CLAIMS OF THIRD PARTIES, EVEN IF THE COMPANY OR AN AUTHORIZED REPRESENTATIVE OF THE COMPANY HAS BEEN ADVISED OF THE POSSIBILITY OF SUCH DAMAGES. IN NO EVENT SHALL LIABILITY OF THE COMPANY FOR DAMAGES WITH RESPECT TO THE SOFTWARE EXCEED THE AMOUNTS ACTUALLY PAID BY YOU, IF ANY, FOR THE SOFTWARE.

SOME JURISDICTIONS DO NOT ALLOW THE LIMITATION OF IMPLIED WARRANTIES OR LIABILITY FOR INCIDENTAL, INDIRECT, SPECIAL, OR CONSEQUENTIAL DAMAGES, SO THE ABOVE LIMITATIONS MAY NOT ALWAYS APPLY. THE WARRANTIES IN THIS AGREEMENT GIVE YOU SPECIFIC LEGAL RIGHTS AND YOU MAY ALSO HAVE OTHER RIGHTS WHICH VARY IN ACCORDANCE WITH LOCAL LAW.

ACKNOWLEDGMENT

YOU ACKNOWLEDGE THAT YOU HAVE READ THIS AGREEMENT, UNDERSTAND IT, AND AGREE TO BE BOUND BY ITS TERMS AND CONDITIONS. YOU ALSO AGREE THAT THIS AGREEMENT IS THE COMPLETE AND EXCLUSIVE STATEMENT OF THE AGREEMENT BETWEEN YOU AND THE COMPANY AND SUPERSEDES ALL PROPOSALS OR PRIOR AGREEMENTS, ORAL, OR WRITTEN, AND ANY OTHER COMMUNICATIONS BETWEEN YOU AND THE COMPANY OR ANY REPRESENTATIVE OF THE COMPANY RELATING TO THE SUBJECT MATTER OF THIS AGREEMENT.

Should you have any questions concerning this Agreement or if you wish to contact the Company for any reason, please contact in writing at the address below.

Robin Short
Prentice Hall PTR
One Lake Street
Upper Saddle River, New Jersey 07458

About the CD

The CD-ROM included with *Oracle Designer* contains a template standards document, an Oracle Designer archive, and two reports. It can be used on Microsoft Windows® 95/98/NT®.

License Agreement

Use of *Oracle Designer: A Template for Developing an Enterprise Standards Document* is subject to the terms of the License Agreement and Limited Warranty, found on pp 770–771.

Technical Support

Prentice Hall does not offer technical support for any of the programs on the CD-ROM. However, if the CD-ROM is damaged, you may obtain a replacement copy by sending an email that describes the problem to: disc_exchange@prenhall.com

1. STANDARDS.DOC

- Author: Kramm & Graziano
- Format: MS Word
- Platform: Windows or Windows NT
- Description: This Word document is a complete enterprise standards document as outlined in *Oracle Designer: A Template for Developing an Enterprise Standards Document*. It is appropriate for use with any project that will use Oracle Designer. The document can be copied from the CD onto a local file system then modified, as needed using MS Word. See Chapter 1 for examples on how this document can be customized to meet the specific needs of an enterprise.

2. DOMAINS.DMP

- Author/Developer: Kramm & Graziano
- Format: Oracle Designer archive file (release 2.1.2)
- Platform: Windows NT
- Description: This file is an Oracle Designer archive file containing a single application system (Domains) with pre-defined domain definitions. The domains contained in this extract are those shown in Appendix C of Standards.doc. Once loaded into a Designer repository, these domains can be shared to other Designer applications and then applied to new or existing column and attribute definitions.

- ❑ Load instructions: Copy the file to a local workstation directory. Start Oracle Designer. In the Repository Object Navigator go to *Applications -> Restore.* Select the local domains.dmp file for import, then restore as you would any other Designer archive. See the on-line Designer help for more details.

3. BUSRULES.RDF

- ❑ Author/Developer: Ken Atkins
- ❑ Format: Oracle Reports 3.0
- ❑ Platform: Windows NT
- ❑ Description: This file is an Oracle Reports source file that when executed will produce a report showing business rules and policies recorded in Oracle Designer. This report assumes that the standards for entering business rules and policies set for the in the book have been followed. If the standard has not been followed exactly, the report can be modified as needed.
- ❑ Execution instructions: Copy the file to a local workstation directory. Execute Oracle Reports runtime, specifying the file name (busrules) and the username and password for a valid Oracle Designer login. Fill in the parameters as appropriate, then execute.

4. BUSRULES.SQL

- ❑ Author/Developer: Ken Atkins
- ❑ Format: ASCII Text
- ❑ Platform: Windows NT
- ❑ Description: This file is SQL text file that can be executed using SQL*Plus. When executed it will produce a report showing business rules and policies recorded in Oracle Designer. This report assumes that the standards for entering business rules and policies set for the in the book have been followed. If the standard has not been followed exactly, the report can be modified as needed.
- ❑ Execution instructions: Copy the file to a local workstation directory. Start SQL*Plus, specifying the username and password for a valid Oracle Designer login. Execute the SQL file, fill in the parameters as appropriate, then execute.